Restaging the Future

performance works

SERIES EDITORS
Patrick Anderson and Nicholas Ridout

This series publishes books in theater and performance studies, focused in particular on the material conditions in which performance acts are staged, and to which performance itself might contribute. We define "performance" in the broadest sense, including traditional theatrical productions and performance art, but also cultural ritual, political demonstration, social practice, and other forms of interpersonal, social, and political interaction that may fruitfully be understood in terms of performance.

Restaging the Future

Neoliberalization, Theater, and Performance in Britain

✦

Louise Owen

NORTHWESTERN UNIVERSITY PRESS
EVANSTON, ILLINOIS

Northwestern University Press
www.nupress.northwestern.edu

Printed in the United States of America

10 9 8 7 6 5 4 3 2 1

Library of Congress Cataloging-in-Publication Data

Names: Owen, Louise, author.
Title: Restaging the future : neoliberalization, theater, and performance in Britain / Louise Owen.
Other titles: Performance works.
Description: Evanston, Illinois : Northwestern University Press, 2024. | Series: Performance works | Includes bibliographical references and index.
Identifiers: LCCN 2023006208 | ISBN 9780810146044 (paperback) | ISBN 9780810146051 (cloth) | ISBN 9780810146068 (ebook)
Subjects: LCSH: Theater and state—Great Britain—History—21st century. | Theater and society—Great Britain—History—21st century. | Theater—Political aspects—Great Britain—History—21st century. | Neoliberalism in popular culture—Great Britain—History—21st century. | BISAC: PERFORMING ARTS / Theater / History & Criticism
Classification: LCC PN2044.G7 O94 2023 | DDC 792.0941—dc23/eng/20230214
LC record available at https://lccn.loc.gov/2023006208

CONTENTS

ACKNOWLEDGMENTS

This book has taken its time. Many people have supported, inspired, and encouraged its realization and I am incredibly grateful to all of them.

The project started its life with Arts and Humanities Research Council support at Queen Mary, University of London. I was extremely lucky to benefit from the intellectual guidance and expertise of Paul Heritage and Nicholas Ridout, whose generosity and kindness I will never forget. Alan Read and Ric Knowles encouraged and inspired the project's next stage. The Department of Drama was the scene of many excellent discussions with Joel Anderson, Giles Brokensha, Sarahleigh Castelyn, Leonore Easton, Tim Edkins, Eirini Kartsaki, Johanna Linsley, Brian Lobel, Megan Macdonald, Jen Mitas, Louisa Pearson, and numerous others, then and since. I am especially thankful for the ongoing scholarly support and kindness of Jen Harvie and Michael McKinnie.

Many people granted me their time, as well as access to archival resources and projects in process at organizations including Artangel, Artsadmin, Creative Partnerships, Dance4, Everyman Archive at Liverpool John Moores University, Greenwich Dance Agency, Immediate Theatre, the Learning Trust, Live Art Development Agency, Liverpool Everyman and Playhouse, People's Palace Projects, Rich Mix, Rising Tide, Sound Connections, and Stoke Newington School. My thanks and appreciation to Maria Ribot, Nicky Childs, Nicky Molloy, Brendan Keaney, Myra Fulton, Mary Bendall, Cressida Hubbard, Michael Morris, Anna Cutler, Lucy Pardee, Pauline Aitken, Bill Calder, Dixon Graterol, Jonathan Hillier, Emma Impett, Anthony Johnson, Rachel Sanger, Carla Martins, Damian Platt, Malin Forbes, Richard Ings, Derek Richards, Jo Carter, EJ Trivett, Chris Westwood, Damian Atkinson, Karen Taylor, Nicola Baboneau, Helen Wood, Peter Leigh, Canan Salih, Gabin Sinclair, Laura Arends, Suzanne Bell, and Esther Wilson.

Countless conversations with friends and colleagues sharpened the development of this book directly and indirectly, including Josh Abrams, Adam Alston, Katherine Angel, Andrew Asibong, Anthony Bale, Heike Bauer, Emma Bennett, Jaswinder Blackwell-Pal, Shane Boyle, Carolyn Burdett, Selina Busby, Melissa Butcher, Luisa Calè, Daragh Carville, Lewis Church, Karen Christopher, Rosie Cox, Ben Cranfield, Isabel Davis, Lina Džuverović, Josh Edelman, David Eldridge, Nadine El-Enany, Stephen Farrier, Marissia Fragkou, Helen Freshwater, Kélina Gotman, Philip Hager,

Anna Hartnell, Wendy Hein, Sophie Hope, Seda Ilter, Dominic Johnson, Lynne Kendrick, Margherita Laera, Louise Lambe, Sarah Lamble, Andy Lavender, Bryce Lease, Esther Leslie, Lorraine Lim, Kate Maclean, Caoimhe Mader McGuinness, David McAllister, Lynne McCarthy, Joel McKim, Andrew McKinnon, Joseph Mercier, Royona Mitra, Aoife Monks, Laura Mulvey, Sophie Nield, Giulia Palladini, Katerina Paramana, Mary Paterson, Jennifer Parker-Starbuck, Timothy Phillips, Flora Pitrolo, Sheila Preston, Prarthana Purkayastha, Dan Rebellato, Scott Rodgers, Theron Schmidt, Rajni Shah, Adam Smyth, Zoe Svendsen, Rob Swain, Michael Temple, Liselle Terret, Karen Tomlin, Aylwyn Walsh, Gareth White, Jo Winning, Elena Yuan, and Martin Young. I am especially grateful to Una Bauer, Broderick Chow, Rachel Clements, Kate Elswit, Tony Fisher, Joe Kelleher, Amanda Stuart Fisher, and Marilena Zaroulia for generously reading drafts, for talking ideas through, and for the joy of company and conversation. I am indebted, too, to Sue Wiseman, Emily Senior, Gill Woods, and Molly Flynn for their wisdom and shrewd critical insights about work in progress. My enduring gratitude belongs to Fintan Walsh for all of the above, for the gift of years of shared endeavor, and for his kindness and support: I can't thank you enough.

At Birkbeck, University of London, I was incredibly lucky to benefit from the expertise, guidance, and friendship of a great many academic and administrative colleagues and to work with wonderful students whose enthusiasm, intelligence, tenacity, and commitment to pursuing ideas and creative practice inspired me daily. Birkbeck's fantastic Department of English, Theatre and Creative Writing and School of Arts offered excellent research support and study leave time that enabled the book to progress.

Restaging the Future was completed at Royal Central School of Speech and Drama, where I was very fortunate to receive a term of research leave, as well as invaluable support toward realizing the book in print. Dan Hetherington and Elaine Henry provided very helpful advice and assistance. I am extremely grateful to Maria Delgado for her generous mentorship and guidance.

Opportunities to work out ideas at various conferences and symposia were incredibly useful for this project: these include Poetics of Globalisation (Southampton University 2007 and 2008), ATHE 2008 (New Orleans), PSi15 (Zagreb), and ASTR 2011 (Montreal). Elements of this text appear in "'The Art of Government': Policy and Censorship in Post-War British Theatre," in *The Cambridge Companion to Post-War Theatre*, ed. Jen Harvie and Dan Rebellato (Cambridge: Cambridge University Press, 2023), 209–28; "'Places, like Property Prices, Go Up and Down': Site-Specificity, Regeneration and the Margate Exodus," in *Performing Site-Specific Theatre: Politics, Place, Practice*, ed. Joanne Tompkins and Anna Birch (Basingstoke, UK: Palgrave Macmillan, 2012), 150–64; and "'In Tune with the Beat of Where They Are': The AfroReggae

UK Partnership in 2007," *PPP Research Bulletin*, no. 4 (May 2008): 1–13. My thanks and appreciations to the editors of all of these texts for their generous feedback.

I am extremely grateful to the Northwestern University Press—in particular to Faith Wilson Stein, Maia Rigas, and the series editors Patrick Anderson and Nicholas Ridout for their supportive critical friendship, patience, and collegiality; and to two anonymous reviewers, whose extensive and valuable feedback made this a much better book.

Both within and beyond academia, many people have influenced the progress of this project in incalculable ways. I will be forever grateful for the years I got to spend at the London Bubble Theatre Company, and for memories of working with Sylvan Baker, Winsome Duncan, Sonia Hyams, Clare Lewis, Kim Lyon, Andrea Mason, Tania Peach, Rebecca Pedlow, Jonathan Petherbridge, Elliot Rose, Andrea Vear, and Theresa Veith. I am indebted to Maxine Mei-fung Chung, without whom I might never have finished writing it at all. My perpetual gratitude and appreciation go to the friendtopia of Louise Foley, James Jackson, Zeinab Lenton, Chris Lenton, and Helen Moore for everything, always, and especially in this instance for dreaming up a title that worked. Likewise, to Donna Wilcox—my oldest friend, and like many of my family members a wonderful teacher. My enormous family is a wellspring of love, support, and boundless creative energy. I dedicate the efforts represented in these pages, with all of my love, to Mark, Paula, Tigere, and Lucy; Graeme, Laura, Elisha, Ezra, Lydia, Ethan, and Jed; Clare, Kevin, Ben, and Georgina; Dee; Lorraine; and to my wonderful parents, Beryl and Roger.

Restaging the Future

INTRODUCTION

Restaging the Future investigates the role of arts practices in the historical process of neoliberalization in Britain—a process that may or may not now be in terminal crisis.[1] The point of departure for the analysis I present here is simple: a set of projects in dance, public art, music, and theater, all of which were commissioned at around the same time in the mid-2000s, a moment well over halfway into the New Labour government's period in office. During these years, as part of its approach to "pro-market governance"[2] and its comprehensive project of "joining up" different domains of government, New Labour enlisted the arts and culture to stimulate and direct aspects of economic productivity and social life: to rejuvenate places, boost economic growth, and catalyze civic engagement. Economic and social aims had long been the purview of state action in relation to the arts and culture in Britain, whether explicitly articulated in terms of cultural policy or not—so in one sense, such an agenda was nothing new.[3] What was new was the expansiveness, reach, and substance of the government's program, and how it imagined and institutionalized active participation in the arts and culture as a mechanism for social and economic change. I examine this moment as part of the decades-long history of neoliberalism as it has unfolded in Britain, addressing projects made at the outset of the twenty-first century in order to write a "history of the present"[4] in relation to them. The turn to arts participation drew sustenance from already existing arts practices linked to "community"—an historically vexed term—and set the course for many subsequent developments. The actions, decisions, and commentary advanced as part of this scene in the mid-2000s built on, modified, or destroyed the ground established by the postwar consensus that preceded it—sometimes incrementally, sometimes with speed and shock. The alterations of this moment and their marketization of social life thereby set the conditions for possible futures, and delimited how they might be imagined.

The projects I discuss in this book, created by La Ribot, Artangel, People's Palace Projects, and the Liverpool Everyman Theatre, were realized through the navigation of a complex set of circumstances. The aesthetic and social visions they staged were distinct but indissociable from the "tangled mess"[5] of neoliberalization, and the specifics of a political and cultural environment which by the mid-2000s was well established. This environment influenced artists and organizations who may or may not have previously engaged with participatory and community-based work to do so, and provided the grounds for existing practices to be reimagined and reworked. Some of the initiatives I examine here involved participants of various ages, with or without formal training in dance, art, theater, and music, who did not identify themselves as professional artists—or at least not yet. In other projects, professional artists sought to represent "real life" by taking people with particular occupations or life experiences as their subjects—a concern with authenticity also reflected in these years, albeit quite differently, in the mass media and other areas of popular culture. Taking these projects as scenes condensing many cultural aspects, I trace the artistic, political, and institutional genealogies of alternative, community, educational, and public arts practice which made them possible, and the developments in culture which they were part of constructing. The projects witness contradictory interactions between artists working in various modes and traditions, between the liberatory ambitions of practitioners associated with arts participation—ambitions elaborated over many years—and a governmental strategy that placed arts and culture in the service of aims that were, in Jim McGuigan's words, "economic, in terms of competitiveness and regeneration, and, to a lesser extent, social, as an implausible palliative to exclusion and poverty."[6] These aims informed much cultural work in the 1990s and 2000s, whether proceeding under the rubric of "community," "participation," "education," or "social engagement," or not—and intersected with histories of arts practice in those areas which were far from mainstream, but which were and continue to be significant.

One such area of practice was theater-in-education (TIE), which was addressed by the theater-maker and writer Tony Coult in an essay compellingly titled "Agents of the Future: Theatre-in-Education" (1980)—a short critical history of what was then a relatively new mode of theatrical performance and participatory work with young audiences in schools. The essay appeared in a collection entitled *Dreams and Deconstructions: Alternative Theatre in Britain*, published a year after the election of Margaret Thatcher's Conservative government. The British TIE movement had been initiated in 1965 at the Belgrade Theatre Coventry—a producing repertory theater whose name was chosen to acknowledge a donation of timber from Serbia, and whose spacious modernist building had been completed as part of the city's program of postwar rebuilding only a few years earlier.[7] Both TIE and the Belgrade Theatre were in different ways cultural manifestations of the postwar social democratic consensus, and were contingent on increased investment in and the reorganization of cultural and educational infrastructure. This reorganization included the 1944 Education Act, which made secondary schooling both mandatory and free, radically affecting both the intake of schools and the constitution of the teaching profession itself.[8] Coult invoked Jean Piaget and Lev Vygotsky's social constructionist theories of education and the democratizing legacies of the 1944 Education Act itself in order to affirm the TIE movement's transformative political aims. Active audience participation was distinctive of TIE's approach, which sought "to nurture creative, sceptical and analytical systems of thought in young people."[9] Performances such as *The Price of Coal* (Belgrade TIE, 1978), which explored the historical and contemporary exploitations of the mining industry, and *Race Against Time* (Greenwich TIE, 1978), which examined immigration and racism, made use of role-playing and theatrical simulation in ways that, in Coult's account, resonate with twenty-first-century immersive theater strategies, but also deployed theatrical reflexivity to speak of the basis of modernity and the capitalist system in historical change. Anticipating the adversities that Thatcherism would bring, Coult concluded that "a greater clarity of vision of the role of all art is going to be necessary for any form of popular art to survive. Creating 'agents of the future' is one of TIE's goals, but it is increasingly clear that it is a goal to be shared by all of the alternative theatre."[10] An agent is the "doer of an action," the "cause of some process or change"—and in more impersonal terms, a force that is "acting, exerting power."[11] Certainly this latter meaning applies to TIE's hoped-for creation of "agents of the future"—young people who would be critically equipped, through their participatory engagement with theatrical representation, to act in the world in a future that would be better than the present, but who could also bring that prospective future into being.

Community arts, an expansive cross-art form that was a "love child of alternative arts and community action"[12] also flourished in Britain in the 1970s, with similar aims. These countercultural movements proliferated in the transition between a postwar moment of "expansion, social liberalism, and relatively high levels of state support for the arts"[13] and the corporatizing institutional changes that would be imposed on the arts as the process of neoliberalization began in earnest in the early 1980s under the Thatcher government.[14] Alison Jeffers and Gerri Moriarty's essential text *Community, Democracy, and the Right to Make Art: The British Community Arts Movement* (2017) provides a rare insight into the rise and decline of community arts, its engagement with state structures, and the persistence of its values in various contemporary practices. In the 1970s and into the 1980s, hundreds of community arts groups and organizations were established all over the country. Working in a range of art forms from film, video, printing, and visual art to theater and dance, artists embraced a variety of political positions which spanned socialism, libertarianism, and craft-driven interest in the time before industry—but all were united in a firm commitment to a thoroughgoing democratization of arts education, production, and presentation, in the interests of overturning the domination of a commodity-driven cultural sphere by an elite minority.[15] As Jeffers shows, both in order to pursue their work and as a matter of survival, community artists relied upon various kinds of state support, in the form of grant-funding for their projects as well as welfare support, and they also often self-subsidized their practice.[16] Thus, the academic and Arts Council member Harold Baldry, author of the 1974 report that first recommended Arts Council funding for community arts, noted in *The Case for the Arts* (1981) that community artists "rarely had a sellable product; when they had an audience, little or nothing could be expected in the way of 'box office returns'; and they could not or would not make a charge for participation in painting a mural or acting a play or making a video programme."[17]

Although its practices continued unevenly to expand in the context of Thatcherism, community arts as a national movement had petered out by the mid-1980s, and by the 1990s the term "community arts" had become almost a pejorative—redolent of infighting, unfashionable political commitments, and what by then seemed to be outmoded forms of cooperative organization—and was increasingly displaced by the less collectivist terms "participatory arts" and "socially engaged practice."[18] In parallel, as the 1980s wore on, theatre-in-education became one of the casualties of the Thatcher government's education policies and its retrenchment of cultural expenditures. In the latter part of the decade, TIE companies were hit hard by cuts to local education authorities, the devolution of budgetary management to schools, and the introduction of a more structured and inflexible National Curriculum, which curtailed the capacity of schools to invite visiting practitioners to contribute to classroom activity.[19] This situation of decline and stagnation was not unique to arts education, but was reflected across the arts sector during the 1980s and 1990s, and especially outside of the capital.[20] Following Thatcherism's attack on publicly funded arts practice in Britain, New Labour's enthusiasm for the arts in the 1990s and 2000s seemed like grounds for optimism and relief.

Neoliberalism and Neoliberalization

Restaging the Future analyzes the conditions and effects for the arts and culture of this renewal of support, and their entanglement in the process of neoliberalization which Thatcher's government had initiated. In David Harvey's oft-quoted definition:

> Neoliberalism is in the first instance a theory of political economic practices that proposes human well-being can best be advanced by liberating individual entrepreneurial freedoms and skills within an institutional framework characterized by strong private property rights, free markets, and free trade. The role of the state is to create and preserve an institutional framework appropriate to such practices.[21]

In the 1980s, the government's imposition of "the features of capitalist business management" on the values, practices, and operations of state-subsidized theater institutions was exemplary of neoliberal policy: the theater sector "would only be subsidized if it accepted the discourse of the 'real' world of the market economy."[22] Jamie Peck's insistence on "the never-inevitable ascendancy of neoliberal*ization* . . . as an open-ended and contradictory process of politically assisted market rule"[23] extends the sense of the temporal emergence engaged in the state's performance of its role in promulgating neoliberal reforms, and its adaptive mutability. Peck and Harvey's definitions treat the intersection between the capitalist system, the state, and neoliberalism as political philosophy as a given. That is the position likewise taken in this book. Capitalism and neoliberalism are sometimes confused with one another, a confusion which is not unreasonable. As Jeremy Gilbert points out, "neoliberalism is the most fanatically pro-capitalist ideology ever, and . . . it has become the default ideology of almost all actual capitalists, and certainly of almost all pro-capitalist political parties."[24] But it is essential, as Harvey does, to distinguish between these three elements: capitalism is a mode of economic organization, the state is a governmental apparatus, and neoliberalism is a normative theory regarding the relationship between the two and their role and function in people's lives, which is then translated into concrete governmental policies and actions.[25]

In historical terms, although neoliberalism as a philosophy originated decades before, the 1973 OPEC oil crisis and Pinochet's coup in Chile in the same year are widely interpreted as a critical turning point in the governmental uptake of twentieth-century political thought advanced in both Europe and the United States that prioritized the "free market."[26] Within Britain, the economic and social problems of that decade are likewise framed as the critical catalyst in the rise of Thatcherism—though Andy Beckett reminds us that between 1979 and the mid-1980s, after the Thatcher government's first two electoral victories, Britain was also riven by a long recession, rising unemployment, and riots across the country relating to economic inequality and the policing of racialized minorities in "a period of economic, social and political crisis that matched, and often eclipsed, anything in the seventies—indeed, anything in peacetime in the modern era."[27] Critics of neoliberalism from the left agree that neoliberalism's broad political project has been to quash the power of labor in the interests of (finance) capital.[28] But within this critical literature, there is no consensus as to the form that neoliberalism has taken in terms of governmental action, or even where in the world it has taken effect. Those averse to neoliberalism as an explanatory framework point, for example, to analyses of state action that contradict one another (neoliberalism being interpreted in terms of both "strong states" and "state retreat") and to mutating appeals since the 1950s to neoliberalism across different national and political domains.[29] By contrast, I find neoliberalism, but more particularly neoliberalization, to be critical in understanding the social, cultural, and political transformations of recent decades, and their consequences for the arts sector and arts practices in Britain. In that respect, I align this project with writers who see in neoliberalism a clearly distinct set of ideological patterns and commonalities, but who also identify and theorize the incidence of tactics and strategies serving this agenda that are contingent on context.

In *Constructions of Neoliberal Reason* (2010), Peck agrees that unspecified assumptions are "indefensible" as the basis for systemic analysis, but contends that neoliberalism's "sprawling yet uneven reach may also signify something perplexingly 'real,' if methodologically inconvenient, about the diverse and tentacular manifestations of market rule."[30] He proposes that neoliberalism is processual, hybrid, and "parasitic"[31] in nature, attaching itself to preexisting formations and shifting unevenly across different national contexts in the endeavor to bring market rule into being, and to manage its attendant crises. For this reason, he emphasizes the expedient and impromptu aspects of "neoliberal*ization*"[32] as a process, and the need for a materialist approach to analysis that is attentive to temporal and historical change, and takes account of the "interstices of state/market configurations."[33] The "free market," the sine qua non of neoliberal ideology, is a utopian chimera, which in practice is "doomed to co-exist with its unloved others, be these the residues of state socialism, developmental statism, authoritarianism, or social democracy."[34] Try as its protagonists might, neoliberalism "can never remake the world in its own image"[35]—a phrase which also points to the imperfectly performative function of representation. To make sense of such processes, an insistence that neoliberalism must be seen to exhibit "a wholly uniform and explicit doctrine, manifested in a homogenous and discrete policy programme"[36] as seen in the critiques of the framework's skeptics, is inadequate at best. The interpretation of neoliberalism advanced by Peck and others is one that I saw materially reflected in the work of the artistic projects I analyze here. These projects emerged in reaction to and in accommodation of new policy and funding agendas, and involved pragmatic approaches on the part of the various agents involved in dealing with the conditions of the time, pursued in relation to their own standpoints and aesthetic and ideological commitments.

A particularly valuable aspect of the line of argument Peck proposes is its identification of broad phases in neoliberalism's development. In the British context, there have been significant differences between Thatcherism's imposition of monetarism, cuts to state spending, and competitive individualism; New Labour's communitarian pro-capitalism; and the Conservative-Liberal Democrat coalition and Conservative enactment of policies of austerity in the 2010s in response to the catastrophe of the 2007–8 financial crisis. Peck and coauthor Nik Theodore have thus roughly periodized three phases: the "rollback" of the 1980s which saw large-scale privatization and deregulation; the "rollout" of the 1990s and 2000s, "neoliberalism's own institution-building moment, pursued through the euphemistic language of partnership, good governance, and helping markets work"; and the post-2008 crisis moment, an authoritarian "'rollover' phase delivered more by force of unilateral action than through democratic consent."[37] In parsing these phases, they build on work published by Peck and another coauthor, Adam Tickell, in 2002, relatively early in New Labour's governmental life, which characterized its approach as "the *rollout* of neoliberalized state forms (themselves partly the outcome of previous tensions and contradictions in the early neoliberalist project)."[38] Meanwhile, neoliberalism's consistent attributes include the inculcation of "individualistic, competitive, acquisitive, and entrepreneurial behaviour"[39] and state intervention, often covered over by rhetoric insisting on the need to reduce the role of the state in people's lives. Systemic reforms such as privatization and deregulation have been framed in terms of "'modernisation,'"[40] a discursive move that, as Gilbert notes, presents such processes as merely technical—though rhetorically speaking, as Alan Finlayson argues, it also harbors other historical associations with nation-building and with party politics.[41]

Restaging the Future is primarily concerned with the cultural practices and rhetorics of the rollout, "institution-building" phase of neoliberalism—the "high point of globalization of the early 2000s" that James Meadway proposes is most critical to an understanding of neoliberal governance.[42] Consider, for example, New Labour's *Create the Future: A Strategy for Cultural Policy, Arts, and the Creative Economy*, a manifesto text published in March 1997. It outlined a raft of measures relating to new media, film, community arts, formal education, the internet, science and technology, and the public library service. The manifesto also declared the party's intention "to revitalize the Theatre in Education initiative."[43] Its frontispiece featured a quotation from John Ruskin: "'A person who every day looks upon a beautiful picture, reads a page from some good book, and hears a beautiful piece of music will soon become a transformed person—one born again.'"[44] Many of the manifesto's twenty-six pages bore the legend "leading Britain into the future." And its introduction stated unequivocally that "our cultural industries are integral to Britain's future economic success. They also give us our sense of identity, define us and articulate our values, beliefs and traditions."[45] The cultural policy summarized in this short text insisted on innovation of thought in relation to the potential of the arts and culture: while "successive Conservative governments have considered it of minimal social and economic importance,"

> we strongly dissent from that view. We believe the quality of our arts and cultural industries, our creative talents exemplify the Age

> of Achievement which will be the hallmark of the next Labour government. They are central to the task of re-establishing a sense of community, of identity and of civic pride, the undermining of which has so damaged our society. They are vital to the creation of jobs and the growth of our economy.[46]

In the work of the cultural (quite rapidly reframed as the creative) industries, creativity, community, and economic productivity would act together as agents of a bright new national future.[47] The opening point of the manifesto's "executive summary" stated: "The arts should be supported by government for their intrinsic merit";[48] the techniques identified as facilitating such support in practice included audit, annual reporting, and public-private partnership. Combining this allusion to Ruskin—and as such, implicit reference to the postwar welfare settlement—with national identity, tradition, and technocratic mechanisms of measurement and assessment, this document is a study in contradiction, and the kind of hybridism that Peck and others have theorized. The stance it expressed manifestly offered reason for hope in relation to neglected values and practices in the arts, especially for the fields of community and participatory arts and education. But those values and practices would be expected to conform to a set of corporate-informed protocols emanating from nearly two decades of neoliberal governmental praxis—a process exemplary of the dynamic of "rollout" neoliberalism.

Culture and the "Third Way"

As is well documented, under Tony Blair's leadership, the rebranded New Labour revised Clause Four, the party constitution's statement of aims and values, in 1995, framing a communitarian politics known initially by the shorthand the "third way."[49] Its agenda, in the phrase of Anthony Giddens, one of its primary academic supporters, sought to move "beyond left and right."[50] The arts sector was decisively implicated in New Labour's "smoothly presented hybrid of neoliberalism and a recalibrated form of social democracy,"[51] as enacted in government when the party gained power in a landslide election victory in May 1997. The *Create the Future* manifesto discussed above built on the Conservative market-led cultural agenda.[52] However, this was only one aspect of a much more comprehensive and transformative cultural policy taking the economic and social future as its object.

In *Creative Britain* (1998) Chris Smith, the first secretary of state for culture in the newly created Department for Culture, Media, and Sport (DCMS), identified "five principal reasons for state subsidy of the arts in the modern world: to ensure excellence; to protect innovation; to assist access for as many people as possible, both to create and to appreciate; to help provide the seedbed for the creative economy; and to assist in the regeneration of areas of deprivation."[53] He defined this as "a profoundly democratic agenda, seeing cultural access as one of the egalitarian building blocks of our society."[54] Refuting Thatcher's aphoristic statement that "there is no such thing as society," he insisted: "We do very definitely believe in society; and cultural activity is part and parcel of that sense of community"[55]—conflating "society" and "community" in a manner that was characteristic of New Labour's centrist brand of neoliberalism.[56] As Robert Hewison notes, in reframing cultural activity in this way, the government not only "placed previously unheard of expectations on the arts and heritage"[57] in relation to its larger social policy goals; it also overhauled institutions and practices. Processes of "inspection, benchmarking, self-assessment, strategic planning, target setting, key performance indicators, and service agreements"[58] were put in place between the Treasury and DCMS to oversee and measure cultural initiatives. Funding infrastructures became increasingly centralized, with the 2002 merger of the Arts Council of England and the regional arts boards to create Arts Council England (ACE). The agenda of "new public management"[59] embraced by Thatcherism was thereby extended—or to restate Peck's phrase, "rolled out"—by New Labour via "an explosion of 'market-conforming' regulatory incursions—from the selective empowerment of community organizations and NGOs as (flexible, low-cost, non-state) service providers, through management by audit and devolved governance, to the embrace of public-private partnership"[60] within the arts sector and elsewhere.

And a crucial aspect of the government's cultural policy agenda that preoccupied both practitioners and critics was the turn to a binary discourse of social inclusion and exclusion—a discourse that is likewise one of the interests of this book. The chapters to come argue for the thoroughgoing influence of this discourse on both the public framing and the material manifestation of the projects they explore. The Social Exclusion Unit was a cross-departmental body which played a critical role in New Labour's vision of government that would be "joined-up"—"an umbrella term describing various ways in aligning formally distinct organisations in pursuit of the objectives of the government of the day."[61] Responding to new theorizations of poverty and its effects, the government defined social exclusion broadly as "a combination of linked problems such as unemployment, discrimination, poor skills, low incomes, poor housing, high crime, bad health, and family breakdown."[62] "Policy Action Team 10: A Report to the Social Exclusion Unit" (1999), a document examining the contribution the arts sector might make to this agenda, consolidated and institutionalized the work of François Matarasso, former community arts worker and author of the landmark study *Use or Ornament? The Social Impact of Participating in the Arts* (1997). This piece of research examined a set of projects in cities across the United Kingdom, and two in Europe and the United States, in order to argue that arts participation strengthened skills, self-esteem, employability, social cohesion, and the cultural life of the nation.[63] Matarasso argued that artistic practice's specific power in this regard was its traffic in "values and meanings," and he insisted that "it is the opportunity to get involved in—indeed to define—what matters that motivates people, transforming them from passive consumers of culture and social policy into engaged participants in arts projects and, by extension, in local democratic processes."[64] His study thus hinted at aspects of the uses that the New Labour government would seek to make of the arts sector in delivering policy goals superficially unconnected to artistic practice, but with hopeful echoes of the political engagement and localism of the alternative and community arts practices of the 1970s and 1980s.

The authors of the "Policy Action Team 10" report made it clear that they did "not believe that every artist or sportsperson should be a social worker by another name, or that artistic or sporting excellence should take second place to community regeneration," but they nonetheless insisted that "arts and sports bodies should acknowledge that social inclusion is part of their business."[65] In the follow-up document "Building on PAT 10: Progress Report on Social Inclusion" (2001), DCMS reported that "the sponsored bodies have accepted social inclusion as a genuine objective for culture and sport."[66] A raft of ensuing documents and research papers all variously referred to the importance of addressing objectives, strategies, and targets associated with social inclusion. However, none of these were especially clear as to what inclusion or social inclusion actually were.[67] As Angus Cameron and Ronen Palan put it in *The Imagined Economies of Globalization* (2004), "inclusion" was thus broadly deployed as "a self-sufficient descriptive noun."[68] Arts practitioners could therefore readily interpret these terms in relation, for example, to identity, or to the lived experience of social marginality—issues informing much participatory arts practice, if not necessarily always other modes of artistic work. But, as Cameron and Palan argue, the implicit logic was this: to be "included" meant to be economically productive—a move that "managed to neatly conflate issues of social citizenship and economic class"[69] while displacing the language of class altogether. Indeed, in 1999, Blair addressed the Labour Party conference with the sweeping claim: "The class war is over. But the struggle for true equality has only just begun." By this he intended "not equal incomes. Not uniform lifestyles or taste or culture. But true equality: equal worth, an equal chance of fulfilment, equal access to knowledge and opportunity,"[70] with "equality" here transfigured as meritocracy.

In *Artificial Hells: Participatory Art and the Politics of Spectatorship* (2012), Claire Bishop interprets the political aims and values of New Labour's inclusion discourse as "a mission to enable all members of society to be self-administering, fully-functioning consumers who do not rely on the welfare state and who can cope with a deregulated, privatized world."[71] She argues that the much-vaunted exercise of "creativity," essential in New Labour's "Creative Britain," similarly disguised an economic agenda, and referred to individuals who must "be entrepreneurial, embrace risk, look after their own self-interest, perform their own brands, and be willing to self-exploit."[72] My argument in this book differs in some respects from Bishop's in *Artificial Hells* and elsewhere in relation to participatory practices themselves, but I agree with her reading of the politics of this terminology. In the four chapters of this book, I examine the ways in which constructs of entrepreneurialism, regeneration, inclusion, and exclusion circulated around and conditioned artistic practices in this period. These constructs were often juxtaposed with "community"—a term whose meaning came to be rearticulated from the grassroots sense, as Raymond Williams put it, of "direct action and direct local organisation"[73] in the 1970s, to a scene of interventionist, top-down "instrumentalism" in the 2000s. For Bishop, the turn to participatory strategies in contemporary art and performance was often irretrievably complicit with this ideological context and signified a "slide into a sociological discourse,"[74] to the detriment of aesthetics and the possibility of cultural critique. She refers to Matarasso's *Use or Ornament* as a founding text in the development of policies of social inclusion in the arts, and argues, with Paola Merli, Eleonore Belfiore, and others, that the study engaged in "proving the positive impact of social participation in the arts"[75] on a spurious basis.

But Matarasso's intervention with *Use or Ornament* was more complex than a straightforward assertion of the value of participation on these terms. Along with its claims regarding social impact, it attempted to stimulate another debate about contemporary cultural practices. Matarasso wrote in his introduction:

> There is nothing reprehensible in artists seeking to extend cultural democracy by opening their practice to others, by sharing their creativity and experience—even, perhaps, by learning from people uninitiated into the mysteries of contemporary cultural discourse. There is obviously bad community art: there is, after all, no shortage of bad art (or bad education, medicine or government, if it comes to that). The argument that community art debases standards raises questions which lie at the heart of the present study: who defines quality, value, meaning?[76]

The use of the term "cultural democracy" positioned the text in relation to the contention between community artists and the Arts Council in the 1970s and 1980s in which an impetus toward transformative "cultural democracy" went head-to-head with the notion of "democratizing culture." The latter construct was criticized by the artist Owen Kelly as a top-down

" 'popularisation of an already decided cultural agenda' "[77] that prioritized the Western canon. *Use or Ornament* featured contributions from figures active in community, education, and alternative arts during this earlier period such as Naseem Khan, author of *The Arts Britain Ignores: The Arts of Ethnic Minorities in Britain* (1976), and Kelly himself. In this light, Matarasso's text might better be understood as an intervention seeking to defend the validity and viability of community, educational, and participatory practices that had suffered under eighteen years of Conservative rule. However, the textual form that mediated its questions about community arts, and through which its argument regarding arts participation's social effects was staged, was an evaluatory study, a choice that demonstrated acceptance of the managerial terms of New Labour's mode of governance. *Use or Ornament* signaled a willingness to engage in attempts to measure and appraise the effects of arts activity, in which processes of quantification would frequently take precedence.

This willingness represented an embrace of what George Yúdice has compellingly theorized as the turn to *culture as resource*, in which cultural practices, broadly defined, became "increasingly wielded as a resource for both sociopolitical and economic amelioration."[78] Writing specifically on the North American context, Yúdice argues that the rearticulation of culture in terms of resource, which intensified in the 1990s, was "due in part to the reduction of direct subvention of all social services, culture included, by the state, thus requiring a new legitimation strategy in the post-Fordist and the post-civil rights era in the United States."[79] *Use or Ornament* was an exemplary modeling of this legitimation strategy in the British context. Framing arts grandees archly as the "priesthood," Matarasso proposed that the "idea of harnessing the forces of art for social democratic purposes is seen by many arts professionals as a debasement of the currency." Furthermore, referring to the short Arts Council report *A Great British Success Story: An Invitation to the Nation to Invest in the Arts* (1985) and John Myerscough's book-length study *The Economic Importance of the Arts in Britain* (1988), Matarasso argued that "in truth, the arts sector has already compromised its principles by embracing an economic case for public funding."[80] But in Britain it was not the case, as Yúdice suggests of the United States, that culture was "no longer experienced, valued, or understood as transcendent."[81] Rather, as I demonstrate below and in chapter 3, in Britain in the 2000s "transcendence" and linked vocabularies would be mobilized by artists, cultural organizations, and even by members of the government itself as a defense against the government's utilitarianism. New Labour's application of market metrics to state-subsidized activities—the key performance indicators, targets, and outcomes discussed earlier—had much in common with governmental practices on the other side of the Atlantic.[82] Meanwhile, invocations of "transcendence," of art's capacity to rise above the machinery of commerce and administration, harked back to the premise of support for the fine arts on which the Arts Council of Great Britain had been founded in 1946—a premise based on an ideology of aesthetic value of much longer standing, as I will show in a moment.[83]

These were the institutional dynamics with which the British arts sector was confronted and in which it participated during the 1990s and 2000s. With the arts now definitively implicated in the project of governance, resources followed—according to one calculation, a real-term increase of 35 percent across the sector between 1998 and 2010.[84] Many artists and organizations benefited anew, ranging from the higher education and training sectors to those working in community and participatory practices and education. One artist respondent in a survey study, for example, alluded to the terminology of inclusion and exclusion as "a bit of a gift for us, in that that's always what we've been about, you know we might talk about the disadvantaged or lacking opportunities, *we've always been working with what we find is now social exclusion*. But I don't think we have a problem with it. I would have a problem with it if I was talking to kids we were working with"[85] (my emphasis). These reflections point to both the revisionist and stigmatizing aspects of the discourse—as Angus Cameron pointed out in a 2006 text, "specifically to label a person or a place as excluded (especially when they are manifestly members of that society) is an act of considerable social violence"[86]—and to the expectations that came attached to increased funding in relation to social and economic goals.

"Complex Historical Geographies"

Restaging the Future is a broadly historicist project that draws methodologically on performance analysis, archival research, historical research, and critical theory. I combine a Foucauldian theoretical approach to power, knowledge, and questions of population with materialist, historical, and geographical scholarship and attention to the live event. I examine the rhetorical presentation of artistic practices in a range of settings—from policy documents to the local, national, and international news—and the ideological underpinnings of discursive interventions made on behalf of art and artists. I juxtapose these with close, situated consideration of performances themselves. By drawing on multiple sources, I seek to understand how and where the voices of artists, cultural policy-makers, producers, and critics diverged and coincided, the political effects of their public utterances and performances, and how these utterances and performances interacted with the broader context of neoliberalization, often to uneasy effect. In her contribution to *Neoliberalism and Global Theatres* (2012), Jisha Menon invokes the "chronotope of palimpsest" as a means of recognizing how cities function "at the conjuncture of temporal and spatial practices—whereas nostalgia and futurity belong to a temporal horizon, palimpsest allows us to attend to the layering of spatiality through temporal traces."[87] Attending to this texture "interrupts the rhetoric of neoliberal progressivism"[88]—a critical agenda that resonates with Peck's assessment that neoliberalization is embodied in "complex historical geographies."[89] The projects I discuss all manifest such spatiotemporal layers, which I have likewise sought to excavate through attention to practice, performance, and discourse.

Using these methods, I historicize and interpret references to entrepreneurialism, exclusion, inclusion, and regeneration. In this period, all these terms quickly became shorthand for complex social phenomena. Such flattening-out is reflected in the "story"[90] of globalization to which the pro-market project of neoliberalization is connected, a story that Angus Cameron and Ronen Palan have scrutinized closely. Rearticulating citizenship in terms of economic participation, the inclusion discourse has been, they insist, indissociable from globalization and its institutional and cultural developments since the 1970s. These developments have been accompanied by an idealized spatial and cartographic imaginary that consists of three domains: "the *offshore*, *private* and *anti*-economies."[91] The offshore economy, a scene of "placeless globality," is framed in this discourse as "an ideal socioeconomic destination."[92] Meanwhile, "excluded communities are rooted to redundant places that have been abandoned by the economic mainstream."[93] Randy Martin put this in a slightly different way, drawing explicit attention to the implication of finance, which "divides the world between those able to avail themselves of wealth opportunities through risk-taking and those who are considered 'at risk' "[94]—a critique that, invoking terminology that is explored later in this book, also demonstrates the centrality of finance to the process of neoliberalization. Between the two is the "private economy" in which the nation's productive citizens engage.

However, the material contours of this domain are mysterious:

> The "normal" state of belonging, conformity, citizenship, economic participation and so on, is not described in territorial terms—the spatial articulation of social inclusion is assumed but never articulated explicitly. Spaces of social inclusion, we must assume, consist of all those other localities and spaces that are not characterized by exclusion.[95]

"Exclusion" signifies the relegation of some people to destitute localities, while "inclusion" signifies the economic and cultural capacity of others to enjoy global freedom to roam. In the years since the financial crisis and now under the conditions of the COVID-19 pandemic, attention from activists, journalists, and politicians to the role and function of tax havens and numerous calls for tax justice have politicized and demystified, at least to some degree, the construct of "offshore." And by examining the legislative histories of tax havens and their relation to colonial structures, Kojo Koram draws crucial attention to "the connection between the offshoring practices of wealthy companies that help produce inequality and Britain's colonial history."[96] But in the 2000s, the assumptions that Cameron and Palan explicate served quite successfully to veil the normative aspects of the inclusion discourse and its basis in ideas of economic subjectivity—what Foucault termed the "abilities-machine"[97] of the self as human capital. The absence of definitions of the term "inclusion" in cultural policy documents in turn effectively elided economic themes and the social and educational ambitions of practitioners. Read in tandem with Koram's work, Cameron and Palan's elucidation of this spatial imaginary gets at the heart of the performative, disciplinary, and postcolonial aspects of the inclusion discourse—themes that run through the chapters that follow. Narratives such as inclusion which have gone to construct globalization are means by which "past, present and future are 're-written' "[98]—or, to put it in terms aligned with the performance practices under discussion here, re-staged.

Cultural work is not reducible to abstractions such as inclusion—and especially not work that by design brings people from different backgrounds, interests, and walks of life together. The projects in dance, public art, music, and theater that I explore in this book were scenes of great intricacy, often involving multiple artistic disciplines, histories, and fields of commitment, as well as moments of friendly consensus, heated disagreement, and sometimes indifference or bafflement. My initial aim with this research was to problematize reflex associations of theater and performance with risk-taking, and to place such associations in their political and economic context. It was informed in part by my experience working for London Bubble, a touring theater and participatory arts company founded in 1972 that was then designated a regularly funded organisation of Arts Council England. Based in Rotherhithe, a historically deprived district in southeast London located close to Canary Wharf, the offices and rehearsal rooms of the company sat on a street between Kingstairs Gardens and a series of exceptionally dilapidated wharf buildings on St. Marychurch Street, built along the banks of the River Thames. During the time I worked for the company (2001–5), these wharf buildings were redeveloped as luxury flats.

Through the summer months, the company's outdoor promenade productions visited public parks across London, performing imaginative adaptations of well-known stories with cross-generational appeal: *Gulliver's Travels*, *Pericles*, *Alice through the Looking Glass*. The company played to audiences of three hundred a night. Its performances approached public space in a manner quite at odds with the modes of gated enclosure imposed by weekend-long music festivals in those same parks from the 2010s on, which were hired out to promoters by local authorities to supplement budgets decimated by central government austerity policies, with the effect of the "creeping privatization" of the parks.[99] Audience members would be given light, portable seating to carry from scene to scene. Minimal, beautifully designed and often mobile scenography, ingenious uses of lighting and live music, and a play with depth and multiple perspectives across the park landscape interacted with a respectful attitude to the public function of the parks and their other users which acknowledged that theater might not be everyone's first priority, that this was a temporary arrangement, and that if you, the person encountering the performance by chance, wanted to stay on to watch, then you were more than welcome, either free of charge now, or from the beginning for a reduced price tomorrow. Meanwhile, the inventive, often groundbreaking participatory work of the company in the early 2000s took place in schools, youth clubs, adventure playgrounds, and the company's own premises. It was positioned by various funders in relation to the vocabulary of "inclusion" explored in this book. My friends and colleagues in other performance contexts would sometimes dismiss participatory theater as complicit, condescending, or just straightforwardly not very good. It seemed to me that often, through their performances and sometimes even in the act of choosing to attend at all, the participants were putting themselves on the line in their social worlds in ways that were as decisive as other modes of performance which more readily attracted the positive descriptor of "risk." A case in point: in 2002, one of my colleagues returned to the office from a primary school in which she had been working with a story. Her drama workshop had been observed by the teacher, who had been astounded to witness a shy and guarded member of the class, who rarely spoke, secure in the fiction of a character she had created, speaking confidently in front of her peers. That same summer, a teenage resident of one of the local housing estates attended a summer workshop series in secret, with his mum fending off calls from his friends in the daytime by claiming he was asleep. My questions departed from observing the confusing confluence of uses of the word "risk" in multiple contexts, competing commitments to artistic work attracting that word, and the omnipresence of aggressive gentrification and capital development.

As the 2000s elapsed, the government's imposition of forms of measurement upon the arts became a point of contention across the sector. Greater investment demonstrably produced positive consequences in terms of the development of new theater and performance work and the strengthening of existing practices.[100] But as Hewison adroitly observes, "by 2003, targets had become a target."[101] To a large degree, government-imposed goals for the arts sector concerned reaching "new audiences"—an aim that the Bubble Theatre, to use its original name, had itself been established in 1972 to achieve.[102] Nonetheless, attempts from the sector to address government agendas did not necessarily emanate from artistic policy and practice, but were framed as audience development work to augment existing programming and as such were delegated to education and marketing departments.[103] To that extent, in "To Hell with Targets," his 2003 "manifesto" in *The Observer*, National Theatre artistic director Nicholas Hytner's critique focused largely on the demographics of the theater's audience.[104] Hytner insisted that "we mustn't judge the success of an artistic enterprise by its ability to pull in an Officially Approved Crowd,"[105] and he proposed that for government, such a crowd now consisted predominantly of young people whose attitudes were to be influenced through exposure to culture, with the work on stage itself strangely of secondary concern. Public objections to government-mandated outreach gradually became more vocal in a debate to which New Labour's second secretary of state for culture, Tessa Jowell, herself contributed a text entitled "Government and the Value of Culture" (2004). This position paper asked "how, in going beyond targets, can we best capture the value of culture?" and offered one answer by unequivocally arguing:

> In seeking access, we want to make sure we are supplying access to the best. Access to the substandard is access to disappointment which will translate into an unwillingness to keep paying. It will not inspire or raise levels of aspiration, and in the end is not worthwhile. That is why excellence has to be at the heart of cultural subsidy, and that is what we must insist on.[106]

The terms of Jowell's analysis point to another binary concept that hedged these debates about: the distinction between the "intrinsic" and "instrumental" value of culture. It was and continues to be a matter of common sense in British arts discourse to counterpose "art as social good" with "art for art's sake." The American literary critic Barbara Herrnstein Smith dubbed this construct the "double discourse of value": the distinction between "valuing things 'instrumentally' or 'as a means to some end,' and valuing them 'for their own sake' or 'as ends in themselves.'"[107] In *Cultural Capital: The Problem of Literary Canon Formation* (1993), John Guillory provides a detailed historical exegesis of the "double discourse" and pays particular attention to "aesthetic value"—terminology that, he shows, tends to be attributed to Immanuel Kant, but was actually predicated on eighteenth-century developments in political economy. Through a complex genealogical treatment of concepts of use, exchange, taste, utility, and production and consumption, Guillory argues that the two sides of the double discourse respectively map onto "the market" and the activities of "civil society," with the latter imagined, in eighteenth-century European culture, to lie outside of the market.[108] Accordingly, "moral philosophy could thus generate as the by-product of a double discourse of value an ontology of objects, a distinction between objects on the basis of whether they were directed to the end of utility (the commodity, the object of craft) or to the end of contemplation (the work of art)."[109] As such, Guillory proposes that "the problem of 'aesthetic value' is not in fact a perennial problem, but can be posed as such only after the divergence of aesthetics and political economy, and as a consequence of the repression of their convergent origin."[110]

In making this analysis, Guillory investigates "the archaeology of that double discourse [which] also unearths the largest aporia of social analysis: the problem of the relation between the economic and the cultural"[111]—an aporia similarly identified by Jean-Christophe Agnew, who argues that by the nineteenth century, "[a]estheticism and economism [had] effectively cartelized the social world by dividing cultural exchange and market exchange into separate disciplinary jurisdictions."[112] In the late twentieth and early twenty-first centuries, governmental demands regarding the use of culture as an inclusionary resource—that is, a resource intended ultimately to engender economic productivity—worked to erode the division between the market and culture which had been established in the nineteenth century. The "juncture of these two aspects of life," as Agnew puts it, had long haunted British cultural discourse irrespective of the inclusion discourse: recall Matarasso's metaphorization of art, quoted from *Use or Ornament* earlier, in terms of currency and its devaluation. But a sign of the struggle around the ideological consequences of the turn to inclusion was the proliferation of position papers, speeches, and policy documents addressing the problem. In these documents, both cultural producers *and* members of the government making these demands attempted to reinstate the familiar market/culture division in their citation of culture's "intrinsic" aspects.[113]

The work of Guillory and Agnew helps to make sense of the acute contradictions found in the debates about cultural value during the 2000s and since. There could be no straightforward solution or answer as to which kind of "value" should take precedence in culture: the instrumental/intrinsic binary emerged from and is sustained by the conditions of capitalist social organization. John Frow's arguments in *Cultural Studies and Cultural Value* (1995) are similarly clarifying. Frow argues against "positing imaginary social unities as the explanatory basis for accounts of cultural texts," and suggests we "think of cultures as being processes that divide as much as they bring together."[114] He proposes that acts of valuation, or determinations of what is to be valued in arts and culture, should not be treated fundamentally as questions of identity but rather of institutional and material interests. To theorize how such acts of valuation proceed, he refunctions Arjun Appadurai's concept of "regime of value" like this:

it is "a semiotic institution generating evaluative regularities under certain conditions of use, and in which particular empirical audiences or communities may be more or less fully imbricated."[115] The inclusion discourse was one such example of an "imaginary social unity" or "regime of value." "Inclusion" delineated the contours of what could and could not be said in this period about the effects of participatory arts in terms of community-building, togetherness, social integration, and personal transformation, and by whom. Bringing material experience, rhetorical performance, and the work of art together, Frow's model is exceptionally useful as a means of problematizing blanket applications of descriptors like "inclusion," and in understanding differences in audience response. And his insights regarding "the possibility that different (institutionally constituted) cultural domains might have quite distinct problematics of form and of audience"[116] strongly resonate with Shannon Jackson's more recent theorization of the reception of "social practice" in art, and "how our varied responses depend upon inherited assumptions about the nature of different art forms and the social function of artistic practice more generally."[117] To this we must add what Frow calls the "indispensable analytic tool" of class in terms of "class-*formation* (including the formation of class interests)"[118]—all of which plays a significant role in shaping the responses and assumptions of which Jackson speaks.

Possible Futures: Summary of Chapters

In the context of New Labour's Britain, the creative industries were envisaged as forms of economic activity whose productivity might be measured and predicted, and entrepreneurialism was vigorously encouraged—an ideology that both conflicted and resonated with existing ideas and practices. The projects I explore thus interacted with neoliberal governmentality and its futural and managerial modes of praxis, which favored "creative uncertainty" over and above the "'rigid' calculative knowledges" associated with the "'welfare-interventionist state'" of the postwar period.[119] The first chapter focuses on the figure of the entrepreneur and the manifestation of entrepreneurship in modes of experimental performance. It takes its lead from the Spanish live artist La Ribot's *40 espontáneos* (2004–7), a work that recruited large groups of non-dancers over the age of forty to stage a theatrical choreography that was explicitly framed as reflecting upon global industrial exploitation but which, I argue, also narrativized entrepreneurialism. I historicize *40 espontáneos*, a performance that hybridized live art and community dance, in terms of the mutual emergence in Britain of experimental and community dance in the 1970s and the institutions that were put in place to support them. I analyze the performance's representational paradoxes in terms of Stuart Hall's theoretical assessment of New Labour's political agenda as one which braided together commitments to marketization and social democracy, as well as the theater as a scene of capitalist value production.

The second chapter turns its attention to themes of regeneration and exclusion through the example of Artangel's *The Margate Exodus* (2005–7), a multi-art form project staged in the deprived seaside town of Margate. This town's identity as a tourist destination has taken various forms since the eighteenth century. *The Margate Exodus* involved large numbers of local participants of all ages in the creation of several works exploring the theme of migration, taking their cue from the biblical book of Exodus. I situate Artangel's interest in ephemeral site-specific work in a trajectory of debate regarding the effects of public and community art for economic and social life in the 1990s and 2000s, and address *The Margate Exodus* in terms of regeneration and political conflict concerning national, racialized, and class identities in a context of anti-immigration.

The third chapter explores People Palace Projects' *Favela to the World*, a transnational youth arts initiative that involved artists and institutions from Britain and Brazil, and which was geared to the "inclusion" of young people "at risk." Having contextualized "inclusion" and "at risk," I examine how national histories, ideologies, processes of nation-building, and forms of racialized identity inform constructs of cultural value, which in turn condition the material possibilities for artistic work in given situations. In Britain, dominant notions of cultural value as either "intrinsic" or "instrumental" particularly impacted the assiduously monitored fields of participatory arts and education.

The final chapter's discussion is prompted by *Unprotected*, a piece of verbatim theater commissioned by the Liverpool Everyman Theatre about street sex work and its regulation in the city, in the run-up to Liverpool's year as European Capital of Culture in 2008. I historicize the increasing popularity of verbatim theater in the 2000s and propose the momentum it gained to be an outcome of the work of primarily London-based institutions. I make a feminist argument regarding the gender politics of theatrically constructed "authenticity" and its interaction with logics of urban regeneration and capital development—a politics sitting in contradiction with the social agenda of the play itself.

In relation to the pursuit of social aims through the arts, one outcome of the turn to "culture as resource"[120] has been the expansion of academic scholarship in the field of community, applied and social theater and performance—and indeed, the elaboration of the category of "applied theater" itself. Some of the key interventions that mapped out this field were published in the 2000s by British and North American authors—for example, James Thompson's *Applied Theatre: Bewilderment and Beyond* (2003), *Digging Up Stories: Applied Theatre, Performance and War* (2006), and *Performance Affects: Applied Theatre and the End of*

Effect (2009); Helen Nicholson's *Applied Drama: The Gift of Theatre* (2005) and *Theatre & Education* (2009); Tim Prentki and Sheila Preston's *Applied Theatre: A Reader* (2008); Philip Taylor's *Applied Theatre: Creating Transformative Encounters in the Community* (2003); and Petra Kuppers's *Community Performance: An Introduction* (2006). This disciplinary expansion crucially enabled analysis of and access to practices that have historically been neglected and under-documented. But I have chosen not to approach the projects I discuss as exemplars of a particular mode of participatory practice or only through the lenses of pedagogy, transformation, and citizenship. Instead, I have treated them as opportunities to ask questions of genre and history within the broader disciplinary contexts of art, theater, and performance. In taking this approach, my investigation of these projects identifies unexpected ideational affinities between practices that have been positioned at odds—for example, between artist-led commissioning and community arts—and forms of historical co-emergence that may not be frequently acknowledged, such as those shared by experimental dance, community dance, and live art. Approaching categories such as "community dance" as in question and under construction facilitates the book's historical questions regarding the development of the practices it surveys, and the multiple scenes of discourse they engage.

Restaging the Future instead participates in what Sophie Nield has called the "strategic broadening" of the field of theater and performance.[121] Theater is only one of several art forms addressed in these pages, but theatricality and the logic of theatrical performance run throughout the book's analysis of both artistic practice and everyday action. For theater is a paradoxical activity that is both oriented towards the future in the subjunctive "what if?" mode which Richard Schechner and others have theorized extensively, and grounded in past action. As Schechner writes of his theatrical and performative concept of "restored behaviour," "to 'make history' is not to do something but to do something with what has been done."[122] Theater's unique capacity as an art form to bring multiple temporal and spatial planes into relation in the moment of live performance is one source of its many fascinations, joys, and frustrations. And theater's play with time, repetition, doubling, and the interplay between "reality" and "fiction" endows it with significant potential for education and learning—a potential embraced by the artists discussed in this book, from those engaged in the alternative arts movements initiated in the 1960s and 1970s, to those working more recently. The material relation between the presents, pasts, and futures imagined by artists and policy-makers during the decades of neoliberalization's unfolding is at the heart of this book's investigation. It embraces ideas of aesthetics, politics, the influence of artistic work on social and economic life—an issue on which there has been substantial disagreement both between and among artists and policy-makers—and the kind of subjects assiduously constructed by neoliberal ideology: citizen-consumers motivated by their own interests, and ready to compete in the global marketplace.

The projects I write about in *Restaging the Future* engaged the architectural and ideational legacies of the bourgeois public sphere of the eighteenth and nineteenth centuries. They bore traces of twentieth-century ideas of social democratic cultural action. They interacted with the material complexities of the built environment and numerous institutional formations. All of these aspects are variously the matter of each chapter's analysis. And though the site of this book's investigation is Britain, it also inevitably involves international issues and questions that were intrinsic to the work of the projects, and which bespeak the nature of capitalism as a global system and Britain's history as a colonial power: international touring practices, pan-European cultural events, transnational arts partnerships, and responses to asylum and immigration policy. Britain's infrastructure for arts production and presentation proceeds on the basis of a mixed economy that combines public funding distributed via central government and local authorities (for which support for the arts is non-statutory), support from trusts and foundations applied for competitively, philanthropic support from the private sector, and commercial engagement. Each chapter touches on this infrastructure, and on many different venues for the presentation of performance, from dedicated theaters on small, middle and large scales to arts centers, museums and music venues, to non-arts environments appropriated for performance—a diverse patchwork of contexts that has materialized unevenly over many decades, in a manner not dissimilar to Britain's towns and cities themselves. In *The Atlantic Sound* (2000), Caryl Phillips explores the city of Liverpool—the setting of this book's final chapter—whose majestic nineteenth-century public buildings were financed by the brutalities of the transatlantic slave trade. He draws his narrative to a close with a walk to Lime Street Station. He writes: "As I turn into the skateboarder's pedestrian precinct, I am struck by how the tall dark buildings of a bygone era, and the ugly concrete and glass ones which represent supposed progress, are all uncomfortably tethered together."[123] How ideas of the future have similarly been awkwardly hitched to the past in the work of performance runs through the analysis that follows.

Chapter 1

✦

"Double Shuffle"

Dancing around Entrepreneurialism

Restaging the Future begins its examination of theater and performance in Britain during neoliberalism's "institution-building moment"[1] with the figure of the entrepreneur. In the nineteenth century, the entrepreneur was idealized as "mythic"—a rare individual possessed of the kind of talent, work ethic, and good economic judgment not granted to all.[2] Contemporary neoliberal politics has sought to normalize competitive individualism and entrepreneurship's purported "flexibility, imagination, inspiration, acuity and inventiveness" as a mode in economic and social life.[3] As Jen Harvie demonstrates of the arts sector, from the 1980s on successive governments impressed upon arts practitioners and organizations alike the desirability of entrepreneurial resilience and responsiveness, taking the artist, an avatar of "creativity," to be the privileged exemplar of such qualities.[4] The pressure to embrace entrepreneurialism has not abated since the mid-2000s, either inside or outside the arts. To that extent, as Pat O'Malley wryly put it in 2004, now "the entrepreneur has to be all of us"[5]—though the more common experience of "entrepreneurship" is not wealth born of innovation, or even profitable self-employment, but "low-wage insecure work."[6]

Here, I consider the mythos of entrepreneurialism in relation to the Spanish live artist La Ribot's *40 espontáneos* (2004–7), a performance intersecting three aesthetic practices—live art, postmodern dance, and community dance. This experimental choreography, for performance by a company of up to forty nonprofessional participants, was inspired by bullfighting, and in particular by the unexpected intervention of the *espontáneo*, described on the artist's website in the mid-2000s as "the person who jumps into the bullring and steals the show from the bullfighter,"[7] and more recently, like this:

> In Castilian "espontáneo" is both an adjective (meaning voluntary or spontaneous) and a noun—it designates a lunatic fringe of

> spectators at bullfights, untrained crazies who leap into the ring and try to steal the matadors' thunder. The stars of La Ribot's *40 Espontáneos*, 2004, are also non-professionals but they perform in a highly co-operative spirit.[8]

In the three years of its life, *40 espontáneos* received thirteen "manifestations" with thirteen different companies in cities across Europe and Latin America, including, in 2005 and 2006, three in Britain—London, Nottingham, and Glasgow. It was first presented in France, Portugal, and Brazil, but the piece had its roots in Britain—it was devised by La Ribot in a series of residencies in 2002 towards the end of the time she spent living in London, a city with a dynamic live art and dance scene.

40 espontáneos was in one sense a community dance performance, and one which provided a generous, supportive, and inspiring encounter between nonprofessional participants and the work of a celebrated contemporary artist. But it was also a piece of live art narrativizing the inexperienced performer as a figure of initiative who "steals the show," who does not officially belong on the stage, thus contradicting one of the key principles of community dance in Britain as it has emerged since the 1970s—that anyone can dance, and should be able to access opportunities to dance. This contradiction is compounded historically by the fact that in 1970s Britain, community dance and experimental modes of postmodern dance, dubbed New Dance, were inextricably connected both formally and institutionally. This was a unique phenomenon, not reflected in other European situations—as illustrated by "Remembering British New Dance," a series of talks curated by Jonathan Burrows and Ramsay Burt in 2012. At the first talk, one audience member asked what its panel members thought would be the equivalent of New Dance in Britain today, hinting that such practice was now largely to be found elsewhere in Europe in the work of conceptual dance artists (*Konzepttanz*, or as Johannes Birringer has described it, "not dance").[9] The choreographer Gaby Agis responded:

> GA: I think one of the things that we do well—I say "we," I mean this country—is diversity. So we have a huge amount of dance going on, we have incredible participation. We have Indian dance, African dance, we have this incredible breadth and width of the country if you want to work with people with Parkinsons, if you want to work with younger children, participation. And then, in a way, a desire to support many, many dance forms. And I think that's what we do well. I think the kind of work that maybe you're interested in—but I don't know—I think it is quite specific, and I think some of the European countries have a concern and a support for that work. But I think within the diversity of our communities within dance,

> within the UK, that kind of work isn't always supported. Some of it is, but I think it's a bigger strategy. So, I feel that's part of what goes on.[10]

Later in the discussion, Jonathan Burrows spoke of New Dance as a "legacy which I had witnessed and been thrilled by and been empowered by" and "this extraordinary radical openness, still, in this country towards access for people of disability, who are older, younger, etc., to dance and move, or dance from different cultures. And it really doesn't exist in the same way elsewhere. It begins to exist." Making reference to Jérôme Bel's *Disabled Theatre* (2012–18)—"quite a shock for cultures which have never seen Candoco, for instance"—he insisted that "access is also a legacy of the same period of time that we're discussing." Agis and Burrows's observations rehearse many of this chapter's themes—the expansive richness of participatory dance cultures in Britain, conflict over the terms and concepts used to describe and delineate dance movement and practice, and institutional dissimilarities between national contexts, made evident in the circulation of artistic work across different territories.

This was the situation in Britain in which *40 espontáneos* arose, and what makes it such an interesting example to explore. In tracing the histories that undergird the piece, I argue that the paradoxes of the performance's particular engagement of nonprofessional participants in the mid-2000s resonated strongly with what Stuart Hall called the "double shuffle" of New Labour's communitarian "rollout" neoliberalism—a dynamic hybrid construct in which values of marketization and entrepreneurialism ran alongside "another, *subaltern* programme, of a more social democratic kind."[11] In the commoditized domain of the theater, the tensions of the double shuffle were expressed in relation to professional artistic identity—a theme that recurs in the chapters of this book. In the political context of the late 1990s and 2000s, institutions increasingly provided access to making artistic work available through programs of education and participation, and rehearsed narratives of openness and community engagement. But for individuals, professional practice and status nonetheless remained the marker of artistic legitimacy—a status made problematic both by forms of artistic experiment seeking to challenge commodity logics, and by structures of insecure freelance employment. And in relation to dance specifically, the practice at the center of this chapter, not only does the professional dancer epitomize the precarious worker but also, "in contrast to other artistic disciplines, the dancer's artistic existence seldom lasts a lifetime"[12]—an existence whose brevity and economic precarity are exacerbated by the occupational hazards of injury and ill health.[13]

In the discussion that follows, prompted by their unusual interaction in *40 espontáneos*, I outline histories of live art, postmodern and community dance, and conceptual dance. Each of these movements has, in different ways, been concerned with what kinds of performance are deemed acceptable within the commoditized domain of the theater for public presentation and consumption. Next, I address some of La Ribot's works preceding the creation of *40 espontáneos* in terms of their engagements with theatricality, and what I interpret as their complex symbolic treatment of the economic predicament of the solo performance artist. Finally, I turn to *40 espontáneos* itself, a performance whose approach to theater as construct I see as enunciating the same theme. I argue that its chosen theatrical metaphor both offered a thoughtful dramatization of the limits of entrepreneurial subjectivity and obscured the complexities of the historical development of community dance in Britain—a field whose beginnings are entwined with the experimental choreography that might now be seen as its opposite. Investigating the histories of performance that in a sense made this piece possible, I take account of their mutating citation of the figure of the entrepreneur and practices of entrepreneurship since the 1970s, the moment of neoliberalization's initial momentum.

Twentieth-Century Legacies

The interdisciplinary practices of live art, postmodern dance, and community dance emerged in parallel and in interaction in the second half of the twentieth century. In defining live art, Dominic Johnson proposes that "in the UK, Performance Art is a formal tradition, while Live Art is a sector."[14] First reluctantly supported by the Arts Council in the late 1960s and early 1970s—initially by the same committee that supported community arts—live art has since grown and developed substantially, informed by European and American visual art, sculpture, dance, and performance art, taking place in a wide range of institutional and non-institutional spaces across the country.[15] The term "live art" embraces an enormous heterogeneity of work. As such, Johnson sees the term only as "a useful label for a context—or a set of contexts—where varied works are presented or received. It is not particularly useful as a concrete description of actual practices or performance."[16] He cautions against treating the assessments of live art that appear in the writings of Lois Keidan, former director of the Live Art Development Agency, as "statements of orthodoxy."[17] But keeping that caveat in mind, Keidan's texts are an essential guide as to how live art was imagined as a contemporary "sector of work"[18] in the 2000s. In 2002, Keidan argued that live art operates "in the cracks in our culture, in the kinds of places synonymous with the innovation, risk, and dissent inherent in radical ideas."[19] In 2005, she described it as a movement which "privileges artists who choose to operate across, in between, and at the edges of more conventional artistic forms."[20] And as she put it in 2006, live art intends "to open up new artistic models, new languages for the representation of ideas, new ways of activating audiences and new strategies for intervening in public life."[21] Both the term "live art" and the Live Art Development Agency itself, established in 1999, emerged to protect the interests of the otherwise vulnerable experimental, and often solo, practitioner. For Keidan, live art functioned as "a cultural strategy to include processes and practices that might otherwise be excluded from more established curatorial, cultural, and critical discourses."[22] Emphasizing outsider status alongside innovation, these statements propose live art as a peculiarly entrepreneurial practice, reflected too in Johnson's thoughts on the sector's "powerful status as a creative engine of sorts, a laboratory of ideas—even a rite of passage—that inspires the development of other artforms."[23]

In some respects, live art bears a resemblance to British postmodern dance, which also emerged in the late 1960s, and was assigned the name "New Dance" in 1977 with the first edition of *New Dance* magazine, a publication which documented its experimental practices.[24] The New York collective Judson Dance Theater is most commonly invoked with regard to the term "postmodern dance"—indeed, the British academic Nick Kaye's *Postmodernism and Performance* (1994) devotes a chapter on dance entirely to Judson and its practitioners—and Judson's work was of significant interest to British dancers in the late 1960s and 1970s.[25] But the roots of New Dance also lay in earlier challenges made by British dancers to the hegemony of classical ballet. The figures for public funding for dance provision readily demonstrate classical ballet's institutional dominance in British dance during the early 1970s: in England, only 4 percent of the Arts Council's grant-in-aid funding was allocated to dance, and of that, 86 percent went to support ballet companies and ballet schools.[26] Judith Mackrell opens *Out of Line: The Story of British New Dance* (1992) with a discussion of Teresa Early's Balletmakers Ltd, a company Early set up in London in 1963 to cater to her interest in classical choreography and movement, despite not being "physically suited to being a professional classical dancer."[27] Open to all, Balletmakers Ltd represented an early move towards democratizing dance and "do-it-yourself" in the face of institutional exclusion.

Stephanie Jordan meanwhile locates the beginning of New Dance in the establishment of the London School of Contemporary Dance in 1966, which "spawned its own creative countermovement and became the centre for choreographic experiment in Britain,"[28] particularly on its move to The Place in 1969. But the decisive moment in the development of New Dance was the founding in 1976 of X6, a dance collective named after the building that its artists occupied: Block X, Floor 6 of a disused tea warehouse in Butler's Wharf, Bermondsey, adjacent to the Thames.[29] When the redevelopment of Butler's Wharf prompted their expulsion, the artists retained the name "X6," while moving to east London to establish Chisenhale Dance Space.[30] As the Chisenhale website explains:

> In 1980 the evicted artists found new premises at the Chisenhale works in Bow, a derelict varnish factory. They surgically removed their magnificent old maple floor, on which they had created so many iconic underground works, and grafted it onto the new location, where it still remains—transferring that experimental spirit up through the feet of a new generation.[31]

Like aspects of the dance scene in New York in the same period, the deindustrialization of London's docks and manufacturing base became the grounds, both metaphorical and actual, for the development of the "experimental spirit" of New Dance.[32] (Jordan notes that the artists did in fact envisage the space as "the British equivalent to the artists' lofts in New York.")[33]

Run on principles of collective organization, X6 provided classes in a wide range of techniques, staged performances within the building and its dockside environs, and hosted visits from European and North American choreographers. It actively embraced interdisciplinary and intermedial work, exhibiting "no concern at all as to whether what was shown fitted established definitions of dance."[34] The collective's politically engaged approach to movement resolutely rejected notions of dance as an after-dinner diversion or entertainment for well-heeled audiences.[35] In 1986, ten years on from the establishment of X6, the founder member Fergus Early delineated New Dance's ethic, with echoes of the manifesto form taken by Yvonne Rainer's "No to Spectacle" (1965)[36]—although not its substantive ideas—at a symposium retrospective at Chisenhale:

> New Dance is not:
>
> baggy trousers, rolling about, chinese shoes, contact improvisation, ballet to rock music, release work, image work, outside performances, post-modern dance, martial arts, self-indulgence, American, non-narrative . . .
>
> New Dance does not exclude:
>
> formal choreography, tap, ballet class, baggy trousers, rolling about, chinese shoes, jazz shoes, no shoes, army boots, self-indulgence, contact improvisation, rock music, virtuosity, stillness, narrative . . .
>
> . . .
>
> The one and only essential concept to New Dance is liberation.[37]

X6's eviction from Butler's Wharf in 1980 meant that the work of the collective as such was short-lived, but as Jordan shows, some of the artists themselves were in any case coming to experience frustration with the collective's politics, its resistance to technique, and their perception of the curtailment of their individual achievement by the prioritization of the collective.[38] In 1992, Mackrell acknowledged the ongoing influence of New Dance on contemporary dance practice, but proposed that "New Dance" had been largely replaced by the term "postmodern dance"; she noted too that, by then, the political vehemence of such works had lessened, and she deplored the ever-increasing economic need for groups to "woo their audiences and sponsors"[39]—a consequence of the marketization of state-subsidized arts practice under Thatcher's government in the 1980s.

Community Dance

The "wooing of audiences and sponsors" is by now a standard aspect of professional artistic practice. And by the 2000s, the interdisciplinary aesthetic concerns of postmodern dance and community dance's emphasis on participation and education no longer seemed immediately related to one another. But in Britain in the 1970s, the two movements developed hand in hand. In *Dance as Education: Towards a National Dance Culture* (1991), Peter Brinson, a passionate advocate of all forms of dance, even suggested community dance in Britain to be a movement of which "in a way, New Dance was a part."[40] However the order of priority is articulated—Mackrell frames community dance as emerging with and alongside New Dance, as does Jordan—the two were intimately connected, with each starting from the premise that "dance is not just an exclusive art form, but an activity that should be open to everyone."[41] And in terms of the development of the infrastructure for dance in Britain, there is a direct genealogical relationship between the earliest iterations of community dance, then connected to New Dance, and the institutions through which audiences and participants now come to see and enjoy multiple forms of dance.

As accounts of his career acknowledge, the importance of Peter Brinson and his work and thinking to the development of both community dance and dance culture in Britain cannot be overstated.[42] In his own writings, Brinson framed dance as an essential part of human experience detrimentally marginalized in industrialized society, and dancers themselves as "prophets of a different future and better humanity in which body, mind, and emotions equally are balanced and valued."[43] In 2006, Christopher Thomson of The Place wrote:

> It was Peter who almost single-handedly created and promulgated the term "community dance," who encouraged the Gulbenkian

> Foundation to make strategic decisions to support the earliest posts and projects, who created the Laban Community Dance course, and who articulated the philosophy and practice of community dance untiringly in his speeches and his writing, throughout the 1980s and 1990s until his death.[44]

Brinson's own Gulbenkian-funded project Ballet for All, launched in 1964 as an adult education initiative at Oxford University, anticipated the community dance movement. With dancers from the Royal Ballet's touring company, including Fergus Early, Ballet for All presented lecture-demonstrations in adult education contexts all over the country, describing, explaining, and performing examples of classical ballet to audiences who might not otherwise have had access to the form.[45] (Early attributed his later experimental engagements with text in the pieces *Two Man, One Man* (1977) and *Manley Struggles* (1978)—New Dance works exploring masculine stereotypes—to his participation in Ballet for All.)[46] The aims and basis of the Ballet for All initiative, which was televised in 1970 with a companion book, were social democratic. As Brinson put it in an article for *New Dance* in 1982, Ballet for All "reflected a feeling that the heritage of classical ballet should be shared more widely and be less elitist," and likewise reflected "a change of emphasis in the British adult education movement during the 1950s, when the practice and appreciation of the arts were added to traditional social and economic studies."[47] In the same article, he theorized what he saw as the contemporary importance of the arts as a peaceful and democratic challenge to power, and an agent of positive social change.[48]

As director of the Gulbenkian Foundation between 1972 and 1982, Brinson oversaw a huge amount of work focused on the linked themes of "community relations, community action, and community arts"[49] in alignment with emphases on these fields in other areas of British social policy and the voluntary sector in the 1970s. But the foundation also sought the integration of "arts education and the practice of art itself,"[50] particularly in the field of dance. The Gulbenkian Foundation supported the Contemporary Dance Trust, Dance Umbrella, *New Dance* magazine, summer schools for artists, and one of the first three dance "animateur" posts in a school in Cheshire in 1976.[51] These posts and the work of the artists who assumed them would become the seeds of the community dance movement, which aimed to open out universal access to dance. Community dance work thus initially proceeded on the animateur model—a construct deriving from a notion of "sociocultural animation" in social policy across Europe during the 1970s, as a means of managing the detrimental effects of postindustrial economic decline and recession, and stimulating social engagement.[52] The community dance movement gathered pace in the late 1970s and early 1980s, and by the mid-1980s around 35 animateurs were practicing across the country with Arts Council support, rising to more than 250 by 1992.[53] The movement and the institutions that developed around it would become the basis for the foundation of the national dance agencies in Britain, which were established following recommendations made by the policy-maker Graham Devlin in an influential dance sector report, *Stepping Forward* (1989). The work of the national and regional dance agencies, spread across the United Kingdom, subsequently combined classes and community outreach with professional development for dancers and performances for audiences.[54] One such agency, Nottingham's Dance4, presented La Ribot's *40 espontáneos* in the context of the festival Nottdance.

As community dance expanded during the late 1970s and 1980s, debates around the practice proliferated. Gradually the discourse on community dance shifted from more radical challenges to institutions and practices, and then to institutionalization itself, as exemplified by the developing conversation around animateurs. Writing in the now-defunct *Dance Theatre Journal* in 1985, Anthony Peppiatt decried what he saw as animateurs' undue focus on contemporary technique in their work with participants: he argued that "the Born Again belief that animateurs are part of a brand new movement is another manifestation of a reactionary and elitist tradition,"[55] and he called for "a community dance policy which puts the individual's and group's needs and potential first and not the art form as a fixed or benign cultural value."[56] In the same journal issue, Brinson himself focused on the less radical matter of the development and evaluation of the field, and the provision of funding and support to mitigate "the frequent isolation of animateurs in their work"[57] as freelance artists. In 1988, Christopher Thomson suggested that "community dance" itself "might better be thought of as indicating a 'family resemblance' between a diverse range of activities, rather than being definable in any narrow way" and drew attention to the questions surrounding the use of the term "animateur," which some practitioners saw as "patronising in its assumption that communities needed animating."[58]

The logic of "animation" was also entrepreneurial, with the etymology of the term "animateur" expressly invoking an action of breathing metaphoric life into the unused or inoperative—and the role itself was cited explicitly in a 1986 evaluation report enumerating how many jobs an animateur was in fact required to do: "administrator, adviser, choreographer, dancer, diplomat, entrepreneur, fund-raiser, politician, promoter and teacher."[59] This dynamic was reflected in François Matarasso's 1994 account of the emergence of dance animateurs offered in a handbook text. Matarasso reminded his readers of the exigencies of Britain's economic circumstances in the mid-1970s, and commended the way in which

> dance practitioners made a virtue of necessity, creating a way of working which was flexible, sensitive to different communities

> and, by developing partnerships, maximised resources. The animateur model, as defined by its pioneering practitioners, won respect on all sides and showed how a relatively small investment could provide a valuable link between artists and arts organisations, local authorities, and the general public. And where there were no arts organisations—as in many rural areas—animateurs became a sort of human arts infrastructure, reaching places and people that others could not.[60]

Matarasso's commendation of the animateur model's entrepreneurialism also demonstrated the rhetorical rise, by the mid-1990s, of themes of value for money, partnership, and flexibility.

Clearly, ideas of community dance's function have come to be debated and remediated over time. But one key principle remains the same: irrespective of age, income, cultural background, or physical capacity, dance is and should be available to anyone. Helen Poynor, director of the Walk of Life center in Dorset and an artist who trained with Anna Halprin, an early figure in American postmodern dance, thus insisted in 2008 that "if we accept that any body is potentially a dancing body (and without this premise it is not possible to work in community dance), then we need also to accept that any movement has the potential to be a dance movement."[61] These principles return us to the vanguardist aesthetic and political principles of postmodern dance of the 1970s, and the joint emergence of New Dance and community dance as democratizing practices. And, as the Foundation for Community Dance's research report "Mapping Community Dance" (2001) had it, the goal of community dance practice, to encourage participants

> to operate as professional artists do—with an artist's questions, perspectives, intuitions, feelings, and responses, to make sense of and create meaning in the world—is of itself a hopeful, empowering, and humanising activity for people to engage with—and by the way you get some good art.[62]

The remark apparently casually tacked on to the end of this statement both asserts social and individual experience as the priority of community dance, and defends against preconceptions of aesthetic mediocrity. This defense points to the wider ideological context explored in the introduction and in chapter 3 of this book—a context in which community-based arts activities have been understood only secondarily as aesthetic practices by virtue of their non-commoditized (or non-commoditizable) status. This is despite the fact that, as Ken Bartlett has written, New Dance and its embrace of strategies such as quotidian movement, contact improvisation, and so on "allowed and encouraged a small number of professional dance artists to see that there were alternative ways of engaging non-professionals not only in dance but more importantly in the art of dance."[63] It was a method by which, as Jayne Stevens has proposed, dance animateurs as practitioners were able "to chart a path between the more radical aspects of cultural democracy and the more conservative aspects of democratisation of culture."[64]

During the 1990s and 2000s, the community dance sector became "adept at arguing the instrumental impact of dance"[65] to government. The focus of these arguments was the self-actualization or empowerment that participants might experience by dancing nonprofessionally under the professional guidance of a facilitator.[66] And accordingly, the professional facilitation of community dance was further institutionalized. By 1996, community dance was framed explicitly as a category embracing "all dance activities at every level but not professional dance performance."[67] "Community" meanwhile came to refer to the promise of the practice: as Christopher Thomson wrote in a 2008 piece, the production of "the experience of *communitas*, of solidarity and significance, in an immediate and grounded way."[68] This account represents "community" not as a vision of an alternative and liberatory mode of dance-making, but as a valued outcome and attribute of "a body of professional practice that is increasingly admired and emulated by dancers and policymakers worldwide."[69] A DCMS document from 2004 similarly described dance's value to the government's inclusion agenda by positing that it "can positively aid social cohesion; it is embraced by different cultural backgrounds and religions; it has no language barriers; it is generally not competitive and anyone can take part; it has positive effects on social behaviour; and, it can encourage people to express themselves through creative experiences."[70] While supportive of dance provision as such, this narrative rejects the idea that different aesthetic languages, traditions, and cultural politics are there to be considered in engaging with dance on a participatory basis, and instead conceives of dance vaguely in terms of creative movement; the key theme is subjective and social transformation.

"Not Dance"

As these developments were unfolding in Britain in the 1990s, the conceptual dance movement in which La Ribot is a significant figure was gathering pace in Europe. André Lepecki, a significant advocate of this "nameless"[71] movement, details a series of characteristics that the works of artists Jérôme Bel, Vera Mantero, and La Ribot in particular share:

> A distrust of representation, a suspicion of virtuosity as an end, the reduction of unessential props and scenic elements, an insistence on the dancer's presence, a deep dialogue with the visual

> arts and with performance art, a politics informed by a critique of visuality, and a deep dialogue with performance theory. The most important element behind all these aspects would be: an absolute lack of interest in defining whether the work falls within the ontological, formal, or ideological parameters of something called, or recognised as, "dance."[72]

Lepecki notes resonances with the performances of Judson in the United States, and Pina Bausch's Tanztheater Wuppertal.[73] This aesthetic logic also bears a clear affinity with New Dance and postmodern dance in Britain—which were likewise concerned to address the politics of dance presented to public audiences. Lepecki begins *Exhausting Dance: Performance and the Politics of Movement* (2006)—an analysis of La Ribot's work and others—with a critique of elements of the mainstream industrial apparatus for producing and consuming dance performance. He juxtaposes the *New York Times*'s Anna Kisselgoff's insistence that dance consists of a "flow or a continuum of movement"[74] with an account of the legal action that attendee Raymond Whitehead unusually launched in regard to the presentation of Jérôme Bel's *Jérôme Bel* (1995) at the 2002 International Dance Festival of Ireland:

> In a statement to the *Irish Times* of 8 July 2004, Mr. Whitehead articulated a clear ontology of dance that was not at all dissimilar to Kisselgoff's. According to the *Irish Times*: "There was nothing in the performance [he] would describe as dance, which he defined as "people moving rhythmically, jumping up and down, usually to music but not always" and conveying some emotion. He was refused a refund.[75]

By denying the legitimacy of intellectually provocative, non-normative dance works, Lepecki argued that critics such as Kisselgoff performed "an ideological program of defining, fixing and reproducing what should be valued as dance and what should be excluded from its realm as futureless, insignificant, or obscene"[76]—an effect reflected in Whitehead's outraged reaction.

Jérôme Bel's first piece, *Nom donné par l'auteur* (1994), was an hour-long performance in which, as the *New York Times* critic Rosalyn Sulcas describes, "two men manipulate household objects—a vacuum cleaner, a dictionary, a hair dryer, a ball, a rug—mostly in expressionless silence."[77] Certainly, this performance bears little relation to dance conceived as "'people moving rhythmically, jumping up and down, usually to music but not always.'"[78] Speaking at "Not Conceptual," a symposium held at London's Siobhan Davies Studios in 2007, Bel ruminated on how, on one occasion, the bewildered audience of the piece got up and left, leaving the work playing to no one.[79] Decades on, that response to such works is no longer the norm. *Exhausting Dance* and its substantial scholarly influence is itself a powerful index of the academy's support of experimental practice, which has arguably acted as an industrial catalyst for more widespread programming and mainstream critical celebration.[80]

Being active in curatorial work, industrial lobbying, and networking, artists have engaged in discursive interventions themselves, such as the "Manifesto for a European Performance Policy" (2002) consulted by Lepecki in an earlier article. This manifesto was devised and published following an artists' symposium at Tanzquartier Wien in October 2001 which La Ribot organized with Bel, Xavier Le Roy, and Christophe Wavelet. The introductory rubric of the manifesto noted that "contemporary performance artists are increasingly concerned with being able to decide on their means of production independently."[81] The manifesto itself, whose primary demand was an end to "the drive by cultural institutions and the art market alike to fix and categorise contemporary art practices,"[82] also rehearsed cultural policy rhetorics:

> Our practices are synonymous with funding priorities in terms of innovation, risk, hybridity, audience development, social inclusion, participation, new cultural discourses and cultural diversity, cultural difference.[83]

The production of contemporary performance art—"an articulate platform from which to challenge the dominant post-colonial narratives and traditional representations of the 'other' "—was thus highly conducive to cultivating interconnected globality:

> We consider the borders between disciplines, categories, and nations to be fluid, dynamic, and osmotic. We produce work that develops partnerships, networks, and collaborations, disregards national borders, and actively contributes to the local, European, and transnational contexts.[84]

The artists called for "a new social status that would acknowledge new concepts of work that have altered the distinction between so-called 'productive' and 'non-productive' periods."[85] In other words, the manifesto accepted globalization as a fait accompli with which, in many respects, its writers' aesthetic interests harmonized. The task at hand was to find structures to accommodate and properly support artists whose practices had complicated the distinction between "work" and "life"—a distinction which, with the entrenchment of digital technologies and structures of insecure employment, was already subject to systematic erosion in social and economic life elsewhere.

La Ribot herself is the celebrated originator of a significant body of performances, whose many awards include the Golden Lion for Lifetime Achievement at the Venice Biennale Danza 2020. Her works have grappled with the status of representation on numerous fronts—critics have interpreted them in terms of time, architecture, melancholia, the canon of Western dance, and modernist intertextuality—and have drawn on and subverted her early training in classical ballet. In view of their particular experimentation with what Lois Keidan calls the "tensions and borders between dance, performance, and visual art,"[86] her performances have primarily been recognized and programmed in Britain as live art.[87] They have also responded to and thematized the experimental solo artist's economic predicament. La Ribot's own career as an artist began in Spain during a period of political and economic upheaval and transformation. In the 1980s, the Spanish government made vast investments in a project to reclaim Spain's cultural "heritage" and in support of national cultural institutions, but in the context of recession in the early 1990s, the government radically scaled back funds and aggressively asserted the desirability of an expansion in private sector sponsorship.[88] José A. Sánchez argues that, like fellow artists who had to employ "survival strategies, such as reducing their work to a much smaller format," La Ribot reimagined her work in response: "If one had to impoverish the conditions of production, then she would go so far as nakedness; and if one had to reduce the format, she would go all the way imaginable."[89] This interpretation is confirmed by the artist herself: "because of the reality of the dance in my country, Spain, at the beginning of 90, I went for rapidity, independence, and the use of solo performer/dancer as well as interdisciplinarity. It was a way to survive but also a way to escape."[90]

Her series *Piezas distinguidas* (*Distinguished pieces*, 1993–2003), an array of works made prior to *40 espontáneos*, typifies this aesthetic approach. Each short *pieza* incorporates nakedness, everyday movement, throwaway props, and cardboard in its action, with gestures of brevity and disposability offering a playful and ironic rejoinder to lengthier works of dance theater.[91] The method of the *piezas*' devising, worked out in the studio, is interdisciplinary and autobiographical, both in terms of the source of the events represented in performance and the objects which feature in them—personal mementoes, clothes with sentimental value, objects with stories attached to them, mediations of events witnessed in the street. While La Ribot narrated her performance of the *pieza* "Another Bloody Mary" at the Centre Georges Pompidou in 2003 live, this information is not always made apparent to audience members, but nonetheless deeply saturates the works.[92] Over the course of the three series of distinguished pieces—*13 piezas distinguidas* (1993–94), *Mas distinguidas* (1997), and *Still Distinguished* (2000), which together comprised *Panoramix* (2003), a three-hour survey event of all thirty-four distinguished pieces that was performed in theaters and galleries across Europe—La Ribot's chosen performance environment shifted. As the video archive of her performances available at the Live Art Development Agency shows, having initially favored frontally oriented theatrical spaces, whose limitations afforded certain opportunities for play with light and spatial depth, she increasingly used the less regimented environs of gallery spaces, enabling audiences to move at will and lending her works a sense of the "happening" in performance.

In aesthetic and conceptual terms, this "reduction" of performative format shows an acute consciousness of the relation between conditions of production and consumption—or in other words, the theatrical dimension of performance. With subtle theatrical imaging and matter-of-fact directness, "Pieza distinguida No. 14" hints at a relation between commoditized sex and the work of the ballerina, and between the categories of role assigned and role performed. First hanging a cardboard sign around her neck which reads SE VENDE, La Ribot then hangs a folding wooden chair around her waist. Having held her arms in fourth position for a moment (and in performance in end-on theater spaces, while walking on tiptoe backwards upstage), she allows her hands to fall to the seat of the chair and slowly begins to open and close it, slowly speeding up to produce a violent clacking and squeaking. Gradually, and with virtuoso control, she descends to the floor to lie supine, battering the chair methodically against her hips to produce what resembles an emotionless and barely consensual sexual encounter.[93] The *pieza* "Outsize Baggage" sees La Ribot tying up her naked body and head with string and attaching a label marked "LHR": its presentation of the naked, unprotected body as air freight might also be thought as a commentary on her status as an internationally touring artist.[94] "Manual de uso," part-slapstick sketch, part-DIY lesson, demonstrates an absurd performance of instructions for a recently purchased appliance, which La Ribot reads aloud and performs: the appliance is the manual user's own body and the instructions, if followed to the letter, will result in the body's suffocation inside a clear plastic rain poncho.[95] For these performances, theatricality's "play of disjunction/unification"[96] mediating the relation between personhood and objecthood functions as a comedic resource; of "Outsize Baggage," for example, Sánchez writes that "'it could be me, but it could also be a package' seems to be the message."[97] "Pa amb tomàquet," the only distinguished *pieza* to take the form of film, reflects explicitly on the reciprocal and contradictory relation between "performer"/"performed" and "consumer"/"consumed." Using a video camera, La Ribot documents her creation of a tomato sandwich made "with" her own body. One unseen hand holds the video camera, while the other awkwardly chops garlic and tomatoes, rubs both all over her naked body, and unscrews and pours upon it a glut of green olive oil from a bottle. The urgent and necessarily jerky camerawork, vibrant color, and spike of accompanying music offer the appearance of a Hitchcockian murder scene—the body gorily smeared with red, blood-like slush but with the real victims, of course, being the tomatoes. Gerald Siegmund writes that in this performance La Ribot "transforms her body into an object ready to be looked at, consumed, and even bought."[98] All these performances suggest the dialogue between production and consumption to be a recurrent, even central theme in her work.

Yet La Ribot has rejected the term "theatrical." In *Live: Art and Performance*, a volume published following the landmark performance festival Live Culture at Tate Modern in 2003, a selection of her writings appeared under the title "Panoramix." One fragment in particular offered insight into her thinking about theatricality:

> I would like to speak about presentation, rather than representation. The quietness can be seen in *Still Distinguished* as a means to speak about presentation—in the sense of being, or of feeling a corporeal presence and of contemplating inside a non-theatrical time, *understanding "theatrical" as something that starts and finishes*. With "stillness" I am trying to convey an approximate time that can break, change, or vary depending on the necessity of each person. I am not enforcing an exact length of time, I am simply giving an approximation, a possible time, in which one must decide while living, doing, observing, changing . . .
>
> *Now the space belongs to the spectator and me without hierarchies*. My objects, their bags or coats; their commentaries and my sound; sometimes my stillness and their movement, other times my movement and their stillness. Everything and everyone is scattered around the floor, in an infinite surface, in which we are moving quietly, without any precise direction, without any definite order.
>
> *The spectator now works in his space and has a relative period of time to use*, a period of time that begins to be understood, and is made up by, each of us individually.
>
> *London, April 15, 2000* (my emphases)[99]

As Adrian Heathfield writes, this is "not the progressive accumulative time of culture, but a time that is always divided and subject to different flows and speeds."[100] As La Ribot framed it above, such a temporality is incompatible with the theater. A linear notion of time is "theatrical" ("something that starts and finishes"), in contrast to undetermined co-presence—or rather, multiple and individualized co-presences. This effect is covalent with audience members' random distribution around and within a performance space. Fixed arrangements between audience and performance are seen meanwhile to produce a sensation of linear time, also understood here in terms of "representation."

Like Lepecki's notion of the theater as a "hierarchical machine,"[101] theatricality in this definition is presented as antithetical to a model of "each of us individually" experiencing performance. Individualized spectatorship itself is imagined as an act of artisanal "work." Heathfield's framing of "progressive accumulation" as the time of "culture" might therefore be thought differently. Instead, the machine-like teleological procedure, the object of La Ribot's critique, is the assembly-line time of Fordism, and the preferred temporal construction is the time of "flexible accumulation": as David Harvey has theorized it, the revolutionizing "'time-space compression'" attendant upon a post-Fordist "'global village' of telecommunications and a 'spaceship earth' of economic and ecological interdependencies," and one associated with the transnational practices of just-in-time production and deindustrialization in the Global North.[102] A critique of the theatrical machine in terms of "progressive accumulation" has little to do with theatricality's cognitive and representational dualisms, which La Ribot's work repeatedly takes up. In its engagements with theatricality, her work seems to address the scenario of post-Fordism in a much more complex way than her definition of theater will allow; as Christian Marazzi writes, "in post-Fordism the *general intellect* is not fixed in machines, but in the *bodies* of workers. The body has become, if you will, the tool box of mental work" (emphasis in original).[103] More faithful to the representational paradoxes at play in her work is this fragment, which also appears in *Live: Art and Performance*:

> There is no more representation, only presentation.
> There is no more magic, only reality.
> There are no more surprises, only variable perceptions.
> There are no more statements, only ambiguity.
> There is no more stability, only imbalance.
> There is no more theatricality, only plasticity.
>
> *London, September 1999*[104]

The statement at the center—"There are no more statements, only ambiguity"—undoes the candidness and incontrovertibility of the others; if each is taken seriously, then none can truly apply.

La Ribot's insightful work and its engagement with spatial, temporal, and commercial constructs embraces fascinating contradictions, both acknowledged and unacknowledged ones. Before moving to the final section of this chapter, I offer one last example: the "distinguished proprietors" project, in which La Ribot offered each of the *piezas distinguidas* for sale to an individual or company for several hundred pounds. Heathfield suggests that this initiative mimics earlier systems of art market patronage, and asks "what could ownership mean in the context of performance, where the work is repeatable but cannot exactly be reproduced, or easily subjected to a capitalist system of exchange?"[105] In a 2002 interview with La Ribot, Goran Serjes Pristaš asked how the notion of ownership operates in the distinguished proprietors project. She framed a clear response:

> The distinguished proprietors are the proprietors of a distinguished piece. They are not the owners because the concept of ownership doesn't exist in the distinguished project. They know where their piece is taking place or being presented because I inform them, and if they want to see their piece they always have a place at the venue. There is a real moment when a distinguished piece is being produced, presented, when it's alive or whatever. Instead of having the detritus or the documents of something that happened, I value "the ephemeral" moment and I sell it as a work of art. I have defined what a distinguished piece is and that is what a distinguished proprietor gets.[106]

The distinguished proprietor thus has a "proprietary" relation to the work's "immaterial" gestures: a relation in which, in paradigmatically theatrical style, it is "as if" he or she is its owner. The item on sale is not the performance "itself" but the idea of the performance's ephemerality. Gerald Siegmund reads this as a critical and subversive gesture, "a performative act that, precisely because it is immaterial, absent, and not an object, will continue to produce new meanings or actions."[107] While in a sense, as Siegmund suggests, the piece does ironize the process of commoditization, it is difficult to see how "distinguished proprietorship" is ultimately different in kind from any other kind of relationship of patronage or sponsorship.

Nonetheless, if artists in the 2000s were "increasingly concerned with being able to decide on their means of production independently,"[108] the "distinguished proprietors" project demonstrates that this did not only concern access to appropriate resources for making performance, but control over discourse. This was the issue at the heart of the controversy over Raymond Whitehead's refused refund, which, though his case was thrown out of court in 2004, cost the International Dance Festival of Ireland 10,000 euros in legal fees. In that instance, Bel's complex address to the performativity of genre ("a set of conventional and highly organised constraints on the production and interpretation of meaning")[109] met Whitehead's outrage at being lured into the theater and separated from his money on a "false" promise, which a critic sympathetic to that outrage described explicitly as a "'breach of contract.'"[110] In this sense, the locus of struggle in Whitehead's case was not the generic recognizability or validity of dance movement per se, but the function of the theater as a scene of economic transaction—which is the institutional construct at the heart of *40 espontáneos*.

"Mission Impossible": *40 espontáneos*

So far, this discussion has traced histories of performance practice. It has considered the heterogeneity of live art and the framing of live art practitioners as marginal and pioneering. It has surveyed the ways in which experimental dance artists sought to democratize access to and definitions of movement practices on stages and in rehearsal rooms in the 1960s and 1970s. It has explored how, from the modest beginnings of community dance in Britain, funded by trusts, foundations, and the public purse, a national infrastructure for dance was established. It has examined how concepts and definitions of community dance have shifted and changed in concert with institutional and political developments—not least the elaboration of policies of social inclusion under the New Labour government. It has touched on European experimental artists' rejection in the 1990s of normative understandings of dance, and how in the 2000s they defended the viability of their practices to policy-makers in the context of globalization. It has noted the uneven and often pragmatic invocation of entrepreneurialism by practitioners across this range of linked domains. And it has offered an analysis of a selection of La Ribot's own performance works in the 1990s and 2000s in these terms. All of these themes come together in this chapter's final example, *40 espontáneos*. La Ribot began research and development for this piece in 2002, and in an interview that year described it as "a piece with a lot of people for the theatre . . . the title could be 'Mission Impossible' or 'Espontáneos.' "[111]

As I described earlier, the bullfight, expertly performed by a matador risking death in the space of the bullring, inspired the work—a practice of historic significance in Spanish culture becoming the basis for a piece of contemporary performance programmed internationally. In an interview with the Spanish magazine *El Cultural*, La Ribot reflected:

> When I asked a bullfighting expert what an "*espontáneo*" was I was answered with a scornful look: "El '*espontáneo*' is the person who jumps into the bull ring and steals the show from the bullfighter, breaking the rules of the game and adding an unnecessary overdose of danger to the celebration so that what is art can become a massacre." The project takes off with this definition, together with a few other questions that have also been raised. What rules of the game? How much dosage of risk and for whom? Is this art, fiesta, life, massacre, or death?[112]

In the corrida, the expertise of the bullfighter enables the audience to experience a thrilling frisson of excitement ("an overdose of danger") in the face of demonstrable threat, while remaining confident that the bullfighter will win through. The practice of "art" lies in the performance of such expertise. The *espontáneo*'s unskilled, if nonetheless planned, blunder into the ring injects an "unnecessary overdose" of danger, resulting not in art but a potential bloodbath. The performers in *40 espontáneos* did not of course encounter a temperamental bull, but performed actions learned in rehearsal. The metaphorical "bull" in this performance was, in which case, the unpredictable live event of performance itself. Speaking about her attraction to the bullfight before the process of making *40 espontáneos* began, La Ribot said that "spontaneity is inside any live performance at some level. It depends how much you appreciate the present, how much you can work with the present."[113] *40 espontáneos* thus told at least two stories: of the dangerous environment of the corrida, and of the professional theater. The *espontáneo* was simultaneously a theatrical character and the real person of the performer who was inexperienced in "work with the present." In the arc of *40 espontáneos*' story—which was not especially clear in the performance itself, but was communicated alongside the work in promotional leaflets, the performance's program, and so on—the performers' transgression resulted in their choreographed "deaths."

40 espontáneos brought live art, experimental choreography, and community dance into a complex exchange. The piece was programmed in Britain as part of the dance and live art festivals Dance Umbrella (London, 2005), Nottdance (Nottingham, 2006), and New Moves (Glasgow, 2006). As I noted at the beginning of this discussion, as a piece of artistic work, and in terms of its institutional connections, in this context *40 espontáneos* appeared definitively as live art. But, in Britain if not elsewhere in the world, by recruiting companies of inexperienced performers, and deploying their appearance as "themselves" as an aesthetic gesture, the piece also exemplified community dance.[114] Supported by the Arts Council's Grants for the Arts scheme, promotions of *40 espontáneos* in Britain rehearsed narratives of empowerment and transformation associated with community dance. For example, in an interview with dance critic Donald Hutera for *Dance Umbrella News*, the festival's newsletter, La Ribot stressed that "it's a generous exchange. I have to be very patient, open, comprehensive. They give me their bodies and minds, I give them confidence. It's a human exchange, about people."[115]

Along with the bullfight, *40 espontáneos* drew performative sustenance from film—specifically, the representational function of the extra, who is incorporated into cinematic spectacle to lend it a sense of reality. In a short British Council-produced documentary about the performance of *40 espontáneos* in Rio de Janeiro, La Ribot noted that "for a film to be real you need extras . . . I like very much these people who are behind the hero, behind the protagonist."[116] A photograph of extras working on Stanley Kubrick's *Spartacus* (1960) depicts a large group of people lying in place on a hillside between takes and, for the benefit of the production team, holding aloft pieces of paper scrawled with identificatory numbers in thick black marker pen. As the documentary shows, La Ribot adapted and choreographed this image for *40 espontáneos*. Calling to mind Number 6's impassioned cry "I am not a number! I am a free man!" in the cult TV show *The Prisoner* (1967–68), the image exemplifies the way in which the performance imagined and constructed the relation between individual and group, while also embracing other humorously unexpected dynamics. The production's entry on La Ribot's website describes how, in this image of people and their numbers, "No. 1 glares furiously over the top of his [piece of paper]; No. 256 uses his as a sunscreen, and No. 19 lazily props his number against his head. The image distils a wonderful set of dichotomies—between individual expression and collectivity, accident and design, reality and fakery, action and inertia, and even life and death."[117]

Meanwhile, the performance's representation of the *espontáneo*'s dash onto the stage and his or her bloody slaughter was more oblique. *40 espontáneos* was structured in sections. Its first phase consisted of the performers walking in and around the stage, seemingly at random. Constantly laughing, they would gradually construct what La Ribot called a "collaboration network"[118] by laying clothes, fabric, and objects across the floor. During this phase, they each dressed using the garments, appropriating clothes others may have laid out, generating a spectacle of constantly churning texture and color. Once all were enrobed, and the floor was covered with fabric, the performers would descend to the floor and fall into a silent sleep for a pause of a few minutes, each holding a number. The next brief phase radically ruptured the scene: the performers were to wake up, very quickly gather up all of the clothes, and dump them in a pile in the middle of the floor. The final phase of the work was "the red moment": "a moment when everything is falling, falling continuously. Very slowly. Everything is falling, falling, falling and laughing, laughing, laughing."[119] The performers would construct a second network, now only with red items from the pile, metaphorizing the spilling of the *espontáneo*'s blood. Scattered around the stage, the participants, laughing again, would "melt" by sliding very slowly down the walls, the sides of furniture, and against other people, occasionally standing upon furniture to survey the stage and its chaotic proceedings. Once the performers had distributed all the red items, they would place enormous sheets of cardboard over the fabric.

While the *espontáneos*' act of trespass was signified by their "not dancing" on the stage, the rehearsal process offered a welcoming, rigorous, and supportive pedagogic encounter with an experimental process. Work in rehearsal taught the structure of the piece, but it also prepared the participants to perform the actions of laughing, walking, and "melting," a preparation which consisted in engagement with two models of corporeality: the one, the body as a site of affective contagion, and the other, a more traditionally choreographic doubling of the body. For laughter to be successfully maintained throughout a given performance without muscular strain or exhaustion, La Ribot advised that it must not be imposed through actorly pretense but "discovered" within the body.[120] At the same time, the movement practice expressly invoked the duality of cognition. Demonstrating, by collapsing against a chair, the action of "melting" to be performed in the final phase of the piece, La Ribot asked the performers to assume a reflexive orientation to their own action:

> Try to make your body go through all the moments, always working much more slowly with the weight, to see where the problems are, where I need to alter my weight so I don't jerk. To overcome the problem. It's slow so we can think with our body.[121]

To encourage such embodied thinking, La Ribot and her three co-facilitators communicated action in terms of metaphor. The collapsing in *40 espontáneos* was conceived as "melting"; balance and confidence "like a tree, fixed, rooted to the ground";[122] stretching legs "as if you wanted to separate it from the body."[123] During rehearsal, the performers stretched, ran around the space together, and "melted" against each other's bodies and surrounding objects, repeatedly testing and exploring their physical limits. This kind of practical engagement is generative: in Susan Leigh Foster's terms, the participating body exercises its capacity as "a body-of-ideas,"[124] becoming more able to work instinctively; furthermore, practice "creates two bodies: one, perceived and tangible; the other, aesthetically ideal,"[125] which become the object of work and attention.

But paradoxically, the physical adaptation and transformation which dance practice encourages was precisely what *40 espontáneos* did not want to stage. In a text about *40 espontáneos*, Jacques Blanc, the director of Le Quartz in Brest, the institution that co-commissioned and programmed the premiere of the performance in 2004, wrote:

> Fame Academy, Pop Idol, Big Brother . . . exhibit non-professionals—humans turned into a merchandise, up for bidding, with nothing in mind but the fake dream of TV celebrity. At the other end of the spectrum, the "40 espontáneos" climb on the stage with all their humanity, with their lives and their emotions.[126]

The signifier supporting this latter narrative is not more visible "humanity," but the absence of training which would render the body "flexible" in both literal and metaphoric senses: the training which equips a person to function as "merchandise" in dance. As La Ribot confirmed in various interviews, non-performers "are more real":[127]

> In the beginning I worked with professional choreographers and dancers. . . . Thanks to them, I realised I have to do the piece with

> people who have no experience on stage. Venues and programmers find them in the community. It makes it much more real.[128]

The "real" body for *40 espontáneos* needed to be unmarked by the disciplinary force of dance training, since such training was evidence of employability in the dance industry, of professional adaptability and flexibility, as Foster elaborates in her discussion of the "hired" body in dance in the 1990s.[129] And to cultivate a sense of greater spontaneity in action, the productions' rehearsal periods were short, numbering no more than five or six evenings, and eventually only people over age forty were invited to perform in the piece.

40 espontáneos in Britain

The calls for performers for *40 espontáneos* emphasized accessibility and the pleasure of new experience. An e-mail bulletin from Artsadmin regarding the Dance Umbrella production of the piece declared: "if you are over 40 and have never performed in public (but have a hankering to)—now is your chance."[130] The New Moves festival in Glasgow departed from the usual format of its Winter School course—generally oriented to professional development for artists, whose contributors the year before were Goat Island, Franko B, Raimund Hoghe, and Lone Twin—to program *40 espontáneos* for

> 40 people over the age of 40, with no performance experience whatsoever! You are someone who would like to work with a major international artist over 5 evenings, culminating in a performance on the Tramway stage at the end of what promises to be an exciting and very rewarding process.[131]

And the Nottdance festival's recruitment flyer made another aspect explicit: the performers would be remunerated.

> Calling all non-performers: If you have a secret desire to get on the stage but usually leave it to others to lap up the attention, then you are exactly the sort of person we are looking for! Nottdance is an annual contemporary dance festival known for offering audiences something innovative and exciting. Taking the theme of Nottingham and its community, internationally renowned artist La Ribot will be inviting 40 over 40s, with no previous performance experience, to work with her on creating a unique piece to perform at the opening of Nottdance06!
>
> *40 ESPONTÁNEOS* will be performed on 28 & 29 April and will require participants to attend rehearsals from 23–27 April at

> Sandfield Theatre from 6–10 pm. Participants will be paid £20 per rehearsal and £40 per performance.[132]

While the trope of community (and the citation of the local area) implies voluntary action, here participation was secured through payment of a modest wage.

And the piece's travels from performance space to performance space ranged internationally across uneven historical, material, and ideological territory. The piece was first staged in 2004 at Le Quartz, a proscenium arch theater in Brest. Martin Hargreaves described its initial scenographic effect as to "particularly violate the architecture of the proscenium. The frontal representational apparatus of the theatre has collapsed, producing a strange feeling of vertigo."[133] The spaces in which it was performed in Britain, meanwhile, were architecturally and institutionally dissimilar with regard to both the proscenium structure and one another. Following its inception in 1993, Greenwich Dance Agency was housed in the former Borough Hall of the London borough of Greenwich, a beautiful Grade II-listed example of Art Deco municipal architecture, built in the late 1930s, which found favor with the architectural historian Nikolaus Pevsner.[134] Greenwich Dance Agency offered a means for people of all ages and abilities to access dance via a range of participatory dance projects, alongside presentations by artists such as Shobana Jeyasingh, Russell Maliphant, and Luca Silvestrini. Akram Khan lent his voice to the organization's promotional DVD, describing a "sense of exchange, between different people, coming into the space, and it almost feels like a people's space, rather than a quite exclusive thing just for professional dancers."[135] Brendan Keaney, the artistic director of Greenwich Dance Agency from 1996 to 2012, argued that one reason for the strength and continuity of the Dance Umbrella festival's relationship with the organization was that "we can offer something that genuinely isn't a theatre, that is a space."[136] The Tramway in Glasgow, a cultural space that prioritizes experimental performance, dance, and visual art, was converted from a late nineteenth-century streetcar shed in preparation for Glasgow City of Culture 1990, following its use to present the only performances in Britain of Peter Brook's *Mahabharata* (1985).[137] And until its closure in 2011 to make way for a private housing development, the Sandfield Centre in Nottingham was a local authority building that also contained a basic black box performance space.[138] My own reception of the performances of *40 espontáneos* in London and Nottingham was ghosted uncannily by familiarity with the venues—the experience of dancing in Greenwich Dance Agency's hall as a participant in a contemporary class, and that of living for two years as a student a few streets from the Sandfield Centre's location in Nottingham.

I watched *40 espontáneos* at Greenwich Dance Agency in October 2005. As I entered the performance space several minutes before the advertised start time to watch the piece, *40 espontáneos* had already begun. From the outset, a part of the action was inaccessible, having taken place in a past to which the audience members now trickling in were not present. Seating lined the back and side walls of the room. Although the relationship between audience and performance was a straightforward thrust arrangement, the location of the entrance required that audience members walk directly across the performance space, which was already peopled with wandering *espontáneos* and a few sparse swatches of colorful fabric. Martin Hargreaves's review of the piece at Le Quartz in Brest described a similar experience: "My ticket (marked *place libre*) doesn't indicate where I'm supposed to sit and the sudden necessity of making a decision about where my proper place is in this transformed space (a place libre) raises some anxiety. Indeed, I see other audience members in a similar moment of suspension; what are we going to watch? Where therefore should we watch it from?"[139] After a moment's hesitation, I selected a seat at the back, adjacent to a gigantic cardboard poster stuffed into a seat, and walked around (not through) the performance space, accompanied by some other audience members who likewise seemed to feel the stage to be an unbreachable zone.

Covered with an artificial material, Greenwich Dance Agency's wooden floor appeared almost entirely black. As the twenty-seven *espontáneos* gradually surged over the stage with seemingly aimless, solitary wandering, I found it impossible not to fix my attention on a single person—a man, constantly laughing, whose face was set in a concentrated, sightless grimace, and whose journey took him all around the space: fetching and carrying strips of fabric, putting on a shirt here, a skirt there, removing a shoe and placing it on the ground, wrapping material around his body, removing it again, finding some more fabric, donning a hat, plucking the hat from his head and placing it on the floor, finding another shoe, putting it on, walking across the floor with a comical gait, one hip high, the other low. Once I had lost interest in tracking this particular individual's movements around the space and turned my gaze to take in the stage, I saw with surprise that it had been entirely swamped by a patchwork sea of fabric. I strove to see as much as I could, yet the events on the stage unconditionally exceeded my capacity to do so, dramatizing the limits of my vision. The performers continued to wander among the upended chairs and tables, an upturned sofa, and piles of huge cardboard posters. At one moment, an older woman grasped the poster adjacent to my seat, looked me dead in the eye, and said "excuse me" as she removed it, an unauthorized act of speech amid the laughter's irrationality that momentarily pierced the piece's aesthetic immersion. Once the performers seemed satisfied that the black floor was sufficiently obscured, they began patchily to sink to the ground.

The laughter faded and an eerie silence took hold. The performers laid themselves down one by one on the bright fabric, an occasional unsettling laugh penetrating the stillness of the space. Each performer held a number, printed boldly on a tatty piece of paper, to their body—402, 13, 666, and so on—the corners unfurling, the folds moving slightly in response to their breath. A final performer stood on top of the block of cardboard sheets, surveyed all that was around her, and laughed: subversive, majestic. The performer joined the group on the floor, and another silence descended for what seemed like forever. Then the performers stirred, got up very quickly, and gathered up every scrap of fabric with speed and care, a rushed swirl of color that formed an elaborate, ragged pile: a dressing-up box in a metaphorical playground. Several participants righted the sofa, chairs, and tables, and each one launched their body at a surface, melting, throwing themselves onto the ground, resting, sliding off the upright furniture, in jerky yet liquid movements taking place in small spots all over the space. Taking the "stowaway"[140] role developed during the various iterations of *40 espontáneos*, two women ran lightly down from the audience and threw themselves into the fray—an uncanny moment that appeared wholly, unspontaneously staged. Another woman melted, laughing, in the arms of another, the one stiff and upright, her arms a cage, the other helpless. By the time the performers began to fetch cardboard sheets from the three piles at the edges of the stage, I had barely noticed that the red fabric had inched its way across the floor. The brown cardboard, laid on top of the vividness of color, swiftly and quietly quashed its loudness. The performers left, leaving two or three lying "dead" on the surface, clutching their numbers silently, a blue light washing over them from the rig above.

Conclusion

In a passage on her website in 2006, La Ribot described her vision for *40 espontáneos*:

> I am speaking of the anonymous, of the person used, or hired, of that person that in the cinema for example, passes by as if he or she did not exist, who drinks in a party or kills a Roman, makes us believe that what we see is more real. I am speaking of the soldier used to defend illegal homelands, the worker who sews T-shirts in filthy factories for somebody else's homeland. I am speaking about the reality that is too big for us, out of our limits, out of our rules, a reality that is interpreted like in the cinema, an "illegal" reality.[141]

The performers and the piece's totalizing aesthetic were to represent the "informal" economy in globalization in a general sense. Ramsay Burt reads *40 espontáneos* and *Laughing Hole* (2006–) in a similar way: "the patient performers in La Ribot's work can thus be seen, in Blanchot's terms, as 'destroyed men' (and women), as people undone by the disaster of modernity."[142] On a symbolic level, these powerful interpretations of the piece's narrative are compelling. But the conditions of *40 espontáneos*' production were specific to a particular phase in this disaster—the moment of "rollout" neoliberalization in Britain, a scene and situation of deep contradiction. Despite the public performance, in this piece, of quotidian movement presented in terms of dance by professional performers elsewhere, the piece narrativized the nonprofessional *espontáneos* as the professional artist's other. The piece allegorized spontaneous action, but in practice it required considerable planning in three different British cities. Its target constituency of non-dancers was more difficult to attract than dancers-in-training, who themselves aspired to enter the dance industry professionally.[143] And in Britain, *40 espontáneos* was neglected by critics, in all likelihood for reasons of the history and familiarity of community dance in Britain, the negative association of community performance practices with aesthetic mediocrity, and the piece's more recent links with the contemporary governmental prioritization of "inclusion," which exerted a clear influence on the presentation of other writings about the project.

For example, Grace Mahoney's "Art Changes Lives"—a piece by a participant in the Glasgow performance—featured unusually on the New Moves website. Mahoney described the experience of participating as "a hugely life-affirming week. . . . I could tell you what the piece was about for me. Birth and death, the journeys in between, meetings and partings, possession and loss. Love and letting go. Joy. Acceptance. Trust. Fate and freedom. The body's wisdom. The soul's movement. This work touched me to the core."[144] As Mahoney's moving text suggests, to a large degree, *40 espontáneos* also enacted the principle informing the work of dance animateurs in Britain in the 1970s and community dance practices since then: to engage participants in dance that was unfamiliar or "new." The words from two of the participants in the Glasgow production also bear this out. In response to my question "What is your strongest memory of from participating in *40 espontáneos*?" one replied

> The training was fantastic. La Ribot (Maria, Tania, Janice) are brilliant teachers. I saw how it was to be a dancer "up close and personal" and that being one transforms one's body and spirit. La Ribot were like magicians, they worked magic on us! The workshops were very important to me. They enabled me to participate in the performance with the audience.[145]

To have perceived "La Ribot" to be a group spoke perhaps to the collectivity of the working process. Another described similar feelings:

> It was intense but very enjoyable. We were very well looked after by the team involved and encouraged and supported all the way. It was physically challenging and stretched muscles I didn't even know I had. Maria is a very warm, passionate and personal teacher, and Tania, her assistant in Glasgow, was fabulously patient and encouraging. It was great to be encouraged to push myself further than I thought I could go by people whose judgement and experience I trusted.[146]

The generosity and joy of the process of making resonates with the "extraordinarily radical openness,"[147] as Jonathan Burrows put it, of contemporary community and participatory dance.

One last thought, then, on the performance's negative idealization of the theater as a proscenium arch subject to catastrophe, and its relation to wider economic imaginaries. This architectural construct, which proliferated in the nineteenth century, invokes a historical moment before time came to be "subject to different flows and speeds"[148] in life and industry in the theater and beyond. Meanwhile, Pat O'Malley shows that in the neoliberal political philosophy that became dominant in the latter half of the twentieth century, "the market was no longer imagined as a space, as it had been under previous liberal rationalities. Instead it was understood as an 'enterprising' mentality articulated with an array of techniques that could be applied anywhere."[149] In spatial terms, we might interpret this transformation as an immersive one, radically weakening the notional boundary between public and private spheres of action, and concentrating focus on the enterprising individual. Consider this idea and aesthetic in relation to Bojana Cvejić's assessment of "the choreography of the 90s":

> The power of self-determination in the concept of dance could be potentially transformative if it also applied to the frame of working, production, and presentation. At the moment, it is capable of articulating something like speech-act: "This is performance, this is choreography," assuming the role of analytical or critical self-interpretation, similar to the conceptualism in visual art. So far it produces open, flexible, and contingent definitions of dance and critique and how we are habituated to perceive it, but it remains dependent on internal, medium-specific matters of dance because operating in the institutional context of theatre makes its critique bound to the theatre *dispositif*.[150]

Earlier in the same text, Cvejić writes that "the only tactic of resisting the institutional market for the freelance artist is to become the mediating machine of him/herself, producing productivity and a self-governed networking."[151] I would define this not as resistance, but as the essence of precarious artistic labor under the conditions of neoliberalization, in which the theater *dispositif* and the body of the entrepreneurial freelance artist are to at least some degree imagined to coincide, thereby mystifying institutional structures and practices—and resonating with O'Malley's insights concerning the re-conceptualization of the market as an "'enterprising' mentality."[152] What then is "the theater" in *40 espontáneos*? In their assessment of anti-theatricality at different historical moments, Alan Ackerman and Martin Puchner propose that "each anti-theatricalism tends to construct its own horror fantasy of the theatre."[153] The ultimate horror fantasy of *40 espontáneos* may thus have been the commercial space of the theater as a "hierarchical machine"[154] which inhibits artists specifically from "being able to decide on their means of production independently"[155]—and a machinic structure disavowed and veiled by a world in which "the entrepreneur has to be all of us,"[156] with each person, artist or not, transformed into "the mediating machine of him/herself"[157] and abandoned to an arena of endless competition.

Live art and experimental and community dance practices have developed with and alongside one another since the 1970s, and the disciplinary segmentation to which the performing arts as industry are now subject serves very effectively to obscure the mutuality of their emergence. As I have shown in this chapter, these practices as they have taken shape in Britain share intriguing historical complicities, including tactics and vocabularies that bear witness to the search for artistic freedom but also intersect with the normalization of entrepreneurialism—even in spite of their demonstrable resistance to or questioning of neoliberalization's market-led transformations of society and culture. Though we might think of live art and experimental dance as more readily embracing an entrepreneurial approach than community dance, given their incursion into new aesthetic or formal territories, entrepreneurialism's logics and practices have been discernible in all three practices, however patchily and unevenly—from the DIY basis of early independent companies to the "animateur" label chosen for community dance practitioners, who were likewise framed as "pioneering." As neoliberalization gathered pace in the 1980s and 1990s, the search for the new and the pursuit of individual achievement became more prominent in discourse about live art and experimental dance practices, while the necessarily more collectively focused practice of community dance asserted its commitments to innovation in terms of its offer to neglected localities and its service in producing forms of communal sociality through dance—one exemplar among many of George Yúdice's "expediency of culture."[158] Yet at all points within these art forms, these discursive moves have been interrupted or challenged—whether in the claims made by community dance practitioners as to their work's aesthetic legitimacy, or in the challenges to commoditized spectatorship levied by live and experimental dance artists, not least La Ribot. To return to Stuart Hall's essay with which I opened this chapter, the "double shuffle"[159] performed in La Ribot's *40 espontáneos* spoke to the specific historical conditions of its creation: the context of "rollout" neoliberalism and its model of predominantly competitive entrepreneurialism and subordinate social democracy. But like the practices with which it was in dialogue, *40 espontáneos* also spoke to the much more long-standing question of the theater as the scene of capitalist value production. The next chapter moves its attention to the seaside town of Margate on England's south coast, to consider how such a dynamic was also engaged in this period in the practice of culture-in-regeneration.

Chapter 2

✦

"Places, like Property Prices, Go Up and Down"

Public Art, Regeneration, and Place

The previous chapter examined experimental and community dance in relation to what Stuart Hall called the "double shuffle" of the "rollout" phase of neoliberalization—in which a dominant ethic of marketization interacted with "another, *subaltern* programme, of a more social democratic kind."[1] The dynamic of the "double shuffle" was also pronounced in the culture-in-regeneration initiatives of the 2000s, such as those connected with this chapter's main example, Artangel's site-responsive project *The Margate Exodus* (2005–7). As the arts journalist Iain Aitch noted, *The Margate Exodus*'s chosen themes of migration, hospitality and exile together represented "perhaps the most controversial tale Artangel could have chosen to tell in Margate."[2] From the 1970s on, many British seaside resorts such as Margate were detrimentally affected by the rise in overseas tourism. Located on the south coast, Margate experienced particularly difficult economic consequences, including high levels of unemployment. As Richard Samuel, the former chief executive of Thanet District Council, wrote in 2010, "by the early 1980s the area had been dubbed Costa del Dole"[3]—a disparaging pun combining references both to benefit claimants and to holidaymakers' turn, ruinous to the local economy, to cheap package holidays to Spain. Former guesthouses, as "homes of multiple occupancy,"[4] became utilized as part of government policy to accommodate vulnerable groups, including refugees seeking asylum. These circumstances interacted with a wider national politics of anti-immigration propagated especially by the tabloid press. As Nadine El-Enany observes of the effects of such politics, "racialized people in Britain, whether categorized as citizens, migrants, refugees, asylum seekers or third country nationals, are habitually understood as having come from somewhere else"; furthermore, those "categorized as migrants are continually scapegoated for societal ills and painted in official and media discourse as taking what is not theirs."[5] Aitch wrote in 2006 that Margate had therefore witnessed a "rise in racial tension which groups such as the National Front have sought to exploit."[6]

The Margate Exodus consisted of a series of participatory works in photography, music, sculpture, and film on themes of "identity, tolerance, and social equality."[7] It was commissioned by one of the most significant and highly esteemed producers of contemporary experimental art and performance in Britain. It took place amid an increasingly overheated property boom which was especially conspicuous in London and the south.[8] In this light, consider these sentences opening a 2006 *Spectator* review of *Exodus Day*, a day of live events staged as part of *The Margate Exodus*: "Places, like property prices, go up and down. Margate, in the most northerly corner of Kent, is just beginning the uncertain journey upwards again."[9] Ruth Guilding's words in this passage demonstrated the prevalent imaginary of place in terms of economic value: assets whose changeable values might be represented on a line graph. Her imaginary graph's X axis, "time," spanned the 1700s to the 2000s: the article's introductory sketch of Margate alluded to Regency architectural grandeur, the former Margate resident J. M. W. Turner, working class and mass tourism of the nineteenth and twentieth centuries, the seafront Turner Contemporary gallery (a new architectural project that was then "stalled"),[10] and processes of immigration and asylum, and concluded by noting that "by southeastern standards, houses are still pretty cheap. Tracey Emin is Margate's only success story."[11] Then the article took a different turn: "This is where that strange, magical organisation Artangel comes in. It aims to make art outside the gallery, matching up artists, contexts, and audiences to get something relevant, democratic, and unmediated."[12]

Guilding's text rhetorically knitted together various cultural and economic priorities of the mid-2000s: rising property values, unmediated experience as democratic encounter (with "relevance" implying "local community"), and art as the impetus for economic transformation. But her reference to Artangel's projects as scenes of unmediated encounter was at odds not only with the conceptual approach of the organization's previous commissions, but also with her own account of class and "cultural tourism"—the latter one of the key components of of culture-in-regeneration.[13] She wrote that on Exodus Day, "in glorious sunshine, London came to watch," where "London" consisted not of ordinary visitors from the city but "coachloads of critics, donors and fashionable types."[14] Nonetheless, the overall tenor of the review, including these aspects, bore a strong affinity with culture-in-regeneration's aspirational and communitarian politics. Culture-in-regeneration was a core cultural policy rationale for the New Labour government and was closely connected to the production of "social inclusion,"[15] a term (as I discuss in the introduction and in chapter 3) that suggests social engagement but also euphemizes economic participation.[16] As a means of "attracting companies and investment; having a role in cultural tourism; adding to land values," policy-makers in this period pitched culture as "a catalyst to turn around whole communities."[17] This claim rearticulated earlier arguments made for culture in urban development in Britain, particularly in relation to programs of public art, but now in a more strongly communitarian register. And in stimulating growth and facilitating public interaction, these policies also imagined culture as a technique for producing "social cohesion" or "community cohesion"—terms used interchangeably throughout the DCMS paper "Culture at the Heart of Regeneration" (2004).[18]

From the early 2000s on, the term "community cohesion" was utilized by government within "the 'new' framework governing race relations policy."[19] In her 2005 analysis, published not long after Labour was elected for its third term, the social policy researcher Clare Worley discussed the problems attaching to the framework's deployment of the word "community": its emphasis on "a place-bound notion of belonging," its construction of identity as "dichotomous," and "the assimilationist tone of much of the rhetoric" which prioritized national identity and occluded the complexity of processes of racial, gender, and diasporic identity formation across contexts and borders.[20] Some of *The Margate Exodus*'s projects addressed themselves precisely to such complexity, and the ways in which, as Worley argues, "identities can be and are transnational, or forged across and through other aspects of identity such as gender or religion."[21] Overall, however, *The Margate Exodus* was strongly associated with the vocabulary of community cohesion. Closely engaged with the national arts education initiative Creative Partnerships, *The Margate Exodus* was positioned in relation to education and community-based art and performance. It sought to involve hundreds of Margate residents. Many appeared in Penny Woolcock's film *Exodus* (2007), an adaptation of the biblical story, and the impetus for the whole initiative and its final and most widely distributed outcome. Comprising several distinct elements and combining the work of internationally renowned artists with local arts education and nonprofessional participants of all ages, *The Margate Exodus* brought various artforms, approaches, and social worlds into contact. To interpret the variable effects of its offerings in situ, I draw on Sophie Nield's materialist argument about site-specific performance: though ephemeral, such performances participate in "a battle for the right to determine, inflect, and produce the site itself."[22] Similarly, Miwon Kwon reads site-specificity not as a generic category but as a "spatio-political problematic."[23] For Kwon, site-specificity refers both to location and the discursive environment in which art makes its intervention; site-specific art thus engages in "the cultural mediation of broader social, economic, and political processes that organize urban life and urban space."[24] Together with Nield's materialist conception of performance, Kwon's approach is useful in addressing an undertaking such as *The Margate Exodus*—a collocation of projects and events that were in dialogue with the resort's cultural and social past and present, and those discourses relating to place-based regeneration.

As part of *The Margate Exodus*'s work, I was able to meet with six participants on three different occasions over the course of a year for conversations towards a short project evaluation for which I had volunteered myself. These conversations demonstrated the town to be a complicated social and historical site, and also showed the ways in which, by accident as well as by design, the project and its practices introduced people who might not otherwise have met, nurtured relationships, and enabled the development of new artistic and technical skills. In short, participants viewed the project in precisely the opposite terms to those of the culture and style journalist A. A. Gill, who deemed it to be "like Victorian cultural imperialism."[25] My purpose here is to understand *The Margate Exodus*'s historical engagement with the force of governmental and cultural discourses and priorities, and to parse references such as these. I begin the discussion by looking briefly at Gill's rhetorical framing of the town and the project, before sketching out Artangel's artist-led commissioning practice. Next, I address disputes in the intersecting fields of public and community art in the 1990s concerning the material resources made available to art, discourses of challenge, utility, and the function of art in the public sphere, and various works' interplay with struggles against racism, their critique of colonialism, and their engagement with constructs of the nation. I consider the implication of ideas and rituals of "anti-tourism" in a selection of Artangel commissions from the 1990s and 2000s, and the role of site-specific artistic interventions in facilitating gentrification. This sets the scene for an analysis of *The Margate Exodus*, which was set in a formerly thriving tourist locality. Its projects' engagement with exclusion and cohesion, and its address to identity, authoritarian oppression and migration interacted ambivalently with "cultural tourism"[26]—a strategy for economic development pursued amid "the contours of geography, history and culture that swirl the globe,"[27] including "Britain's post-colonial articulation of its borders and their dispossessory effect."[28]

"Impresarios of the Avant Garde"

A. A. Gill's 2006 feature article on *The Margate Exodus* for *The Sunday Times*—a paper not ordinarily quick to report on community arts events—meditated on Margate wistfully:

> The moment you walk out of the train station, Margate hits you with the Proustian nostalgia of the English seaside. There's the whiff of ozone, rotting seaweed, and chip fat, the ambient static of the waves, predatory herring gulls, and the mechanical chatter and pop from dozing amusement arcades. And there's the bright, bounced, magical light, the North Sea horizon gleaming

> like polished steel. The light is astonishing—it was this light that turned on Turner.[29]

This sentimental narrative stages a melancholic hankering after simple tourist pleasures, haunted by a mild sense of threat. In print, the article's text was juxtaposed with a photograph of the author standing on a seafront street, seemingly looking out to sea, his eyes trained through fashionable black-rimmed glasses at something on the horizon. Photographs from one of *The Margate Exodus*'s projects, Wendy Ewald's *Towards a Promised Land* (2005–6), are affixed to a concrete building and are blurrily visible behind him in the image. Gill is clad in a dark 1950s single-breasted suit, collar, tie, and immaculate pocket-square, with a pristine cone of chips in hand—a persona evoking Pathé newsreels and the anthropological curiosity of a mid-century flâneur. In this pre-austerity moment in 2006, mid-century modernism was not yet in style, so the glasses and suit registered not as fashion but as costume, and his appearance as a pastiche of tourist identity.

Revealing the artist Wendy Ewald to be his cousin, Gill used his article to critique her work and *The Margate Exodus* more generally as "exactly the sort of civilised aesthetic outreach concerned people yearn for."[30] He described Artangel co-director Michael Morris as someone who

> believes in moving art out of its building box and putting it into communities, ones that don't get much access to culture or anything that looks nice or relevant to them. This is a good thing, a fine ambition, and who is to gainsay him even if, here on the seafront, he does look like a windblown Dr. Livingstone offering missionary art to the natives?[31]

These assertions read strangely. Artangel's stated mission was then "to take art 'beyond the white walls of the gallery'."[32] Gill's phrase "missionary art" refers to this project's community-based focus. Colonial metaphor functioned in this passage to position contemporary art in relation to class—a choice which, in its orientation towards both the project and the town's residents, obscured Margate's changing economic status over the centuries, including its historical implication in colonial exploitation. For example, in 1766, a wealthy East India Company trader retired to Margate—then a modish therapeutic coastal retreat for bourgeois visitors—and, with the proceeds of a tea plantation, built a property called India House modelled on his home in Calcutta.[33] The property may have been used administratively by the East India Company decades into the nineteenth century; Margate's bank similarly had connections to the East India Company.[34] By the nineteenth century Margate's identity had changed: it had become a cheap and convenient destination for working people to spend their leisure time in activities that did not necessarily involve the "rational recreations" imposed by religious reformers and the middle class in that period.[35] Critics have polemically drawn connections between New Labour's social and cultural policy, participatory practices, and nineteenth-century reformist intent.[36] But Gill's piece did not seem aligned with such critiques—instead it looked back anachronistically to 1970s discourses of "access," articulated them in terms of nineteenth-century reformism and colonial intervention, and in turn mis-associated them with Artangel in regard to *The Margate Exodus*'s presumed "civilised aesthetic outreach."[37]

For anyone familiar with Artangel's previous commissions, this surely will have been a baffling analysis. Under Michael Morris and James Lingwood's co-directorship, Artangel's predominant interest was in commissioning experimental site-specific works "born from an open-ended commissioning process with an artist offered the opportunity to imagine something extraordinary,"[38] which could take any form at all—a practice hailed by critics as transformative of the scene of public and site-specific art in Britain.[39] In a piece in *The Times* previewing an Artangel commission, Hans Peter Kuhn's *Five Floors* (1992), Robert Hewison offered a dismal diagnosis of the state of the arts in 1990s Britain: an endless parade of safe theatrical classics on the National Theatre stage and the reliably consistent presence of long-running West End musical shows, a stagnant scene enlivened only by the occasional gallery closure. But there was a glimmer of hope:

> In the depths of this imaginative depression we are witnessing the emergence of a new breed of artistic entrepreneur, someone neither artist nor bureaucrat, who will take the risks and make the judgements that the institutions seem too distracted to make. Engineers of the imagination, impresarios of the avant-garde, they are independent producers who will work with the institutions without turning into one. Typical of this new breed are Michael Morris and James Lingwood.[40]

If the "artistic entrepreneur" was novel in the early 1990s, this figure has since become ubiquitous, with the professional role of creative producer now common. Founded in 1985 by Roger Took, the Artangel Trust made use of private sponsorship to "fund the unfundable"[41] in contemporary visual and conceptual art, with works frequently engaging in a critique of the constitution of the public sphere and its privatization.[42] Before Morris and Lingwood assumed co-directorship of Artangel in 1991, Lingwood had been curator of exhibitions at the Institute for Contemporary Arts (ICA) and a director of other significant place-based public art projects.[43] Morris worked at the ICA as the director of performing arts, diversifying and extending the institution's performance program into spaces beyond the building.[44] He established Cultural Industry in 1987, an independent company producing the work in Britain of international figures in experimental performance such as Pina Bausch, Robert Lepage, and Robert Wilson.[45] Cultural Industry was the producer of Improbable Theatre's acclaimed "junk opera" *Shockheaded Peter* (1998), a touring theater piece whose gradual emergence Morris described in an interview in terms characteristic of Hewison's risk-taking cultural entrepreneur:

> The resulting show was not initially auspicious. "I well remember the awful night when our PR man came to see a dress rehearsal," Morris recalls. "He was horrified to find that everything was made of cardboard and string. I even had to convince myself that it would be alright on the night." It certainly was: a smash-hit in several countries besides Britain, it's now licensed to 12 German theatres.[46]

Artangel's work sought to fulfill what its 2006 promotional brochure articulated as "the need for an arts organisation that is inspired and shaped by the vision of artists, and is committed to realising them, no matter how challenging or ambitious they may be."[47] This ethic of practice entailed difficulty and sometimes bewilderment for both producer and artist. Morris's comments regarding *The Margate Exodus* in a discussion with his regular collaborator Brian Eno, appearing in *The Producers: Alchemists of the Impossible* (2007), describe insomnia and anxiety, "waking up in the middle of the night yet again and thinking I will never again allow myself to be in this position, where it feels so difficult."[48] In the mid-1990s, Artangel invited Robert Wilson to make what ultimately became the celebrated installation piece *H.G.* (1995), a collaboration with Hans Peter Kuhn, staged in the Clink Street Vaults near London Bridge. Wilson's praise for Artangel evokes the exercise of freedom as overwhelming and confusing: "they say you can do whatever you want. I had no idea what to do. I didn't know whether it should be indoors or out, in a park or a factory building or someone's house."[49] Conspicuously absent from Wilson's list are the gallery and the theater: Artangel's commissions in the 1990s and 2000s consistently made temporary use of industrial, postindustrial, and disused spaces, or rearticulated institutional ones. To take a couple of examples, an early commission, Melanie Counsell's *Coronet Cinema* (1993), responded to a derelict Mile End film house by requiring audiences to navigate an unusual journey through the space to witness a thirty-minute film representing "the gradual evaporation of a liquid from a small glass" from its upper circle, in a staging of "the intense interaction between the spectator and the screen."[50] Fifteen years later, Roger Hiorns's Turner Prize-nominated *Seizure* (2008–9) introduced 75,000 liters of copper sulphate into the interior of an "abandoned"[51] council flat near London's Elephant and Castle area, producing the growth of a defamiliarizing layer of blue crystals all over the flat, which audience members, equipped with Wellington boots, could enter free of charge.

Art in Public Space

In a 2002 roundtable discussion, Lingwood described Artangel's aims for engaging audiences, and noted too the performativity of policy discourses:

> It's hard not to use certain buzz-words of the moment. We do have an ambition that the projects should have the potential to be genuinely inclusive. It's important that they can engage people who come intentionally—and often with a considerable amount of previous knowledge—and those who arrive accidentally.[52]

Rachel Whiteread's *House* (1993) was exemplary: staged well before the term "inclusion" had become common currency, this provocative commission catapulted Artangel into wider public awareness, and, as Lisa Jardine remarked in the same roundtable discussion, "for better or worse is equated with Artangel precisely because it includes that relationship with the rest of the world."[53] It also triggered a fierce debate on art's position in the public sphere and how it should be supported. Whiteread cast the interior of a soon-to-be demolished terraced house in the east London district of Mile End in concrete. The resulting sculpture foregrounded the aesthetics of Victorian architecture, the meaning and significance of home, and, by virtue of its presence, the absence of both the other houses in the former terrace and the house which had itself been cast. In November 1993 Whiteread received the Turner Prize, but the Bow Neighbourhood Committee, which oversaw the site, resolved to destroy the sculpture on the agreed schedule, despite months of initial delays and its newly award-winning status.[54]

Public reaction erupted stormily, and in this pre-internet moment in 1993, in among the sculpture's voluminous press coverage, a tussle between Artangel and Councillor Eric Flounders, leader of Tower Hamlets Council, played out in the letters' pages of *The Independent*. Flounders wrote, on November 25, 1993:

> Surely those like Mr. Glendinning [author of another letter to the newspaper] should not be whining about a local authority wishing to stick to a universally agreed contract, but should be grateful that this piece of experimental nonsense which they love so much was permitted to exist in the first place. The antics of Artangel in failing to abide by the agreement, of course, will make this and other councils wary of such agreements in the future.[55]

James Lingwood, on November 30, 1993, replied:

> Once more, Eric Flounders conflates private prejudice with public interest (Letters, 25 November). The decision by the Bow Neighbourhood Committee, on his casting vote, not to allow Rachel Whiteread's *House* a briefly longer life takes no account of the prodigious interest this sculpture has generated. Only last weekend more than 3,000 people signed a petition on site in only 12 hours. Many of these were not representatives of the "chattering classes" whom Mr. Flounders acknowledges may be interested, but people who live and work locally.[56]

In these texts, competing articulations of class, cultural capital, power, and the public good vie for authority. But the argument that haunts both is one of utility: the appropriate expenditure of public resources on something of value.

Ash Wall (1993), a permanent public sculpture by Vong Phaophanit situated by the Thames Barrier in Charlton in southeast London, was launched only weeks before *House*. (Phaophanit was also nominated for the 1993 Turner Prize for his work *Neon Rice Field*.) Less publicly controversial, *Ash Wall* was vandalized and eventually demolished only a few years later. In an article published in relation to the launch of Sara Selwood's text *The Benefits of Public Art* (1995), Patrick Wright noted the glass sculpture's intended response to the Thames: "Since the river had long been a route of migration, trade, and colonization, it would evoke the idea of a frontier that was both real and illusory."[57] He interviewed people working near the location of *Ash Wall*, by then abandoned and dilapidated:

> The attendants at the Thames Barrier last week described the vandalism as "disgusting." The men at the nearby salvage yard, CJ Wreckers, were more contemptuous of Vong's efforts. "Everyone thinks it's rubbish," said one, "a waste of taxpayers' money, total crap. Nobody understands it. All we know is that we went out one day and there it was." Told that this extra-terrestrial visitation had cost £60,000, he ventured that the money should have been given to Greenwich Hospital.[58]

The art critic Richard Cork praised *Ash Wall* as "elegiac";[59] Wright's article conjures a similar appreciation of the work as part of a critique of the economic and socially regenerative claims made on behalf of public art, and insists that "art work like *Ash Wall* needs proper security and maintenance, certainly, but the redevelopment of a sunken area also demands education, and thorough-going economic and social reform: 'You can't raise a place with a work of art alone.' "[60]

But to go back to *House*, Councillor Flounders advanced a blunter view about the sculpture in an interview with *The Guardian* as the renegotiated demolition date in 1993 drew nearer. Asked what his response would be to a request from artists for a grant to produce the "sentimental Victorian paintings" of his preference, he declared he would "tell them to fuck off. It is nothing to do with what I like or don't like, it has got to do with reality and funds not being diverted from real needs."[61] *House*'s entanglement in this ongoing debate became inscribed on the sculpture's surface, with one graffiti tag reading "WOT FOR" on one side of the building and beneath it, a response, "WHY NOT?" with the "O" in "not" the basis of a jolly cartoon stick figure with large ears and a cheeky smile. Other posters and placards glued to the sculpture protested the M11 Link Road development, and made demands regarding housing provision.[62] For geographer Doreen Massey, the latter issue was especially pivotal to the sculpture's cultural politics and signification locally, given that housing shortages had been exploited by the far-right British National Party (BNP) to narrowly win a local council seat in Millwall, in east London, in September 1993.[63] Though *House* exercised undeniably powerful effects in querying the meaning and symbolism of home, it did not grapple with how "the iconography of house and home performs a crucial role in the various imagined pasts of this part of London"—a place where " 'tradition' " can evoke both "radicalism and ethnic diversity or racism and community closure."[64] She concluded that, despite the sculpture's inattention to the history of its east London location, by confounding its numerous audiences, *House* had circumvented being co-opted as a project of nostalgia for a "mythical white past": the work was "a glorious combination of the evocation of tradition precisely in a non-traditional form of 'art.' "[65]

The debate regarding *House*'s status as art was perhaps not "a sterile confrontation in its own terms,"[66] as Massey put it, but was intimately connected to the interarticulated questions of state support, approaches to public space, and the performative effects of art. Two linked assumptions underscore the dominant responses to the works of art discussed above: on the one hand, art is a special kind of human activity and product, and therefore vandalism to it is especially "disgusting"; and on the other hand, without "real" effect in the world, art is a pointless activity. This pervasive binary clearly relates to the "double discourse of value"[67] discussed in the introduction. Beyond this binary, in an article for *The Times*, Lingwood theorized the politics of the controversy regarding *House* as it related to public art as a genre:

> It seems that in this particular local contest (I am not prepared to generalise about the attitudes of local authorities), contemporary public art must aspire to anonymity if it is to be allowed to exist at all. In short, it is only OK if it is close to meaningless. This

> culture of the lowest common denominator is exemplified by the decision of three councillors of Bow neighbourhood to insist on the immediate demolition of *House* on the same night that Rachel Whiteread was awarded the Turner Prize.[68]

When introducing the book of essays, photographs, and press cuttings documenting the project, Lingwood extended this argument further: "*House* did not seek to manufacture some confectionary consensus, as many public works of art are compelled to do. Indeed, it laid bare the limits of language and expectation which afflict the contentious arena of public art."[69] This assessment resonated with Richard Serra's similarly controversial *Tilted Arc* (1981), which, as Lingwood notes, was also referenced in arguments about the project. A gigantic metal post-minimalist sculpture, *Tilted Arc* sliced uncompromisingly across Federal Plaza in New York, and became the subject of a protracted legal action regarding its removal that the artist ultimately lost. As Miwon Kwon argues (following Rosalyn Deutsche), Serra's sculpture represented a model of site-specific art "without obvious utilitarian payoffs, one that critically questions rather than promotes the fantasies of public space as a unified totality without conflicts or difference."[70]

Public Art, Community Art

Let's move now to consider the institutional elaboration of public art more broadly and its relation to the vexed term "community." In a 1990 discussion on the topic of public art, Lesley Greene, director of the Public Art Development Trust, commented that "ten or fifteen years ago, it was actually very hard to interest first-rate artists in making public commissions; the activity was too closely associated with community art."[71] By the 1990s, "community art" was a term that had come to be rejected even by artists working in community contexts in Britain.[72] From the 1970s on, groups like Free Form and Greenwich Mural Workshop had positioned themselves and their work outside of institutional frameworks for art, and sought to offer people "a chance to reclaim their environment"[73] by staging cross-art form festivals, developing local resources such as community gardens, and adorning buildings with intricate murals depicting events or people of significance.[74] The participants in the 1990 discussion hazarded a series of suggestions as to the failure of community art as a movement: a confusion between aesthetic critique and political attack upon community art makers themselves, the movement's reluctance to question its own ideologies, and "amateurism." Malcolm Miles (then director of British Health Care Arts) suggested that these factors had "actually distracted attention from the more interesting problems of what artists might really be adept at addressing. It's about chemistry, and you don't get a chemical reaction without different elements."[75] Lingwood agreed, arguing here too that the "directional pull of most community arts has been towards a lowest common denominator, the desire not to displease"; instead, he advocated that works "should show that the meanings of places are in contest."[76]

An important example that counters such a narrative of community arts is Dave Binnington, Desmond Rochfort, Paul Butler, and Ray Walker's *Cable Street Mural* (1983), a work whose methods made it "significant in the development of community-led initiatives."[77] Based on archival research and conversations with local people, the mural paid tribute to the antifascist 1936 Battle of Cable Street in which, in the wake of systematic fascist aggression against Jewish people and communists in east London, a counter-demonstration of thousands of people presented united resistance to a march through the area by members of the British Union of Fascists and the police assigned to protect it.[78] The mural commemorating the battle was defaced with ultra-nationalist and racist slogans before it was finished in the early 1980s, and the artists themselves faced aggression from the BNP during the year-long process of its creation.[79] The mural was paint-bombed in 1987 and again in 1993, and in restoring it that year, Paul Butler confronted threats from BNP supporters.[80] (The restoration was unfolding at the same time as the negotiations over *House*, which would be presented less than two miles away in Mile End.) For a 2016 *Guardian* article reflecting on Cable Street's history, decades of far-right violence against Jewish and South Asian people in east London, and the mural (restored again by Butler in 2011), David Rosenberg interviewed Cable Street residents who had been involved in the artwork's origination. They expressed their admiration for the mural's politics and longevity: the painting represented an "extraordinary landmark [which] has survived the rapid gentrification that has swept aside communities, cultural memories, and sites of struggle"—and, in the words of a local teacher reflecting on her pupils' interpretation, was a work "not only about racism but also about solidarity."[81]

The creation of *Cable Street Mural* in the early 1980s was funded by grants from the Arts Council, Greater London Arts Association, Greater London Council, and various trusts and foundations.[82] In the wider industrial scene of public art, by the early 1990s, new forms of funding—percent-for-art, private commissions, and publicly funded regeneration initiatives—had diversified and shifted the practice of public art, consolidating the economically developmental justifications of support for the arts, and making public art more attractive to artists who did not wish to align themselves with the more marginal movement of community art.[83] A key intervention was the Arts Council report *An Urban Renaissance: The Role of the Arts in Urban Regeneration: The Case for Increased Public and Private Sector Co-operation* (1988), which argued for the arts' capacity to produce entrepreneurializing social effects, and claimed that the arts create "the 'can do' attitude essential in developing the 'enterprise culture' this government hopes to bring to deprived areas . . . The arts provide a means of breaking this spiral and helping people believe in themselves and their community again."[84] Yet, Sara Selwood proposes that despite their industrial marginality, lobbying from various groups, including community arts, as part of the 1991 National Arts and Media Strategy—"youth arts, community arts, folk arts, Cypriot culture, amateur arts, arts in rural areas, arts and disabilities and women and arts"[85]—also provided the conditions in which the Arts Council embraced "work promoted in 'non-art' contexts, including art employed in urban regeneration."[86] Both Lingwood and Morris situated Artangel's particular approach to commissioning artist-led projects in the specificities of this changing industrial landscape, responding, in particular, to culture-in-regeneration's growing impetus and legitimacy in the lead-up to and aftermath of Glasgow's year as European City of Culture in 1990, and navigating a "patchwork" of public and private funding sources.[87]

In this changeable scenario, and in "non-art" contexts, it was necessary for a producer to generate a sense of affinity for a project among multiple "stakeholders." Morris writes:

> You have to communicate with them, gain their trust, and ask them to help you do things that appear quite mad, actually. And you've got to position the whole project so that it has credibility with all of its constituents. It can take a very long time.[88]

Michael Hardt and Antonio Negri influentially termed such a process "affective labour," which produces "social networks, forms of community, biopower"[89] and thus in this case the conditions for contemporary artists to pursue their creative practice. Despite differences in the cultural positioning of artist-led commissioning and community arts, the process of slowly cultivating relationships that Morris describes above is common to both of them. As Justin Lewis wrote in 1990 of community arts groups across the country, "the more experienced groups in the field emphasise two broad principles for outreach work: establishing *credibility* and giving people *confidence*. Building up credibility and trust can take time."[90] And community arts work and artist-led commissions each emphasize the nurture of creative vision and capacity. In an article responding to Roy Shaw's *Arts for All* (1985), and doubling as advance notice of the Shelton Trust's text *Culture and Democracy: The Manifesto* (1986), the community artist Owen Kelly insisted that "our concern is not with producing the 'right art,' but rather with producing the right conditions within which communities can have their own creative voices recognised and given sufficient space to develop and flourish."[91] The resonance with Lingwood's 2002 reflections is striking: "We always started with the artist and his or her ideas and let things emerge."[92] But as in the case of the community dance practices I discussed in chapter 1, the community arts movement sought to radically democratize the notion and practice of artistry to produce not wider access to artistic work produced by select and privileged voices, but cultural democracy: "everyone is an artist."[93]

Anti-Tourism

If community arts work proceeds largely within a particular place or context, one of the most enticing aspects of Artangel's site-responsive commissions has been their invitation to audiences to travel to unusual locations, or to reframe those locations through artistic experiment. Distancing itself from the start from "early 1970s rhetoric"[94] concerning art's oppositionality, Artangel's concern in many of the works it commissioned in the 1990s and 2000s was to explore a postmodern "seepage of the work into the world and vice versa."[95] In a 2002 piece, Claire Bishop favorably compared this interest to Allan Kaprow's use of the installation space as a training ground for audience members to test and thus develop a more flexible approach to dealing with the uncertainties of everyday life.[96] Works as diverse as Tatsuo Miyajima's remote-control car LED installation *Running Time* (1995) staged in the Queen's House, Greenwich; Gabriel Orozco's *Empty Club* (1996), a reimagining of a disused gentlemen's club at 50 St. James's Street; and Jem Finer's thousand-year digital sound work *Longplayer* (2000) can be interpreted as responses to the uncertainties of the contemporary, while nonetheless their "choice of environment irreducibly shapes the final work, making uprooting or relocating often impossible."[97] For Bishop, these projects reflexively offered up "the 'experience of experience' ": "the whole experience of visiting each work acquires a purposive character comparable to that of a pilgrimage. You need your London *A-Z* and your wits about you."[98]

Roughly coinciding with the release of Penny Woolcock's film *Exodus* in autumn 2007, Artangel staged another work that took up themes of national identity, but from an alternative angle: Paul Pfeiffer's *The Saints*, a sound and video installation about England's 1966 World Cup victory, which focused not on the game but on the crowd. The piece was presented in an empty retail unit adjacent to Wembley Stadium, sitting, as the program notes put it, "in the shadow of the new stadium, and on the footprint of the original Empire Exhibition."[99] The recorded noise of the crowd was in part simulated: it was "outsourced" to "a crowd of young Filipinos . . . brought together in Manila, an outpost of a different Empire, to chant and cheer their way through the experience of 1966."[100] In a similar way to the expeditions Bishop describes to visit Artangel pieces, my journey to Wembley to attend *The Saints*, alone in the dusk of a chilly evening, acquired the magical character of a desolate urban fairy tale, with each moment experienced on the way woven tightly into its narrative. A request for directions from a station guard and his sexist response, my precarious descent in foolishly chosen shoes down the steep granite steps of the Jubilee underground line development, and a missed turning in an industrial estate resulted in my stumbling, improbably enough, upon an audition line for a forthcoming series of *The X Factor*. These events became as much a part of the encounter, aesthetically and critically, as the mustiness of the carpet in the cold retail unit, my solitude within it, the tiny grey TV screen bearing the solitary moving figure of footballer Bobby Charlton blinking from a partitioned area at the back of the unit, and the disembodied echoes of exuberant cheers rebounding from its high walls. The installation's strategies were deeply theatrical—presenting, as one critic put it, "an uneasy dialectic of presence and absence through this act of both displacement and reconstruction, reconfiguring an iconic moment to produce a situation of physical and psychological estrangement."[101]

In her 2002 text, Bishop suggested that the experience of subjective decentering modeled by performance and installation works of this kind offers a critique of contemporary capitalism, in part by affording reflection on the movement of history in and through the defunct urban spaces appropriated for the works, much in the manner of the "chance encounter" with the outmoded prized by the Surrealists and the Benjaminian *flâneur*. "Although it is imaginary," she wrote, "this 'fantasy' experience of decentring may nonetheless prompt not only memory but a questioning and re-evaluation of our environment."[102] This claim to such works' oppositionality is debatable at best. Even in 2002, it was optimistic to see these strategies as questioning capitalist development so straightforwardly. The reevaluation of "outmoded," "marginalised," or "abandoned" sites is the essence of gentrification.[103] Works temporarily presented in sites of "anti-tourism" within the grander touristic site of the capital have therefore more plausibly operated both as cultural critique and in ritual complicity with the logic of postindustrial capitalist expansion, a process unfolding over many years. Likewise in 2002, Morris reflected that the mid-1980s "was a time when the lure of an untouched Docklands provided performance spaces both large and small. A time when Royal Victoria Docks hadn't made way for a City Airport and Butler's Wharf had not yet been colonised by Conran."[104] These words allude to the possibilities that derelict industrial sites opened up to artists in that period and to those sites' subsequent gentrification, with an apt vocabulary of colonial seizure.

Though perhaps a little less conspicuous in the late 1990s and early 2000s, in the aftermath of the financial crisis of 2007–8, the broader connection between these processes and "art-washing"—a spin on the corporate practice of "greenwashing"—became conspicuous with the acceleration of the turn of local authorities to private development in the domain of housing. This turn has had destructive consequences for people on low incomes and in need of secure and affordable accommodation, priced out of new private developments in a process epitomizing "accumulation by dispossession."[105] One such area is Elephant and Castle, a deprived district bordering central London. According to the 2011 census, the district had more than three times the national average of social housing tenancy; the census found "social renting and private renting rates that vary considerably across ethnic groups."[106] Following years of struggle over its future, between 2011 and 2014 the Heygate Estate in Elephant and Castle was gradually demolished—a large social housing block that prior to its removal had accommodated more than 3,000 people.[107] In 2013, Artangel controversially attempted to utilize the site for a Mike Nelson work, an action strongly contested by local and former residents "decanted" from the estate.[108] In his analysis of the dispute, Alberto Duman argues that the impermanence of Artangel's commissions had previously "sheltered their work from association with more vulgar imagery blatantly connecting public art and urban development speculative activities."[109] Nonetheless, he suggests that throughout the 1990s and 2000s, the organization, "in their constant search for London properties in a state of transition, became the high-end precursors of 'interim-use' as value-incubator for developments to come, all of which perhaps explains [artist] Richard Wentworth's jokey reference to their specific brand as "the art world's estate agents."[110]

Writing from the perspective of the artist-producer, Gregory Sholette discusses the work of his own company REPOhistory and public art's compromised implication, in the late 1990s, in urban transformation and clearance in another rapidly gentrifying financial center, New York. Sholette examines the struggle over the site of the Millennium Hotel, an upscale urban retreat in Times Square now occupying the site of what until the mid-1980s was four hotel buildings accommodating the working poor. In 1998, REPOhistory attempted to memorialize developer Harry Macklowe's dangerous and unauthorized 1984 leveling of the four buildings with a piece of public art signage. The piece was produced as part of a larger project, "Civil Disturbances: Battles for Justice in New York City," which was supported by New York Lawyers for the Public Interest. The Millennium Hotel had REPOhistory's sign peremptorily removed and relocated away from the hotel on the basis that "REPOhistory was damaging hotel business."[111] Sholette's analysis makes the stakes of rewriting place narratives, and the wider transformations they facilitate, acutely clear:

> Like an arcane plot out of a Philip K. Dick novel, the very visage of the city I knew was being transmuted from lead to gold. The more I looked, the more I saw. Quaint Cafés replaced actual coffee

shops. Futuristic bars and art galleries took over food processing and light industrial shops. An ersatz cosmopolitanism was everywhere and the Millennium was a part of this larger whole that involved wiping clean not merely the physical traces of the past, but its memories.[112]

For Sholette, the semiotic and material overhaul of the public realm delivered through artistic work was highly likely, ultimately, to overwrite the political commitment and intention of the artists making it: to that extent, "I had indeed found the enemy: it was me."[113] Sholette's account demonstrates the dynamics of art's implication in gentrification as they were shared in cities in the Global North in the 1990s and 2000s. In relation to these processes of re-signification, a more appropriate metaphor than selling real estate—brokering access to property—may therefore be property development itself.

"Places, like Property Prices, Go Up and Down"

If "sophisticated and fleeting spatial interventions"[114] in the financial centers of London and New York encouraged a kind of anti-normative urban tourism, what of *The Margate Exodus*'s brief appearance in the seaside tourist town of Margate? As historian John Walton argues, the seaside resort is both a place of escape and of industry.[115] From its earliest days, coastal tourism in Britain enabled people at leisure to shed the "leaden constraints of day-to-day identity"[116] and become carnivalesque "holiday role-play fantasists"[117] on leave from their quotidian responsibilities. Margate's own complex identity as a tourist destination dates from the early eighteenth century.[118] To accommodate wealthy visitors from the 1730s on, the early decades of the resort saw the construction of townhouses in the image of Georgian London, and, alongside its sea-bathing facilities, the development of venues for bourgeois entertainments—assembly rooms, a theater with a royal patent, and subscription libraries.[119] In the nineteenth century, with the introduction of steamships and, later, the railway, wider public access to the resort caused its aura of gentility to evaporate.[120] In *Sketches by Boz* (1836), for example, Charles Dickens refers to the resort for satirical effect: the Tuggs family, in receipt of an inherited fortune and intent on social climbing, shun Margate as a new place to live in their quest for status distinction:

> "Gravesend," mildly suggested Mr. Joseph Tuggs. The idea was universally scouted. Gravesend was *low*.
>
> "Margate," insinuated Mrs. Tuggs. Worse and worse—nobody there but tradespeople.[121]

As leisure time became more widely available to waged workers in the late nineteenth and early twentieth centuries, and legislation such as the 1938 Holidays with Pay Act was introduced, Margate developed and prospered as a lively venue of popular tourism, despite blows sustained during the Second World War.[122]

In the early 1960s the resort thrived, and visitors were entertained by stars of music, stage, and screen at the 2,500-seat Winter Gardens, and by the roller coasters of the Dreamland amusement park. Built on the site of the former Hall by the Sea, a pleasure palace developed in 1863, Dreamland became one of the resort's chief attractions; it opened for business in 1920 and provided thrills and spills to millions as the decades unfolded. Mildly saucy tourism films presented and endorsed by such popular cultural luminaries as Kenneth Horne and Michael Aspel promoted Margate's beaches, donkey rides, trampolines, and nightlife.[123] Margate's history thus encompasses the elements of "defensive gentility, precarious respectability, chromium-plated glamour, earthy humour, and raw sexuality"[124] that Walton suggests make up the twentieth-century popular cultural imaginary of the British seaside. All of these elements are represented in "The Jolly Boys' Outing" (1989), a landmark Christmas special of *Only Fools and Horses*, the popular and long-running BBC television series. The special featured the show's working-class heroes on an outing to Margate. Created during the town's decline, the episode resisted dramatizing Margate as "that favourite symbol of seaside economic collapse."[125] Margate's facilities now include the Turner Contemporary gallery, which opened in April 2011; the gallery continues to present its work in terms of "driving the social and economic regeneration of Margate and East Kent and transforming lives in one of the most deprived areas of the UK."[126] And Dreamland and its Grade II-listed Scenic Railway (an early roller coaster) were refurbished and reopened in 2015—the outcome, by contrast, of many years of grassroots lobbying and successful application for big coastal renewal funds.[127]

In 2006, while still closed and their future uncertain, the Dreamland site and the Scenic Railway acted as a base and public stage for *The Margate Exodus*'s events. For its producers, Margate's resonance for the project as "a perfect place to explore issues of identity, tolerance, and social equality" had less to do with the town's history as a popular resort than with immigration, an issue that the project's website proposed had "never been more meaningful than it is today."[128] This claim alluded implicitly to conflict in Margate, exacerbated by a wider environment of anti-immigration politics. This environment was and continues to be conditioned by Britain's colonial past, the ways in which the nation has been constructed as postcolonial in public discourse and in law, and the persistence of a "colonially ordered Britain"[129] in the present. In *(B)ordering Britain: Race, Law and Empire* (2020), Nadine El-Enany unfolds a detailed history of immigration law, spanning the 1905 Aliens Act, which "set a legislative precedent for immigration control"; the 1981 British Nationality Act, which disaggregated Britain from its former colonies and "raised for the first time the spectre of a post-imperial, territorially defined and circumscribed Britain";[130] and the subsequent 1996 and 1999 acts passed under Conservative and Labour governments to define and limit asylum and immigration.[131] She argues in the specific case of asylum that "the omission in mainstream discourse of the colonial context for the presence of asylum seekers and other people without a legal status in Britain enables them to be presented as a drain on resources understood as belonging to Britons."[132] Mainstream discourse thus turns histories of colonial dispossession upside down.[133]

Towards the end of the 1990s, violence in the Margate area became more prevalent, inflamed by bigoted statements in the media—for example, the *Dover Express*'s notorious 1998 article headlined "'We Want to Wash Dross Down Drain,'" which described "asylum seekers" (along with "illegal immigrants," "bootleggers," and "scum of the earth drug smugglers") as "a nation's human sewage."[134] In 2000, a National Front march on Margate's seafront prompted the *Isle of Thanet Gazette* to respond in an effort to explode "urban myths" about "asylum seekers" being automatically "given council houses, mobile phones, free food, free taxis"[135]—an emphasis on resources that corroborates El-Enany's argument above. In the 2000s, Margate's Nayland Rock Hotel was used as an induction center. In 2003 the tabloid newspaper *The Sun*, appalled that as recently as 1991 the hotel had hosted Mick Jagger and Jerry Hall's wedding banquet, ran a story with the headline "Our Heritage Is Crumbling" and ominously referred to "the invasion of Margate by an army of immigrants, said by even conservative estimates to number 3,000."[136] This handful of examples relating to the town affirms the argument made by Rosemary Sales in 2002 that "the terms of mainstream political debate have been predicated on the notion that the majority of asylum seekers are 'bogus' and therefore undeserving of entry into Britain and of social support."[137] The continued incidence of racist and xenophobic hostility in Margate in 2006 was evidenced by the graffito "Go Home Kosovans" sprayed on the wall of a car park by the seafront.[138]

In common with other arts projects and campaigns, *The Margate Exodus* sought to challenge racism, and was made possible by the national arts education program Creative Partnerships, which was designed to introduce artists to schools in the thirty-six most deprived areas of the country. Thanet, the most deprived district of Kent, was one such area; Creative Partnerships Kent itself was based in Margate. Initiated in 2002, Creative Partnerships was aimed at "nurturing the creativity of learners and educators, and developing creative approaches to teaching all aspects of the curriculum"[139] by inviting artists to respond to settings' specific needs in situ. Appointed as the director of Creative Partnerships Kent, Anna Cutler's intention was to collaborate with artists "with the aim of raising the quality of work in schools and with the community as well as increasing the capacity of arts practice in Kent."[140] During a chance telephone conversation she had in 2002 with Michael Morris, a short-term education project was initially mooted; ultimately,

> what actually arose from this conversation, and a follow-up visit from Michael, was the decision by them in agreement with Channel 4 to work on a film commission with Penny Woolcock for the summer of 2006. This film was to involve the entire local community in a contemporary re-telling of the epic *Exodus*. This shifted the project from a stand-alone education project within schools into a significant piece of art in the public domain that impacted on the community at large and fed in to the ongoing regeneration of the area.[141]

Filmmaker Penny Woolcock had utilized documentary methods in the creation of both documentary and fictional works since early in her career.[142] The film *Exodus*—a project that a promotional flyer advertised as "the biggest community feature film ever made in the UK"—would be the outcome of a four-year process in Margate that incorporated several other projects as well. The American photographer Wendy Ewald made *Towards a Promised Land* (2005–6), a photography and public art project working with young arrivals to Margate encountered in schools, the Nayland Rock Induction Centre, and a facility for "unaccompanied" children. Antony Gormley's *Waste Man* (2006), a giant temporary sculpture, was created entirely from waste materials, and was burned spectacularly on the grounds of Dreamland in the context of other live events on *Exodus Day*. With contributions from a range of celebrated musicians, *Plague Songs* (2006) was a concept album release inspired by the biblical plagues. A series of smaller projects was created in schools. The works reflected, directly and indirectly, on Margate's engagement in global processes of migration and the lived experience of social marginality.

Representing "Excluded" Communities

Wendy Ewald's *Towards a Promised Land* rejected stereotypical understandings of Margate and its newer residents, and instead sought to work with "a group of children in Margate uprooted from wherever they called home, a group whose common emotional experiences might cut across the divisions of race, faith, politics and circumstance."[143] Some of the project's participants were living in Margate with or without their families, having fled situations of conflict in places as far-flung as Northern Ireland, the Democratic Republic of the Congo, and Afghanistan. Others, more prosaically, had moved to be closer to other family members, or because of their parents' employment. With an aesthetic similar to that of Dorothea Lange's photographic documentation of migrant workers in 1930s America, Ewald's bold, monochrome portraits of the young people were the most publicly visible aspect of an initiative which, like many of her other projects, also involved the children's own creative work.[144] The photographic portraits were blown up to enormous size and staged as large-scale outdoor banners in Margate in 2005 and again in 2006.[145] During the course of *Towards a Promised Land* in 2006, on turning the corner from the station, the visitor arriving in the town from elsewhere would be greeted by the contemplative gaze of a young white boy, whose gigantic image was secured to the side of Dreamland's cinema tower. As if opening a tale of adventure, curving around the boy's face was the handwritten legend: "It happened that we had to leave our lovely city." The writings on other images ranged from optimism ("I helped mum pack. I hoped for luck and success") to wonder ("I didn't believe it—me, in Europe? No, it's not me!"), mundanity ("I feel the same really, except I drink tea"), and forthright exasperation ("I didn't like English. It gave me a headache").[146] The autobiographical relation suggested between the statements and the images invited imaginative projection while at the same time being vulnerable to reductive discourses of "reality": assertions of Margate as located in "Europe" and the difficulties encountered in learning another language complicated narratives of nation, cultural homogeneity, and integration.

In visual and spatial terms, the enormous size of the images had a peculiar scalar effect: from a distance, they were the only perceptible detail of the buildings, which now, accordingly, seemed almost miniature, while up close, they both towered over the spectator and dominated the buildings. The hypervisibility and longevity of the project, described as "monumental"[147] by the artist, metaphorically asserted the continued "presence" of the young people in the town, eliciting questions and comments from passersby during the installation process, and, once they were in place, an angry objection from one local couple: "We know there are asylum seekers, and we've accepted that, but we don't want it rubbed in our face."[148] Others replied with physical violence to the symbolic confrontation the photographs staged, repeatedly burning a portrait of a Muslim girl from South Africa which was displayed on Margate's seawall. The project directors attributed these particular actions to the exact coincidence, in 2005, of the images' public installation and the London bombings of July 7, which, in their account, further politicized an already contentious project.[149] For one academic commentator, the project's exposure of the images of the young people to such actions was deeply problematic.[150] Other members of the public praised the ongoing project and its various elements as brave and informative.[151] If the acts of destruction to the banners signaled a generalized "antipathy toward immigrants and strangers who represent the involution of national culture,"[152] the project demonstrated that, as Paul

Gilroy insists, "it is the workings of racism that produce the order of racial truths and not the other way around."[153]

Several other filmmakers have favored Margate as both a source and location for cinematic interrogations of twenty-first-century poverty, adversity, and Britishness, dramatizing the effects of the unequal distribution of wealth, along with questions of racial identity, ethnicity, and nationhood.[154] The film *Exodus* (2007) was no exception to this, and for Woolcock there was a narrative continuity between this project and her earlier documentary-informed works. In the DVD extra "The Making of Exodus," Woolcock framed *Tina Goes Shopping* (1999), a story about a professional shoplifter made with the residents of a Leeds housing estate, as the project's precursor:

> A few years ago I did this film called *Tina Goes Shopping*, which was this improvised drama on a housing estate, and right the way through to the editing stage it was called "Exodus." And what interested me was this idea of people kind of being in exile in their own country and you know the whole "us and them" thing. The thing with Moses is that he's brought up in this very affluent place; in the original story in the Old Testament he thinks that he's the Pharaoh's son. And then he discovers actually that he's a Jew, he's not one of us, he's one of them, if you like. So this idea that there is no difference between us, it's just who you think you are, and the kind of judgements that you might be making about other people are often so mistaken. So that idea of migration and identity—seems to me it's completely timeless.[155]

With more in common with Alfonso Cuarón's dystopian *Children of Men* (2006) than, say, the social realism of Alan Clarke or Ken Loach, the hyper-real science fiction of *Exodus* transposed the biblical story to contemporary Britain. The oppression of the Hebrews was narratively adapted and articulated as the confinement of "all undesirables"[156] to a shantytown. It thus framed exile as equivalent to the position of a notional underclass: a state of exclusion. The shantytown "Dreamland" is established by the fascist leader Pharaoh Mann (Bernard Hill), having secured electoral victory on an ultra-nationalist political platform ("we've become the dustbin of the world! . . . sinking under the weight of people nobody else wants!").[157] Moses (Daniel Percival) ultimately leads the Dreamlanders in a revolutionary uprising, which explodes in a violent encounter between "Mods" and "Rockers" on the beach, recalling the riots in Margate of 1964.[158]

Like A. A. Gill's *Sunday Times* article discussed at the beginning of this chapter, many commentators on *The Margate Exodus* framed the town of Margate in its entirety as representative of the excluded state on which the film's concept was based. One exception was the arts journalist and author Iain Aitch, originally from Margate himself, whose review of *Exodus Day* appeared in the *Isle of Thanet Gazette*. Ruminating on the surreal experience of his "worlds colliding," he remarked that

> the oddness began at the lunch for journalists and Artangel patrons at the Greek Taverna, which afforded a great view of [Antony Gormley's] *Waste Man* from its lofty position in Grosvenor Place. Playing dumb, I listened intently as one art fan painted a picture of Margate as a place where semi-literate locals spent most of their time burning tyres in gardens or banging rocks together. She also expressed surprise at how many white faces she had seen on her way along the seafront, as she assumed the town's population was 95 per cent refugees. Another particularly haughty diner said: "Yes, I thought you looked out of place" when I revealed my place of birth.[159]

Ewald's *Towards a Promised Land* had tested "the limits of language and expectation"[160] attending Margate in the public representational context of the street, and in that respect had much in common with projects like Whiteread's *House*. Media treatment of *The Margate Exodus* as a whole meanwhile broadly and decisively represented it as a scene of transformative social integration. Articles ranged from local stories in *The Margate Exodus*'s media partner, the *Isle of Thanet Gazette*, to broadsheet commentary and magazine diary listings—including, extraordinarily, an editorial listing in *Vogue* and reporting on *Exodus Day* in the *New York Times*.[161] On the process of participation, the coverage favored tropes of breaking down barriers in a project that "would involve people from all walks of life."[162] Iain Aitch's own piece in *The Guardian* referred to "community cohesion" as the "responsibility"[163] of the project's assistant casting director and outreach worker Lucy Pardee. Resonating with Stuart Hall's "double shuffle," this integrationist narrative ran alongside another narrative, that of competitive excellence. Michael Morris in the *Thanet Extra* observed:

> The *Waste Man* is a very strong image and it will be remembered forever. But the real legacy is in the communication between people who live in the same town, who live next to each other but don't know each other. All the way through we have been making alliances between people at the top of their game with people who have never had any opportunity to show their talents.[164]

The author of the blog *Turneround Margate*, a participant in the project, enthusiastically vouched for the beneficial effects Morris described.[165]

Meanwhile, in advance of the project, in a slightly different approach to the project's showcasing of "talent," several article headlines in the *Isle of Thanet Gazette* calling for participants appealed to its readers' sense of celebrity, now largely in relation to the film itself: "Your chance to be a star," "Be a star in movie of town," "Chance for all to shine with film project," "Your invitation to create an art legend."[166]

Antony Gormley framed *Waste Man*'s theme as "the displaced and disadvantaged everywhere . . . shouting out 'I want to be recognised! I want to belong! I want to be part of this world!' "[167] On his website, Gormley writes of the piece: "Some works are made in wax to be cast in bronze; this was made in domestic waste to be cast in fire."[168] The sculpture was torched and burned spectacularly before a sizeable audience in Dreamland's car park on *Exodus Day*, resulting in further waste in the form of piles of ash, an event which in Michael Balfour's reading produced "an odd form of communion."[169] The evanescence of the sculpture in its "made" form, which burned for only half an hour, gestured towards transience, appearance, and disappearance, but the predominant impression was of the volatility of material structures and their meaning. The rapid transmutation of the work in performance from wood to fire to ash belied the complex and laborious technical process of its making, which the professional production company Unusual managed with assistance from several local volunteers—and not, as Madeleine Bunting wrote in *The Guardian*, undertaken by local volunteers spontaneously responding to Gormley's call in the local news.[170]

Exodus Day

The live event *Exodus Day* took place on September 30, 2006, a few days into the seven-week shoot of Penny Woolcock's *Exodus*. I caught the midday train to Margate from Charing Cross; supplementing the scheduled train departures was a dedicated National Express coach, the "Exodus Express," running from London to Margate. On board, Lyn Gardner's preview in *The Guardian Guide* encouraged anticipation of a day of theatrical performance:

> Artangel is responsible for some of the most stupendous live art events of the last decade, and this two-day performance, taking place as part of the filming for Penny Woolcock's film, should be a genuine marvel . . . a fiesta of performances, speeches, songs, processions and even plagues.[171]

An hour and a half later I disembarked onto a crowded train platform. Having progressed through the swing doors of the station, past one of

Wendy Ewald's pictures displayed behind glass in the lobby, a representative of the Margate Town Centre Regeneration Company approached, pressing a leaflet into my hand encouraging subscription to their events text-messaging service. Unsure of the direction to take next (the crowd by now had dispersed into the streets beyond), I followed the sunlit sweep of road down towards the Victorian clock tower on the seafront. An encounter with a T-shirted guide provided a *Margate Exodus*-branded map of the town bearing a schedule for the day and a similarly branded stick of rock candy. Thus equipped, I made my way towards the shopping precinct where the first staged piece would take place.

En route, in the recess of a doorway were two homeless people, and a garish neon election campaign poster featuring actor Bernard Hill as the fascist leader "Pharaoh Mann"—with the legend "NOB" scrawled across it—was posted on a doorway just above them. As the fiction-effect of the poster registered—and a moment's indecision regarding the status of the people beneath—I recognized that the town was being presented as the immersive site of the film's action, and its visitors as its characters. Approaching the entrance to the precinct, a narrow, covered arcade, I waited for a woman with a pram to come through, and, while waiting, read the full text of a sign displayed at the opening of the arcade's passageway:

> PLEASE READ THIS NOTICE CAREFULLY
>
> TODAY'S EVENTS ARE BEING RECORDED AND MAY FORM PART OF A FILM
>
> BY ENTERING THIS VENUE YOU ARE CONSENTING TO OUR INCLUDING YOU IN OUR RECORDING OF THE FILM AND YOU FURTHER IRREVOCABLY AND UNCONDITIONALLY GRANT TO US ALL CONSENTS WHICH MAY BE REQUIRED FOR OUR EXPLOITATION OF YOUR PERFORMANCE BY ALL MEANS AND IN ALL MEDIA WHETHER NOW KNOWN OR HEREAFTER DEVISED THROUGHOUT THE WORLD FOR THE FULL PERIOD OF COPYRIGHT, INCLUDING ALL EXTENSIONS, REVIVALS, REVERSIONS, AND/OR RENEWALS IN PERPETUITY.
>
> WE HOPE THIS WILL NOT INCONVENIENCE YOUR VISIT
>
> THANK YOU

The "crowd release notice" is a standard supplement to acts of filming in confined, quasi-public places.[172] In the context of *Exodus Day*'s address to its audience as a live event, its simultaneously theatrical and economic implications were thrown into relief by the sign. If the event's framing of the town theatrically hypothesized its visiting spectators as "characters," then this preemptive staging of the shopping precinct, a zone now discursively partitioned, or better, enclosed from the surrounding environment, promised swiftly to divest the "actors" of the rights to the image that their public "performance"—their mere presence—might produce.

Within, a more explicit form of "character" asserted itself: a line of uniformed actors performing as military police secured the interior of the precinct. A large podium festooned with posters would accommodate Woolcock's character Pharaoh Mann. After a brief period of waiting characteristic of a film set, the crew shot Bernard Hill's rendition of Mann's election speech, a torrent of fascist rhetoric, before its live audience of "real" people. The speech concluded with the news that Mann had won the election and then a celebratory explosion of streamers popped into the air, whose ungovernable distribution mitigated against the possibility of restaging the scene. Like the staging of speeches from the belly of Gormley's *Waste Man* and the sculpture's burning later that day, this was filmmaking in a definitively "live" mode: there would be no second takes of this moment. During the shoot, however, after a particularly incendiary passage of fictional hate speech, a member of the crew called "cut" and took to the stage, assuring the assembled audience that "this is just a film, we don't endorse any of these views"—and Bernard Hill interjected, "Particularly me! Especially me!"—"We love everybody, we're peaceful people,"[173] to a gale of laughter. The scene complete, Mann and his entourage dismounted from the podium, and the crew invited the audience to follow the victorious politician down towards Dreamland, with some carrying placards bearing his "election poster." As the crowd made its unhurried journey, the "police" would seize and assault "dissenters," the holiday atmosphere in uncomfortable dialogue with acts of staged and filmed violence being perpetrated in the immersive environment of "the street."

Maddy Costa's disappointed review of *Exodus Day* appeared in *The Guardian* the following Monday, her critique based largely on her sense of listless inaction during "great expanses of time when it's clear that we are just sitting on the sidelines of a film set, waiting, bored, for the cameras to roll."[174] The burning of Gormley's sculpture was the day's high point:

> An awe-inspiring spectacle, a lifetime of Guy Fawkes Nights all rolled into one. What it all means, though, is anybody's guess. And that's the problem with *Exodus Day*. It is not designed as a piece of integrated street theatre, so audiences have no narrative to follow, no sense of how each scene fits in with Woolcock's story . . . the common cry, heard throughout the day, is: "I'm confused." The day needed more cohesion, more activity—more theatre, essentially—for audiences truly to feel involved.[175]

If the day's disparate proceedings lacked an intentional and unified narrative construction—what Costa suggestively called "cohesion"—they did not lack theater. At the most straightforward level, the staging of the journey from London to Margate both cited and materially performed a model of tourism—a day trip to the seaside—whose participants not only consisted of pleasure-seeking city-dwellers intent on a day at the beach, but a group including myself whose (professional) interest in common was *The Margate Exodus* as art. More than this, the immersive sense of the "town-as-set" was the work of theatrical production, entailing acutely contradictory effects. *Exodus Day*'s immersive staging of the town was an increasingly ubiquitous gesture in contemporary installation and performance in the 2000s, but its basis here was the representational imperative of making a film in the realist mode, in a process that corroborates Sophie Nield's materialist theorization of performance and site as a "mutual process of construction—action determining space, which reciprocally determines action."[176] While trading on the site as aesthetically "real" in order to produce the film—a work that explicitly challenged authoritarian politics—the event's makers also needed to intervene in the "really real" public space of Margate's shopping precinct to confirm Pharaoh Mann's fascist rhetoric to be "theater."

Morris published a rejoinder to Maddy Costa's critique of the day in *The Guardian* a few days later:

> It never occurred to those of us involved in the planning and execution of the day that we were engaged in producing "street theatre," a quaint term that has little resonance for today's highly sophisticated, visually literate, and rapidly expanding public, hungry for immersive cultural experiences. Those who came from far and wide to Margate—just like those who came in their thousands to witness an outsize romance between an elephant and a child on the streets of London in May—were not looking for a storyline. Nor did they come just to see a film being made. What they discovered was an emotional connection, not only with the unfolding live events but also—and perhaps most importantly—within the crowd itself: large numbers of people from very different backgrounds coming together fearlessly to transform a public space in a fleeting but unforgettable moment. In Margate on Exodus Day, themes of violence to achieve political ends were explored—but they were never intended to be part of a narrative . . . In another *Guardian* article about *Exodus Day*, Madeleine Bunting understood that work like this means "the walls between the elite who produce art and those who observe it are disappearing." Equally, the dividing line between where art stops and where the world begins is breaking down, a belief that has been at the core of Artangel's work since the early 1990s.[177]

In referencing the Artichoke-produced *The Sultan's Elephant* (2006), Royal de Luxe's ambitious, expensive, and spectacularly well-attended four-day event in London, Morris presents the public as consumer group in search of new experience. A spectatorial desire for aesthetic immersion is radical and fresh. While readily prepared to engage in innovative experiences as consumers, the members of this public are fearful of one another. The public space of encounter is a site of intersubjective uncertainty which in this argument may be briefly sutured—cohered into a community—by the effects of live performance: an argument which resonated with other citations of liveness and spontaneity in regard to the project's work.

The first screenings of Penny Woolcock's film *Exodus* in 2007 took place in Dreamland's cinema to an appreciative audience of the film's participants. Towards the end of her introductory speech, as Woolcock thanked everyone present, a voice from the back called "No, thank *you* Penny!" eliciting a loud murmur of assent and warm, resounding applause. A couple of months later, following the selection of the film in the Orizzonti section of the 64th Venice Film Festival in 2007, an e-mail bulletin announced:

> Inspired by the biblical story of Exodus and shot in the derelict Dreamland funfair in the English coastal town of Margate, *Exodus* explores timeless themes of identity, migration, and great movements of people across the globe. Leading actor Bernard Hill takes the part of Pharaoh and Ger Ryan plays Pharaoh's wife, Batya. RADA-trained actor Daniel Percival plays Moses' brother Aaron. All other speaking parts and the many hundreds of extras are all non-actors from Margate and the Isle of Thanet. The Orizzonti section of the Venice Festival aims to provide an overview of new trends in cinema, and in particular cinema which merges fiction and documentary. It was set up by Marco Müller in 2004 during his first season as director of the Venice Film Festival.[178]

The announcement demonstrated the project's commercial engagement with domestic and international scenes, and professional training, celebrity, and innovation took the stage.

Conclusion

The Margate Exodus was a complex project, combining the professional work of commissioned artists and multiple modes of nonprofessional participation, arts education, and representation. Cultural, social, and class differences were writ large throughout it, amid the rearticulation of community on various fronts. In 2007, Michael Morris suggested that Jeremy Deller's *The Battle of Orgreave* (2001)—the renowned Artangel-produced participatory reenactment of the 1984 clash between striking miners and police—and *The Margate Exodus* each "have tried to rethink what used to be called community art: how a disenfranchised or deprived group of people can view itself differently with the collaboration of an exceptional artist."[179] The "rethinking" of community art here appears as a rejection of aspects of the earlier movement's politics, and a restatement of the artist/community split. "Exceptionality" replaces the older construct of "genius," a move Nicholas Garnham proposes to be characteristic of the rhetoric of New Labour's "creative industries."[180] Of his project, Deller himself wrote that he "wanted the re-enactment of the Battle of Orgreave to become part of the lineage of decisive battles in English History,"[181] and elsewhere he spoke of the work as "digging up a corpse and giving it a proper post-mortem, or a thousand-person crime re-enactment."[182] But despite such ideological differences, in terms of industrial history, as this chapter's discussion has noted, there are several affinities between the superficially distant practices of artist-led site-specific art and community art—not least the fact that community art played a substantial role in producing the conditions for the emergence and consolidation of culture-in-regeneration in Britain which has facilitated much site-specific work.

Although culture-in-regeneration and its promotion of cultural tourism have been strongly associated with the paradigm of globalization—an aspect that also comes into focus in chapter 4—issues of national identity, power, and the continued impact of the colonial past also insistently recur in the works surveyed here, including *The Margate Exodus* itself. This is the case in applications of colonial metaphors to both *The Margate Exodus* and processes of corporate redevelopment, but also to the thematic content and venues of works throughout the 1980s, 1990s and 2000s: trade routes (*Ash Wall*), antifascist resistance (*Cable Street Mural*), the private club (*Empty Club*), the 1966 World Cup (*The Saints*), and housing stock (*House*, *Seizure*). The aesthetic approach of *Cable Street Mural* is quite different from the reflexive, sometimes melancholic problematization of site seen in the Artangel commissions discussed here, interested as these were in "the dividing line between where art stops and where the world begins"[183]—a representational approach arguably more amenable to rewriting narratives of place. But common to these public art works, albeit mediated differently, is the issue of social reproduction—of ideas, cultural and social practices, access to institutional power, and access to resources and to dwellings. All these aspects intersect with the construct of the nation and forms of racialized identity. And social reproduction is intimately bound up with another topic foregrounded here: the dominance of a utilitarian imaginary which presents artistic practice in binary opposition with "real needs"[184] such as health care and housing, with implications for the distribution of state resources and the contention around them inside and outside the sphere of art.

Resisting the more romantic citations of community seen in other commentary on the project, Iain Aitch concluded that "whether the *Margate Exodus* has any regenerative or community benefit remains to be seen, but what *Exodus Day* did prove was that Margate has the potential to be a successful venue for large-scale arts events. If the event is good enough, then the curious will come, stay and spend."[185] Intriguingly, the day's events modeled other aspects of tourism. The narrative theme of *Exodus Day*'s events, which involved the production of Penny Woolcock's film, was unquestionably "violence to achieve political ends"[186] which were authoritarian in nature. But the day's immersive representational approach, deployed to produce a piece of cinematic realism, also reflected the kind of "place-making" semiotic activity that creates tourist sites: the theatrical construction of "real" venues for spectacular consumption. The staging and restaging of this "real" with signage and speech during *Exodus Day* dramatized the contingency of such constructions. Wendy Ewald's *Towards a Promised Land*, meanwhile, disclosed conflict that would rupture such a scene of consumption. In this respect Ewald's project also interrupted the discourse of cohesion—a discourse interested not in the nuances of racial and diasporic identity that her work addressed, but in a more reductive and assimilationist construct of British national identity. In a 2006 critique, Angus Cameron proposed that "inclusion as cohesion is achieved when specific social problems are removed or rendered invisible such that they no longer deviate from, or threaten, the 'reasonable' norms of national society"[187]—norms such as "morality, responsibility, independence and competitiveness,"[188] the character traits of neoliberalism's ideal subject, and arguably the ideal tourist.

On *Exodus Day*, an unexpected disruption to the scene of immersion on the street drew attention precisely to the necessity of social and economic support beyond the trope of the self-sufficient, responsibilized, competitive individual. As the crowd progressed towards Dreamland, we reached a crossroads. There I noticed a set of other placards competing for attention with those of Pharaoh Mann—handmade fluorescent orange signs wielded by a group of protesters. These read:

> ACTION NOW! WE NEED YOUR SUPPORT
> HOUSES HOUSES HOUSES HOUSES
> WHERE'S THE DOCTOR, DENTIST, HOSPITAL AND WATER?

The protesters, from an association called Save Thanet, had chosen to intervene in the public events to advance their cause, a fight against a planning authorization for 4,000 houses in the Thanet area. This was not a spontaneous incident of protest: Save Thanet had launched its intervention with an announcement in the local newspaper *Kent News* about their plans the day before *Exodus Day*:

> "We know the film-makers are planning some spectacular public events for Saturday in Margate, and we aren't going to spoil the fun," said organiser Norman Thomas, "but we are going to make our voices heard. After all, the theme of Exodus is all about people looking for a promised land. The problem for Thanet is that our land has been promised away to be built over—and we are not prepared to accept this. All over Thanet housing developments are springing up. We have to say enough is enough . . . Thanet depends on tourism and visitors. Who's going to want to come and visit a huge urban sprawl?"[189]

At that moment in 2006, in the midst of the housing boom, acts of protest addressing these issues were infrequent, despite the increasing evidence of the entrenchment of inequality—one of the most decisive outcomes of decades of neoliberalization.[190] The placards' protest against property speculation in search of quick profits asserted Thanet as an area in need of basic amenities for all. The supplementary press coverage strategically framed Thanet as a place where people live and work, whose economy is based on acts of travel. And on location, the demonstration also had the effect of denaturalizing the fake placards. It confirmed public space, a site of struggle over the terms of social life and its material shaping, to have representational properties akin to the theater.[191] Like Ewald's photographs, this moment dramatized "site" not as a commoditized parcel of land, or as a theatrically produced "experience," but as a scenario engaged with social and economic change and struggle—one distinctly at odds with the *Spectator* critic Ruth Guilding's framing of place as asset. The next chapter likewise takes up questions of site, culture, identity, and value, but begins several thousand miles across the Atlantic, in a rather more glamorous coastal city, Rio de Janeiro.

Chapter 3

✦

"Double Discourse"

Culture and Value across Borders

The previous chapter investigated histories of public and community art, and the interaction of a project in the seaside town of Margate with narratives of "community cohesion" and "exclusion." This chapter turns to two more constructs that were also highly conspicuous in neoliberalism's "institution-building moment"[1] in the 2000s: "inclusion" and "youth at risk." These terms were not unique to the British context. *Favela to the World*, the project I analyze here, referred to both constructs, and was a transnational collaborative initiative involving artists and participants in Britain and Brazil, produced by the British arts organization People's Palace Projects. The project was inspired by Grupo Cultural AfroReggae—a Brazilian group established in 1993 as a small participatory percussion project in the suburban favela (shantytown) of Vigário Geral in Rio de Janeiro. By the mid-2000s, AfroReggae had expanded to become a sizeable organization with a critically celebrated, internationally touring band. The band's first two albums were released by Universal and Warner Music Brazil; the group's day-to-day arts work in the favelas of Rio de Janeiro sought to offer young people an alternative to working in the drug trade which had violently colonized the settlements. In October 2007, I made a short visit to Rio de Janeiro with People's Palace Projects to write a research bulletin about *Favela to the World*'s activities. On what proved the hottest day yet of the visit, we drove an hour from the glittering beaches and hillsides of Copacabana to visit AfroReggae's cultural center in Vigário Geral, located in the deprived north of the city. Having disembarked from the rented minibus at a nearby gas station, we walked into the center of the silent favela down a series of interconnected concrete thoroughfares. The last of these, bright white in the sunlight, was empty but for an armed teenager standing alone.

Inside AfroReggae's Centro Cultural Vigário Legal—the word *legal* ("cool") substituting for Geral in the center's name—I stood with my two British companions in the intense heat, watching a group of teenage participants dance in a workshop accompanied by live percussionists, some clad in AfroReggae's branded T-shirts. In what to me were deeply unfamiliar circumstances, I was surprised to experience an uncanny sensation of "home." In the mirrored dance studio, I looked at AfroReggae's mission statement, prominently stenciled on the center's wall:

> Nossa Missão: Promover a inclusão e a justiça social, utilizando a arte, a cultura Afro-Brasileira e a educação como ferramentas para a criação de pontes que unam as diferenças e sirvam como alicerces para a sustentabilidade e o exercício da cidadania.
>
> Our Mission: To promote inclusion and social justice, using art, Afro-Brazilian culture, and education as tools to bridge differences and serve as foundations for sustainability and the exercise of citizenship.

By then, the ubiquitous term "inclusion" had become a reflex descriptor in Britain for artistic work with nonprofessional participants—or, to put it another way, members of the "community." Encountering the textual form of the mission statement was unexpected, and especially AfroReggae's citation of "inclusion"—albeit alongside "social justice," a term not often seen in similar statements in Britain. Painted on the wall of the center, beside the logos of AfroReggae's sponsors Natura, Banco Real, and Petrobras, "inclusion" appeared as a jarring reminder of the slick corporate presentations of contemporary British arts organizations. In this moment in 2007 I dismissed this apprehension of sameness, assuming that like histories of "citizenship," "inclusion" must have a different meaning in Brazil.[2]

Back in Britain, *Favela to the World* worked with a wide range of British artists and organizations gathered under the heading of the AfroReggae UK Partnership. Among the participants in the project were companies devoted to working with young people (Immediate Theatre, Contact Theatre, Bigga Fish, Asian Dub Foundation Education), larger cross-disciplinary arts institutions (Barbican, Theatre Royal Stratford East, Rich Mix), and, outside of the arts sector, advocacy groups (Careif, Metropolitan Black Police Association), schools, and education authorities. Most of the arts organizations were London-based, and several took arts education to be their central or founding purpose; their histories and artistic interests encompassed a mix of alternative, underground, popular, avant-garde, and classical theater, film, and music cultures. During *Favela to the World*'s talks and debates in 2006 and 2007, participating practitioners paid most attention to the many differences between Britain and Brazil, both in terms of everyday culture and the example of AfroReggae itself. In conversations about the relative affluence and consumerism of British society, differing modes of social comportment, and the makeup of urban space in Rio and London, they also asked: how has AfroReggae so successfully combined "artistic excellence" and "community action," ambitions we also share? Can we, as practitioners working in Britain, meaningfully emulate the group's model? During the activities and talks addressing these questions, practitioners did not discuss the terms "inclusion" or "youth at risk." These words' shared status as items in national and transnational vocabularies seemed entirely unremarkable.

I argue here that, far from being unremarkable or irrelevant, this terminology was critical to the transnational dimension of *Favela to the World*'s exchange. When viewed as shorthand for social engagement in the arts, "inclusion" seemed to represent common ground between British and Brazilian artists. I suggest that social engagement in this narrow definition was only part of the story: "inclusion" was also a sign of the global reach of neoliberalization and its institutional cultures. As I noted in the introduction, despite its associations with democracy, the word "inclusion" also connotes economic productivity.[3] *Favela to the World* pointed to the homogenizing ideological functioning of "inclusion" as a globally circulated discourse—by bringing together practitioners working in different countries, and by creating a situation in which, through its work, national discourses of culture and value could be juxtaposed: that is, a decontextualizing concept of culture as either intrinsically or instrumentally valuable with ideological roots in eighteenth-century Europe, and a postcolonial construction of culture as mixture, responding expressly to European discourses of cultural universality. These discourses have informed assumptions about artistic practice and conditioned the circumstances in which arts work is pursued, including that taking place in "community" contexts, in ways that in the 2000s were not always immediately obvious. The interactions between artists and cultural organizations bringing different sets of intellectual, historical, and cultural assumptions with them to the project's work threw into relief the debates that raged in Britain regarding the "intrinsic" and "instrumental" value of culture. In this regard, "inclusion" and "at-risk" were false friends. They appeared to have the same meaning in radically different contexts—and in one sense they did, given their implication in the functioning of the capitalist system. But they were deeply reductive, decontextualizing lived experience and concealing historic inequalities. More than that, the economic logic of this terminology was obscure: as Angus Cameron wrote in 2006, those in possession of wealth and able to engage in tax avoidance via legal "loopholes" practice a "mode of voluntary exclusion [which] also represents the ultimate expression of social inclusion"[4] in these terms. None of this was explicit in the uses of inclusion as "as a self-sufficient descriptive noun"[5] in the arts sector, where for practitioners it signified engaging with participants who may or may not have had previous arts experience. In context, as this project showed, both terms could be imbued implicitly with distinct and heterogeneous histories. Encompassing a great diversity of scenes of practice in Britain and Brazil, *Favela to the World* demonstrated "culture" to be less a weapon—the title of a book about AfroReggae by Patrick Neate and Damian Platt—than a matter in question.[6]

First, I contextualize the constructs "inclusion" and "youth at risk." Next, I historicize the discourses of culture I refer to above, noting how they were taken up in the cultural policy arena in Britain and Brazil in the early 2000s. Finally, I turn to the projects themselves, offering a brief historical account of AfroReggae's work prior to this moment in the mid-2000s, and how *Favela to the World* and its structures and texts responded to it. As in the previous chapters, theater and theatricality are critical to my analysis in two respects. *Favela to the World* demonstrated "inclusion" to be an object amenable to staging: animated by its contexts, and a construct onto which various values and ideas could be projected. And the action of the projects engaged theatricality in a similar manner to Augusto Boal's famous characterization of "*metaxis*": "the state of belonging completely and simultaneously to two different, autonomous worlds: the image of reality and the reality of the image."[7] As Warren Linds has written, *metaxis* entails that theater can act as "the space for interplay between the actual and the imagined, the tangible and the ephemeral,"[8] revealing possibilities for theater's intervention in constructing alternative worlds in the reality beyond the stage, by virtue of that reality's already theatrical status. Discussing *Favela to the World* in 2007, Derek Richards, an artist and former director of creative at Rich Mix arts center in east London, remarked upon how the group had inspired the British practitioners in terms that resonate with this idea:

> The impetus, the energy they have, and the willingness to accept and even incorporate the emotional engagement in what they do. And that's what made the environment upstairs what it was, and that's what made the environment in Hackney Free School in 2006 what it was. And so yeah, you forget about those things until you're introduced to something that comes from outside what has developed here, and kind of punctures that bubble.[9]

These reflections point to what, in *Theatricality* (1972), sociologist Elizabeth Burns called "the social reality of the patterned world of institutions,"[10] as well as sensibilities conditioned by convention and lived experience—the overall matter of this chapter and its exploration of this example of cultural work under the conditions of "rollout" neoliberalization.

Discourses of Culture and Value

In *Inclusion and Democracy* (2002), Iris Marion Young described inclusion as a "norm often invoked by those seeking to widen and deepen democratic practices."[11] She considered the inclusion discourse in order to distinguish it from her own concern, the incidence of what she called "*political* exclusion and marginalization in particular":[12]

> The promotion of inclusion in some of this discourse, or "social cohesion," as it is sometimes called, refers to a diverse set of policies, social services, and civic education aimed to support such populations ["misfits, particularly immigrants experienced as racially or culturally different and unemployed youth"] and ease their interaction with better-off citizens. Policies and policy proposals in this context, however, sometimes appear to aim at making social and economic deviants fit into dominant norms and institutions, as well as to give them opportunities for political participation, educational development, and welfare benefits.[13]

For Young, the use of "exclusion" and "inclusion" in descriptions of "deviancy" and "normativity" was unhelpfully sweeping, and she insisted: "Where the problems are racism, cultural intolerance, economic exploitation, or a refusal to help needy people, they should be so named."[14] George Yúdice's pathbreaking book *The Expediency of Culture: Uses of Culture in the Global Era* (2003) is acutely attentive to the performativity and contextuality of discourse, but in its examination of reframings of culture in terms of "resource," the text, like Young's, tends to deploy the term "inclusion" positively to denote involvement in society or at least its potential—however compromised such involvements may be in practice.[15]

I follow Angus Cameron and Ronen Palan by approaching inclusion as a neoliberal discourse of value that is constructed, unevenly and incrementally, in relation to a constellation of other (cultural) values.[16] To be "included" in this sense means to enjoy the benefits of "modes of postnational social integration (economic participation and wealth, lifestyle, consumption, the internet, networked urban societies and so on) most commonly associated with globalization."[17] The cognate discourse of "international development," as Regina Gagnier puts it, signifies "economic transformation, specifically the integration of less developed states into the global market or, in fully depoliticized terms, the 'war on poverty.'"[18] Though invested with meaning locally, and also having real resonance with democratic questions, the capacity of "inclusion" to travel across national borders—the source of its uncanny appearance as I saw it in AfroReggae's Centro Cultural Vigário Legal—suggested the term to possess a similar representational function to the logos of the group's corporate sponsors: that of the "hyper-socialized, de-territorialized factory"[19] of the brand.[20]

The category "youth at risk" meanwhile represents a group teetering on the brink of "exclusion." The phrase first gained currency in the west in the 1980s, designating, like Charles Murray's "underclass," "a new class of untouchables."[21] In 1990, the American education researcher and campaigner Joy G. Dryfoos defined "at risk" youth as

> young people who are functionally illiterate, disconnected from school, depressed, prone to drug abuse and early criminal activity, and eventually, parents of unplanned and unwanted babies. These are the children who are at high risk of never becoming responsible adults.[22]

Though herself a progressive, Dryfoos's summary of the problems faced by such young people resonates nonetheless with the "new managerialism" of neoliberal governmentality. Most significantly, it frames young people experiencing these problems as dysfunctional "human capital," whose "future status and work potential"[23] is compromised, and thus, in the words of another American writer on the topic, the future of "America's position as a world economic power."[24] The deployment of the phrase "youth at risk" in a 2007 World Bank policy document addressing Brazil is identical to Dryfoos's use of the term, but the larger consequence of "academic underachievement" is made even more explicit: "Low human capital accumulation among today's young people is producing a generation of Brazilians that will not be able to compete in either the region or the world."[25]

In Britain, though the *Oxford English Dictionary* dates the earliest use of the phrase "at-risk" in public discourse to 1965,[26] the specific construct "youth at risk" seems to have been taken up significantly later.[27] In the 2000s it became an organizing concept of New Labour's inclusionary social policy, contradictorily encompassing the holistic dictates of the 2003 Green Paper *Every Child Matters: Change for Children* ("being healthy; staying safe; enjoying and achieving; making a positive contribution; and achieving economic well-being")[28] and punitive reforms made to the youth justice system, including increased surveillance, increased powers of imprisonment, and the Anti-Social Behaviour Order (ASBO).[29] In the arts sector, Arts Council England responded to *Every Child Matters* and "youth at risk" by collaborating with the structures of the youth justice system. It framed artistic work with young people in quite different terms, however, from the discourses of risk and blame on which youth justice reforms were based, asserting that "the arts can address the whole person *without prejudice*. In other words, rather than identifying young people with their current or past behaviour, artists and arts organisations address their potential as creative people and as learners."[30]

Chapters 1 and 2 of this book examined the interaction of the inclusion discourse with dance and public art practices in Britain in the 2000s, and the ways in which the "double shuffle"[31] between its entrepreneurial mandate and ethic of social democracy played out. The transnational work of *Favela to the World* revealed another dimension to this discourse: how concepts of culture and value closely interact with national and imperial imaginaries. As People's Palace Projects artistic director Paul Heritage puts it, "for over 500 years, Brazil has been repeatedly 'discovered' by those who travelled there—many against their will—from Africa, the Americas, Asia, and Europe. Brazilians also became 'discoverers' of their vast continental-sized country, hidden from itself by geographic, social, economic, cultural, historical boundaries."[32] In early twentieth-century Brazil, *mestiçagem* (miscegenation) became a problematic but defining feature of narratives of modern national identity in a country grappling with the violent legacies of colonialism and slavery.[33] In cultural practice, *antropofágia*, a notion of "cultural cannibalism," was conceived by the Brazilian modernist poet Oswald de Andrade and enthusiastically taken up by many Brazilian artists in the decades afterwards.[34] In his "Manifesto Antropófago" (1928), he recommended that Brazilian artists voraciously "eat" colonial influence in producing art and culture—with the line "Tupy, or not Tupy that is the question"[35] wittily questioning the ontology of Brazilian culture by hybridizing the name of a reputedly cannibalistic indigenous tribe with one of the most famous declamations in the English dramatic canon.[36]

In her discussion of "*mestiço* nationalism," Styliane Philippou notes that *antropofágia* "proved to be the most important, most effective, most radical, most enduring and ingenious theoretical tool of Brazilian Modernism that would ensure the ingestion of European models and a national Brazilian modernity rooted in native traditions."[37] Producing a "contamination of colonial/hegemonic univocality,"[38] *antropofágia*'s exponents ranged across artistic, scholarly, and political domains. They included artists in the early period of Brazilian modernism, the anthropologist Gilberto Freyre, theorist of the "luso-tropical," and the populist dictator Getúlio Vargas, who, in an effort to materialize Freyre's theory of "racial democracy," institutionalized many formerly marginal and illegal cultural practices that are now understood as typically Brazilian.[39] Movements in music and art in Brazil have thus grappled successively with post-coloniality by practicing and interrogating cultural "cannibalism."[40] Popular music plays an important role in this history, constituting "an essentially contradictory phenomenon in Brazil, one that invariably produces multiple political effects."[41] In the case of "cultural activists of the *favela*"[42] such as the renowned rap artists Nega Gizza and MV Bill, the values of the mystificatory "racial democracy" have been vigorously rejected in favor of discourses informed by civil rights.[43] And, to take an earlier example of the agonistic cultural politics associated with *antropofágia*, Gilberto Gil, an exponent of *tropicalismo* who was imprisoned by the military dictatorship in 1968 and subsequently exiled from Brazil, reports that his efforts in the 1960s "to try to bring rock 'n'roll elements into Brazilian music, as well as the experiments of Stockhausen and the avant-garde, and use open speech to talk about society, politics, and the source of life itself"[44] met with disapproval from his socialist peers: "They reacted negatively. Electric guitars were considered imperialist, and there was this idea that Brazilian music should be kept pure. But Brazil has never been pure."[45]

In his official capacity as Brazil's minister for culture in President Luiz Inácio da Silva (Lula)'s government (2003–8), Gil gave speeches hybridizing *antropofágia* with other discourses. In a 2003 address in Rome,[46] for example, alongside rhetoric refuting the Thatcherite discourse of "there is no alternative,"[47] Gil also framed culture in terms highly conducive to the ongoing project of neoliberalization: culture was a "dynamic sector of the economy,"[48] a "front upon which to combat social exclusion,"[49] and a "space in which to realize full citizenship."[50] His speech's argument was underscored by a fundamental understanding of culture as mixture. Gil invoked *antropofágia* to historicize Brazil as "both son and product of the first great planetary tide of globalization"[51] and to underline the importance and necessity of "cultural transfusions."[52] He reflected on Brazil's connection to the continent of Africa as enduring and genealogically critical:

> As a result of the transatlantic slave trade, people from countries like Nigeria, Benin and Ghana are present in our genetic and symbolic codes. As you know, despite all the systemic violence of colonial slavery, Black people in these regions and their descendants were active and vital subjects in the process of constructing and inventing Brazil and Brazilian culture. From Zumbi to Pelé.[53]

And culture should be seen, categorically, as "inclusive." It should be viewed

> not only as the limited array of traditional cultural forms canonized by Western Europe, but as a dynamic constellation in which all the creative acts of our people appear. From architecture to *candomblé*, from *capoeira* to literature, from samba to theater, from town planning to crafts, from heritage to laser art, from the aesthetic of the *favelas* to culinary techniques, from the cultural fragments of street children to the way of life of the Xinguano, from football to carnival, from scientific research to the knowledge of Amazonian healers.[54]

Gil's inaugural address in Brasília in January 2003 took a similar position: culture represents "the people's factory of symbols, culture as a set of symbols belonging to each community and each nation, culture as the meaning behind our actions, as the sum total of our gestures, as the meaning behind our ways of being"[55]—a radical understanding of culture shared by figures of the twentieth-century British left like Raymond Williams.[56]

In the 1990s and 2000s, New Labour's adoption of "inclusion" did not carry the same popular and heterogeneous cultural valence. Many cultural producers, most often those working in the largest institutions, interpreted the government's "inclusive" cultural policy directives as a threat to the "intrinsic worth"[57] of culture. By coincidence, a month before Gil's speech in Rome in 2003, the British think tank Demos convened a symposium entitled "Valuing Culture" in collaboration with the National Gallery and the National Theatre; the symposium was designed precisely to interrogate these moves in policy, and to defend the interests of cultural producers. Adrian Ellis of AeA Consulting characterized the dispute then in play:

> The very strong emphasis in current policy on the actual and potential contribution of arts organisations to wider social and economic goals leaves under-articulated and, given an environment where there is a strong bias towards the quantifiable, undervalued the intrinsic worth of these organisations and their activities. Further, many of the broadly instrumental arguments in support of public expenditure are themselves neither soundly constructed nor empirically well-supported—cultural organisations are blunt and often unproven instruments of social and economic policy.[58]

Alongside its critique of the co-optation of cultural organizations as agents of policy delivery, this account exemplifies Barbara Herrnstein Smith's "double discourse of value": the distinction between "valuing things 'instrumentally' or 'as a means to some end' and valuing them 'for their own sake' or 'as ends in themselves.'"[59] Despite some important differences in their approaches to the matter of culture, all the contributors to the symposium—not all of whom represented "elite" cultural institutions—reiterated this binary. The cultural references some employed point to its historical basis: Nicholas Hytner referred to *Hamlet* ("we want to hold as 'twere the mirror up to nature")[60] and Keats ("I felt embarrassed, as I first tried to articulate what I thought the National Theatre was for, to say up front that I thought it was more exciting to live in a society that's actively engaged in wondering what's truthful and what's beautiful"),[61] while Chris Smith quoted Hazlitt ("'It may be said of the Fine Arts that they 'toil not, neither do they spin,' but are like the lilies of the valley, lovely in themselves, graceful and beautiful, and precious in the sight of all but the blind'").[62] These references illustrated the "double discourse" running hand-in-hand with a universalizing liberal humanist ideology of "art for art's sake." As the introduction to this book discussed, the cognate categories of "aesthetic value" and "excellence," also cited by the majority of the contributors, have conceptual antecedents in eighteenth- and nineteenth-century European thought that elaborated artistic practice as a preserve entirely separate from the rest of social and economic life.[63]

The binary discourse of cultural value as either intrinsic or instrumental also intersects with the matter of racial identity and its administrative definitions. At the "Valuing Culture" symposium, Deborah Bestwick, director of Oval House Theatre,[64] which since the 1960s had been one of London's most important venues for what was formerly called "alternative theater" practice, made clear the consequences of attempts to measure inclusive engagement in terms of identity:

> We are obliged to monitor all users by race, preferably along the CRE[65] model. As this prescriptive tick-box format consigns many of our carnival participants (Trinidadians of Indian racial background) to the OTHER box, we invite people, in an open question, to self-define. Even so, in a survey of people who were eloquent in [and] enjoyed sharing their response to the theatre they had seen, 34% declined to give their racial background, while NONE declined to give their age. In [the] bid to INCLUDE we find yourselves supporting mechanisms which exclude, stigmatise, or just "other-boxify" ordinary citizens of this country. They are subjected to monitoring and special audience development schemes, as if the problem is somehow with them and their recalcitrant stubbornness to buy a ticket.[66]

In Bestwick's critique, two important normative aspects of the British cultural scene are writ large. First, participation in culture is understood to consist primarily not in the making of art and performance, but in audience membership. Second, this audience can, and—to evidence the success of efforts to encourage a diverse attendance base—must be analyzed with statistical tools that reproduce what Paul Gilroy describes as "the fragmentation and division of racial thinking."[67] Critics have powerfully demonstrated that in Brazil, the construct of harmonious "racial democracy" has occluded and entrenched multiple intersecting inequalities based on racialized identity and class.[68] The managerial administration of state-funded projects in Britain, statistically producing a different variety of abstract individual in terms of racialized and ethnic identity, exposed anxiety with regard to multiculturalism and integration. Here the legacies of discourses of "race" and "culture" meet, inflected too (as Bestwick hints above) with the issue of class identity and cultural consumption.

Of course, *Favela to the World* was not "about" these matters of culture and value. It was established to facilitate young people's access to making theater, music, and visual art. However, I argue that attending to these discourses is critical to understanding the conditions of the project's efforts to translate practice from one country to another, the conversations about practice that it hosted, and the institutional and political environment in which its projects for "youth at risk" were pursued. By the mid-2000s, the lethal incidence of knife crime and gang warfare in Britain had acquired the status of a moral panic focused on racialized identity, with increasingly sensational headlines in the press. In 2007, Blair called on "the black community" to tackle the problem, attributing violence to "specific groups that for specific reasons have gone outside of the proper lines of respect and good conduct towards others and need by specific measures to be brought back into the fold," eliciting anger from figures in government, law enforcement, and charitable organizations.[69] *Favela to the World* didn't position AfroReggae's artistic work as a privileged means of addressing issues of violent crime and gang formation in Britain. Instead, the project proposed that AfroReggae might act as a catalyst for new ways of working and thinking about the role of artistic work in education and "outreach."

In researching the second year of the *Favela to the World* project, I interviewed various British artists, producers, teachers, and funders and documented the project's talks, seminars, workshops, and performances.[70] The reflections of practitioners offered a bleak sense of the institutional culture of arts education. Though arts education had come to attract more resources than ever before as part of the "inclusion" agenda, the bureaucracy and short-termism attending the distribution of those resources were seen to serve practitioners and participants poorly. If conditions of work were inhospitable, practitioners were driven by a love of their chosen art forms and their vocations as educationalists. In "Can Culture Be Our Weapon?" a panel discussion hosted by the Barbican arts center in May 2007, participants and attenders debated the application of "key performance indicators" and collusion with counterproductive governmental processes. Among the participants was Camilla Batmanghelidjh, the former director of Kids Company, whose 24-hours-a-day model of practice with deprived and vulnerable children and young people bore the most resemblance to AfroReggae's own practices. The discussion's contributors also invoked the distance between the "creative industries" and the street, which, as Jeremy Weller of the Grassmarket Project put it, "is part of the culture that actually many of us never enter . . . a subsection to our society that we're in the Barbican right now discussing, but it's outside the door in its raw reality."[71] In this context, in which "excellence" had also once again become a primary theme in public discussion of the arts in Britain, a simultaneous embrace of community work in conditions of great exigency and commercial success was seen to hold out much promise.

"Culture Is Our Weapon"

In 2007, Frederick Moehn summarized the Brazilian political context since the mid-1980s in these terms:

> Democratization and political stabilization (with a new constitution in 1988); currency reform and the taming of hyperinflation; market-oriented economic policies (generally referred to as neoliberalism) with limited economic growth and modest progress in reducing inequality; the increased importance of social movements and non-governmental organizations (NGOs); a sharp rise in violence associated in part with escalating drug trafficking, and seen by many as a threat to the full realization of modern citizenship; and various developments associated with globalization such as the increasingly complex international dynamics of finance, communications, the media, and social activism and policy.[72]

AfroReggae's grassroots formation and expansion as a social organization took place in these conditions. It was founded in January 1993 as a free monthly newsletter, *AfroReggae Notícias* ("a communications vehicle for Afro-Brazilian culture"),[73] which was distributed by hand in Rio's favelas.[74] Following a brutal police attack on Vigário Geral in August 1993, in which armed police killed twenty-one civilian residents, two initiatives were established in the favela: the Movimento Comunitario de Vigário Geral (Mocovige) and the Casa de Paz (House of Peace), a community center based in a home formerly occupied by a family killed by the police.[75] With funding from the NGO Viva Rio, Mocovige invited AfroReggae to run participatory drumming workshops, which the group offered in partnership with fellow company Afro Tafaorogi.[76] With the support of celebrated figures in contemporary Brazilian culture—Waly Salomão, Caetano Veloso, and Regina Case—Grupo Cultural AfroReggae gradually expanded to run *nucleos* (centers) in favelas across the city. These were modified from existing buildings or built from scratch, and offered carefully designed programs of work formulated to bridge the gulf between the *morro* (*favelas* on the hills) and the *asfalto* (asphalt-paved city) in the *cidade partida* (divided city), described as such by the journalist Zuenir Ventura in response to the Vigário Geral massacre.[77]

At the beginning of *Nenhum motivo explica a guerra* (*No reason justifies war*) (2006), the second film documenting AfroReggae's work, the band's lead singer LG argued:

> We do not only have the issue about criminality, issues about negative things in the *favela*, what we have are great groups which are trying to show that all the *favelas* have something good to offer.[78]

Like other cultural organizations and NGOs working in the favelas—theater company Nós do Morro established in Vidigal in 1986, CUFA (Central Única das Favelas) founded in 1999, and the NGO Luta Pela Paz, initiated in Complexo da Maré in 2000—AfroReggae sought to rewrite the racist and classist narratives of endemic marginality and incapacity that had been ascribed to the favelas and their residents in different forms since the settlements first began to emerge informally in the late nineteenth century—at first to house demobilized troops, and then expanding more rapidly in the mid-twentieth century in response to Rio's industrialization.[79] With the colonization of the favelas by drug gangs in the 1980s, these narratives also became entwined with organized crime. Damian Platt writes that the takeover was a gradual process in which the booming international trade in cocaine, the sale of arms, and the criminal gangs first established in prisons came to occupy the favelas; by the end of the twentieth century, the favelas had become "the dominion of highly organized, heavily armed informal armies."[80] Those most likely to be employed in the *tráfico*—a means of quickly earning a relatively high wage—were "young, poor, non-white men"[81] whom Elizabeth Leeds characterized—referring to the gangs' approach to these favela residents as a labor force—as "a reserve army for drug traffickers, with children in that army becoming increasingly younger."[82] The mortality rates from violence in the favelas rivaled those seen in war zones.[83] In these circumstances, AfroReggae's programs in percussion, dance, drama, digital technology, radio production, hip-hop, and circus sought to cultivate in participants feelings of belonging to a group, an understanding of Afro-Brazilian cultural histories, and skills leading to employment. As Olivia Maria Gomes da Cunha shows, the group had espoused this mission since its founding in the 1990s: departing from 1970s collectivist discourses, AfroReggae articulated its antiracist aims in terms of providing "'work,' 'education,' and the generation of income—conditions necessary for the activation of citizenship status"[84] as imagined in the context of neoliberalization. In a 2006 article, Silvia Ramos concurred: foregrounding black identity, the group's agenda was the creation of "powerful images of young people of the favela who, against all expectations, become filmmakers, stage actors, or musicians," meaning that "the media, success, and fame are understood as ingredients of political militancy."[85] AfroReggae took "the shantytown as a geographical reference and the 'community' as a political reference."[86] A central facet of AfroReggae's strategy—and a point essential to the argument here regarding "inclusion"—was its ongoing insistence on the necessary and active participation of the favelas and the organization itself in a global economic and cultural scene.

In its everyday participatory work and musical experimentation, the group embraced multiple cultural forms that were characteristic of *antropofágia* as both practice and concept. In *Da favela para o mundo:*

A historia do Grupo Cultural AfroReggae (2004), founder Jose Júnior wrote that during the 1990s, as Banda AfroReggae developed its fusion of hip-hop, reggae, ragga, and Afro-Brazilian percussion, its members "listened to various musical genres from inside and outside Brazil. It was all good, all there to be taken advantage of: drum 'n' bass, *maracatu*, rap."[87] Alongside these references, the turntablism and video animation in their shows in the 2000s recalled artists on the British Ninja Tune label like DJ Shadow and Mr Scruff, and their aesthetic hybridity and play with costume, color, and dance evoked artists from the *tropicália* movement. One nod in the band's performances at London's Barbican Centre in 2006 and 2007 was MC Anderson Sá's military coat with golden epaulettes, similar in style to that of Gilberto Gil on the cover of *Gilberto Gil* (1968).[88] Meanwhile, those performances also insistently staged the band's favela roots. Dominating the stage at the opening of their show at the Barbican in 2006 was a huge projection of a world map, whose focus zipped from city to city—Johannesburg, Los Angeles, Paris—and finally alighted on Rio de Janeiro. Then it zoomed in on the favela of Vigário Geral, while three percussionists, diminutive before its scale and with their backs to the audience, drummed rhythms on the instruments slung around their waists before launching into the gig's first song. This performance did not represent the favelas as chronically excluded and parochial, but as sites no less internationally engaged than the band's touring practices in venues across the world.

That AfroReggae's development interacted with neoliberalization in Brazil is reflected too in Olivia Maria Gomes da Cunha's finding that AfroReggae's "'myth of origin' was grounded precisely in dance parties and celebrations, in leisure and entertainment."[89] And, as AfroReggae's practitioners and biographers have noted, the group engaged its context through pragmatic and deft acts of mediation and networking across all the scenes of its practice. With the growth of the organization, these partnerships included international collaborations with NGOs, university institutions, the state, and big domestic and international brands, including the Spanish banking group Santander, to whom AfroReggae provided support in introducing a local branch to the favela of Complexo do Alemão in 2010.[90] While George Yúdice more cautiously weighed the threat of AfroReggae's discursive co-optation by both NGOs and commercial organizations, Patrick Neate enthusiastically foregrounded AfroReggae's embrace of economic and cultural globalization in an evocative 2003 account of a visit to Vigário Geral.[91] For Neate, AfroReggae represented a highly effective "oppositional voice that stands against exclusion with full knowledge of the possibilities of imagined identity and the value of its capitalized reputation"; as Neate and Platt put it in their later text on AfroReggae, the proliferation of coverage of the group in the news media and scholarly settings acted as a "kind of 'cultural asset base.'"[92] In 2009, AfroReggae's identity was licensed by the Brazilian clothing company Hering for the production of a line of T-shirts—corroborating Silvia Ramos's argument regarding the "market-oriented" stance of groups like AfroReggae: this stance was "the opposite of the 'non-profit' culture that characterizes the Brazilian NGOs."[93]

Fashion functioned for the group in the day-to-day as an activist device: "real" costumes of branded sportswear were means both to attract young participants and to demonstrate the costumes' "fictionality." As Júnior wrote in *Da favela para o mundo*:

> We use branded clothes, because we like them and because also in this way we can arouse greed, vanity, and self-esteem in the young people. Our major objective is that young people in the *favelas* no longer only have drug traffickers as their idols. In place of rifles, we would offer them musical instruments. Our power was not of death, but of life. We would engage in a traffic of dreams, of possibilities, and of culture.[94]

The political concern here was the violent consequences, locally speaking, of consumerist desire—or as Altair Martins put it: "if Nike only knew the evil they do in these communities"[95]—where the desire for consumer goods might be redirected to encourage young participants to engage with their programs of artistic work in the service of transformation for the better. In *Nenhum motiva explica a guerra*, Martins reflected:

> That's the power of AfroReggae, because Júnior is something else, Eduardo [Tafaorogi's percussion instructor] too, at the time, out of sight, of making you believe even in the things that you . . . even in the things that you aren't, because I had never played any kind of percussion instrument, never not even rapped on a table and I don't have any special gift. A lot of people are born with a gift. I wasn't born with any kind of gift for music or percussion, but he saw something in me and made me believe that I was a leader from the first day.[96]

The process of encouraging self-belief discussed here is performative inasmuch as "saying" does indeed "make it so."[97] In relation to artistic practice, this process is radically egalitarian: it insists that, given the appropriate conditions of production, the ability to create meaning through artistic work that is taken seriously is available to anyone—a critical value at the heart of community arts movements. The capacity to produce art is not mysterious, or predicated on social status, but is the outcome of work, triggered (if necessary) by a psychic investment which, though it may be based in fiction, activates in the "actor" a productive reflexive attention to themselves, and their capacity for action. *Nenhum motiva explica a guerra* itself dramatizes representational reflexivity: a second camera regularly stages its interview subjects speaking to the camera. The effect is to signal the film's constructedness, but in so doing, also to suggest that to be represented on film in this way is, in effect, to be a subject worthy of being represented on a global stage.

"Can Culture Be Our Weapon?"

AfroReggae's successful navigation of local and global scenes of practice provided the impetus for *Favela to the World*, run by People's Palace Projects. The academic and theater director Paul Heritage founded People's Palace Projects in 1997.[98] Based at Queen Mary, University of London, it took its name from the philanthropic institution founded there in 1887. Explicitly addressing "young people at risk," the AfroReggae UK Partnership put together collaborations between arts, public, and voluntary sector institutions from divergent, if occasionally overlapping domains—to take one small grouping, the multidisciplinary Barbican Centre; the Shoreditch Trust, a New Deal for Communities agency;[99] and Immediate Theatre, a community-based theater company. In this sense, the partnership reflected aspects of neoliberalism's uneven historical geography, which, as Jamie Peck notes, is "replete with examples of crisis-induced and pragmatic adjustments, uneasy marriages with coexistent ideologies and practices, and context-specific experimentation, often played out across transnational terrains."[100] The 2007 *Favela to the World* activities which I researched towards the bulletin for People's Palace Projects offered a view of the complex negotiations required to make participatory arts projects happen in Britain—both to set them up, and to attract young people to work on them. Though many of the organizations involved were community-based, the project itself did not emanate from a single context. The sixty or so practitioners who attended the project's Training Forum in 2007 represented enormous organizational diversity—ranging from building-based organizations based in local areas, to local authorities, large production companies operating out of offices and studios, schools, to smaller companies and freelancers moving between contracts and projects. One or two arts organizations had long-term relationships with partner schools. Others developed relationships by tailoring programs of work to harmonize with a school calendar or curriculum. Outside of the school setting, others entered into projects with predetermined partners, developed projects in collaboration with government or non-statutory agencies, or worked as freelancers across all kinds of settings—youth centers, pupil referral units, theater organizations. Some had international links and toured their work overseas. While schools and school-based projects could assemble groups of young people relatively easily, other projects worked hard to attract participants by offering taster workshops, by networking with teachers, youth workers, members of the youth justice system, and local organizations, by using the internet, or simply by talking to people in the street. This diffuse and fragmentary field of work was made more complex by the short-term nature of projects and funding cycles, and the limited time available to overstretched institutions.

In this context, the AfroReggae UK Partnership represented a redistributive innovation designed to benefit young people living and being educated in London's poorest and most racially and ethnically mixed boroughs—for the most part, settings in Tower Hamlets and Hackney; and it sought to benefit artists by facilitating transnational exchange and the circulation of resources and knowledge among the most and the least powerful institutions, not their transfer from the least to the most. For the Barbican to be working reciprocally with schools in Hackney and much smaller arts organizations like Immediate Theatre both asserted and complicated notions of specialized function, and cultural "center" and "margin." The Barbican's enthusiastic support of the project and its endorsement of AfroReggae as artists and activists was critical to the project's initial success. The Barbican Centre is among the best resourced of London's arts institutions: in the financial year 2006–7, the period under discussion here, the Barbican's total expenditure on arts programming and marketing was £12.8 million.[101] With an artistic policy of internationalism, the institution was in a position to provide an appropriate venue for AfroReggae's large-scale performance. Flying AfroReggae's artists over from Brazil to England to perform enabled their work with other, much smaller British institutions to take place—an act described by producer Malin Forbes as a "baseline engine"[102] for the project.

The events of *Favela to the World* in 2007 began with a panel discussion before an audience in the Garden Room of the Barbican Centre: taking its cue from the phrase "Culture is our weapon," the discussion's title asked, rather more tentatively, of the assembled artists, teachers, politicians, and police, "Can Culture Be Our Weapon?" The Barbican's artistic director Graham Sheffield[103] introduced the discussion, remarking that

> the educational mission of this place is very close to my heart, but I'm also delighted to note that culture is really climbing up the political agenda now in a way that I think was impossible to imagine a decade ago, not only in its own right but I think also as an integral and not peripheral part of an approach to key issues in society.

But, he continued,

> this approach has often been dubbed "instrumentalism" and it's become in some areas a pejorative term, and I think in the wrong hands and with the wrong artistic leaders and minds it can lead to some mediocre results. But with great artists, great musicians, great organisations working together, led by the vision of AfroReggae, I think it's proved possible and will prove possible to harness the power of the arts to make a real difference to society without compromising the spirit or the integrity of the art itself, and that surely is key to all this.[104]

This is a model articulation of the "double discourse of value."[105] Here, "the arts" appear as autonomous, but also as precarious and corruptible. They represent a "power" not directly produced by human action, but which might be "harnessed" by it: a singular entity in possession of a "spirit," whose "integrity" suggests a state of already being fully formed. The image gives the sense of Eurydice tentatively emerging from the depths of Hades, who with a single look from her mortal partner will be sent scuttling back into the shadows; or a mercurial genius who needs careful handling by expert managers to produce goods that are not "mediocre." Such a view of artistic work is unable to account for gradual and grassroots development, or for the voracious assimilation of multiple aesthetic forms and the effects of the process of making performance, which was jokingly described by the percussionist Juninho at the launch of the AfroReggae UK Partnership events in 2008 at the Toynbee Studios in London as "a lot of noise and a lot of mess."

Sheffield's reflections enacted a separation between artistic product and material context while also naturalizing the language of entrepreneurship closely linked to "inclusion." The words of finance director Sandeep Dwesar in the Barbican's annual report for 2006/07 likewise reflected that separation: "we let our programmers dream their dreams and find fresh ways of testing the Finance Director's nerves. And I wouldn't have it any other way."[106] The globalized cultural politics of inclusion were similarly articulated by an article celebrating Barbican International Theatre Events (BITE), written for a 2007 brochure marking the Barbican's twenty-fifth anniversary. Its author, the theater-maker Mark Espiner, described BITE as "a visionary performing arts infrastructure" that offered theatergoers an experience of "sharing a space with fellow travellers."[107] He first briefly reviewed the diversity of its program, in which the works of Steve Reich, Duckie's Christmas cabaret *C'est Barbican!*, solo performers like Ursula Martinez and Laurie Anderson, a Beckett retrospective, and Shakespeare commingled with "the full-on pounding power of massed drums mixed with video visuals from a collaborative band of musicians born out of the slums of Rio de Janeiro."[108] At its expansion in 2002, following the departure of the Royal Shakespeare

Company as the Barbican Centre's resident company, BITE became, he suggested,

> less of a festival and more of a cultural identity. It came to signify quality work that embraced the performing arts without feeling a need to pigeonhole them by style, genre or, indeed, language.[109]

In this imaginary, political and ideological differences are neither here nor there. Instead, the defining characteristics of this "cultural identity" are cosmopolitanism and quality of experience directed at an audience of discriminating "fellow travellers." In other words, in its offer to culturally literate arts attenders, BITE represented a paradigmatic model of inclusion. The festival did not refer to itself in this way—the notion that it participated in the globalized scene of "inclusion" went without saying.

Meanwhile, an in-depth evaluation report on the AfroReggae UK Partnership projects in 2006 more explicitly narrated its discursive partner, "exclusion." This text was written by Richard Ings, the author and editor of publications addressing the field of British community arts practices over many years as an independent researcher and consultant. The report's title, *From the Favela to Our Manor: Translating AfroReggae: The Impact and Implications of an International Intervention in Arts Work with Young People at Risk* (2007), indicated that the text would describe the AfroReggae project's translation of practice from Brazil to Britain. But it also suggested the report itself to be an agent of translation between different domains of practice—the scene of artistic production and the report's main target audience of policy decision-makers. For the research bulletin I prepared in 2007, I interviewed Karen Taylor, formerly inclusion officer at Arts Council England. She described the prevalence of skepticism in the policy arena:

> It does feel that there has never been so much art in public spaces, but we struggle to make the case for creative practice in our everyday lives and to make this integral to running those spaces and services . . . There is a sense that arts and creativity is frivolous, a needless and wasteful use of resources that could be used more appropriately. Evaluation plays a part in challenging these ideas, but it is only through enabling the policy-makers and funders to witness or experience projects that we will make significant breakthroughs in changing policy and practice.[110]

By the mid-2000s, project evaluation, whether publicly disseminated or not, had come to be seen as a normative ingredient of publicly funded arts projects in Britain—a means of measuring their "impact" and as such also an ideologically freighted tool of advocacy.

Just as Taylor staged and refuted the intrinsic-instrumental binary—here in the form of frivolous art for consumption as opposed to the serious work of delivering public services—*From the Favela to Our Manor*'s narrative textual form bore little resemblance to social scientific and statistical models which appeared to offer a more legitimate means of evaluating publicly funded work (recall Adrian Ellis's observation regarding the "strong bias towards the quantifiable"[111] in public discourse). For Ings, the narrative form of his evaluative writing represented an activist gesture, producing "a critical object. It's criticising implicitly what happens elsewhere in the system—it's criticising the way these young people are treated, it's criticising attitudes toward creativity in the mainstream classroom"[112] which have historically marginalized arts-based pedagogical approaches that might enable children and young people to develop skills differently. In Ings's *Creating Chances: Arts Interventions in Pupil Referral Units and Learning Support Units* (2004), for example, this critique took the form of attention to young people's art practice and behavior in the settings as social performance. In this text, Ings surveyed ten projects taking place in PRUs and LSUs across the country. The journalistic idiom of his writing offered a narrative-driven, even poetic understanding of the various projects, locating the voices of practitioners and pupils at the center of the discussions, and drawing upon cultural and political information by way of support. Its gentle and often moving account sensitively dramatized the cultural situations of the various settings. In paying attention to contextual dynamics and the detail of human relationships, Ings aimed pragmatically to use the evaluatory text to strike a middle path by "taking two cultures, two sets of languages and assumptions . . . trying to find some common ground, trying to find a way of speaking to both at the same time."[113]

Though Ings's national survey of PRUs and LSUs inevitably embraced cultural and regional differences, the AfroReggae UK Partnership, the subject of his longer study, *From the Favela to Our Manor*, was a much more geographically expansive and complex cultural exchange. Taking account of the considerable cultural differences between Brazil and Britain, the common ground this report found between AfroReggae and the British cultural sector was the presence of qualitatively, if not quantitatively equivalent pockets of social exclusion in both locations of practice, an account reflecting the terms of inclusion discourse. If "inclusion" is predicated on competitive national economies participating in a single global market, its counterpart, exclusion, as Angus Cameron argues,

> has been ascribed a specific if ambiguous "local" geography. Whatever else it might be, social exclusion is routinely couched in terms of "communities," "neighbourhoods," "worst estates" and so on (all understood to be small, subnational territorial spaces).[114]

As noted in chapter 2, Cameron contends that in such a scenario "inclusion" doesn't represent the mobility of the globally networked subject, but instead doubles as "cohesion."[115] The purchase of this construct in public discourse about the arts in Britain—with and alongside that of the binary of "instrumental" and "intrinsic" value—was reflected in *From the Favela to Our Manor*'s own narrative. In alignment with "inclusion as cohesion," the report treated arts education as supplementary to productive economic activity, but not in and of itself oriented toward professional artistic practice. *From the Favela to Our Manor* discussed the favela as an economic context but held AfroReggae's participants at a distance from commercial performance work, providing a conceptual frame for the subsequent account of the projects in Britain:

> A young man, Jonathan, shows us proudly around the centre [in Cantagalo]. Jonathan is my first personal encounter with the powerful ethos that drives AfroReggae. As he shows us the history of the organization in photographs that are mounted in the reception area, he explains that young people come here not to be artists *per se* but to value themselves and to develop personally and socially.[116]

Nonetheless, Jonathan himself was "now studying at the Escola Nacional de Circo (national circus school) and taking the equivalent of his GCSEs there."[117] The report did not position this in terms of training. Occluding the question of paid work, *From the Favela to Our Manor* trained its critical focus on how the values that AfroReggae embody might assist in mending dysfunctional social relationships.

The report asked, rhetorically, of Shoreditch and Hackney, "Our own *favela*?"[118] Adjacent to a full-page image of a person creating a graffiti tag—"HACKNEY"—the next section was headed "Working with the 'worst.'" It opened with a quotation from Altair Martins of AfroReggae: "The first thing we saw in Hackney Free was a fight, so we knew we had a lot of work to do."[119] Referring to the scale of young people's criminalization through the use of the Anti-Social Behaviour Order, Ings argued that

> something must have decayed within our social fabric to have allowed this to happen on such a scale and we all have a responsibility for it—and repairing those communal bonds. So, allowing for the difference in the scale and intensity of the social problems in Rio, there is still, many believe, an urgent need for intervention here of the kind provided by AfroReggae in the *favela*, not just so that young people can be drawn away from criminal and anti-social activity but in order to demonstrate to government that there are more imaginative and sustainable ways of achieving this than increasing punishment and extending custody.[120]

As David McNally shows of the United States, "neoliberals' preferred disciplinary institution has been the prison: it is there that the 'undisciplined,' particularly young people of colour, are to be taught the price of not functioning as obedient cogs in the machinery of capitalist production."[121] The relevance to Britain of McNally's insight regarding the increased use of incarceration in the United States is corroborated by British Ministry of Justice statistics: between 1993 and 2012, the prison population in England and Wales almost doubled.[122] *From the Favela to Our Manor* argued strongly for alternative models of criminal justice, and condemned the public humiliation of young offenders through electronic tagging. But it also advanced community as a solution, and suggested that in "relying more and more on the state and its agents to take on the functions of the traditional community and the private citizen, in everything from supporting our elders to tackling anti-social behaviour, we may have learned, in effect, to be individually helpless in the face of social challenge and risk."[123] This passage resonated with a wider governmental concept of community in relation to antisocial behavior—"as a community you are not performing as you should if you cannot stop people behaving badly"[124]—as seen in John Muncie's summary of the rationale underpinning New Labour's youth justice reforms:

1. Communities should take primary responsibility for crime prevention.
2. Individuals should be held responsible for their own actions.
3. Families, in particular parents, have a responsibility to ensure their children do not develop anti-social tendencies.[125]

From the Favela to Our Manor concluded that "what is missing in this country is the political will to recognize, as Brazil seems to, that culture is central to the health and development of the country, not simply a middle-class pastime, and that artists can provide lasting social benefits whilst continuing to pursue excellence."[126] But the report's demand for cultural work to be properly recognized and supported also implied counterproductive assent to the dominant understanding of artistic practice in Britain: an understanding of "lasting social benefits" and "excellence" as two different categories of experience.

Social Mobility

Attention to structural questions tells an alternative story regarding "exclusion" and its dynamics. "Inclusion" imagines a mobile subject whose movements and social relations traverse boundaries of place, where mobility is a function of access to exchange value. David Harvey analyzes the relation between exchange value and lived experience:

> Low income populations, usually lacking the means to overcome and hence command space, find themselves for the most part trapped in space. Since ownership of even basic means of reproduction (such as housing) is restricted, the main way to dominate space is through continuous appropriation. Exchange values are scarce, and so the pursuit of use values for daily survival is central to social action. This means frequent material and interpersonal transactions and the formation of very small-scale communities. Within the community space, use values get shared through some mix of mutual aid and mutual predation, creating tight but often highly conflictual interpersonal social bonding in both private and public spaces. The result is an often intense attachment to place and "turf" and an exact sense of boundaries because it is only through active appropriation that control over space is assured.[127]

This passage resonates strongly with the emergence of territorial subcultures in British cities with postcodes (postal codes) as their focus, compellingly illustrated by Robyn Travis in his memoir *Prisoner to the Streets* (2013).[128] Travis gives an autobiographical account of growing up in Hackney and participating in the postcode warfare of the 1990s and 2000s. His narrative is largely concerned with dramatizing the "mutual aid and mutual predation" to which Harvey refers. The text offers devastating glimpses of the victimization to which members of the National Front subjected Travis's family in the 1980s, and later, the racism of police and employers, and the implication of gangs in wider transnational criminal networks. Travis thus subtly refuses to disentangle the experiences of young people living in east London in highly circumscribed conditions from global cultural, political, and economic forces. Despite differences in cultural circumstances, compare this observation about Rio's favelas: in his text *Children of the Drug Trade* (2003), Luke Dowdney wrote that "in *Comando Vermelho* (Red Command) *favelas*, youth may use the word '*vermelhou*' to refer to something good. Literally translated, this means 'to become red,' as anything that becomes red (such as a *Terceiro Comando* community that is taken over by the *Comando Vermelho*) is perceived as being positive."[129]

To loosen the hold of such narratives (the "pursuit of use values," in Harvey's terms),[130] AfroReggae's practices sought to cultivate in participants an "exchange mechanism," akin to the "feel for the game"[131] of Bourdieu's *habitus*—that is to say, comfortable conversancy with cultural codes and practices. During the UK Partnership discussions in 2007, the

AfroReggae artist Johayne Hildefonso described its practices in terms that invoke Harvey's thinking regarding spatial appropriation:

> The first thing we do in the workshops is move—percussion, theatre, dance, circus. Only bit-by-bit when we have trust . . . but it's not that we try to change them, we try to mould them. We show that you don't necessarily have to be a part of the fiction that controls the area. It's not a quick process—there are parents and other influences—it takes a long time, and it's not an easy process.[132]

Artistic practice was imagined as going hand-in-hand with forms of social and educational training. The task of artistic work was to bring the existing knowledges of the young people of their lives into dialogue with art—as one artist put it, "to be better able to bring their universe into the universe of popular dance, to work with young people's capacity to confront the new"[133]—the "new" in this case being knowledge of much older Afro-Brazilian dance traditions. Many practitioners participating in the UK Partnership events in 2007 shared this ethical orientation to making performance with young people. But the institutional environment in which AfroReggae-inspired projects took place in Britain was different in many important respects. Conspicuous among these were the interconnected aspects of short-term funding cycles and complex systems of monitoring and reporting—systems that constructed participants less as proto-entrepreneurial subjects than as figures of socially cohesive compliance.[134] The artistic practice itself, by contrast, sought to encourage in participants an orientation to the self as a thinking artist.

One of the AfroReggae UK Partnership projects to be established was the samba-reggae drumming initiative run by the Hackney-based Immediate Theatre.[135] Creating theater projects almost exclusively in partnership with the public, education, and voluntary sectors, in 2007 Immediate was entirely funded on a project-by-project basis. Jo Carter, its artistic director, indicated that the company's substantial half a million-pound annual turnover consisted of a variety of different grants, all of which were monitored in "a complicated process addressing lots of different outputs."[136] In 2006, the Shoreditch Trust put the delivery of a project "to tackle the youth guns and gangs issue through positive activities"[137] out to tender. Immediate was one of a handful of organizations that responded. In view of Immediate's work on housing estates and with young people outside of formal educational settings in Hackney, the Shoreditch Trust felt it to be the only organization with the relevant experience and knowledge.[138]

In collaboration with Taru Arts,[139] a Brazilian performance company located in Woolwich in southeast London, Immediate Theatre initially ran weekly workshops at the Blue Hut, a youth center on Provost Street near the Murray Grove estate, in the densely built-up inner district of Hoxton in the London borough of Hackney. Hackney is one of London's most diverse boroughs, and during the 2000s it had one of the highest numbers of people living in poverty.[140] Hoxton itself was an area that in the 1990s and 2000s became synonymous with gentrification and the figure of the hipster, mercilessly parodied in Charlie Brooker and Chris Morris's TV comedy *Nathan Barley* (2005), but which was also in the top 3 percent of the most deprived areas in England.[141] In relation to the running of the project, the Blue Hut was too small to accommodate the specified group size, and local residents did not welcome the noise generated by the drums in the early evening workshops. When Immediate moved the sessions to Hoxton Hall,[142] a theater less than ten minutes' walk away, attendance dropped off sharply. Staff attributed this outcome to the "invisible lines"[143] of gang rivalry and territorialism. Meanwhile, the strategic change sought by the Shoreditch Trust was the increased employability of the young participants. The short narrative about *Favela to the World* in the Shoreditch Trust's "Delivery Plan 2007/08" assumed a corporate voice. Opening with a vision statement ("Our vision for Shoreditch is a strong, safe, healthy and just community, led by local people to make it a better place for all who live and work here"),[144] the document described the project "applying the highly successful Brazilian *favellas* [sic] approach, and using their methods and leaders."[145] The outputs assigned to Immediate's project included a set numerical target of participants, with a specific focus on attracting young people who were not in education, employment, or training (NEET), and the project's participation in the "peer mentoring" scheme Youth Music Mentors, delivered by Sound Connections, which could garner credit for the nationally recognized Arts Award qualification for participating Peer Mentors.[146]

The complexity of these overlapping administrative structures, directed at the economic productivity of the young participants, endorsed Karen Taylor's assertion that, in Britain, what she called "arts and inclusive" projects were "heavily scrutinized because they are complex and there is an expectation that they will deliver on many levels/outcomes."[147] While the project's funders exercised tight control over the definition of its targets, the artists and young people were not able to exercise a similar control over the spaces for making their work. To take a small but symptomatic example, a session I attended at Hoxton Hall concluded with the caretaker entering at precisely 9:00 pm and beginning to switch off the lights while the group, finishing the post-workshop meal provided each week as part of the project, were still in the room.

In December 2007 Immediate Theatre's group, led by artists from Taru, staged *Festa das Ruas* (*Festival of the Streets*), a sharing of their work followed by food at Hoxton Hall. A young person who had stopped attending the workshops came along with his mother. The performance, given to an intimate audience of friends, family members, and representatives from agencies connected to the project, felt relaxed and welcoming. With drums made from found materials, artist Rudi Rocha encouraged the audience to experiment with a simple samba rhythm—"HELLO / HOW DO YOU DO / LET US PLAY THE SAMBA NOW!"—suggesting one rhythm for the bass drums made from large cardboard cylinders with layers of cling-film stretched across, and another for the snares made from biscuit tins and washers, in patterns of call and response. Rocha would pick individuals from the audience to improvise for a moment, single voices speaking through percussion amid the group rhythm. Then a young performer gave a complicated performance of body percussion, accompanied by the now more confident audience. At first it didn't work: the bass rhythm we were playing as audience members, slightly too fast, sat stubbornly out of joint with the beats he was producing. And then almost imperceptibly the rhythms found a harmony, and fell in time with one another. It was beautiful; in a meeting later, Rocha said it seemed "like magic, somehow."[148] But the prosaic reality is perhaps more exciting—moments like this one are the result of the work of listening and responding that is an integral part of musical performance: the outcome of practice.

Conclusion

The conditions of work in which the *Favela to the World* project was pursued amply demonstrate the extension and entrenchment of managerial discourses of value for money during the 1990s and 2000s in Britain, which constrained cultural practitioners' freedom to develop projects with and for young people—a turn reflected in youth work more generally since the 1990s.[149] Within the arts specifically, these discourses also interacted with the "double discourse" of "intrinsic" and "instrumental" value. As I noted in the introduction, a long-standing preoccupation with "quality" (often doubling for "intrinsic value") in the cultural sphere is the basis of community arts and education practice's comparatively low status in Britain—a preoccupation reflected, for example, in *Artificial Hells: Participatory Art and the Politics of Spectatorship* (2012), where Claire Bishop's remarks about the community arts movement ("by avoiding questions of artistic criteria, the community arts movement unwittingly perpetuated the impression that it was full of good intentions and compassion, but ultimately not talented enough to be of broader interest")[150] imply "excellence" to be contingent on talent, a naturally occurring phenomenon, the luck of the draw. Working effectively in situations of war, Grupo Cultural AfroReggae's structures and practices in this same period meanwhile resonated with British youth work and associated initiatives of the mid-twentieth century, in which "little was expected or demanded by the state"[151]—though a different set of representational limits and stereotypes relating to histories of racialized identity, internationalism, and development attended their work. George Yúdice characterized such limits acidly in terms of an "NGOized depiction of development, worth, and self-esteem."[152] For AfroReggae, the chosen escape route from the "double-bind of representation"[153] was the pursuit of commercial success. To function as the mobile subjects of global capitalism was to evade reification within imaginaries of deprivation, of visions of "*favelados* in rags, children with dirty noses and rotten teeth."[154]

AfroReggae's mission statement, with which this discussion began, aligned "social justice" and "citizenship" with "inclusion" and "sustainability." Miranda Joseph writes that this latter term is

> often associated with the notion that development should sustain the lives of the poor and the health of the environment. It is also used with regard to the management of NGOs, suggesting that they should be if not actually profitable, then at least not ongoingly dependent on philanthropy. However, I would suggest that it is the sustainability of capitalism that is really at stake.[155]

The doubling of meaning that Joseph excavates here was also present in "inclusion": a discourse resonating with democratic engagement but invested in facilitating globalization. In this context, and to tell a different story regarding Rio's favelas, AfroReggae argued that "the talent of young slum dwellers is a resource"[156] and sought "a quiet revolution, the revolution of the social capitalist movement."[157] A moment from AfroReggae's Barbican concert in 2008 illustrates the limits of "inclusion" in these terms. For this occasion, AfroReggae had created *Favelization* (2008), an entirely new show directed by Jose Júnior and designed by the internationally renowned artist and scenographer Gringo Cardia. The show featured extraordinary digital projections that showed international landmarks being gradually overwhelmed by creeping shantytown dwellings. Following performances of AfroReggae's own material, which was juxtaposed with harsh, stark line drawings and photographic images of slavery and poverty, the singers made swift costume changes to preppy slacks and jumpers, to give tongue-in-cheek renditions of disco and soul classics—Earth Wind and Fire's "Let's Groove" (1981), Marvin Gaye's "Sexual Healing" (1982)—on the Barbican Theatre's stage. The ironic appropriation of popular, globally recognizable songs was expertly pitched.

The show had opened with seventy participants from the schools and youth settings involved in the UK Partnership performing a samba routine before the safety curtain. It was to close with "sounds and images from young performers in East London, inspired by AfroReggae."[158] The Bigga Bloco—an AfroReggae UK Partnership project run by the participatory arts company Bigga Fish—were clad in branded orange T-shirts. They casually entered the stage from the wings playing a simple, unaccompanied samba rhythm. After two phrases of this rhythm and a moment's pause, Blackstreet's "Don't Leave Me" (1997) euphorically kicked in. A perfectly judged citation of a late-90s example of U.S. new jack swing, it brought a paradoxical sensation of "London" rushing into the gig and the cheering audience to their feet. The young performers scattered across the stage, beating their sticks together to produce a rhythm in time to the tune in an exhilarating moment of "cultural invasion" evoking AfroReggae's own. As they performed their fusion of samba reggae and funky house—Crazy Cousinz featuring Calista's "Bongo Jam" (2008) and Donaeo's "Devil in a Blue Dress" (2008) accompanied by the lyricist and producer himself—the projections behind this group were not the sophisticated digital designs produced by Gringo Cardia. An unsophisticated revolving series of slides of rehearsal images was accompanied by text showing the names of the various schools and theater companies. This design decision as the backdrop for the young people's performance instituted an unfortunate hierarchy, accentuating, given their more limited experience, the necessarily less accomplished appearance of their musicianship than that of AfroReggae and AfroLata (a younger AfroReggae group which had performed earlier playing instruments made entirely of recycled materials). Within the sphere of commercial spectacle, this moment and its visual aesthetic metaphorized the functioning of capitalist competition—the fundamental underpinning, as this chapter has argued, of the discourse of inclusion. The next and final chapter turns to the city of Liverpool to examine a documentary theater piece, similarly caught up in competitive dynamics, that likewise sought to amplify the voices of marginalized people.

Chapter 4

✦

"Privatised Politics"

Verbatim Theater in the Public Sphere

The previous chapter addressed the cultural politics of two terms in the neoliberal lexicon of governance: "inclusion" and "youth at risk." Through the example of a transnational youth arts project bringing practitioners from Britain and Brazil into dialogue, it examined how those terms have served to articulate people and their lives in relation to the economy, and the interaction of both terms with much older cultural discourses. The final chapter of *Restaging the Future* returns to the implication of culture in processes of place-based regeneration during the 2000s, now addressing questions of gender, sex, and public space in that moment of commercial development and expansion. Its focus is a theater project in the city of Liverpool—a place that in 2003 won the coveted title of European Capital of Culture 2008. Instituted as European City of Culture in 1985, and reconceived as a competitive award in 1991, the European Capital of Culture title has functioned for cities as a valuable opportunity for international place marketing and a lever for inward investment.[1] Staged two years before Liverpool's festival year as "Liverpool 08" officially began, *Unprotected* (2006, Liverpool Everyman Theatre) was a verbatim theater piece about street sex work in the city. As this discussion shows, "verbatim theater" is a term whose use and meaning shifted in Britain between the 1980s and the 2000s, but here is an initial definition of the practice: theater that uses recordings of the spoken word as source material. The play's name, *Unprotected*, carries various connotations in relation to sex and sex work ranging between contraception, legal rights, and social solidarity. It also referred to a short-lived political debate in Liverpool in the mid-2000s regarding the possible institution of a managed zone for street sex work, which in part responded to the brutal murders of women working in Liverpool's street sex trade. The discussion about the managed zone catalyzed the play's commissioning by the Liverpool Everyman. Supported by the Liverpool Culture Company, the play was also materially connected to the city's repositioning as a destination for culture and consumerism in the run-up to Liverpool 08.

In the 2000s, critics hesitantly credited verbatim theater works with reviving British theater's capacity for political engagement by reporting forms of injustice, exploitation, and inequality to audiences.[2] In parallel, and with similar hesitancy, academic theorists of verbatim theater noted that its "practitioners solicit the unsolicited, giving those voices a public place, and perhaps then rewriting the dominant narratives in the process (narratives of history, social justice, community)."[3] Furthermore, in their encounters with documentary theater, audiences could be "actively engaged in dialogue as citizens and putative participants in the public sphere."[4] In the context of public disillusionment with governmental "spin"—the satirical target of Armando Iannucci's political comedy *The Thick of It* (2005–12)—and a seemingly insatiable appetite for reality television and celebrity gossip, verbatim theater held out the promise of accessing more complex and unpalatable truths of contemporary experience. Despite reports of verbatim theater's subsequent decline, the genre continued to flourish in the 2010s, with more productions staged than at its supposed height in the mid-2000s—suggesting that verbatim theater did not so much diminish in popularity as become a less novel feature of the theatrical landscape.[5]

Prompted by the example of *Unprotected* and its context, I historicize "verbatim theater" in this moment of neoliberalization's trajectory. Following Stephen Bottoms's critique of the masculinism of David Hare's notion of verbatim theater practice—metaphorized by the playwright as an injection of virility, of "pumping red cells into the dramatic bloodstream"[6]—I argue that the preoccupation with the authenticity of captured speech-acts evident in British verbatim theater of the 2000s exemplified a "'patriarchal principle'"[7] in dialogue with what Rebecca Schneider calls "a cultural habituation to the imperialism inherent in archival logic."[8] For Schneider, claims regarding performance's intrinsic ephemerality buttress archival logic; instead, she proposes an analytical approach to performance that foregrounds repetition and iteration. Despite verbatim theater's prioritization of the "privileged, 'savable' original,"[9] projects in this mode inevitably engage the acts of repetition that Schneider theorizes, and not only in terms of their artistic realization. As a project, *Unprotected* itself encompassed contradictory dynamics of local campaigning, national and international competition, and institutional rearticulation.

The gender politics attaching to verbatim theater's investment in authenticity were reflected in processes determining urban development and the regulation of city life. The moment of *Unprotected*'s commissioning witnessed "the forging of new patriarchal arrangements in Western post-industrial societies."[10] In *The Aftermath of Feminism* (2009), Angela McRobbie influentially theorized the cultural developments of the 1990s and 2000s in terms of an incremental "undoing" or "disarticulation" of earlier feminist political demands regarding work, family, representation, sexuality, and inequality.[11] "Elements of feminism," she wrote, "have been taken into account, and have been absolutely incorporated into political and institutional life. Drawing on a vocabulary that includes words like 'empowerment' and 'choice,' these elements are then converted into a much more individualistic discourse."[12] Simultaneously, feminism's associations with earlier forms of organized resistance to patriarchal social relations were demonized as "hideous spectres" or "monstrous ugliness,"[13] and relegated decisively to the past. McRobbie thus argued that these ambivalent conditions produced the naturalization in the 1990s and 2000s of "a patriarchal order which is dissolved, decentralized, and nowhere to be seen."[14] Transformations specifically implicated in this chapter's example included the overhaul, refunctioning, and securitization of city centers to encourage consumer spending, the expansion of indoor adult entertainment venues in those locations serving a largely male clientele, and the displacement of street sex work, the issue at the play's center. Meanwhile, sex work regulation continued to sharply demonstrate the material existence of this now mystified patriarchal order and its double standards: as Julia Laite wrote in 2006 in relation to the constructs "common prostitute" and "public nuisance," "the same laws that existed in 1824 and 1839 still exist in a form only slightly modified today."[15]

In this cultural context, *Unprotected* grappled with the incidence of gender-based violence and stigmatization. But I argue that in this regard, its documentary methodology represented a contradiction. The monologue-based dramaturgical approach taken in this play—in common with numerous other verbatim theater productions of the time—was not the neutral method its makers proposed, but of a piece with the individualization implicated in the "aftermath of feminism" and in processes of neoliberalization more broadly. First, I discuss the elaboration of the verbatim theater genre in Britain. I identify how the label "verbatim" shifted from theater engaged in local oral history amplifying lives lived in non-metropolitan contexts from the 1960s on, to gain a different meaning and momentum in public discourse in the 2000s, to a large extent because of the work of London-based institutions and critics. For *Unprotected*, the use of verbatim theater to bring to light stories of oppression in Liverpool was influenced by this momentum. I consider verbatim theater's anti-theatrical investment in authenticity alongside the discursive construction of the street sex worker as, in the words of Lisa E. Sanchez, a "figure of eternal otherness who makes it possible to imagine the inner dimensions of community, politics and nation."[16] My aim is to historicize the uses of "verbatim theater" as a term, and to raise questions regarding the cultural effects and paradoxes of the practice as a campaigning theatrical mode in a context of commercial development, the insistent entrepreneurialization of cities and cultural institutions, and the wider obfuscation of historic and continuing inequalities.

The Emergence of "Verbatim Theater"

"Verbatim theater" is a kind of documentary performance based on recorded speech which, by 2005, national arts critics were calling a "growing canon."[17] Though practiced in the 1960s and 1970s, it had yet to be explicitly named at that time. The Victoria Theatre in Stoke-on-Trent (founded in 1962) and the Everyman Theatre in Liverpool (founded in 1964) incorporated spoken utterances into works that ranged between iconoclastic comedy, local history, and socialist intervention, and did not advertise themselves as "verbatim." As a *Daily Post* article reported, to create *The Mersey Funnel* (1967), a piece marking the building of the new Metropolitan Cathedral in Liverpool, the Everyman company conducted on-street interviews with around seventy people, whose tape-recorded words were "woven into the dialogue"[18] of a comedic historical treatment of the cathedral's fraught emergence. Running in and out of the theater during rehearsals to inspect the new cathedral only a hundred yards away, the piece's seventeen-year-old stage manager created the designs for an imitation cathedral to be built onstage during the performance. This "at the cost of less than a pound with tea chests and wooden oddments, takes only three minutes to erect—compared with the £4,000,000 original which took four years to complete."[19] Two days before its first performance, the cathedral celebrations committee had "not yet seen a script of the play."[20] According to Doreen Tanner, theater critic of the *Daily Post*, the resulting "uneven, episodic but rather endearing slice of living history" was an anarchic mess—"Ian Taylor has directed the piece; no one actually seems to have written it[21]—whose charm would probably be lost on those with only a passing acquaintance with Liverpool, with the show functioning as "a kind of in-joke—in, that is, for everyone in the city."[22]

Initiated in November 1973, *The Fight for Shelton Bar* (1974) was a musical documentary project with which the Victoria Theatre responded to the imminent loss of 2,000 jobs at the British Steel Corporation's Shelton works in Stoke-on-Trent, Staffordshire. The play was to be made "entirely from the words of the workers involved and, if they agree to participate, the BSC officials."[23] The Victoria Theatre's artistic director, Peter Cheeseman, regarded the theater as being in service to the economic and social particularities of its local community in the county of Staffordshire. In a 1968 interview with *The Stage*, he reflected: "There's a saying here, 'Clogs to clogs in three generations': a man could be a pot works owner one day, and bankrupt by the misfiring of one kiln the next. There's a curious absence of a culture-seeking middle class grouped together coherently in sufficient droves of white collars and little black dresses to make any real social impact."[24] In another interview, with the *Leicester Student University Newspaper* in 1966, he argued:

> Our job is to be the theatre artists of North Staffordshire. Any excellence we may attain, any accolades we may receive from the critical pundits, are neither here nor there. If, by the end of my life, we have got a significant place in the community, and are considered to be as useful in this community as the milkman, or the miner, or the grocer, then our lives will not have been lived in vain.[25]

Nearly fifty years on, the economic insecurity epitomized by "clogs-to-clogs" seems far less anachronistic than these notions of continuity, stability, indifference to public relations, and the uniform dress code of a theater-going middle class. And as I will show, the institutionalization of the term "verbatim theater" in the 2000s was in large part contingent on the work of contemporary "critical pundits" in the national press.

Derek Paget's 1987 article "'Verbatim Theatre': Oral History and Documentary Techniques" is generally acknowledged to be the first sustained analysis of the form and its "*use of vernacular speech*."[26] Paget sought to categorize the works made in the 1970s and 1980s that used new, easily portable cassette recorders to capture the voices of "'ordinary' people, done in the context of research into a particular region, subject area, issue, event, or combination of these things."[27] The Sheffield-based playwright Rony Robinson, whom Paget credited as "a pioneer of the method,"[28] reflected on his work: "You get a grim sense of people fighting against the dark to remember the past. And that seems to be one of the functions of what the actual play is doing, to deliver it back with a bit of *light* on it to the people who have experienced it . . . That seems like a very democratic and decent thing to do."[29] Social media and mobile telecommunications have since entirely changed how everyday life is documented, remembered, and publicly circulated. These early "verbatim" works and their social historiography speak to a different time. Paget's account described how practitioners like Robinson, Chris Honer, David Thacker, and Ron Rose made works in Chester, Sheffield, and Lancaster in the 1970s and 1980s on topics such as Cheshire's educational system (*Down at Our School*, 1978), life between the two world wars (*The Rose between Two Thorns*, 1980), and city dwelling (*One Day in Sheffield*, 1977). For these artists, Cheeseman's work was formative, and that of his forebears and influences, Joan Littlewood, Ewan MacColl, and Charles Parker.[30] Paget distinguished between such companies undertaking local histories, the results of which were then "fed back" in performance to local audiences, and work he characterized as "*present* national 'controversy'" plays—for example, the documentary piece *Falkland Sound/Voces de Malvinhas* (1983) produced by the Royal Court and directed by its artistic director, Max Stafford-Clark.[31] As Paget noted, *Falkland Sound* was also broadcast on television, offering it a platform for access by a much larger audience.[32] Taken together, these productions represented for Paget a scene of broader and longer-term struggle for cultural audibility, in which London had thus far inevitably won out over the more marginal "regions."

The democratic ambitions of the artists Paget interviewed sat in an uneasy relation with their class positioning and their knowledge of local vernacular. Rony Robinson's account of Cheeseman's approach to the production of *The Fight for Shelton Bar* (1974) signals this cultural distance: "What I found there was this, I would say 'puritanism' about it . . . the meticulous way in which the material had to be collected, had to be transcribed—and certainly at that stage they were using the methodology of linguistics to actually *annotate* the stuff, so that you can see how you speak it" (emphasis in original).[33] Similarly, "restraint" had to be taken on the part of actors in performance, to avoid the sense of "middle class actors taking the mickey out of working class people or whatever," with their role in gathering interviews endowing "the same sort of respect that comes with that puritanism for people's memories."[34] Despite such asymmetries of class and cultural capital, Paget insisted along with Cheeseman that verbatim theater could confer "that sense of pride and self-confidence that every district outside of London desperately needs—so you don't feel you're a nonentity."[35]

Cheeseman wished the Victoria Theatre to be organically responsive to its region and its histories: "a community theatre, particularly in a district where there is only one of them (as in most British towns)," he wrote, "has a responsibility to its rate and taxpayers to reflect the past *and* the present: to preserve what is best of the past, to re-enact our ancient rituals if you like, and to reflect, consider, and celebrate the present."[36] These civic commitments resonated with the political currents of the time. Jennie Lee, the first minister for the arts appointed by the Labour government in 1964, had negotiated a threefold increase in the Arts Council's funding from government and had instituted redistributive measures that favored the regions; between 1958, the year in which the first regional repertory theater, the Belgrade Theatre in Coventry, was built, and the early 1970s, as many as a hundred new theater buildings were created across the country.[37] Jen Harvie writes of this moment in cultural policymaking that these initiatives demonstrated "a prevailing national 'edifice complex.'"[38] In this context, "verbatim theater" practices represented a more flexible form of artistic response: as Robinson put it, they were "an area of the theatre that should be throwaway, that should have a journalistic touch" and which might enable the local histories they narrated to become "part of the air again . . . *talk* again."[39] Yet, as Paget noted, these productions could equally be seen to serve a pragmatic agenda in which "new, or newish, civic repertory theatres, partly working off fringe theatre methodology, sought to justify their claims to serve a region by demonstrating their willingness to go *outside* their immediate bricks-and-mortar environment and into the community."[40] Paget nonetheless concluded on the side of verbatim theater's oppositional potential: it "involves nothing less than the continued reclaiming and celebrating of that history which is perennially at 'the margins of the news' "[41]—and in particular histories and experiences outside of the capital city.

"Verbatim Theater" Revived

Andy Lavender launched the 2006 symposium "Verbatim Practices in Contemporary Theatre" by drawing attention to the importance of Paget's article as the earliest example of scholarship addressing the by now flourishing genre of verbatim theater. Reporting on the symposium for *Contemporary Theatre Review*, Chris Megson described Paget's article as "prescient,"[42] and positioned documentary theater practices in the 1990s and early 2000s in parallel to other forms of contemporaneous theatrical production in much the same way as Paget did in 1987:

> If the first performance of Sarah Kane's *Blasted*, at the Royal Court Theatre in January 1995, has taken its place in the glittering pantheon of premières that help constitute post-war theatre historiography, so might a very different kind of performance that took place over six months before. *Half the Picture*, compiled by the *Guardian* journalist Richard Norton-Taylor (with contributions from John McGrath) and directed by Nicolas Kent at the Tricycle Theatre, in June 1994, offered a meticulous re-enactment of the Scott Arms-to-Iraq Inquiry and drew heavily on spoken testimony reproduced from the inquiry itself. An alternative narrative of British theatre in the 1990s might be grounded in this moment: *Half the Picture* was the first of the so-called Tribunal plays to be staged at the Tricycle, and this model of testimonial theatre, with its roots in the European documentary tradition, has been adopted or adapted by a great many practitioners and companies in the ensuing period.[43]

In a 2008 article on the ubiquity of documentary performance, the playwright David Edgar similarly treated the terms "verbatim," "documentary," "witness," "fact-based," and "reportage" as synonymous prefixes for "theatre."[44] Paget's article had addressed a small group of artists and defined "verbatim" specifically as speech acts recorded on cassette out in the "field." Edgar and Megson's texts meanwhile suggested a historical continuum, playing down the genealogical complexity of practices—the kind of complexity that Megson's subsequent, more detailed examination of *Half the Picture* (1994) unfolded.[45]

And in fact by the mid-2000s, the director Nicolas Kent and writer Richard Norton-Taylor would themselves associate the tribunal plays, made from 1994 on, with the term "verbatim theater" quite routinely.[46] In 2007 Norton-Taylor wrote of the plays: "this is 'verbatim' theatre, an art form critics credit the Tricycle with pioneering."[47] But initially the plays were not called "verbatim theater" by their makers, nor did they attract that label in critical discourse. In the 1990s, Norton-Taylor's own journalistic writings on these projects made no mention of the term at all.[48] *The Times* characterized *Half the Picture* as "gripping courtroom drama,"[49] and the *Daily Telegraph* critic Charles Spencer's review used "verbatim" only in relation to the court transcripts themselves ("two hours of edited but verbatim highlights").[50] In an article previewing the subsequent tribunal plays *Srebrenica* (1996) and *Nuremberg* (1996), Mark Lawson described the works as "verbatim plays,"[51] but other critics did not pick up the term. Three years on, the next tribunal play, *The Colour of Justice* (1999), addressed the racially motivated murder of Stephen Lawrence via what *The Observer*'s theater critic Susannah Clapp called "a dramatised reconstruction of the inquiry."[52] The play received substantial national press attention, but with barely any reference to "verbatim" except again in relation to the court transcripts ("verbatim words from the actual inquiry," "verbatim extracts from last year's inquiry").[53] And *Half the Picture* was not the first of Nicolas Kent's theatrical experiments with courtroom proceedings. In a 1996 interview, he described his interests as a director in the 1970s:

> At the Traverse we used to do what we called Traverse Trials on Sunday evenings. We had subjects such as "Scottish Oil for Scotland," "Should We Abolish the Monarchy?" They weren't scripted but we had a prosecutor and a defence lawyer, and the audience was the jury. They were enormously popular. So when I went to Oxford and *The Romans in Britain* obscenity trial was on, I had the idea of putting together the transcripts each day and presenting them on the stage night by night. We had two reporters in court transcribing evidence, and someone edited it on the train up to Oxford.[54]

The solicitor representing conservative campaigner Mary Whitehouse, who had brought the action against *The Romans in Britain* (1980)—the last such example following the abolition of formal censorship of the theater in 1968[55]—went so far as to allege that the production placed Kent in contempt of court.[56] Though it fell well within the period it reviewed, Paget's survey did not mention this controversial early tribunal piece. If Kent had staged tribunal productions much earlier than 1994—works which had no apparent connection with the "verbatim" theater-makers Paget discussed and which had not been consistently described as verbatim theater—then why, in 2006, could *Half the Picture* be claimed as a founding text in the contemporary proliferation of verbatim theater?

I argue that these changing narratives were an effect of the canon formation emerging from the programming decisions of London theaters and companies, in concert with the responses of theater critics in the 2000s. In this respect, a formative addition to the "pantheon of premières"[57] would be *Waiting Room Germany* (*Wartesaal Deutschland*),[58] a piece by the German playwright Klaus Pohl, first staged by the Royal Court's international department as a single rehearsed reading in translation in the Theatre Upstairs, also in 1995.[59] It starred the playwright and actor Robin Soans, who narrates the story of the show's presentation in his contribution to *Verbatim Verbatim: Contemporary Documentary Theatre* (2008)[60]—a text which gathered together interviews with documentary theater practitioners Max Stafford-Clark, David Hare, Richard Norton-Taylor, Nicolas Kent, and Alecky Blythe, thereby contributing to that process of canon formation. *Waiting Room Germany* consisted of a series of monologues researched via interviews with people across Germany about their responses to and experiences of reunification, delivered to the audience in direct address. Following disruptions to the production process of *Harry and Me*, the next piece slated for the Theatre Downstairs, Soans recalls that the Royal Court offered *Waiting Room Germany* a full run. As a member of the acting company of *Waiting Room Germany*, he describes the experience of performing the work, in a production for which few had any expectations of success, as a moment of epiphany:

> A few lines into my first long monologue, I became aware that the audience was listening. And not just listening, but *really* listening . . . During my second monologue, the account of a man who'd endured a great deal in striving for the welfare of the town where he lived, I got to the point where he said, "Yesterday I submitted nomination papers, and I'm going to stand for Mayor," and the whole audience burst into applause. If there has ever been a defining moment in my induction as a verbatim actor and dramatist, that spontaneous reaction was it.[61]

For Soans, the piece and its subsequent box office success were extraordinary and radical, eliciting not the self-regarding connoisseurship in audiences that he had encountered as an actor on similar stages, but "an unsophisticated attention which was new to me."[62]

The experience inspired Soans to research and write similar works. As he describes in *Verbatim Verbatim*, the Royal Court commissioned him to produce a similar project during the theater building's period of closure and refurbishment: *Across the Divide* (1996, Duke of York's Theatre) staged the reflections of constituents in the London parliamentary constituency of Brent East about their political affiliations in the run-up to the 1997 general election. Max Stafford-Clark (by now the artistic director of Out of Joint) then invited Soans to write a piece to run alongside the revival of Andrea Dunbar's *Rita Sue and Bob Too* (1982), whose first production Stafford-Clark had directed at the Royal Court. For this purpose, Soans created *A State Affair* (2000)—a piece based on three weeks of interview research on Bradford's Buttershaw Estate, where Dunbar had lived and where her play was set. In the manner of *Waiting Room Germany*, he composed the piece largely of monologues from individual "characters." *A State Affair* staged their narratives of experiences of poverty, addiction, and violence in the context of a stage design featuring a concrete backdrop housing ten television monitors which displayed images of tuning failure "snow"—a gesture towards postindustrial disintegration as a material and psychological phenomenon.[63] The play opened at the Liverpool Everyman Theatre, and toured nationally with a run at London's recently relaunched Soho Theatre (co-producer with Out of Joint) midtour. Critics described it as "verbatim theatre" with assurance. While Lyn Gardner, for example, had characterized *Waiting Room Germany* as "staged verbatim interviews,"[64] she reviewed *A State Affair* decisively as "a piece of verbatim theatre created via interviews with people who live in Buttershaw today."[65] In his five-star review, Phil Daoust pronounced the piece "a magnificent endorsement of what Out of Joint describes as 'verbatim theatre,' "[66] commentary which more clearly references the company's active discursive framing of the work: Elaine Aston and Janelle Reinelt note that the program distributed with the play incorporated both performed playtexts and explanatory notes.[67] "The interrupted narratives maintain the suspense," Daoust continued, "and director Stafford-Clark has eliminated any trace of actorliness from his uniformly excellent cast. . . . By the end of it, you just might feel like crying."[68] *A State Affair* received a second national tour and a longer run at Soho Theatre at the end of 2001.

The German critic Thomas Irmer casts Soans's view on the "potent and relevant"[69] innovation of documentary direct address to audiences into relief: he reads Klaus Pohl's *Wartesaal Deutschland* not as radical theatrical ethnography but as "a series of well-made character monologues"[70] by a prominent figure in German theater, and as such, a safe choice for the numerous German repertory theaters that programmed the play in 1995. Irmer contrasts Pohl's work with documentary experimentation by German artists of the 1990s and 2000s who were "searching for forms that radically depart from these known formulas": among others, Hans-Werner

Kroesinger, Roland Brus, and Rimini Protokoll.[71] In Britain, however, as verbatim theater became increasingly popular in the early 2000s, the monologue became established as its normative mode of presentation. To this extent, speaking at the symposium "Verbatim Practices in Contemporary Theatre" in 2006, the actor Lloyd Hutchison, who performed in both David Hare's *The Permanent Way* (Out of Joint and National Theatre, 2003) and Robin Soans's *Talking to Terrorists* (Royal Court and Out of Joint, 2005), wryly described his yearning as a performer, following these experiences, "to look into another actor's eyes."[72] In his 2008 survey, David Edgar observed:

> The big subjects of this decade appear to lend themselves to traditional, mimetic representation. So why have so many post 9/11 plays presented their research interviews as reportage rather than dramatising them in scenes? Why is the first question for an audience at a contemporary political play not "how have they shown the horrors of terrorism and war?" but "will it be stools or chairs?"[73]

In *The Permanent Way*, directed by Max Stafford-Clark, and in Victoria Brittain and Gillian Slovo's *Guantánamo: "Honour Bound to Defend Freedom"* (2004, Tricycle) and the New York-based theater-makers Jessica Blank and Erik Jensen's *The Exonerated* (2005, Queen's Hall, Edinburgh), the monologue was the central dramaturgical unit—with onstage movement at its most limited in *The Exonerated*, where the actors remained seated in a row throughout, reading from scripts placed on lecterns before them.[74] In 2006, British arts critics heralded *The Exonerated* as "the latest example of verbatim theatre,"[75] despite the show having been initiated several years earlier, toured in the United States, and dramatized as a 2005 film starring several famous Hollywood actors.[76] In 2002, the *New York Times* had described the piece simply as "an intense and deeply affecting new documentary play."[77] Meanwhile, Edgar's distinction between "reportage" and "drama" reflected the widespread perception of verbatim theater as individuals relaying information to audiences in a more or less unmediated manner.

Reenacting the Real

Despite such claims to immediacy, in both preparation and performance these productions used a mix of visual, textual, and performative rhetorics that engaged realism, theatrical reflexivity, or sometimes a combination of the two. As Edgar points out, the Tricycle Theatre's tribunal plays were the most straightforwardly anti-theatrical in their staging of source material and their hyper-naturalistic representation of the courtroom environment.[78] Symptomatic of this was the extraordinary request made to the Tricycle by the International Criminal Tribunal for the former Yugoslavia in The Hague after the staging of *Srebrenica* (1996), which Nicolas Kent described in a 2004 interview:

> A year or so later, when the trial of Slobodan Milošević was about to begin, Kent received a phone call from the administrator of the court asking if he still had the desks used in the production. "Then he asked if he could send a United Nations lorry to pick them up," explains Kent. "It turned out that the trial was going to be bigger than the previous hearings and they didn't have enough desks. Although we hadn't actually used mahogany, we had reconstructed the furniture very carefully and we did still have them. So the lorry came and as far as I know the desks are still in Hague being used for the trial of Slobodan Milošević.[79]

Edgar celebrated David Hare's *The Permanent Way* (2005) as "the kind of in-depth, investigative, historically analytical job on a contemporary political story that conventional journalism rarely does anymore, occupying space abandoned both by long-form print journalism and by traditional television documentary."[80] Here Edgar obliquely referred to the investigative reporting of the 1970s and 1980s that he had engaged as a dramatist himself with *I Know What I Meant* (1974), a TV drama on the subject of Watergate edited from White House taped transcripts.[81] But in fact, *The Permanent Way* followed the research and development model that Max Stafford-Clark had deployed in his work with Robin Soans on *A State Affair*, which hybridized ethnographic practice and realist theatrical technique. *The Permanent Way* company member Bella Merlin described how the actors met and interviewed their various subjects during a short two-week period, and brought their research back to the rehearsal room not as audio recordings but as improvised reenactments.[82] When performed for the creative team, their utterances were transcribed by Hare and fashioned into a drama in what Merlin called "the 'verbatim' style.' "[83] Of the process, Merlin wrote: "our imaginations as actor-researchers served as a creative filter for that which we deemed sufficiently theatrical or dramatically provocative to pass on to Hare as the writer."[84] Conversely, Stafford-Clark characterized the play's " 'embarkation point' " as one of " 'surrender' " ("both actors and writer are going to surrender themselves to the words that they find [and] surrender themselves to the material in terms of the story").[85] Stafford-Clark thought of that research material as "raw": "really what a verbatim play does is flash your research nakedly. It's like cooking a meal but the meat is left raw, like a steak tartar. It's like you're flashing the research without turning it into a play."[86] The chosen metaphors in this passage problematically construct a dynamic of domination, exposure, and spectacularization.

In the finished playtext of *The Permanent Way*, not all the members of the creative team were seen to "surrender" to the material: the research was heavily implied to be the fieldwork of a single researcher, author David Hare, through the insistent repetition of his name by the characters ("Because, David, what I do now is manage contracts," "But then you work on from there, David," "It's very English, David").[87] The playtext didn't represent its characters talking to the actor-researchers, whose performances in rehearsal had mediated those dialogues, but to a single quasi-journalistic commentator. In performance, as in so many verbatim theater works, *The Permanent Way*'s characters talked directly to the audience. The play effectively assigned to the audience the role of interviewer, thereby consolidating and legitimizing, through its spectrality, Hare's role as author and his public identity as a theatrical "'moral watchdog'"[88]—or alternatively, as Stephen Bottoms puts it, as "some all-seeing, godlike figure, hovering invisibly somewhere in the auditorium."[89] As text, *The Permanent Way* disavowed the complex processes of theatrical engagement and reenactment that went towards it and crafted an alternative narrative for public reception—its critical points being the unmediated facticity of speech, the interchangeability of the theatrical and the journalistic, and the primacy and legitimacy of the (male) author as cultural critic or commentator.[90] Merlin's reference to an extraordinary piece of rehearsal room shorthand reflects the project's masculinism. In one scene, alongside two male colleagues she played one of three characters—an "Investment Banker," a "Senior Civil Servant," and a "High-Powered Treasury Thinker"—which in rehearsal "became known colloquially as 'The Three Wise Men.'"[91]

Rather than connoting oral history conducted in non-metropolitan contexts, "verbatim theater" thus came to function simply as a catch-all term for contemporary documentary theater using recorded speech, sometimes in juxtaposition with other archival materials. The practice attracted significant attention, and as the 2000s unfolded, the popularity of verbatim theater took off, reaching critical mass in 2005 with at least nine pieces being produced that year.[92] The majority were presented in London theaters, and two by the Royal Court alone: Alan Rickman and Katharine Viner's *My Name Is Rachel Corrie* (2005) and Robin Soans's *Talking to Terrorists* (2005), the latter's run at the Royal Court opening days before the London bombings of July 7. Meanwhile, other companies' adoption of the Tricycle's tribunal model readily attracted the verbatim label. To this extent, reflecting upon *Beyond Belief* (2004), a theatrical restaging of the Harold Shipman inquiry directed by Chris Honer (one of the practitioners Paget had interviewed) at the Library Theatre in Manchester, critic Alfred Hickling mused dryly that "it's increasingly the case that no official enquiry can be considered complete until it has been transcribed, condensed, and turned into a piece of verbatim theatre."[93] The actor-turned-writer Alecky Blythe's first "recorded delivery" play, *Come Out Eli* (Arcola Theatre, 2003), was an edited reenactment of responses from on-street witnesses to a fifteen-day siege in Hackney, east London, that Lyn Gardner felt moved "beyond normal verbatim theatre."[94] Blythe's works, based in performance on actors' precise imitations of recorded interview speech received via earpieces in real time, derived their method from the practices of the American actor and performance-maker Anna Deavere Smith.[95] (Smith's own work was otherwise not especially prominent in these discussions—she had not performed in Britain since 1993, with *Fires in the Mirror* at the Royal Court.) From 2006, other projects similarly began to distance themselves from what had become established as verbatim theater's conventions, and used alternative dramaturgical strategies. Among these were the National Theatre of Scotland's *Black Watch* (2006, Traverse Theatre, then tour), a hybrid of realism, symbolism, contemporary choreography, and military song addressing Scottish troops' deployment in Iraq; Look Left Look Right's *Caravan* (2008, Pleasance Courtyard; 2009, Royal Court and Roundhouse), a piece about the 2007 floods in Britain presented to small audiences in the immersive context of a caravan; and *Geoff Dead: Disco for Sale* (2008, Live Theatre, Newcastle), which approached the Deepcut army barracks scandal with the use of "dramatic reconstruction, chronologically mixed reports, and forays into expressionistic nightmare sequences."[96]

In the 2000s, theatrical productions either using or attracting the term "verbatim theater" thus demonstrated considerable aesthetic differences. But they shared a preoccupation with communicative authenticity based on what was understood to be the unmediated spoken word, with effects ranging between captive attention on the part of audience members, the production of verisimilitude, and "unself-conscious and incredibly free"[97] performances from actors. Authenticity was seen to reside in the recorded words communicating experience, to be corroborated or disrupted by the aesthetics or discursive framings of the works. And even the most representationally non-naturalistic or experimental works treated the discursive status of testimony as beyond representation. DV8's impressionistic and virtuosic dance theater documentary *To Be Straight with You* (National Theatre, 2007–9)—followed by the documentary works *Can We Talk About This?* (National Theatre, 2011–12) and *John* (National Theatre, 2014–15)—was framed by a clear statement regarding the work's basis in interviews and other documentary material. *Black Watch*'s realist passages presented the troops' experience of conflict in Iraq as beyond the comprehension of the fictionalized researching writer, whose inept efforts as an interviewer form one of the play's points of critique of the verbatim theater genre. In an early scene, soldier 'Stewarty' barks "Go tay fucking

Baghdad if you want tay ken what it's like,"[98] at the earnest 'Writer.' Program notes featuring Frantic Assembly's Stephen Hoggett, the associate director on *Black Watch*, reflected that conception of testimony and experience: "It's very tricky to honour somebody else's words and still make the show what you mean it to be."[99] Reviewing Robin Soans's *Life after Scandal* (2007), *The Independent*'s Kate Bassett contended: "Anthony Clark's direction doesn't always feel sufficiently naturalistic to inspire complete trust."[100] Lyn Gardner's review of Look Left Look Right's *Yesterday Was a Weird Day* (2005), a theatricalized series of witness accounts of the London bombings, likewise emphasized "trust" and "transparency": "simply staged, this is vivid and honest, made more transparent by the fact that the transcript of interviews is available in the foyer."[101] In this example, spectacularity and archival logic collide: the document, staged in the space of the everyday, is imagined as evidence of the real, not as a representational supplement to the work's truth claims.

Writing on nineteenth-century naturalism, Kirk Williams argues that its "abjuration of theatricality and the presentation of 'reality' on the stage was meant to herald and bring about more truthful communal interactions and a less 'theatrical' structure of social subjectivity."[102] The same is arguably the case with these British verbatim theater works, which were made in a context of mid-2000s consumerist excess and political spin. Indeed, as Kenneth Pickering and Jayne Thompson show, verbatim theater shares numerous methodological affinities with naturalism and its antecedents: plays by Büchner, Hennique, Brieux, and Hauptmann drew on documentary materials and trial transcripts, with the perceived authenticity of the latter reportedly producing a "thrill" for audiences.[103] Within verbatim theater, the basis for the "less 'theatrical' structure of social subjectivity"[104] was the presentation of the individual voice. Verbatim theater practitioners in the 1970s and 1980s were likewise interested in accessing "the authentic,"[105] but their approach was informed by class and linked notions of collectivity—whether in the selection of topic, the methodology, a desire to "bring working-class history to the stage,"[106] a focus on locality, or the negotiations and anxieties expressed regarding the class positioning of artists in relation to their interviewees. In 1990, Paget argued that the documentary "true story" mode represented "a completion in the present century of that valorization of the individual which began with the rise of the bourgeoisie as a class"[107]—a dynamic similarly manifest in these works. In the 2000s, verbatim theater practices tended to prioritize the individual utterance, or the representation of narratives produced through individuals' interactions with unforgiving, monolithic systems. In a 2008 critique, Paget therefore suggested verbatim and tribunal works to be "plays in the service of a distinctively new privatised politics": in this context, where "the collective now seems an absent presence," artists found recourse to "the figure of the *witness* as the last best hope of oppositional information."[108] A 2006 interview with Nina Raine, the director of *Unprotected*, bore out Paget's remarks: "I wonder whether what we're seeing with all these types of plays is a hunger for the kind of engaged, agit-prop theatre of the 1970s . . . Except that playwrights today are often much less willing to be on the nose about politics. Verbatim is a way of getting around that. It fills the void."[109]

The "Excluded Exclusion"

At what then seemed the apex of the trend for "the deeply fashionable form of verbatim theatre,"[110] the Liverpool Everyman Theatre staged Esther Wilson, John Fay, Tony Green, and Lizzie Nunnery's *Unprotected* (2006)—three years after Liverpool's unexpected victory in the competition for European Capital of Culture 2008.[111] Using techniques of documentary research, the project responded expeditiously to changing decisions regarding the regulation of street sex work in the city. In 2004, the Home Office Green Paper *Paying the Price: A Consultation Paper on Prostitution* (2004) had been published, as had Liverpool City Council's own *Consultation on a Managed Zone for Sex Trade Workers in Liverpool* (2004)—a study commissioned from Liverpool John Moores University regarding the possible introduction of a managed zone for street sex work in "an agreed non-residential area."[112] This text represented the zone as "a safer environment for street sex trade workers to operate in whilst removing the nuisance of prostitution from residential areas," while a "zero tolerance approach to prostitution" would apply in all other locations—echoing the moral and regulatory stance of the Home Office's *Paying the Price*.[113] The proposals in Liverpool had gained momentum following the deaths of Hanane Parry and Pauline Stephen, two women working in Liverpool's street sex trade who had been brutally murdered by the same client.[114] As a *Guardian* interview discusses, Dianne Parry, the mother of Hanane Parry and one of the central interviewees portrayed in *Unprotected*, had contributed to the campaign for the institution of a managed zone following the loss of her daughter.[115] In September 2005 a third street sex worker, Anne Marie Foy, was killed—a person who had herself participated in *Unprotected*'s research process as an interviewee. Published in January 2006, the Home Office's *A Coordinated Prostitution Strategy* (2006) ruled out the possibility of managed zones—a development which occurred during research for the full production of *Unprotected* at the Everyman and necessitated further interviews on the part of the writing team.[116]

In July 2006, Lyn Gardner previewed the Edinburgh Festival Fringe run of *Unprotected* at the Traverse Theatre, describing it as "theatre telling it straight from the horse's mouth."[117] She added that "the great thing about the play is that it presents all sides of the argument for and against protected zones and always shows the human face of the statistics about drug-taking, family breakdown, and violence that are always quoted when prostitution is mentioned."[118] Suzanne Bell, the literary manager of the Everyman and Playhouse theaters and the play's dramaturge, echoed Gardner's position in the playtext's preface. "Sex as a commodity," she wrote, "is not something people want to talk about; they want to hide behind statistics and close their ears to the human story. Verbatim theatre enabled us to go to the heart of the issue, giving a voice to those most involved with and affected by street sex work."[119] These reflections contrast statistics with the singularity of human experience, and emphasize communicative immediacy and humanity. Bell wrote that the shock of the news of Anne Marie Foy's death had "brought the situation into startling focus, spurring all on to give this issue a voice that spoke louder than government wrangling and political correctness."[120]

Verbatim theater was thus conceived as an effective communicative means of amplifying the lived realities of street sex work. The epistemology of verbatim theater is paradoxically anti-theatrical in essence, in seeking to use the tools of theatrical representation to provide access to the real or authentic. Like naturalism, its logic proposes that theatricality is exclusive to the domain of the theater—and for theater to be more like real life outside of the theater, certain modes of representation must be employed. Yet as all four chapters of this book have sought to argue, theatrical representation is not unique to the theater. It is fundamental to both modern social structures—to refer again to Elizabeth Burns, theatricality is implicated in "the social reality of the patterned world of institutions"[121]—and to social interaction in the public sphere. With echoes of Brecht, John Frow puts it like this:

> The public sphere is constituted in a process of alienation from self-identity (which of course we may in turn want to understand as similarly constituted); and that such a division of the self in the "moment of special imaginary reference" is a proper use of the suspension of belief and passion that allows the fictions of sociality to work. This suspension, let me emphasise, is as ordinary and trivial a thing as the willingness to hold two contradictory beliefs at the same time, or rather simultaneously to believe and not to believe; and yet it is this moment of paralogic that makes possible any complex co-existence with others.[122]

Sophie Nield argues similarly that the theatrical constitutes "a set of qualities, practices, and forms of spatialisation which may certainly be present in, but are by no means restricted to, the practices of the theatre."[123] Nield's reference to spatialization—a Lefebvrian concept that connotes the active production of space—is crucial to the circumstances that *Unprotected* addressed: the regulation of public space in relation to the street sex trade in the form of a managed zone. Nield applies this theory of the theatrical to citizenship, asking what refugee status reveals about representational processes at state borders, and therefore the constitution of border space as such. Requiring the presentation of passports and papers, state borders produce "a space in which identity can be doubled; in which it is possible, indeed necessary, to be present in more than one way; in which one must simultaneously be present and be represented."[124]

The dynamics Nield describes likewise apply to the aggressively policed and regulated field of sex work. In English law, selling sex is legal—or, more accurately than "selling sex," the client's temporary acquisition of "powers of command"[125] over the sex worker's actions in exchange for money. Julia O'Connell Davidson thus problematizes the popular terminology "selling her body": "It is not that the prostitute contract allows the client to buy the *person* of the prostitute, while the employment contract merely allows the employer to buy the worker's fully alienable labour power. Both contracts transfer powers of command from seller to buyer (the extent of those powers and the terms of the transfer being the subject of the contract), and so require the seller to temporarily surrender or suspend aspects of her will."[126] A "façade of voluntarism"[127] is established by this contractual exchange, but illegal activities such as soliciting and kerb crawling are also necessitated by the sex trade. Accordingly, as Phil Hubbard, Roger Matthews, and Jane Scoular wrote in 2008, "it has proved virtually impossible for women to sell sex without breaking a number of laws."[128] As numerous analyses attest, stigmatizing ideologies of sexual morality meet processes of criminalization so that sex workers, and in particular those who work on the street, constitute, in the words of Hilary Kinnell, "a class of women who are designated as the recipients of violence and abuse, and for whom the law offers no protection and little redress."[129] Kinnell's detailed sociological analysis in *Violence and Sex Work in Britain* (2008) specifically addressed female sex workers, but she added that "the available information indicates that the issues for male and trans sex workers are similar."[130] Since it is conducted in place, the sex trade does not involve the same kinds of border-crossing and authentications of identity as those discussed by Sophie Nield—though in the 2000s, human trafficking became a primary concern in the regulation and policing of sex work in the United Kingdom and Europe.[131] However, the relation between "presence" and "representation" strongly applies.

Lisa E. Sanchez draws out this point in her discussion of a Prostitution-Free Zone Ordinance enacted in Portland, Oregon, in 1995—a measure not dissimilar to the proposed Liverpool plans, to which she briefly refers.[132] She contrasts Portland's burgeoning private sex industry with the banishment of sex workers from the city's public spaces in the 1990s, and identifies the ordinance as having a twofold effect. First, it assigned a reified public identity of "prostitute" to women and men, thereby denying the legitimacy of their other nonprofessional identities and activities within the zone.[133] In Britain, a study of a street sex work controversy in Balsall Heath, Birmingham in the mid-1990s found a similar dynamic. A sex worker harassed by local residents seeking to eradicate street sex work from the area explained: "I will be walking up the road with my daughter and they will stop me. I say to them at night when I am on my own and I am dressed in mini-skirts then they have got a right to stop me but not at 3 o'clock in the afternoon, with my baby in the push chair with about six carrier bags. I mean am I really doing business in that state?"[134] The person of the sex worker is conflated with their job, and "presence" and "representation" accordingly collapse into one another. Furthermore, Sanchez writes that the Portland ordinance displaced on-street sexual transactions to less populous areas where the risk of arrest was more slight, but which exponentially increased the risk of violence to the sex worker. In effect, it produced "nomadic and anarchistic spaces outside [of the zero tolerance zone] where men can execute their own private sovereignty upon the bodies of prostitutes, through violence, rape, mutilation, and murder."[135] The horrifying exercise of such sovereignty was precisely what impelled Councillor Flo Clucas, the Liberal Democrat executive member for social care at Liverpool City Council, to support the plans for a managed zone in Liverpool as a possible technique for increasing the safety of street sex workers, and to consent to participate as a pseudonymously represented interviewee in *Unprotected*. In an interview with *The Guardian*, Clucas commented: "'My position is that I am a married, middle-class Catholic morally opposed to prostitution. But,' she says, 'I am even more strongly opposed to girls being raped, murdered and mutilated on my doorstep.'"[136]

Such vulnerability to violence and the debates about the regulation and policing of sex work hinge on questions of social belonging, citizenship, and power. Sanchez argues that the feminized figure of the sex worker in effect constitutes an "*excluded exclusion*"[137]—an insight she develops in a brilliant reading of Giorgio Agamben's influential text *Homo Sacer: Sovereign Power and Bare Life* (1998). Agamben theorizes *homo sacer* as a figure of "bare life," a person "who may be killed but not sacrificed," consigned to a "state of exception," to the "zone of indistinction between outside and inside, exclusion and inclusion" in the structures of the state.[138] In making her own argument about the discursive construction of the refugee, Nield likewise takes up Agamben, when he writes that the refugee "should be considered for what he [or she] is, that is, nothing less than a border concept that radically calls into question the principle of the nation state."[139] Nield's insertion of the feminine pronoun into Agamben's sentence here bears out Sanchez's argument regarding the gendered aspects of his thinking. In this regard, Sanchez contends that *homo sacer* is not in fact a figure of exclusion but of displacement. In the paradoxical, liminal position of being included-through-exclusion, *homo sacer* "retains within his body the possibility of return to the social, thereby maintaining a special entitlement to the male outlaw as errant, but not as alien or inhuman. He is a figure of displacement relative to the 'foreign' or 'other'—that is, to the figure of the racial, the hybrid, or the woman outside."[140] The same entitlements are not accorded to such "others," who are imagined as fundamentally exterior to the social; the feminized figure of the sex worker in effect constitutes one such "excluded exclusion that makes *homo sacer*'s displacement and return to the social possible."[141]

Sanchez illustrates this point with an incisive deconstruction of Agamben's account of the medieval French myth of Bisclavret. This parable of sovereign power and the distinction between "nature" and "culture" features a wife who, in league with a male companion, successfully attempts to stop her noble husband's periodic transformations into a rapacious werewolf. As part of the process of her violent husband's restoration to land, title, and humanity by the king, she is punished and expelled as a figure of "feminine betrayal and excess; she subverts the law of patriarchy."[142] Agamben's treatment of the wife's fate in the myth is peremptory ("The inevitable encounter with the ex-wife and the punishment of the woman follow"),[143] and his focus is devoted instead to the exercise of sovereign power over the male subject. Sanchez accordingly argues that "Agamben himself reenacts the very terms of displacement and exclusion I have been trying to expose . . . [his] abrupt dismissal of the woman in the text as not part of 'what is important' is symptomatic of precisely the kind of erasure we see repeated in the myths and legends of our history."[144]

Repetition and Erasure

Sanchez's description of Agamben's erasure of "the woman in the text"[145] in terms of reenactment echoes Rebecca Schneider's thinking regarding the recursive, iterative nature of cultural practices, and the gendered aspects of archival logic. Schneider proposes an alternative to constructions of performance in terms of "disappearance" and theorizes the embodied practices of repetition and reenactment as forms of historical knowledge. She writes: "According to the logic of the archive, performance is that which does not remain. Radically 'in time,' performance cannot reside in its material traces, and therefore it 'disappears.' "[146] If ritualized action and its material traces (such as embodied memory) are illegitimate as evidence of history, we are left instead with the archival trace: "the solidification of value in ontology as retroactively secured in document, object, record."[147] Seen in this light, endorsements of performance's ephemerality do not present resistance to but confirmation of archival logic. The archival trace is of course key to verbatim theater practice, in which the "unique" event of the speech act is captured as a recording and then utilized in performance. Schneider draws sustenance for her argument from Jacques Derrida's *Archive Fever* (1995), in which he contends that the exercise of permanent patriarchal "domiciliation"—as Schneider puts it, "the domiciliation of this flesh with its feminine capacity to reproduce"[148]—is constitutive of the ontology of the archive as an institution. (The "feminine capacity to reproduce" might be read here not only in terms of gestation, but also as a more general process of vital fleshly renewal conceived as feminized.) Derrida proposes that "the structure of the archive is *spectral*. It is spectral *a priori*: neither present nor absent 'in the flesh,' neither visible nor invisible, a trace always referring to another whose eyes can never be met."[149] Repetition is intrinsic to the functioning of the archive: as Schneider writes, the archive constitutes "an architecture housing ritual, rituals of 'domiciliation' or 'house arrest'—continually, as ritual, performed."[150] Domiciliation is thus a process engaging restriction of movement, discursive governance, cultural domination, and value extraction.[151] These are all concepts likewise implicated in the regulation of street sex work, and the measures taken to "purify" contemporary cities of street sex work represent ongoing processes of reenactment and repetition in which the figure of the sex worker, to return to Sanchez, is given to constitute "eternal otherness."[152]

In a 2005 article exploring Liverpool's proposed managed zone in *The Times*, interviewees holding radically different political views averred a connection between the proposals and the impending European Capital of Culture festivities in the city.[153] A residents' action group argued that the managed zone scheme represented a "'politically correct experiment'" in international public relations, while a sex worker suggested that, on the basis of her experience of working in Manchester during the Commonwealth Games in 2002, it was a scheme designed straightforwardly to "clean up the streets."[154] Elsewhere, Cari Mitchell of the English Collective of Prostitutes argued that "Liverpool should be addressing the core issues that drive women into prostitution, such as homelessness, domestic violence, debt, and poverty."[155] In contrast to the managed zone's supporters, she framed schemes like the zone as "dumping grounds for working women away from the eyes of the community"[156]—a metaphor that also resonates with Sanchez's reading of the sex worker's public identity under the conditions of zero tolerance as reified and unchangeable, or, to put it another way, as "real." Meanwhile, in a 2004 article addressing sex work in New York, Paris, London, and Liverpool, Phil Hubbard historicized and theorized the postindustrial displacement of sex work from inner city red-light districts to private sites and peripheral public locations. These were strategies implicated in "gentrification and the re-aestheticisation of the central city,"[157] and represented "the reinscription of a virile masculinity, the authority of which was seriously undermined in the economic crises of the 1970s and 1980s (with the disappearance of a once familiar division of labour organized around the labouring male body and a procreative female body)."[158] The "lively streetlife and high-quality public realm" recommended to Liverpool City Council by cultural consultants influenced by Richard Florida's "creative class" thesis in these terms appears both highly gendered and highly securitized.[159]

Liverpool's year as European Capital of Culture sought to redefine the city as a prosperous scene of contemporary culture, and in doing so, to attract capital investment. The festival's January 2008 launch event, The People's Opening of Liverpool, expressly drew attention to the still-unfolding changes to the city's built environment. Featuring digital animations, aerialists, local up-and-coming bands, and contributions from children and young people from across the city, with a finale from Ringo Starr, the launch was staged around and upon the neoclassical St. George's Hall and Liverpool Lime Street Station. In his somewhat noncommittal review, *Liverpool Daily Post*'s arts editor Phil Key noted that the celebration "was also a show that seemed to mirror Liverpool's current reputation as the City of Building Sites. There were huge cranes swinging around, a container, scaffolding, and many of the performers, including the compere, were attired in hard hats."[160] The shipping container in question, emblazoned with the label "PRECIOUS CARGO," formed a spectacular, trompe l'oeil mode of transportation by which artists and local dignitaries made their appearance onstage—with the shipping container a defiant if unsubtle signifier of globalization and Liverpool's post-imperial decline in particular.[161]

Alfred Hickling similarly described the concluding Transition ceremony, a light and film show staged on the waterfront against the unfinished Museum of Liverpool and the Three Graces, as a "building site ending."[162] Yet, he wrote,

> it is hard not to be taken aback by the transformation of the city as a result of the £4bn of investment that has poured in since it won the title in 2003. For the majority of the population, the most significant event of 2008 was neither a concert nor an exhibition, but the unveiling of the £1bn Liverpool One development, which catapulted the city from 15th to 5th in the UK retail league, and put it third in Conde Nast Traveller's list of desirable UK locations (behind London and Edinburgh).[163]

Enhanced private securitization accompanied these developments in consumerism: a public realm agreement had delegated the security and management of the forty-two acres occupied by the Liverpool One mall—formerly public streets with public rights of way—to the private developer Grosvenor.[164] Meanwhile, throughout the year, visiting national journalists talked up the city's luxury hotels, cocktail culture, fine dining, and shopping opportunities, as well as its art experiences. One critic enthused about "the stunning views of the sunset over Albert Dock. If it wasn't for the instantly recognisable Liver Building, a snapshot of this view could easily be mistaken for Barcelona or New York."[165] Alongside a defense of the Capital of Culture's local significance in terms of engagement with schools, its creative director Phil Redmond insisted: "I think we finally proved that culture brings in people, and people bring their cash. I predicted 10 million visitors and we actually got 15 million. We spent £125m and made an £800m impact on the economy."[166] As 2008 drew to a close, in the context of what was then being called a "credit crunch," healthy seasonal shopping statistics in Liverpool were greeted with relief as Christmas Eve front-page news.[167] On New Year's Day 2009, the leader of Liverpool City Council argued that "our year as European Capital of Culture will help protect us from the worst effects of the global credit crunch,"[168] and cited increased domestic tourism as a prospect.

In the years anticipating Liverpool 08, *Unprotected* played a small but not insignificant part in reshaping the identity of the Liverpool Everyman Theatre in the context of the transforming city. Founded in 1964, the theater was a place of popular, radical, and multidisciplinary performance that in recent years had struggled; after a period of financial instability during the 1990s, the Everyman and Playhouse theaters were relaunched together in the 2000s.[169] In 1999 the newly incorporated Liverpool Merseyside Theatre Trust had assumed the management of the two theaters, and the trust's board of directors, Arts Council England, and the Liverpool City Council formulated a policy that prioritized new writing, appointing Suzanne Bell to the newly created post of literary manager in 2001.[170] The theater returned to producing following the joint appointment of Gemma Bodinetz and Deborah Aydon in 2003 as artistic and executive directors, respectively; each of them had worked for high-profile theatrical institutions connected with new writing in Britain and Ireland.[171] Their appointment garnered substantial attention in the national press, and various articles celebrated the revival of regional theater's fortunes, particularly in the north of England, and pointed to the beneficial effects of the £25 million uplift awarded to regional theater following the recommendations of the Arts Council's Boyden Report in 2000.[172] Quoted in *The Guardian* in 2004, Gemma Bodinetz said that "Liverpool has been theatrically underachieving for so long that audiences have lost the habit. Our job is to win them back, and the Theatre Review has been the cash and confidence-boost which enables us to do it."[173] Not long after her appointment in 2003, in a *Liverpool Daily Post* piece previewing a reading at London's Soho Theatre of the work of three Liverpudlian writers developed as part of Bell's program, Bodinetz framed the theater's new function with an entrepreneurial language of excellence and renewal: "Our city is renowned for its strong voice. By the time Liverpool holds the Capital of

Culture title in 2008, we hope to have positioned the Everyman and Playhouse as one of the leading centres for new writing in the whole of Europe. I really believe we are on the threshold of a dynamic new era."[174] These words resonated with the Everyman and Playhouse's mission—"to create theatre of the highest quality which is firmly rooted in our community, yet both national and international in scope and ambition."[175]

Unprotected

With regard to *Unprotected*, the decision to produce a piece of verbatim theater came before the selection of the topic of the piece. At "Verbatim Practices in Contemporary Theatre," a 2006 symposium at Central School of Speech and Drama, Suzanne Bell discussed the choice to pursue verbatim theater in terms of "something that was happening a lot in theatre across the country, and Gemma and I wanted to celebrate the political and also social history of the Everyman."[176] The first phase of *Unprotected*'s development was entitled the Headlines project; members of a small team of writers were each asked to pitch an idea, with the brief "a local headline with a national resonance."[177] Esther Wilson had recently interviewed a sex worker in a witness protection program, with the prospect of developing their conversation into a piece of radio drama.[178] This theme, and the debate regarding the managed zone, was chosen for the prospective piece: Bell reflected that "it was something that touched on many of the issues we had talked about in terms of regeneration, of where the city was."[179] Esther Wilson argued that the verbatim method represented a means of focusing on the experiences of street sex workers "because so often those voices get sanitised or edited into non-existence."[180] Each writer was allocated a category of person to research: "residents, sex workers, police, politicians, punters, outreach workers."[181] Following a rehearsed reading of an in-progress draft, the play was developed further as a BBC radio commission and for the stage.[182] Esther Wilson was nominated as the lead writer. The full-length version of the play staged narratives from three key interviewees. "Diane" and "Pat," the mothers of Hanane Parry and Pauline Stephen, discussed their daughters' lives and the abusive events that led to their addictions to heroin, which both serviced through street sex work. A third central character, "Ali," discussed her own addiction to heroin, her work with clients, and her survival of a horrifying experience of violent abduction, rape, and attempted murder. These narratives were juxtaposed with reflections from other interviewees, with the play's scenes addressing a range of themes in turn. The play was presented at the Liverpool Everyman Theatre in March 2006, and at the Traverse Theatre as part of the Edinburgh Festival Fringe, where I saw the play, in August 2006.

The byline on the flyer advertising the Edinburgh run read: "*It could be anyone's daughter . . . it could be any city.*"[183] A knowledge of *Unprotected* reveals this to be a reference to its discussion of addiction as a catalyst for street sex work, but superficially it implied female subjectivity as fundamentally precarious and the local specificities of its story to be geographically transferable. Through the positioning of bland, generic office furniture, *Unprotected*'s stage was divided into four rough quadrants. A square office table and two chairs sat in each corner of the stage, each bearing various objects (an urn, a photograph on a tray, a polystyrene cup containing plastic spoons, a box of tissues); at the center was a plant, also surrounded by four plastic chairs, and before this, downstage center, was a round table also bearing a plant. At the back of the stage was a slightly raised, thin platform, immediately above which was a neutral backdrop, and before this, directly behind one of the four tables, a bench, such as you might find in a public park, divided into seats. The effect, viewed from the raked seating of the Traverse, was of gazing into a dreary public sector waiting room, with the anomalous bench barely registering at the beginning of the performance. The play's action opened here, at "The Drop In." "Ali" entered and engaged in a casual exchange with the outreach worker "Colin" about medical support and, more obliquely, the recent death of a fellow sex worker:

> ALI: (*inspecting candles, chocs, etc.*) Oh, is all this for—
> ANDY: Yeah. Wanna light a candle for her?
> ALI: Fuckin 'ell! Gis' a minute.[184]

This conversation—which dispatched any sense that the play would offer sentimental representations of camaraderie or idealism—established a theatrical "fourth wall" which it quickly proceeded to interrupt.

> ANDY: (*gesturing to audience*) Have you heard about the project that these're doing?
> ALI: (*in a mock St Helens accent*) No.
> ANDY: Are you taking the piss out of my accent?
> ALI: (*in the same voice*) No love.
> ANDY: Are yer interested?
> ALI: No.
> ANDY: (*laughing*) I didn't think ye would be.
> ALI: (*in her own voice now*) What is it love?
> ANDY: If I talk scouse will you talk to me?
> ALI: Yeh. Go 'head. Alright then.
> ANDY: They're doing a project about managed zones.
> ALI: Yeh? So what happens?

ANDY: Well they're gonna get actors and actresses to portray your words.

ALI: And what do we get, like?

ANDY: Goody bags, what they brought today.

ALI: (*inspecting the pile of stuff*) Three lippy bits and a bracelet? That's crap! (*Coming forward.*) My face isn't going to be on that is it? It's just using the voices, isn't it? Okay. That's cool. Alright. Cool. Cool. (*Speaking to audience*) I don't think that a managed zone's any good because alright, it's legal in Amsterdam, but people are on holiday there, they're home here, de ye know what I mean? Like if anyone got murdered, say if they wanna vehicle recognition—registration and all that—people getting letters through the door. Now I wouldn't want that if I was a family man, de ye know what I mean?[185]

"Ali's" agreement to participate and this first moment of interview material marked the transition from a mode of realism, which opened the play's two acts, to the familiar monologic mode of verbatim dramatization.[186] The words' veracity was corroborated by the realist representation of character onstage. "Ali," who appeared without makeup and with her hair roughly scraped into a ponytail, wore a thin jersey top, tracksuit bottoms, and a grubby pale blue coat with a fur-trimmed hood. Leanne Best, the actor who portrayed her—and the only actor in the company of six who did not double as another character—was from Liverpool herself, and had been selected in consultation with Wilson during casting for the play in London.[187] Performed in the Traverse—"Scotland's new writing theatre"[188]—the play's opening moments located its action and interests firmly in Liverpool.

As the "verbatim" sections began, the ceiling-to-floor backdrop at the rear of the stage became a surface for real-time video projection: of cars driving around a green, of people walking. The theater space made a transition from a room that was the object of a voyeuristic theatrical gaze—a voyeurism interrupted by the outreach worker's acknowledgment of the audience's presence and our interpellation as interviewers—to a porous site in which the action unfolding on the stage coincided with events taking place "elsewhere," with the outside coextensive with the conversations staged in the theatrical space. By contrast with "Diane" and "Pat," who were seated in imagined domestic spaces in the quadrants of the stage to which their characters had been assigned, "Ali" could roam about the stage unrestricted, a choice that suggested her (to use Victorian terminology concerning sex work) as a "public" woman.[189] The projections' presentation of visual information did not show consistent fidelity to the real-time conceit but strategically showed different locations, serving ambiguously to display exterior contexts and to orient and locate us as audience members. When the "punters" appeared in the first act, the projection shifted to the interior of a car moving down a road, with the street at night visible through the windscreen, placing the audience in the position of a "kerb-crawler." A view of Liverpool's grey governmental buildings from above introduced the politician's contribution; it gradually zoomed in more closely, both endowing the audience with a God's-eye perspective and representing the administrative process as solid, immovable, immense. Its representations emphasized chance incident, imaginatively dissolving the spatial boundaries of the theater building. In this visual context, and through the stories the characters told, the play gradually mapped out mother-daughter attachments, relationships of dependency and exploitation, justifications of violent misogyny, the catastrophic social and psychological consequences of racism, the role of fantasy and reenactment in constructing sexual desire, and the interplay between emotional need and addiction. The play invested heavily in the realistic representation of character and the uniqueness and authenticity of the verbatim text—the source of the "red cells"[190] so highly prized by David Hare. But despite the project's emphasis on communicative immediacy, the reflections on which the play was based and which it shared in performance both exposed ideological difference and delineated repetition as intrinsic to selfhood and sociality.

As the play reached its conclusion, "Diane" and "Pat" gave devastating accounts of the brutality of their daughters' murders. The play ended with an "epilogue." Police officer "Kevin" read from the text of two official statements about the deaths of the women and that of Anne Marie Foy, which segued into a playback of the recording of Anne Marie Foy's voice, taken in 2005.

> ANNE MARIE (VO): You're never safe. Ye know out there, ye—it's—it's—it is—like every every car you get into ye don't know whether ye gonna get out of it. It's it's dangerous all the time, ye don't realize how dangerous. And me of all people do realize 'cos I have been in situations where I've nearly died.
>
> (*A projection shows the dates of* ANNE MARIE'S *life.* ALI *comes forward.*)
>
> ALI: It could be anyone's daughter, I know but . . . people don't see it like that. You're just dirt to them. (*Pause.*) My dad said . . . he never mentioned it until he was dying . . . he said . . . 'Listen, I've never spoke to you about it but . . . you never changed in my eyes. That's all I needed to hear from him, do you know what I mean? It killed me, but I really needed to hear it from him.
>
> (*Lights fade.*)[191]

As the final gesture of a play that had engaged directly and indirectly with many of patriarchal society's violent consequences, and represented alternative modes of social support and solidarity, this shattering moment was acutely contradictory. But the emotional force of the production was strong: by the end of the performance, like many audience members around me, I was overwhelmed with tears.

In *Autobiography and Performance*, Deirdre Heddon proposed this critique:

> Hearing Foy's voice, having just learnt of her death, is shocking, particularly given her prophetic vision . . . This appeal to the real is precisely the powerful potential of auto/biographical performance; but this close proximity to the real also encourages a realist mode of representation (including the recordings, videos, and photographs) which risks masking mediation and construction. Though the real voice may be heard, or the real photo projected, the image may nevertheless be the playwright's (and surely the fact that these plays carry playwrights' signatures is clear evidence of this). Also, what agency does Anne Marie Foy have here? Is she used, even in death, for emotional effect and impact?[192]

The responses the play received from those close to the people it discussed during the run at the Liverpool Everyman Theatre compellingly demonstrated another set of standpoints and questions with and beyond those of criticism and authorship. At the "Verbatim Practices in Contemporary Theatre" symposium, Leanne Best reflected on performing the work and the strength of reaction it elicited. One performance was attended by Anne Marie Foy's daughters. Following her recounting, as "Ali," of an account of the memorial laid out for Anne Marie Foy where her body had been found, Best heard cries of anguish and grief rise up in the auditorium: "there was this weeping, and I went offstage. It was the only time in my working life I've ever thought, 'I can't go back on.' And this isn't me as an actor; this is me as a human being, having to go on stage. And I don't want to cry because that devalues what we are doing."[193] In view of the pain that family members expressed in this and other moments, and at the performance's conclusion in response to the recording, the producers asked whether they felt the play should be changed or indeed canceled altogether; their response, as Nina Raine reported at "Verbatim Practices in Contemporary Theatre," was "Do not take these voices out; do not take this material out."[194] Best described how Anne Marie Foy's daughters sought her out in the bar after the performance and thanked her: "I wanted people to hear what happened to my mother because nobody is listening to me."[195] Interviewed in *The Guardian*, Dianne Parry said that through the play's public presentation, she felt that her own daughter Hanane Parry "got her name back."[196]

Conclusion

Unprotected's verbatim theater approach encompassed numerous contradictions in its treatment of gendered inequality and violence. Part of verbatim theater's national revival, the play sought to enable "the real people involved to speak for themselves"[197] on the issue of the implementation of a managed zone for street sex work in Liverpool. However, the play and the theater that produced it were also contradictorily caught up in schemes of regeneration and capital development that were actively hostile to street sex work in cities. The Liverpool Everyman Theatre had a forty-year history of popular, multidisciplinary, and politically engaged performance but, as artistic director Gemma Bodinetz put it, people had "lost the habit" of attending.[198] In the run-up to Liverpool 08, the production of *Unprotected* played a part in attracting new audiences and developing the theater's new writing agenda. The play was also critically celebrated. It won the Amnesty International UK Award for Freedom of Expression 2006, and Nina Raine was named Best Director at the 2006 Theatrical Management Association Awards. Liverpool Culture Company funded *Unprotected* to tour to the Traverse Theatre, the first play ever to be staged by the Everyman at the Edinburgh Festival Fringe. Robyn Archer, then director of Liverpool Culture Company, reported the tour as evidence of the Capital of Culture's success, and speculated that "more and more productions will be exported out of the city as the success grows."[199] In a *Liverpool Daily Post* article, headlined "Liverpool Artists Stage an Invasion of Edinburgh," executive director Deborah Aydon framed the festival as "a shop window"[200] for the Everyman to access fellow artists and international audiences. Until the late 2000s, a quotation from Susannah Clapp's review of the play in *The Observer* appeared on the Everyman's website:

> The Everyman in Liverpool is living up to its name. Thanks to a new play, it is doing what theatres all over the country dream of: pulling in scores of first-time theatre goers alongside loyal subscribers . . . blazes with energetic intelligence . . . this will change people's hearts and minds in unexpected ways.[201]

This endorsement reflected a wider context in which accessing new audiences was an institutional priority, and warmly demonstrated the Everyman's success in fulfilling it.

In this discussion, I have sought to trace the synergies between verbatim theater's purportedly neutral monologic conventions, the entrenchment of individualism, and the insidiousness in the 2000s of "a patriarchal order which is dissolved, decentralized, and nowhere to be seen."[202] I have asked what this combination of elements might have meant for a production with gendered inequality as its focus. Given its basis in repetition and reenactment, there were many aspects of verbatim theater in these years that interrupted or contradicted emphasis on the "red cells"[203] of authenticity, despite its insistent reiteration by theater-makers and critics. As Rebecca Schneider has argued, "performances-as-remains are suited to psychoanalytic analyses of traumatic repetition, to Althusserian analyses of the ritual tracks of ideology, and to Austinian analyses of enunciation, or citationality: repetitive *act*."[204] And in any case, the dominant mode of verbatim theater in Britain—of people talking directly to the audience about lived experience—sat in an uneasy relationship to the individualizing ideological conditions of the 2000s. Verbatim theater was a form that sought to activate public and political engagement at a moment when "the collective now seem[ed] an absent presence,"[205] and when a focus on the authenticity of the individual voice, as Nina Raine put it, "fill[ed] the void"[206] left by a reluctance to attend to questions of politics. In these terms, *Unprotected*'s staging choices echoed that of other verbatim theater productions staged elsewhere. Given the subjection of sex workers to the cruelty of performative, realist representation in spaces beyond the theater, I see the terms of the play's engagement with verbatim theater and the visual representations it employed as impossible—if not actively counterproductive—as an ideological challenge to the laws and social norms that construct the sex worker (to return to Lisa Sanchez's words) as a figure of "eternal otherness who makes it possible to imagine the inner dimensions of community, politics, and nation."[207]

However, readings of verbatim theater's aesthetics and methods alone are not adequate to understanding the range of its paradoxical effects on audiences or their potential meanings in people's lives, perhaps especially those close to the people represented onstage. In *Unprotected*, these effects were predicated precisely on its realist methodology and its sharing of stories of lived experience. The production's audiences also included sex workers and support workers invited by the Liverpool Everyman Theatre as guests. For Leanne Best, the run saw "a lot of evenings where it wasn't like a performance: it was like an event."[208] Of those evenings, which involved audiences talking back to the actors, shouting in recognition, and so on, Esther Wilson reflected on their social dynamics as public occasions: "there was this human interaction of . . . It's not a celebration, it wasn't a celebration. . . . It was an affirmation of their existence."[209] These audience interactions revealed the "authenticity" of words communicated "straight from the horse's mouth"[210] to be acutely theatrical—because of course any "conversation" staged via the verbatim monologue did not really invite a response. At the same time, verbatim theater made those interactions possible. As Duška Radosavljević suggests in her reflection on a powerful performance of *Deep Cut* (2008, Sherman

Cymru)—whose story of the death of soldier Cheryl James ended with her bereaved parents taking to the stage and her father's delivery of the final speech ("It stops when it's over. / It stops when it's over . . . / When it's over . . .")—here "theatre asserts itself as being no longer a place of inconsequential entertainment, but a place where we are brought together around a shared concern and brought together in our experience of just being human."[211] I interpret "our experience of just being human" in this case as connoting both compassion for the James' struggle for justice, and awareness of vulnerability to harm—a vulnerability that, as this chapter has discussed, is systematically and unequally distributed. These moments in the theater recall Peter Cheeseman's ambition for the Victoria Theatre in Stoke discussed at the outset of this chapter: to make of the theater not a machine for producing value which is yet to come, but a place and environment in which to consider the present.[212]

CONCLUSION

What does it mean for the future to be restaged?

Restaging the Future has explored how professional and nonprofessional artists, participants, policy-makers, commentators, and artistic practices were implicated in the marketization of social life in the 2000s. This was a process of social transformation that was both material and ideational, involving institutional change, the development of policy frameworks, and forms of artistic and cultural re-imagining and re-articulation both on- and offstage. The governmental task assigned to the arts was to assist in solving social and economic problems of the past and present. This task was mandated explicitly in the form of aims and targets, or implicitly, with reference to wider priorities and cultural emphases. This directive, managerial process was quite different from the one imagined by Tony Coult in his argument about theater in education, which I discussed at the beginning of this book. For Coult, the practice of theater would instantiate another kind of social agency. Theater would endow young audiences with historical knowledge, and exposure to its techniques of representation and storytelling would cultivate their critical and political intelligence: accordingly, they would become able to assume some control over their destinies and contribute to the realization of a better world. Taking a historical view of that article, and thinking about the broader shifts of culture, society, and economy that subsequently took place, it is striking that the primary school-age children that Coult was talking about in 1980 would have fallen within the bracket of Generation X—the label popularized by Douglas Coupland's 1991 novel, and which quickly became 1990s shorthand for disaffected cynicism, detachment, and hedonism. In 1990s Britain, its pop culture-defining members included figures like Oasis front man Liam Gallagher, the "ladette" DJs Sara Cox and Zoe Ball, and the Spice Girls. Of the same generation in the political sphere was Ed Miliband, who would become Labour leader in 2010, but who in the 1990s was building his political career behind the scenes as a speechwriter for MP Harriet Harman.[1]

During the 1990s and 2000s, "dynamism" and "innovation" were rhetorical watchwords inside and outside of the arts. At the same time, reflected in the cynicism characterized by Generation X and the popular culture associated with it was a kind of defeatism that Mark Fisher called "capitalist realism": "the idea that, whether we like it or not, the world is governed by neoliberal ideas, and that won't change."[2] For Fisher, in its surrender to and entrenchment of the pro-market philosophy and policy initiated under Margaret Thatcher, New Labour exemplified capitalist realism. "Labour's painful journey from unelectability in the 1980s to government in the 1990s," he wrote in 2013, "ended up consummately proving Thatcher's point that there is no alternative. When Thatcher first made that remark, she was saying that there is no viable alternative to neoliberal capitalism. By 1997, there was no imaginable alternative."[3] The example Fisher takes is the bureaucratic overhaul of the education sector in the image of the private sector—an overhaul which was described to teachers such as Fisher by the managers implementing changes, reluctantly or otherwise, as simply "how things were to be done now."[4] Such processes had numerous counterparts in the arts sector. And as I've discussed, processes of performance measurement and management attached to funding were extensively applied in participatory, educational, or community-based contexts which could not be dynamized by the search for profit on a commercial model of performance as commodity. The future that was imagined in the 2000s was constrained by the market-based protocols set in place by neoliberalism, which appeared to have emerged victorious.

These changes didn't take place overnight. Culture is the complex site of many overlapping historical and ideological formations, and the actions taken under neoliberalization's "rollout," its "institution-building moment,"[5] necessarily had to engage with the structures that preceded them. My argument in *Restaging the Future* has been premised on the predominance of neoliberal ideology and practice at the level of government, which set priorities for the arts sector organized around a series of key discourses—entrepreneurialism, inclusion, exclusion, and regeneration—all of them underscored in different ways by an ethic of competitive individualism. One of my aims has been to trace how these discourses were taken up rhetorically and in performance by the projects I discussed in the wider context of competitive individualism and its other manifestations: consumerism, celebrity culture, reality television. My aim has been to demonstrate the contingent performative pressure of a powerful discourse such as "inclusion" and how other discourses, practices, and histories engaged in a particular project existed in alignment with it, at a distance from it, in active antagonism to it. Each example I have discussed was a crucible of such forces. These dynamics meant that neoliberalization's processes as they unfolded in and through these projects, though dominant, were not totalizing. And then there is the issue of purpose. Jeremy Gilbert has written that discussions he and colleagues had with British government ministers in the early 2000s revealed that, despite accommodating to the legacy of Thatcherism, those ministers understood themselves to be pursuing a social democratic agenda, without recognizing that "in the process they were normalising an individualist ideology which could only ever undermine their own best intentions."[6]

Two years after I started my research on this project, the financial crisis that began to make itself felt in 2007 took many people entirely by surprise—though not economists such as Ann Pettifor, whose incisive book *The Coming First World Debt Crisis* (2006) had been published the year before. The crisis appeared to initiate a radical break from the norms of neoliberal political culture. But as the months and years went by, it became clear that, as Jamie Peck wrote in 2013, "a new normal was taking shape, as the costs of restructuring and insecurity were visited (once again) on the poor and the vulnerable, as austerity programming, entitlement cutbacks, and radical reforms of the public sector were once again raised to the status of non-negotiable imperatives."[7] In the arts sector, London Bubble, the theater company I worked for in the early 2000s, was one of 194 organizations to bear the brunt of the first wave of cuts in 2008: it lost the entirety of its annual Arts Council England grant, and shortly afterwards, its London Councils grant—a serious crisis that the company was able to weather in that period, but not without layoffs. Several of the venues and institutions involved in the projects I have discussed in this book have also since closed or have had their public funding withdrawn. Creative Partnerships, the national scheme that facilitated *The Margate Exodus*, was scrapped in 2010 as a consequence of cuts imposed by the Coalition government's first Comprehensive Spending Review.[8] The Sandfield Centre in Nottingham, where La Ribot's *40 espontáneos* was presented in 2006, was closed in 2011; Nottingham City Council granted planning permission to Persimmon Homes to develop the site as private dwellings in 2017.[9] In 2015 Rich Mix, the host of the AfroReggae UK Partnership events in 2007, was threatened with closure owing to a legal and financial dispute with its local authority funder, the London Borough of Tower Hamlets—a dispute that fortunately was resolved, enabling Rich Mix to continue to operate.[10] In Arts Council England's 2017 funding round, cuts to regional dance agencies were announced: Greenwich Dance Agency—which had also been closely involved with the production and presentation of *40 espontáneos*—would lose its National Portfolio Organisation status and 100 percent of its Arts Council England funding from April 2018, along with Merseyside Dance Initiative and Dance Manchester.[11]

This handful of examples goes to underline the finding reported in "Arts Council England: Sector Dialogue on Funding 2018 and Beyond" (2016), a consultation with cultural organizations across the country: "challenges to funding for the arts and culture sector more broadly are seen to be creating fundamental instability."[12] Arts Council England support was cut by 36 percent between 2010 and 2015, and local authorities continued to radically reduce their non-statutory arts support thereafter.[13] As reported in 2019, £400 million of local authority arts spending had been cut across the country since 2011, and 37 percent of local authorities had abolished the post of arts officer altogether.[14] In the words of one commentator, the 2010s under Coalition and Conservative governments saw, in place of cultural policy, "a governmental war of attrition on public services"[15]—a substantial change from New Labour's approach to culture, but one wholly in line with neoliberalism's ideological orientation towards the market.

Legacies

Part of this book's critical agenda has been to reject linear narratives of cause and effect in the domain of arts and culture, and instead pay attention to dynamics of influence, repetition, and recursion, noticing how new formations interact with older ones—which is not to deny the obvious force of political decision-making, or the brutal effects of retrenchment imposed under the conditions of austerity and its intensification of marketization. With these thoughts in mind, in July 2017 I visited Margate for the first time since the screening of Penny Woolcock's *Exodus* that I had attended at the Dreamland Cinema ten years previously. I was curious to see how the town had changed, and what the Turner Contemporary gallery and the relaunched Dreamland amusement park would be like.

The weather that afternoon was glorious—perfect for a trip to the seaside. On this occasion, the image displayed behind glass in Margate's train station lobby was a photograph of the clean lines of the town's new-ish art gallery, set against a clear blue sky. The floor-to-ceiling poster read:

> Welcome to Margate
> Home of Turner Contemporary

Approaching the seafront, on Royal Crescent Promenade, I came across a piece of public art I hadn't seen before on any of my visits: *Standing Stones*, a trio of short menhirs, arranged in a circle. As I approached them, the words on one of the stones came into focus. Inscribed in a medieval script reminiscent of the gravestones in Victorian churches, with a cartoonish impression of sandwiches etched in one corner, it read:

> My cheese & pickle sandwiches made by mum are heavy in my lap

The plaque adjacent explained the piece:

> The words on the stones ahead of you arose out of a public art project carried out in 1997.
>
> Writer Suzannah Dunn worked with local children at Artwise Youth Club in Ramsgate and other venues to explore ideas and

> thoughts about Margate, people, and feelings in words, stories, and poetry.
>
> From all the words written down and spoken by the children Suzannah has drawn together a poem, which has been carved into stone by sculptor Paul Wehrle.

All six surfaces of the menhirs bore similarly sweet, somewhat nostalgic texts—about the sound of the sea, the sun's glare, the flavor of chips, candyfloss, ice cream. One was slightly spikier—"Insects are divebombing me, and I am spooked by the crisp, sharp sound of leaves creeping over the ground." I thought of the Second World War and the sources of "Englishness." The stones were set in a pebble-dashed circle of concrete, with a semicircular metal bench adjacent for visitors, against the backdrop of the busy road and its traffic, some shrubs, and a sign to Arlington car park. The stones' diminutive size suggested them as shrunken aestheticized counterparts of other stones that have been standing in far-flung rural places since the Neolithic age. It seemed to me to be an utterly strange, time-traveling work.

The accommodation where I had booked a room was located in Cliftonville, a few minutes' walk up the coastal road from the Old Town. Cliftonville West, the electoral ward in which the accommodation was located, continues to be one of the most deprived in the country. The Old Town had many more cafés and restaurants than I remembered. Between the Old Town and Cliftonville, a sparse smattering of newly opened independent shops selling things like artisanal coffee and mid-century teak furniture strongly indicated speculation and creeping gentrification, and stood in stark contrast to signs of the area's deprivation and decline: the defunct Lido and seawater baths, uncollected waste, and run-down Victorian dwellings. Even so, these buildings still possessed a sense of grandeur. In the late nineteenth century, Cliftonville had been the scene of "Margate's best hotel" and "a higher quality of holiday and living experience" owing to its distance from the station and thus the incursions of day trippers.[16] In a 2018 piece, Iain Aitch—whose articles on Margate and *The Margate Exodus* I consulted in chapter 2—described Cliftonville West as the seat of the town's new reputation as "Shoreditch on Sea," given its "affordable six-bedroom former B&Bs, plentiful studio space, and urban grit."[17]

Inside, the person checking me in asked about the reason for my trip. I said a few words about *The Margate Exodus* and Dreamland, and how I'd not yet managed to visit the revamped amusement park. By the mid-2010s, in no small part due to the success of Dreamland and Turner Contemporary, Margate had acquired cachet as "the new hipster's paradise."[18] As one 2014 *Vice* feature had it, "it's like London before everything started to look like Angel."[19] Our conversation encompassed the amusement park's renovation process, and the transformation that programming live music and festival events at the Dreamland park had brought about for the hospitality trade, causing a spike in business, with audiences traveling from all around to attend. He referred to Margate's historically low rents for private accommodation, and how that was now changing, which, he averred, was probably a good thing on balance, because £200 a month for a two-bedroom flat was really "not enough."

Having checked in, I walked back down the coastal road toward Turner Contemporary. Directly outside the Winter Gardens—a large venue for dancing and performances established in Cliftonville in 1911 with municipal support[20]—was a beautiful period bus stop with a rounded cast-iron metal roof. Inside, the walls enclosing the staircase leading to the venue from the high coastal road were emblazoned with black-and-white stencils of modern and contemporary popular performers. All of them had entertained audiences in the Winter Gardens' sizable theater at various points in the twentieth century: Morecambe and Wise, Ronnie Corbett, Arthur Askey, Laurel and Hardy, Lulu, Danny La Rue, Tommy Cooper, Paul Merton. Back on the road, the sun shone on a banner advertising a forthcoming attraction—Elaine Paige in Concert. The image of the singer herself featured an exuberant twirling moustache that someone had drawn on.

Turner Contemporary is located directly adjacent to the beach, slightly up the slope of the coastal road. As I entered it from the heat of the day, the art gallery's cool air was calming. Installed on the ground floor of the gallery was a new commission, Kashif Nadim Chaudry's *The Three Graces*—a huge, stunningly intricate, and vibrant set of textile sculptures incorporating bones, beads, multicolored printed silk, and lace in earthy, metallic, and crimson hues. The work had been created in collaboration with Turner Contemporary's The Studio Group, consisting of nineteen local artists. "Chaudry's Three Graces," the rubric read,

> are intentionally full of contradictions. He describes them as "queer assemblages," "Graces gone wrong," and "redundant deities." Their skull heads suggest something crumbling or decaying beneath the decorative surface, reflecting the fragility of the belief systems we construct our world upon.

The sculptures were both delicate and outrageous—speaking of death, ceremony, and life. From one of the Graces, hanging high against the gallery's white wall, tumbled a series of globular structures of varying sizes, enclosed in ornately embroidered fabrics which, the rubric confirmed, signified "multiple breasts, testicles, or gourds"—some distended, others more demure.

Upstairs, the main exhibition, entitled *Every Day Is a New Day*, juxtaposed sculptures by Phyllida Barlow—whose exhibition *Folly* was then occupying the British Pavilion at the 2017 Venice Biennale—with works by the painter Michael Armitage, watercolors by J. M. W. Turner, and a selection of pieces by local young people. Barlow's imposing sculptures, Armitage's uncompromising address in painting to violence, sexuality, and inequality in East Africa, Turner's landscapes, and the works by young people still in school were thus placed in direct conversation—an intervention that would have been highly unusual to see twenty years previously. On the same floor as this exhibition was another space featuring a project entitled Art Inspiring Change—"a child-led learning initiative to inspire the whole town to engage with art, transforming Margate through physical and social change." Funded by the Paul Hamlyn Foundation, Art Inspiring Change—"Turner Contemporary's most ambitious project to date"—had Young Arts Leaders of six and seven years of age at its center. Its eighteen months of activity were outlined by a vertical banner featuring a timeline of actions, including the establishment of City and Guilds qualifications for adults, meetings with Thanet District Council regarding requests for land for regeneration through art, and the presentation of "social return on investment" research at the Houses of Parliament.

The exhibition *Every Day Is a New Day* was located down the corridor. The display of artworks by the young people was connected to a schools' competition called Portfolio, which had then been running for a decade, alongside the MASK Prize, "open to young people living in Africa and of African origin." The young people's works were displayed on white plinths and on the gallery's walls with a kind of curatorial rhetoric similar to those used for the artists of international renown staged elsewhere in the exhibition. The artworks were impressive. One of the pieces I found most affecting was entitled *A Bag for Life*, created by Sarra Bird of Otford Primary School. Sitting atop a sizeable square plinth, the piece was presented at about waist height. A realistic-looking stuffed turtle was resting upon a watercolor in a black frame that lay flat on the plinth. The watercolor consisted of a series of blue, grey, green, and pink curving stripes. It offered the impression of plants growing in the bed of a shallow river or stream being moved gently in one direction by the flow of the water—as if the spectator were looking into that stream on a sunny day. Meanwhile, the frame's glass resembled the still surface of a pool, giving the whole piece a vague sense of the uncanny. The handles of a plastic bag, which featured some kind of regal insignia on its exterior, were wrapped around the turtle's neck. They were not wound tightly enough to indicate strangulation, but to imagine the turtle swimming in the nonexistent water was to imagine its neck becoming more and more tightly gripped by the plastic. *A Bag for Life* seemed to me to be not only an ecological statement, but also a contemplation of art's own function, and the limits of its capacity to represent the cost and consequences of human reliance on plastics for other living creatures. It was quite brilliant: thoughtful and incredibly sad.

As daylight drew in, I returned to my room, watched a few episodes of *American Gods* on the Amazon Prime-equipped television, and got an early night.

The next morning, I went down for breakfast. On the television in the breakfast room, a news channel broadcast images of the G20 protests in Hamburg. I drank coffee as next to me an older couple engaged in conversation with another person about the notion they were contemplating, of moving from Scotland to the south. They were discussing purchasing property. The couple's interlocutor described how she and her husband attended auctions where ex-council properties could be picked up for a song. It was, she said, a question of holding steady, of being prepared to take risks. They talked about on-street parking, the necessity of enough space for a car. The thought occurred to me: if I were in a writers' room for a show about gentrification, rocketing economic inequality, and the generational divide, and proposed this as a scene, it would be rejected for being too obvious.

I gathered my possessions and walked from Cliftonville along the beach towards Dreamland at its opposite end. In beautiful morning sunlight, I passed the Flamingo arcade with its vibrant red and yellow sign, a branch of the fast food restaurant Wimpy, and the Mechanical Elephant pub, where a celebratory drinks party had taken place after the screening of *Exodus* at Dreamland Cinema in 2007. I turned left down Hall by the Sea Road into the amusement park grounds. A small sign at its entrance read:

> By entering the Dreamland site you are agreeing to be filmed and photographed and so release Dreamland, its contractors, its employees, and third parties involved in the creation or publication of marketing materials.

Within the grounds, signs encouraged attenders to "Share your *Dreamland memories" (Instagram), "Check in and start Dreaming!" (Facebook), "Snap us your Dreamland stories!" (Snapchat), and "Join the #Dreamland conversation!" (Twitter). In September 2006, when the filming of *Exodus* had required its own crowd release notice, Facebook had been launched to members of the public only days before, and Twitter was only a few months old; Snapchat and Instagram did not yet exist.

The concrete floor of the café and arcade was studded decoratively with pennies, a cute gesture that implied cascades of coins emanating from slot machines. A neon sign indicated the presence of a roller disco at its far end. Outside, with the sun increasingly intense, the park was yet to become too busy. Its environment was colorful and spacious but still quite intimate, featuring rides like the Chair-o-Plane and Dodgems alongside the park's star attraction, the restored Scenic Railway. I made a beeline for the Big Wheel where, given the relative slowness of custom, the attendant let me stay on for a couple of extra rotations. The view across the town was stunning. I gazed down upon Dreamland's car park. I recalled meeting the participants on the film set's site for the project evaluation I had written ten years previously, and the burning of Antony Gormley's *Waste Man* on *Exodus Day*. Disembarking from the ride, I absorbed the text adjacent to it:

> At thirty five metres high, our Big Wheel is the King of all he surveys. And that means the most beautiful stretch of Kent coastline: rich golden sands, sparkling silver water, and the rosy glow of England's finest seaside town enjoying a deserved period of regeneration . . . on a really clear day, you can even see the house prices going up! Our Wheel is big, but the biggest of all time was the first to be built: a 1,300 ton monster designed by George Washington Ferris. At the top, passengers could see for a whopping 50 miles. Eagle-eyed wheel-spotters will notice that our current structure is not the one which featured at Dreamland in the eighties. Rest assured, he is alive and spinning, enjoying the ex-pat life at a theme park in Mexico. Olé olé!

I paused on the underline under the word "clear." Why was this word highlighted thus? Was the writer of this text making a subtle jab at gentrification, and the processes by which bricks and mortar become gold mines of exchange value—a thing impossible to see in and of itself? Probably not. I noted the nomenclature of "ex-pat," and considered the doublethink the term performs in relation to other migrant identities, the racialized hierarchy of legitimacy it refers to and creates—all the more pernicious in the context of the "hostile environment" and the concomitant rise in race-related aggression and violence.[21] I thought of the anti-immigration UK Independence Party (UKIP) winning control of Thanet District Council in 2015 (which returned to the Conservatives in 2018).

Two friends who lived in Canterbury, a city a few miles away from Margate, arrived to meet me in the park. We enjoyed a couple of rides, and then got chips and sat on the sun-bathed beach for the afternoon, trying and failing to keep grains of sand out of the food.

Futures

The legacies of the 2000s were visible everywhere on this trip. Most conspicuous was the use of cultural investment for regeneration, manifest in the foregrounding of Turner Contemporary at the train station, conversations, the presentation of artworks, the blurb attached to Dreamland's Big Wheel. Closely linked to that discourse, in the work of Turner

Contemporary's Art Inspiring Change project, were themes of leadership and the delegation of leadership to young people, and the uses of art as a pathway to professional qualifications or academic awards—mechanisms that were likewise a strong feature of the *Favela to the World* project discussed in chapter 3. Here, notions of art as a form of ethical training and productive economic contribution coincide, along with the prioritization of leadership, a mode that is heroic and individualizing.

This consolidation of arts education and the change in its status was arguably one of the most substantial transformations at the level of cultural institutions consequent upon the period I've discussed in *Restaging the Future*. The exhibitions I enjoyed at Turner Contemporary in 2017 witnessed the integration of education and community-based work in the gallery's activity on a number of levels, as well as a defense of the public realm as one of many voices and histories, of migration in particular. The works demonstrably asserted the multiplicity of identities, the validity of embracing and exploring them through art, and the importance and necessity of programming work by practitioners above and beyond a canon of white male artists. It also presented the practice of those who live and work locally, or who may still be very young, as integral to the gallery's work as a public institution. *Standing Stones*, a multidisciplinary work made in 1997 in collaboration with a youth club, was artist-led, and realized ultimately by a writer and a sculptor. Though hardly a rejection of the gallery system of the sort community artists called for in the 1970s, in *Every Day Is a New Day*, the young people's own work was presented with and alongside that of other artists. And, though the 2000s were undoubtedly a period in which arts education enjoyed much greater institutional and financial prioritization than ever before owing to the cultural changes explored here, this book has presented evidence that arts education and community-based work played a formative role in the gestation of many aspects of the cultural sector in Britain in the postwar period. From the development of infrastructures and institutions for performance, to the emergence of culture-in-regeneration in its earliest iterations, the influences of arts education and community-based practices are sometimes subtle but are undeniably present, though they so often depart from the dissenting politics of the movement as those were expressed in the 1970s.

Yet as Eleonora Belfiore argued in 2012, the legacy of this period was also "the paradox of a cultural sector that has experienced a remarkable growth in funding, a more prominent political profile and, indeed, a golden age, yet [which] also appears to be consistently on the defensive, vulnerable, and lacking in confidence when it comes to articulat[ing] its own value."[22] In a situation in which market logics predominate, she continued, "the possibility of a constructive notion of cultural value that does not derive legitimacy from exchange value becomes undermined."[23] With John Guillory, whose compelling argument I discussed in the introduction to this book, I would go further: the possibility of a discourse of cultural value unattached to exchange value has always been unavailable within the context of capitalist society, precisely because exchange value is the precondition for the discourse's emergence. And the abstraction "cultural value" goes nowhere near expressing what is important about the process of making and watching artistic work, of being able to make sense of the world and communicate with other people through aesthetic means that aren't only based in words, or which operate on multiple levels. Artistic practice is never only about "art," which is one of the many reasons why the category of "intrinsic value" is problematic, and is also what sets the conditions for the co-optation of artistic practice by other forces, including the discourses explored in this book.

In researching and writing *Restaging the Future* I engaged in "close-focus, experience-near, low-flying methods," combined with an account of neoliberal ideology, whose continued hegemony in the 2010s was "manifest in the form of unrelenting political pressure for market-oriented and voluntarist modes of governance."[24] While pretending to economic common sense, the implementation of austerity in Britain has devastated lives and communities and decimated public institutions.[25] In 2011, Stuart Hall acknowledged that, despite the political continuities between Thatcher, Blair, and Cameron's regimes, which he framed in terms of "the long march" of neoliberalism, the New Labour government had instituted valuable progressive changes such as the establishment of a minimum wage and expanded support for the National Health Service—while noting too that these changes were inextricable from marketization at the level of institutions.[26] The subsequent drive for austerity sharpened and redirected "neoliberal logic": it was based on attacks on those reliant on state provision, with particularly brutal impact upon women, and upon the mass privatization of services, and had an emphasis on "localism," "voluntarism," and "phoney populism" as ideological cover, all in the service of a pro-market "permanent revolution."[27] In 2013, Jamie Peck—whose thinking about neoliberalization has been decisive for my argument about culture—had this to say on the question of the future:

> The residues of pre-existing social formations will never be entirely erased or rendered inert. Double movements against the overextension of market rule will not only continue, but can be expected to intensify, presenting new challenges but also opening up new moments for social action. Crises, in forms old and new, will recur. Realistically speaking, it is on this uncertain and uneven terrain that all forms of post-neoliberal politics will have to be forged.[28]

Peck proposed that in this context "actually existing alternatives (progressive and otherwise) will never be completely expunged."[29] With crucial exceptions, the alternatives to have been realized electorally in recent years are decisively "otherwise." In 2017, Ann Pettifor observed that "millions of people are in open revolt, backing populist, mostly right-wing political candidates. They hope these 'strong men and women' will protect them from hard-headed neoliberal policies for unfettered global markets in finance, trade, and labour."[30] In 2019, writing prior to the general election of that year, Jeremy Gilbert discussed "the very strong evidence for the breakdown of neoliberal hegemony within mainstream British politics in recent years, as the neoliberal consensus has given way to a sharp polarisation between a newly radicalised Labour Party, an extreme English nationalist wing of the Conservative Party and an increasingly isolated and impotent neoliberal 'centre.' "[31] This represented a radical shift from the conditions of the 2000s, when globalization and its associated discourses seemed unshakeable, and pervaded the examples I have explored in this book. In reaction to these developments, this neoliberal "centre" in Britain has assiduously sought an encore, borne out by this report from the *Evening Standard* in July 2023: "Labour is wooing businesses and bankers as it readies itself for office in a repeat of the 'prawn cocktail offensive' by Sir Tony Blair and Gordon Brown to get finance on side before their 1997 victory."[32] Yet we are now also in the wake of the COVID-19 pandemic—an unprecedented catastrophe that Adam Tooze has theorized as "a comprehensive crisis of the neoliberal era—with regard to its environmental envelope, its domestic social, economic, and political underpinnings, and the international order."[33] Neoliberalism may be facing its demise, but that by no means inevitably portends transformations for the better.[34]

Restaging the Future has focused on artistic practice and public culture in the context of neoliberalism's "long march."[35] It has theorized them in terms of the theatrical, an everyday practice that forges and sustains forms of identity and sociality—a social constructionist approach which, as noted at the beginning of the introduction, has long been at the center of progressive arts pedagogy, and which has a far longer precedent than that. To bring the discussion to an end, I refer again to a text written by John Frow in 1999, in which he reworked a phrase commonly associated with theatricality. The "suspension of belief," he argued, is fundamental to the operation of the public sphere in modernity: it is "as ordinary and trivial a thing as the willingness to hold two contradictory beliefs at the same time, or rather simultaneously to believe and not to believe; and yet it is this moment of paralogic that makes possible any complex co-existence with others."[36] Frow argued that under the conditions of neoliberalism, the "spectacularization" of political figures threatens to bypass such paralogic.[37] The aesthetic preoccupations with authenticity and immersivity seen across the projects I have examined in this book likewise speak to this representational bypass—and the interruptions to them, seen in on-street protests, disruptions to theatrical ritual, and so on, to the socially constructed, changeable fabric of everyday life. Frow thus proposed in 1999 that this reality placed "a methodological imperative on us not to separate the study of the political from the study of mass culture"[38]—an imperative that without doubt remains. The projects under discussion here were hardly examples of mass culture, and this study approached New Labour not in relation to a culture of spin, information management, and iconicity but to select policy rhetorics. But on whatever scale they might have done so, and whatever the magnitude of their effects, these and many other initiatives in the 2000s sat at the nexus of culture and politics, contributing to the advancement and challenge of market rationality, and sometimes both at the same time. We are living in the future thus restaged.

NOTES

Introduction

1. During 2021, various commentators debated whether neoliberalism is being superseded by "the age of national capitalism" (George Eaton, "Is the Neoliberal Era Finally Over?" *New Statesman*, June 16, 2021), "mutant strains of neoliberalism" (Quinn Slobodian, "Hayek's Bastards: The Populist Right's Neoliberal Roots," *Tribune*, June 15, 2021), "authoritarian capitalism" (Grace Blakeley, "Covid-19 Is Not the End of Neoliberalism," *Tribune*, May 28, 2021), or, as James Meadway proposed (citing all three), an "*anti-neoliberal* offensive" (Meadway, "Neoliberalism Is Dead—and Something Even Worse Is Taking Its Place," *Novara Media*, June 29, 2021). In September 2021, Meadway argued that "it is too early to say that neoliberalism is dead, and a revival in some form—at least at the national level—cannot be completely ruled out," but he nonetheless insisted "neoliberalism is dying, if not yet dead" (Meadway, "Neoliberalism Is Dying—Now We Must Replace It," *Open Democracy*, September 3, 2021).

2. Jamie Peck, *Constructions of Neoliberal Reason* (Oxford: Oxford University Press, 2010), xi.

3. See, for example, Janet Minihan's detailed analysis of legislative and institutional transformations in nineteenth and early twentieth-century British cultural production, *The Nationalisation of Culture* (London: Hamish Hamilton, 1977).

4. David Garland, in "What Is a 'History of the Present'? On Foucault's Genealogies and Their Critical Preconditions," *Punishment & Society* 16, no. 4 (2014): 373, outlines this Foucauldian critical practice thus: "A history of the present begins by identifying a present-day practice that is both taken for granted and yet, in certain respects, problematic or somehow unintelligible—the reformative prison in the 1970s, for example, or the American death penalty today—and then seeks to trace the power struggles that produced them. Genealogy is motivated not by a historical concern to understand the past—though any historical claims it makes must be valid, verifiable ones—but instead by a critical concern to understand the present. It aims to trace the forces that gave birth to our present-day practices and to identify the historical conditions upon which they still depend. Its point is not to think historically about the past but rather to use historical materials to rethink the present."

5. Peck, *Constructions of Neoliberal Reason*, 15.

6. Jim McGuigan, "Neoliberalism, Culture, and Policy," *International Journal of Cultural Policy* 11, no. 3 (2005): 238.

7. Belgrade Theatre Coventry, "About Us | History," http://www.belgrade.co.uk/about-us/history/.

8. Tony Coult, "Agents of the Future: Theatre-in-Education," in *Dreams and Deconstructions: Alternative Theatre in Britain*, ed. Sandy Craig (Ambergate, UK: Amber Lane, 1980), 76–77.

9. Coult, "Agents of the Future," 84.

10. Coult, "Agents of the Future," 85.

11. *OED Online*, December 2022, s.v. "agent, n.1 and adj.," https://www-oed-com.ezproxy.lib.bbk.ac.uk/view/Entry/3859?rskey=llAgRA&result=1&isAdvanced=false.

12. R. G. Gregory, quoted in Alison Jeffers, introduction to *Culture, Democracy, and the Right to Make Art: The British Community Arts Movement*, ed. Alison Jeffers and Gerri Moriarty (London: Bloomsbury Methuen, 2017), 3.

13. Stephen Lacey, "British Theatre and Commerce, 1979–2000," in *The Cambridge History of British Theatre, vol. 3: Since 1895*, ed. Baz Kershaw (Cambridge: Cambridge University Press, 2004), 427.

14. D. Keith Peacock, *Thatcher's Theatre: British Theatre and Drama in the Eighties* (Westport, CT: Greenwood, 1999), 33–63.

15. Jeffers, introduction to *Culture, Democracy*, 10, 1.

16. Jeffers, introduction to *Culture, Democracy*, 15–17.

17. Harold Baldry, quoted in Alison Jeffers, "The Community Arts Movement 1968–1986," in *Culture, Democracy, and the Right to Make Art: The British Community Arts Movement*, ed. Alison Jeffers and Gerri Moriarty (London: Bloomsbury Methuen, 2017), 41.

18. Jeffers, "The Community Arts Movement 1968–1986," 41–43; Alison Jeffers, "Then and Now: Reflections on the Influence of the Community Arts Movement on Contemporary Community and Participatory Arts," in *Culture, Democracy, and the Right to Make Art: The British Community Arts Movement*, ed. Alison Jeffers and Gerri Moriarty (London: Bloomsbury Methuen, 2017), 136–39; Sophie Hope, "From Community Arts to the Socially Engaged Art Commission," in *Culture, Democracy, and the Right to Make Art: The British Community Arts Movement* (London: Bloomsbury Methuen, 2017), 204.

19. Helen Nicholson, *Theatre and Education* (Basingstoke, UK: Palgrave Macmillan, 2009), 37–39.

20. Baz Kershaw, "Discouraging Democracy: British Theatres and Economics, 1979–1999," *Theatre Journal*, no. 51 (1999): 280.

21. David Harvey, *A Brief History of Neoliberalism* (Oxford: Oxford University Press, 2005), 2.

22. Peacock, *Thatcher's Theatre*, 49, 50.

23. Peck, *Constructions of Neoliberal Reason*, xii.

24. Jeremy Gilbert, "'Neoliberalism' and 'Capitalism'—What's the Difference?" *jeremygilbertwriting*, July 14, 2015, https://jeremygilbertwriting.wordpress.com/2015/07/14/neoliberalism-and-capitalism-whats-the-difference/.

25. For an examination of the "state apparatus" as a construct, see Mark Whitehead, Rhys Jones, and Martin Jones, *The Nature of the State: Excavating the Political Ecologies of the Modern State* (Oxford: Oxford University Press, 2007), 117–22.

26. For a detailed intellectual history of neoliberalism as a political and governmental project, see Quinn Slobodian, *Globalists: The End of Empire and the Birth of Neoliberalism* (Cambridge, MA: Harvard University Press 2018).

27. Andy Beckett, *When the Lights Went Out: What Really Happened to Britain in the Seventies* (London: Faber and Faber, 2009), 518.

28. Alfredo Saad-Filho and Deborah Johnston, introduction to *Neoliberalism: A Critical Reader*, ed. Alfredo Saad-Filho and Deborah Johnston (London: Pluto, 2005), 1–6; Stuart Hall, Doreen Massey, and Michael Rustin, "After Neoliberalism: Analysing the Present," in *After Neoliberalism: The Kilburn Manifesto* (Chadwell Heath, UK: Soundings, 2013), 1–20, https://www.lwbooks.co.uk/sites/default/files/00_manifestoframingstatement.pdf.

29. Bill Dunn, "Against Neoliberalism as a Concept," *Capital and Class* 41, no. 3 (2017): 435–54; Taylor C. Boas and Jordan Gans-Morse, "Neoliberalism: From New Liberal Philosophy to Anti-Liberal Slogan," *Studies in Comparative International Development* 44, no. 2 (2009): 137–61.

30. Peck, *Constructions of Neoliberal Reason*, 15.

31. Peck, *Constructions of Neoliberal Reason*, 30.

32. Peck, *Constructions of Neoliberal Reason*, 19.

33. Peck, *Constructions of Neoliberal Reason*, 16.

34. Peck, *Constructions of Neoliberal Reason*, 7.

35. Peck, *Constructions of Neoliberal Reason*, 7.

36. Jeremy Gilbert, "What Kind of Thing Is Neoliberalism?" *New Formations*, no. 80-81 (2013): 7.

37. Jamie Peck and Nik Theodore, "Still Neoliberalism?" *South Atlantic Quarterly* 118, no. 2 (2019): 259.

38. Jamie Peck and Adam Tickell, "Neoliberalizing Space," *Antipode* 34, no. 3 (2002): 396.

39. Gilbert, "What Kind of Thing Is Neoliberalism?" 9.

40. Gilbert, "What Kind of Thing Is Neoliberalism?" 11.

41. Alan Finlayson, "Tony Blair and the Jargon of Modernisation," *Soundings* 10 (1998): 11–27.

42. "After Neoliberalism, with James Meadway," *Politics, Theory, Other*, July 25, 2021, https://soundcloud.com/poltheoryother/after-neoliberalism-w-james-meadway.

43. Labour, *Create the Future: A Strategy for Cultural Policy, Arts, and the Creative Economy* (Labour Party, 1997), 15.

44. Labour, *Create the Future*, 3.

45. Labour, *Create the Future*, 9.

46. Labour, *Create the Future*, 9.

47. Nicholas Garnham, "From Cultural to Creative Industries," *International Journal of Cultural Policy* 11, no. 1 (2005): 15: "In the arts policy documents produced by the British Labour Party prior to its 1997 election victory, it used the term 'cultural industries' to describe the range of activities with which it was principally concerned (Labour Party 1997). In the government policy documents it produced after victory in that election, the organising term shifted to the "creative industries" (DCMS 1998)."

48. Labour, *Create the Future*, 7.

49. Clause Four had been a part of Labour's constitution since 1918 in this form (quoted in Michael White, "Blair Defines the New Labour," *The Guardian*, October 5, 1994): "To secure for the workers by hand or by brain the full fruits of their industry and the most equitable distribution thereof that may be possible upon the basis of the common ownership of the means of production, distribution and exchange, and the best obtainable system of popular administration and control of each industry or service." The revised version moves its focus away from industry ("Labour Party Rule Book," 2013, 3): "The Labour party is a democratic socialist party. It believes that by the strength of our common endeavour we achieve more than we achieve alone, so as to create for each of us the means to realise our true potential and for all of us a community in which power, wealth and opportunity are in the hands of the many, not the few. Where the rights we enjoy reflect the duties we owe. And where we live together, freely, in a spirit of solidarity, tolerance and respect."

50. Anthony Giddens, *Beyond Left and Right: The Future of Radical Politics* (Cambridge: Polity, 1994).

51. Peck, *Constructions of Neoliberal Reason*, xvi.

52. The manifesto's coauthor, Mark Fisher, said of the arts: "The Labour government will be sympathetic because we know the cultural economy is not only good for the cities but it affects investment. Culture creates jobs." Quoted in Polly Toynbee, "A Good Home's Where the Art Is," *The Independent*, May 29, 1997, 21. Toynbee is reporting on the publication of François Matarasso's *Use or Ornament?* (1997), in which Mark Fisher's statement also appears.

53. Chris Smith, *Creative Britain* (London: Faber and Faber, 1998), 18–19.

54. Smith, *Creative Britain*, 3.

55. Smith, *Creative Britain*, 16.

56. Rob Imrie and Mike Raco, "Community and the Changing Nature of Urban Policy," in *Urban Renaissance? New Labour, Community, and Urban Policy*, ed. Rob Imrie and Mike Raco (Bristol, UK: Policy, 2003), 7.

57. Robert Hewison, *Cultural Capital: The Rise and Fall of Creative Britain* (London: Verso, 2014), 29.

58. David Hesmondhalgh, Melissa Nisbett, Kate Oakley, and David Lee, "Were New Labour's Cultural Policies Neo-Liberal?" *International Journal of Cultural Policy* 21, no. 1 (2015): 105–6.

59. Eleanora Belfiore, "Auditing Culture: The Subsidised Cultural Sector in the New Public Management," *International Journal of Cultural Policy* 10, no. 2 (2004): 187–92.

60. Peck, *Constructions of Neoliberal Reason*, 23.

61. Tom Ling, "Delivering Joined-up Government in the UK: Dimensions, Issues, and Problems," *Public Administration* 80, no. 4 (2002): 616.

62. Office of the Deputy Prime Minister, *Breaking the Cycle: Taking Stock of Progress and Priorities for the Future: A Report by the Social Exclusion Unit* (London: Office of the Deputy Prime Minister, 2004), 3. See Ruth Levitas, *The Inclusive Society? Social Exclusion and New Labour*, 2nd ed. (Basingstoke, UK: Palgrave Macmillan, 2005), for an essential critique of New Labour's adoption and mobilization of the exclusion discourse and its basis in the work of sociologists such as Peter Townsend.

63. François Matarasso, "Summary," in *Use or Ornament? The Social Impact of Participating in the Arts* (Stroud, UK: Comedia, 2003).

64. François Matarasso, "Conclusions," in *Use or Ornament?* para. 10.3, 79.

65. Department for Culture, Media, and Sport, "Policy Action Team 10: A Report to the Social Exclusion Unit," London, 1999, 5.

66. Department for Culture, Media, and Sport, "Building on PAT 10: Progress Report on Social Inclusion," London, 2001, 4.

67. For example, *The Arts and Social Exclusion: A Review Prepared for the Arts Council of England* (2001), *Count Me In: A Review of the Dimensions of Social Inclusion through Culture and Sport* (2002), and Helen Jermyn, *The Art of Inclusion*, Research Report 35 (London: Arts Council of England, 2004).

68. Angus Cameron and Ronen Palan, *The Imagined Economies of Globalization* (London: Sage, 2004), 158.

69. Cameron and Palan, *The Imagined Economies of Globalization*, 147.

70. "UK Politics: Tony Blair's Speech in Full," *BBC News*, September 28, 1999, http://news.bbc.co.uk/1/hi/uk_politics/460009.stm.

71. Claire Bishop, *Artificial Hells: Participatory Art and the Politics of Spectatorship* (London: Verso, 2012), 14.

72. Bishop, *Artificial Hells*, 16.

73. Raymond Williams, *Keywords: A Vocabulary of Culture and Society* (London: Fontana/Croom Helm, 1976), 66.

74. Bishop, *Artificial Hells*, 17.

75. Bishop, *Artificial Hells*, 14.

76. Matarasso, *Use or Ornament?* 5.

77. Baz Kershaw, *The Politics of Performance: Radical Theatre as Cultural Intervention* (Abingdon, UK: Routledge, 1992), 184.

78. George Yúdice, *The Expediency of Culture: Uses of Culture in the Global Era* (Durham, NC: Duke University Press, 2003), 9.

79. Yúdice, *The Expediency of Culture*, 11.

80. Matarasso, *Use or Ornament?* 13.

81. Yúdice, *The Expediency of Culture*, 12.

82. Wendy Brown's *Undoing the Demos: Neoliberalism's Stealth Revolution* (New York: Zone Books, 2015) focuses extensively on this process.

83. Ruth-Blandina M. Quinn, *Public Policy and the Arts* (Aldershot, UK: Ashgate, 1998), 103–4.

84. Hesmondhalgh, Nisbett, Oakley, and Lee, "Were New Labour's Cultural Policies Neo-Liberal?" 100–101. See Jen Harvie, *Fair Play: Art, Performance, and Neoliberalism* (Basingstoke, UK: Palgrave Macmillan, 2013), 150–91, for a discussion of the mixed economy of arts funding in Britain and the cuts made following the emergence of the financial crisis in 2007–8.

85. Jermyn, *The Art of Inclusion*, 26.

86. Angus Cameron, "Geographies of Welfare and Exclusion: Social Inclusion and Exception," *Progress in Human Geography* 30, no. 3 (2006): 403.

87. Jisha Menon, "Palimpsestic City: Nostalgia in Neoliberal Bangalore," in *Neoliberalism and Global Theatres*, ed. Lara D. Nielsen and Patricia Ybarra (Basingstoke, UK: Palgrave Macmillan, 2012), 237.

88. Menon, "Palimpsestic City," 237.

89. Peck, *Constructions of Neoliberal Reason*, 20.
90. Cameron and Palan, *The Imagined Economies of Globalization*, 3.
91. Cameron and Palan, *The Imagined Economies of Globalization*, 17.
92. Cameron and Palan, *The Imagined Economies of Globalization*, 17.
93. Cameron and Palan, *The Imagined Economies of Globalization*, 145.
94. Randy Martin, *An Empire of Indifference: American War and the Financial Logic of Risk Management* (Durham, NC: Duke University Press, 2007), 8.
95. Cameron and Palan, *The Imagined Economies of Globalization*, 144.
96. Kojo Koram, *Uncommon Wealth: Britain and the Aftermath of Empire* (London: John Murray 2022), 184.
97. Michel Foucault, *The Birth of Biopolitics: Lectures at the Collège de France 1978–79*, ed. Michel Senellart (Basingstoke, UK: Palgrave Macmillan, 2008), 229.
98. Cameron and Palan, *The Imagined Economies of Globalization*, 11.
99. Dan Hancox, "Revealed: Creeping Privatization of London Parks in Summer," *The Guardian*, July 5, 2019, https://www.theguardian.com/cities/2019/jul/05/revealed-how-london-parks-are-partly-privatised-festivals-wireless-finsbury-park.
100. Liz Tomlin, *British Theatre Companies: 1995–2014* (London: Methuen, 2015).
101. Hewison, *Cultural Capital*, 121.
102. See Louise Owen, "The Witness and the Replay: London Bubble," in *Performance and Community: Commentary and Case Studies*, ed. Caoimhe McAvinchey (London: Bloomsbury Methuen, 2014), 155–87, for a historical account of the company's emergence.
103. Leila Jancovich, "Great Art for Everyone? Engagement and Participation Policy in the Arts," *Cultural Trends* 20, no. 3-4 (2011): 272.
104. Hewison (Cultural Capital, 129) observes that its "misleading but effective" title was an invention of a sub-editor.
105. Nicholas Hytner, "To Hell with Targets," *The Observer*, January 12, 2003.
106. Tessa Jowell, *Government and the Value of Culture* (London: Department for Culture, Media, and Sport, 2004), 18, 16.
107. Barbara Herrnstein Smith, *Contingencies of Value: Alternative Perspectives for Critical Theory* (Cambridge, MA: Harvard University Press, 1988), 126.
108. John Guillory, *Cultural Capital: The Problem of Literary Canon Formation* (Chicago: University of Chicago Press, 1993), 296, 308.
109. Guillory, *Cultural Capital*, 308.
110. Guillory, *Cultural Capital*, 303.
111. Guillory, *Cultural Capital*, 316.
112. Jean-Christophe Agnew, *Worlds Apart: The Market and the Theatre in Anglo-American Thought, 1550–1750* (Cambridge: Cambridge University Press, 1986), 6–7.
113. Jowell, *Government and the Value of Culture*; Estelle Morris, "Estelle Morris: 'There Is Something Inherently Good and Valuable in Art': From a Speech by the Arts Minister at the Cheltenham Festival of Literature," *The*

Independent, October 17, 2003; Sir Brian McMaster, *Supporting Excellence in the Arts: From Measurement to Judgement* (London: Department for Culture, Media, and Sport, 2008).

114. John Frow, *Cultural Studies and Cultural Value* (Oxford: Clarendon, 1995), 13.

115. Frow, *Cultural Studies*, 144.

116. Frow, *Cultural Studies*, 21.

117. Shannon Jackson, *Social Works: Performing Art, Supporting Publics* (Abingdon, UK: Routledge, 2011), 19.

118. Frow, *Cultural Studies*, 98, 104.

119. Pat O'Malley, *Risk, Uncertainty, and Government* (London: Glasshouse, 2004), 174, 59.

120. Yúdice, *The Expediency of Culture*, 9.

121. Sophie Nield, "On the Border as Theatrical Space: Appearance, Dislocation, and the Production of the Refugee," in *Contemporary Theatres in Europe: A Critical Companion*, ed. Joe Kelleher and Nicholas Ridout (Abingdon, UK: Routledge, 2006), 63.

122. Richard Schechner, *Between Theatre and Anthropology* (Philadelphia: University of Pennsylvania Press, 1985), 51.

123. Caryl Phillips, *The Atlantic Sound* (London: Vintage, 2001), 92.

Chapter 1

1. Peck and Theodore, "Still Neoliberalism?" 259.

2. O'Malley, *Risk, Uncertainty, and Government*, 57.

3. O'Malley, *Risk, Uncertainty, and Government*, 59.

4. Harvie, *Fair Play*, 62–74.

5. O'Malley, *Risk, Uncertainty, and Government*, 57.

6. Elizabeth Cotton, "Self-Employment Is Precarious Work," *LSE: Surviving Work in the UK*, September 12, 2016, https://blogs.lse.ac.uk/businessreview/2016/09/12/self-employment-is-precarious-work. In this 2016 text, Cotton noted acidly that "self-employed people on average earn half the wage of people with a contract of employment. Hardly Dragons' Den then." In a *New York Times* op-ed, "Entrepreneur or Unemployed?" (June 1, 2010), Robert Reich similarly argued that the proliferation of new start-ups in the United States in 2009 could be accounted for by the rise in unemployment in the context of the financial crisis, and organizations rehiring workers as temps.

7. La Ribot, http://www.laribot.com.

8. La Ribot, "*40 espontáneos*," https://www.laribot.com/work/12.

9. Johannes Birringer, "Dance and Not Dance," *PAJ: A Journal of Performance and Art* 27, no. 2 (2005): 10–27.

10. Siobhan Davies Studios, "New Dance and the Visual Arts," *Remembering British New Dance*, June 2012, https://www.siobhandavies.com/relay/events/remembering-british-new-dance/.

11. Stuart Hall, "New Labour's Double Shuffle," *Soundings*, no. 24 (2003): 19.

12. Gabriele Klein, "Dance in a Knowledge Society," in *Knowledge in Motion: Perspectives of Artistic and Scientific Research in Dance*, ed. Sabine Gehm, Pirkko Husemann, and Katharina von Wilcke (New Brunswick, NJ: Transaction, 2007), 31.

13. The title of the dance sector organization Dance UK's health and well-being handbook, *Your Body, Your Risk* (2001), identifies these circumstances bluntly. An earlier, more detailed study partly commissioned by Dance UK is Peter Brinson and Fiona Dick's *Fit to Dance? The Report of the National Inquiry into Dancers' Health and Injury* (London: Calouste Gulbenkian Foundation, 1996).

14. Dominic Johnson, "Introduction: The What, When, and Where of Live Art," *Contemporary Theatre Review* 22, no. 1 (2012): 7.

15. Graham Saunders, "The Freaks' Roll Call: Live Art and the Arts Council, 1968–73," *Contemporary Theatre Review* 22, no. 1 (2012): 32–45; Heike Roms and Rebecca Edwards, "Towards a Prehistory of Live Art in the UK," *Contemporary Theatre Review* 22, no. 1 (2012): 17–31.

16. Johnson, "Introduction," 7.

17. Johnson, "Introduction," 9.

18. Beth Hoffmann, "Radicalism and the Theatre in Genealogies of Live Art," *Performance Research* 14, no. 1 (2009): 100.

19. Manuel Vason, Lois Keidan, and Ron Athey, *Exposures* (London: Black Dog, 2002), 2.

20. Lois Keidan and Daniel Brine, "Live Art in London," *Performing Arts Journal*, no. 81 (2005): 74.

21. Lois Keidan, "This Must Be the Place: Thoughts on Place, Placelessness, and Live Art since the 1980s," in *Performance and Place*, ed. Leslie Hill and Helen Paris (Basingstoke, UK: Palgrave Macmillan, 2006), 9.

22. Keidan, "This Must Be the Place," 9.

23. Johnson, "Introduction," 10.

24. Stephanie Jordan, *Striding Out: Aspects of Contemporary and New Dance in Britain* (London: Dance Books, 1992), 58.

25. Jordan, *Striding Out*, 63, 83–84.

26. Arts Council of Great Britain, *Opera and Dance: Report of the Study Group: February 1983* (London: Arts Council of Great Britain, 1983), appendix A.

27. Judith Mackrell, *Out of Line: The Story of British New Dance* (Binstead, UK: Dance Books, 1992), 4.

28. Jordan, *Striding Out*, 13.

29. Jordan, *Striding Out*, 62.

30. Mackrell, *Out of Line*, 26; Peter Brinson, *Dance as Education: Towards a National Dance Culture* (London: Falmer, 1991), 30.

31. Chisenhale Dance Space, "History," https://www.chisenhaledancespace.co.uk/about/our-history/.

32. Randy Martin, "A Precarious Dance, a Derivative Sociality," *TDR* 56, no. 4 (2012): 71. This example corroborates Randy Martin's thinking about the relation between contemporary dance practices and "derivative logic" ("reinventions as things for themselves into matters of interest for others," 67), the floor of Chisenhale literally deriving from Butler's Wharf.

33. Jordan, *Striding Out*, 62.

34. Jordan, *Striding Out*, 72.

35. Mackrell, *Out of Line*, 28.

36. Yvonne Rainer, in "Some Retrospective Notes on a Dance for 10 People and 12 Mattresses Called 'Part of Some Sextets,'" *Tulane Drama Review* 10, no. 2 (1965): 178: "NO to spectacle no to virtuosity no to transformations and magic and make-believe no to the glamour and transcendency of the star image no to the heroic no to the anti-heroic no to trash imagery no to involvement of performer or spectator no to style no to camp no to seduction of spectator by the wiles of the performer no to eccentricity no to moving or being moved."

37. Mackrell, *Out of Line*, 1. Rainer's manifesto is a strident statement of anti-theatricality, while Early's paradoxical text is both a rejection of genres and styles and a refusal to exclude them. The objectifying description "chinese shoes" presumably refers to flat-soled slippers.

38. Jordan, *Striding Out*, 84–87.

39. Mackrell, *Out of Line*, 136, 139. See also Judith Mackrell, "Post-Modern Dance in Britain: An Historical Essay," *Dance Research: The Journal of the Society for Dance Research* 9, no. 1 (1991): 40–57.

40. Brinson, *Dance as Education*, 31.

41. Mackrell, *Out of Line*, 40.

42. Richard Ralph, "Peter Brinson," *Dance Research: The Journal of the Society for Dance Research* 15, no. 1 (1997): 4–12; Ann Nugent, "In Memoriam: Peter Brinson (Born Lladudno, Wales, 1923—Died London, 1995)," *Dance Research Journal* 28, no. 1 (1996): 126–29.

43. Peter Brinson, "A Culture of Mind and Body," *Dance Now* 2, no. 3 (1993): 52.

44. Christopher Thomson, "We Are a Dancing Nation," *Animated*, Spring 2006.

45. Brinson discusses Ballet for All in detail in "Reaching Out from London: Gulbenkian Grant for the Opera House," *Dancing Times* 54, no. 642 (March 1964): 290; "The Audience of the Future: The Royal Ballet Demonstration Group's Work and Progress," *Dancing Times* 56, no. 669 (June 1966): 455–56; and "Stimulating Audiences: Peter Brinson Talks to Dance and Dancers about Ballet for All," *Dance and Dancers* 18, no. 11 (November 1967): 22–23. This collection of articles offers a fascinating insight into the institutional politics of the period and the struggles that Brinson faced in mediating with the dance establishment.

46. Jordan, *Striding Out*, 75.

47. Peter Brinson, "The Nature of Collaboration," *New Dance* 22 (June 1982): 9.

48. Brinson, "The Nature of Collaboration," 8.

49. Robert Hewison and John Holden, *Experience and Experiment: The UK Branch of the Calouste Gulbenkian Foundation, 1956–2006* (London: Calouste Gulbenkian Foundation, 2006), 88.

50. Hewison and Holden, *Experience and Experiment*, 120.

51. Hewison and Holden, *Experience and Experiment*, 120–24; Jordan, *Striding Out*, 81; Veronica Lewis, "Fundamentally Embodied," *Animated*, Autumn-Winter 2016/17, https://www.communitydance.org.uk/DB/animated-library/fundamentally-embodied?ed=41635.

52. Jayne Stevens, "The National Association of Dance and Mime Animateurs (1986–89): A Community of Practice," *Dance Research* 31, no. 2 (2013): 158.

53. François Matarasso, *Regular Marvels: A Handbook for Animateurs, Practitioners, and Development Workers in Dance, Mime, Music, and Literature* (Leicester, UK: Community Dance and Mime Foundation, 1994), 11–12; Stevens, "The National Association of Dance and Mime Animateurs (1986–89)," 163. For other detailed accounts of the origins and development of the community dance movement, see Christopher Thomson, "Community Dance: What Community . . . What Dance?" in *Young People Dancing: An International Perspective*, vol. 3: *Dance: A Cultural Phenomenon and Community Dance* (Oxford: Dance and the Child International, 1989), 88–98; Julie Tolley, "The Dance Animateur: A British Phenomenon," in *Young People Dancing: An International Perspective*, vol. 3: *Dance: A Cultural Phenomenon and Community Dance* (Oxford: Dance and the Child International, 1989), 103–11; and Linda Jasper, "Tensions in the Definition of Community Dance," in *Border Tensions: Dance and Discourse, Proceedings of the Fifth Study of Dance Conference, University of Surrey 20–23 April 1995*, ed. Janet Adshead-Lansdale (Guildford, UK: University of Surrey, 1995), 181–90.

54. People Dancing: The Foundation for Community Dance, "Dance Agencies," https://www.communitydance.org.uk/useful-contacts-and-links/dance-agencies.

55. Anthony Peppiatt, "Speaking in Tongues," *Dance Theatre Journal* 3, no. 3 (1985): 27.

56. Peppiatt, "Speaking in Tongues," 27.

57. Peter Brinson, "The Making of Dance Animateurs," *Dance Theatre Journal* 3, no. 3 (1985): 26.

58. Thomson, "Community Dance: What Community . . . What Dance?" 89–90. The first of these statements represents a gentler version of Beth Hoffmann's theorization of live art's sectoral representation in "Radicalism and the Theatre in Genealogies of Live Art," *Performance Research* 14, no. 1 (2009): 101–2: "Specifically within the British context, at least, live art emerges not from a model of positive affinity and formal resemblance among works but from a principle of non-identity, the lack of definition outside the negation, subversion or transgression of a received practice or set of practices."

59. Stevens, "The National Association of Dance and Mime Animateurs (1986–89)," 163. The *OED Online* offers this etymology: "French *animateur* organizer, promoter (1914 or earlier; 1801 denoting a person who brings something to life)." *OED Online*, December 2022, s.v "animateur, n.," http://0-www.oed.com.catalogue.libraries.london.ac.uk/view/Entry/248726?redirectedFrom=animateur.

60. Matarasso, *Regular Marvels*, 11.

61. Helen Poynor, "Yes, But Is It Dance?" in *An Introduction to Community Dance Practice*, ed. Diane Amans (Basingstoke, UK: Palgrave Macmillan, 2008), 88.

62. Foundation for Community Dance, "Mapping Community Dance: A Research Report for the Foundation for Community Dance," Leicester, 2001, 17.

63. Ken Bartlett, "A Workforce for the Future?" *Animated* (Spring 2009): 33.

64. Stevens, "The National Association of Dance and Mime Animateurs (1986–89)," 168.

65. Bartlett, "A Workforce for the Future?" 32.

66. Sara Houston, "Participation in Community Dance: A Road to Empowerment and Transformation?" *New Theatre Quarterly* 21, no. 2 (2005): 170.

67. Anthony Peppiatt, "What Is a Framework and Why Does It Matter?" in *Thinking Aloud: In Search of a Framework for Community Dance*, ed. Chris Jones (Leicester, UK: Foundation for Community Dance, 1996), 3.

68. Chris Thomson, foreword to *An Introduction to Community Dance Practice*, ed. Diane Amans (Basingstoke, UK: Palgrave Macmillan, 2008), xi.

69. Thomson, foreword to An Introduction to Community Dance, x.

70. DCMS/DfES, "Government Response to the Culture, Media, and Sport Select Committee Report on Arts Development: Dance (HC 587), Session 2003–2004" (London: TSO, 2004), 5.

71. André Lepecki, "Concept and Presence: The Contemporary European Dance Scene," in *Rethinking Dance History: A Reader*, ed. Alexandra Carter (London: Routledge, 2004), 171.

72. Lepecki, "Concept and Presence," 173.

73. Lepecki, "Concept and Presence," 173.

74. Anna Kisselgoff, quoted in André Lepecki, *Exhausting Dance: Performance and the Politics of Movement* (London: Routledge, 2006), 1.

75. Lepecki, *Exhausting Dance*, 2.

76. Lepecki, *Exhausting Dance*, 4.

77. Rosalyn Sulcas, "Unless You Have Another World, Dance Will Do," *New York Times*, February 24, 2008, https://www.nytimes.com/2008/02/24/arts/dance/24sulc.html.

78. Lepecki, *Exhausting Dance*, 2.

79. "Not Conceptual," symposium held on February 22, 2007, presented by Jonathan Burrows at Siobhan Davies Studios, part of Parallel Voices 2007: A Public Season of Talks and Events, https://www.youtube.com/watch?v=EkdI-87T2z0.

80. When Sadlers Wells programmed *Nom donné par l'auteur* in 2008 as part of a retrospective of Bel's works staged at the Lilian Baylis Theatre, a substantial proportion of the audience for the sold-out event consisted of academics and students. Una Bauer, in "The Movement of Embodied Thought: The Representational Games of the Stage Zero of Signification in Jérôme Bel," *Performance Research* 13, no. 1 (2008): 41, comments that "Bel is still touring extensively with most of his works, some of them dating from 1994 or 1995, which, especially in the field of dance, even more than theatre, is not a minor achievement. Numerous theoreticians, dance scholars, and artists from around Europe have written articles or book chapters about his work." In several reviews, the 2015 Candoco Dance Company's restaging of *The Show Must Go On* (2001) in Britain was described as a "revival," which speaks to a process of canon formation.

81. "Manifesto for a European Performance Policy (2002)," http://www.freietheater.at/?page=kulturpolitik&detail=61304&jahr=2002.

82. "Manifesto for a European Performance Policy (2002)."
83. "Manifesto for a European Performance Policy (2002)."
84. "Manifesto for a European Performance Policy (2002)."
85. "Manifesto for a European Performance Policy (2002)."
86. Keidan, "This Must Be the Place," 9.
87. While a couple of La Ribot's early performances in Britain were presented at The Spitz—a long-standing and iconic music venue in London's Spitalfields which was made to close in 2007 by its landlord—her performances have more frequently been supported by institutions and festivals such as the South London Gallery (London), Southbank Centre (London), ICA (London), Arnolfini (Bristol), Fierce (Birmingham), Nottdance (Nottingham), the National Review of Live Art (Glasgow), and SICK! (Manchester). A retrospective of her work, Panoramix—which I discuss later in this chapter—was featured in the three-day event Live Culture (2003) staged at Tate Modern, a landmark festival marking collaboration between the fields of visual art and performance.
88. Emma Dent Coad, "Artistic Patronage and Enterprise Culture," in *Spanish Cultural Studies: An Introduction: The Struggle for Modernity*, ed. Helen Graham and Jo Labanyi (Oxford: Oxford University Press, 1996), 373–76.
89. José A. Sánchez, "Distinction and Humour," in *La Ribot*, vol. 2, ed. Claire Rousier (Pantin: Centre National de la Danse, 2004), 43.
90. Goran Sergej Pristaš, "'Whispering with Our Bodies': Interview with La Ribot," *Frakcija magazin za izvedbene un jetnosti: Performing arts magazine* 24/25 (2002): 22.
91. Adrian Heathfield, "After the Fall: Dance-Theatre and Dance-Performance," in *Contemporary Theatres in Europe: A Critical Companion*, ed. Joe Kelleher and Nicholas Ridout (Abingdon, UK: Routledge, 2006), 195.
92. La Ribot, quoted in Laurent Goumarre ("Die Another Day," in *La Ribot*, vol. 2, ed. Claire Rousier, 61–62): "'OK. I take the blond wig that I used in my first distinguished piece, 'Muriéndose la sirena.' I take my place here for 'Another Bloody Mary.' I begin by spreading out over the floor all the red things that I have with me, with a lot of caresses, if you can say that: red velvet, a magnificent red that I like very much. I spread out these red things, side by side, on the floor, like this box that contains all sorts of plastic objects, big, small, medium-sized, sand moulds for playing at the beach, a red CD, a theatre programme from Vienna that I'm very fond of, with a cover showing a hammer and lipstick (a parody of communist imagery), my son's Lego, and a toy in the shape of a London telephone box. I'm not sure what these are called, oh yes, rollers for women, for their hair, to give a bit of volume. I like these very much."
93. A controlled descent to the floor, appearing repeatedly in the pieces, constitutes, Laurent Goumarre suggests, a historical critique of the falling female body in classical dance, for whom, as in the case of *Giselle*, to fall means, helplessly, to die. According to Goumarre ("Die Another Day," 68), La Ribot "knows she is breaking a taboo; that she is rewriting history; and if she keeps her posture, it is because she now knows she will not die during the first act."
94. Thanks to Joel Anderson for this observation.
95. In the interview with Pristaš ("Whispering with Our Bodies," 21), La Ribot comments on her work with manuals: "For a long time I've been

creating instructions for the body to dance, to eat . . . Finally I used the instructions for a body to die, to become extinct. I liked it better that way."

96. Josette Féral, foreword, *SubStance* 31, no. 2-3 (2002): 12.

97. Sánchez, "Distinction and Humour," 40.

98. Gerald Siegmund, "Emblems of Absence: La Ribot's *Piezas distinguidas*," in *La Ribot*, vol. 2, ed. Claire Rousier (Pantin: Centre National de la Danse, 2004), 81.

99. La Ribot, "Panoramix," in *Live: Art and Performance*, ed. Adrian Heathfield (London: Tate Publishing, 2004), 30.

100. Adrian Heathfield, "In Memory of Little Things," in *La Ribot*, vol. 2, ed. Claire Rousier (Pantin: Centre National de la Danse, 2004), 26.

101. Lepecki, *Exhausting Dance*, 77.

102. David Harvey, *The Condition of Postmodernity: An Enquiry into the Origins of Cultural Change* (Malden, MA: Blackwell, 1990), 147–72, 240.

103. Christian Marazzi, *Capital and Language: From the New Economy to the War Economy*, trans. Gregory Conti (Los Angeles: Semiotext(e) 2008), 44. Paolo Virno, in "General Intellect," an entry in Zanini and Fadini's *Lessico Postfordista*, defines "general intellect," a concept from Marx's *Grundrisse*: "This is the knowledge objectified in fixed capital and embedded in the automated system of machinery. Marx uses an attractive metaphor to refer to the knowledges that make up the epicentre of social production and preordain all areas of life: general intellect."

104. La Ribot, "Panoramix," 30.

105. Heathfield, "In Memory of Little Things," 25.

106. Pristaš, "Whispering with Our Bodies," 22.

107. Siegmund, "Emblems of Absence," 85.

108. "Manifesto for a European Performance Policy (2002)."

109. John Frow, *Genre* (New York: Routledge, 2006), 10.

110. Paul Ben-Itzak, quoted in Una Bauer, "The Movement of Embodied Thought: The Representational Games of the Stage Zero of Signification in Jérôme Bel," *Performance Research* 13, no. 1 (2008): 35.

111. Pristaš, "Whispering with Our Bodies," 23.

112. La Ribot, "Los cuarentones son más auténticos con sus cuerpos," *El Cultural.es*, October 19, 2006, https://www.laribot.com/work/12.

113. Pristaš, "Whispering with Our Bodies," 22.

114. Heidi Wilson, in "Community Dance in Performance," in *An Introduction to Community Dance Practice*, ed. Diane Amans (Basingstoke, UK: Palgrave Macmillan, 2008), 70: "A community dance performer lacking the cover of perfectly executed technique behind which to hide is more likely to appear as him or herself in performance. Their body becomes the medium and the subject of the dance."

115. Donald Hutera, "Pregnant with Possibilities," *Dance Umbrella News*, Autumn 2005, 3.

116. "La Ribot," in *Panorama Rioarte de Danca Workshops: La Ribot—Pacitti Company—Gary Stevens*, DVD, dir. Nelson Enohata (London: British Council, 2004).

117. La Ribot, "*40 espontáneos*," https://www.laribot.com/work/12.

118. "La Ribot," in *Panorama Rioarte de Dança Workshops.*

119. "La Ribot," in *Panorama Rioarte de Dança Workshops.*

120. La Ribot's subsequent piece, *Laughing Hole* (2006–), redeploys laughter in the context of interrogating the limits and content of speech. In an interview about *Laughing Hole*, La Ribot argues that "[l]aughter is not just funny. It's not something directly related to the comic. It is just a sound and because it's a sound we can understand that it is also a muscle that we have to warm up and treat in the same way that we treat our body. It has flexibility and is affected by cold or warm—it is dynamic and with energy. It's very close to how we work with the body." "On the Concept of Laughter in Laughing Hole: An Interview with La Ribot, Edited by Abi Weaver," *Contemporary Theatre Review* 23, no. 2 (2013): 259.

121. "La Ribot," in *Panorama Rioarte de Dança Workshops.*

122. "La Ribot," in *Panorama Rioarte de Dança Workshops.*

123. *40 espontáneos* rehearsal session, October 26, 2005.

124. Susan Leigh Foster, "Dancing Bodies," in *Meaning in Motion: New Cultural Studies of Dance*, ed. Jane C. Desmond (Durham, NC: Duke University Press, 1997), 236.

125. Foster, "Dancing Bodies," 237.

126. La Ribot, "*40 espontáneos*," https://www.laribot.com/work/12. The full text was available on the website in October 2005; it is now quoted in the production description in brief.

127. Samantha Ellis, "Spontaneous Co-operation: Maria Ribot Takes on Untrained Performers for Her Dance Work about Bullfight Spectators, Reports Samantha Ellis," *What's On in London*, October 26, 2005.

128. Hutera, "Pregnant with Possibilities," 3.

129. Foster, "Dancing Bodies," 253–55.

130. Artsadmin Events, "La Ribot Comes to Greenwich," received via e-mail September 27, 2005.

131. New Moves, http://www.newmoves.co.uk/PageAccess.aspx?id=345.

132. Dance4, "Exciting Opportunity to Perform at Nottdance06," publicity flyer.

133. Martin Hargreaves, "Laughing, Crying, Contagion, Collapse," *Dance Theatre Journal* 20, no. 2 (2004): 35.

134. Historic England, "Meridian House (Former Greenwich Town Hall)," http://list.historicengland.org.uk/resultsingle.aspx?uid=1213855.

135. Greenwich Dance Agency, promotional DVD.

136. Interview, Brendan Keaney, gDA, April 2006.

137. Tramway, "Tramway—A History," http://www.tramway.org/Pages/Tramway---A-History.aspx.

138. Nottingham City Council, "Development of Sandfield Centre, Sandfield Road, Nottingham," 2012, http://open.nottinghamcity.gov.uk/comm/download3.asp?dltype=inline&filename=52591/sandfieldreport.pdf).

139. Hargreaves, "Laughing, Crying, Contagion, Collapse," 33.

140. Another passage on La Ribot's website in 2006: "A new role has come up in the last performances, the 'stowaway,' who has joined the spontaneous and who jumps onto the stage halfway through the performance as if he/she were a real spontaneous, bringing us back again to the first and most

important question of the piece. The spectator. The spectator and his/her role as such, a creator and an interpreter."

141. La Ribot, http://www.laribot.com.

142. Ramsay Burt, "Preferring to Laugh," *Parallax* 14, no. 1 (2008): 16.

143. Interview with Nicky Childs, Artsadmin, July 2006. In response to some questions about the piece via e-mail, Nicky Molloy of Dance4 reflected that "it is actually quite hard to get people with no experience involved in something like this (would have been easy to get someone already interested in performing to do it)."

144. Grace Mahoney, "Art Changes Lives," *New Moves*, http:/www.newmoves.co.uk/PageAccess.aspx?id=36.

145. *40 espontáneos* e-mail questionnaire, May 2006.

146. *40 espontáneos* e-mail questionnaire, May 2006.

147. Siobhan Davies Studios, "New Dance and the Visual Arts."

148. Heathfield, "In Memory of Little Things," 26.

149. O'Malley, *Risk, Uncertainty, and Government*, 60.

150. Bojana Cvejić, "Collectivity? You Mean Collaboration," Transversal Texts, January 2005, https://transversal.at/transversal/1204/cvejic/en.

151. Cvejić, "Collectivity? You Mean Collaboration."

152. O'Malley, *Risk, Uncertainty, and Government*, 60.

153. Alan Ackerman and Martin Puchner, "Introduction: Modernism and Anti-Theatricality," in *Against Theatre: Creative Destructions on the Modernist Stage*, ed. Alan Ackerman and Martin Puchner (New York: Palgrave, 2006), 12.

154. Lepecki, *Exhausting Dance*, 77.

155. "Manifesto for a European Performance Policy (2002)."

156. O'Malley, *Risk, Uncertainty, and Government*, 57.

157. Cvejić, "Collectivity? You Mean Collaboration."

158. Yúdice, *The Expediency of Culture*.

159. Hall, "New Labour's Double Shuffle," 19.

Chapter 2

1. Hall, "New Labour's Double Shuffle," 19.

2. Ian Aitch, "Culture: Plagues of Frogs and Lice . . . and Artists, including Antony Gormley and Rufus Wainwright, Have Descended on Margate. Ian Aitch on a Huge Project That's Transforming the Town," *The Guardian*, September 26, 2006.

3. House of Commons Communities and Local Government Committee, *Coastal Towns: Second Report of Session 2006–07* (London: Stationery Office, 2007), 3, https://publications.parliament.uk/pa/cm200607/cmselect/cmcomloc/351/351.pdf; Richard Samuel, "Thanet," in *Coastal Regeneration in English Resorts—2010*, ed. John Walton and Patrick Browne (Waterside South, UK: Coastal Communities Alliance, 2010), 82–83, https://www.coastalcommunities.co.uk/wp-content/uploads/2015/07/coastal-regeneration-handbook.pdf.

4. Shared Intelligence, "Margate Renewal Study," 2008, 18–23, https://democracy.kent.gov.uk/documents/s6101/Item%209%20App%202Thanet Shared%20Intelligence%20Report.pdf.

5. Nadine El-Enany, *(B)ordering Britain: Law, Race, and Empire* (Manchester: Manchester University Press, 2020), 187–88.

6. Aitch, "Culture: Plagues of Frogs and Lice."

7. *The Margate Exodus*, http://www.themargateexodus.org.uk/about.html.

8. Sandra Haurant, "Average House Price Breaks £200,000 Barrier," *The Guardian*, November 8, 2006.

9. Ruth Guilding, "Unforgettable Fire," *The Spectator*, October 7, 2006, 56.

10. Guilding, "Unforgettable Fire," 56.

11. Guilding, "Unforgettable Fire," 56.

12. Guilding, "Unforgettable Fire," 56.

13. I use "culture-in-regeneration" as a catch-all term here. Graeme Evans and Phyllida Shaw's research report, *The Contribution of Culture to Regeneration in the UK: A Review of Evidence* (London: Department for Culture, Media, and Sport, 2004), identifies three models: "culture-led regeneration' (exemplified by stand-alone capital projects such as the Tate Modern in London and the Lowry Centre in Salford), "cultural regeneration" (cultural provisions well integrated into local planning), and "culture and regeneration" (culture as an "add-on') (5). *The Margate Exodus* represents a mix of the second and third models.

14. Guiding, "Unforgettable Fire," 56.

15. Department for Culture, Media, and Sport, *Culture at the Heart of Regeneration* (London: Department for Culture, Media, and Sport, 2004), 32.

16. Steven Miles and Ronan Paddison, "The Rise and Rise of Culture-led Urban Regeneration," *Urban Studies* 42, no. 5-6 (2005): 836.

17. Department for Culture, Media, and Sport, *Culture at the Heart of Regeneration*, 21, 3. Like many other local authorities and agencies, the Thanet District Council, the Kent County Council, and SEEDA (South East England Development Agency) developed cultural strategies for the areas they oversaw. For Thanet, culture represented a means to attract visitors to the area and to rejuvenate Margate's Old Town, in concert with other economic activity. See Kent County Council, "Regeneration of East Kent Coastal Towns: A Review by a Select Committee Appointed by the Strategic Planning Policy Overview Committee," August 2004; and New Economics Foundation, "Coasting Along: A Study of Business Impacts and Regeneration in South East Coastal Towns: A Report from NEF (the New Economics Foundation) for the South East Enterprise Development Agency (SEEDA)," August 2005.

18. Department for Culture, Media, and Sport, *Culture at the Heart of Regeneration*, 9.

19. Clare Worley, "'It's Not about Race. It's about the Community': New Labour and 'Community Cohesion," *Critical Social Policy* 25, no. 4 (2005): 483. See also Nasar Meer and Tariq Modood, "The Multicultural State We're In: Muslims, 'Multiculture,' and the 'Civic Re-balancing' of British Multiculturalism," *Political Studies* 57 (2009): 473–97.

20. Worley, "'It's Not about Race. It's about the Community," 489, 491.

21. Worley, "'It's Not about Race. It's about the Community," 489.

22. Sophie Nield, "Siting the People: Power, Protest, and Public Space," in *Performing Site-Specific Theatre: Politics, Place, Practice*, ed. Anna Birch and Joanne Tompkins (Basingstoke, UK: Palgrave Macmillan, 2012), 232.

23. Miwon Kwon, *One Place after Another: Site-Specific Art and Locational Identity* (Cambridge, MA: MIT Press, 2004), 2.

24. Kwon, *One Place after Another*, 3.

25. A. A. Gill, "Something Biblical for the Weekend? As Margate Prepares for a Plague of Frogs and Lice, A. A. Gill Asks: Can They Be Serious?" *Sunday Times: Culture*, August 27, 2006, 7.

26. Department for Culture, Media, and Sport, *Culture at the Heart of Regeneration*, 21.

27. John Urry, *The Tourist Gaze*, 2nd ed. (London, Thousand Oaks, and New Delhi: Sage Publications, 2002), 142.

28. El-Enany, *(B)ordering Britain*, 150.

29. Gill, "Something Biblical for the Weekend?" 6.

30. Gill, "Something Biblical for the Weekend?" 6.

31. Gill, "Something Biblical for the Weekend?" 6.

32. Alice Jones, "Arts: Behind Closed Doors: Installation: Gregor Schneider's Mysterious Terrace-Based Project Is Set to Intrigue," *The Independent*, September 21, 2004, 18.

33. Nigel Barker, Allan Brodie, Nick Dermott, Lucy Jessop, and Gary Winter, *Margate's Seaside Heritage* (Swindon, UK: English Heritage, 2007), 12, https://historicengland.org.uk/images-books/publications/margates-seaside-heritage/margates-seaside-heritage/.

34. Barker et al, *Margate's Seaside Heritage*, 12; "India House: A Short History, Compiled by Ian Priston, Boys & Maughan Solicitors, September 2017." https://www.margatelocalhistory.co.uk/Articles/India%20House%20by%20Ian%20Priston.pdf; R. C. Osborne, The Margate Guide; Or, Isle of Thanet Directory (1835), https://www.google.co.uk/books/edition/The_Margate_Guide_Or_Isle_of_Thanet_Dire/rqhYAAAAcAAJ?hl. According to "India House: A Short History," the last owner of India House before its acquisition by Boys & Maughan Solicitors in 1920 was music hall actress and Gaiety Girl Phyllis Broughton, who had requested Lt. General Coote Synge-Hutchinson to buy the property for her as a trustee. The document notes that "as a Major in the Second Dragoon Guards, Coote Synge-Hutchinson was awarded the Indian Mutiny Medal, with Lucknow clasp, for his service with the 2nd Dragoon Guards at the Siege of Lucknow during the Indian Rebellion of 1857." R. C. Osborne's 1835 text notes that the proprietors of the town's bank "Messrs. Cobb & Son are also Agents to Lloyd's and the East India Company, and French, Dutch and American Consuls" (21).

35. Barker et al., *Margate's Seaside Heritage*, 1; Edward Royle, *Modern Britain: A Social History, 1750–1985* (London: Edward Arnold, 1987), 247; John K. Walton, *The English Seaside Resort: A Social History, 1750–1914* (Leicester, UK: Leicester University Press, 1983), 162–63.

36. See, for example, Andy Hewitt, "Privatizing the Public: Three Rhetorics of Art's Public Good in 'Third Way' Cultural Policy," *Art and the Public Sphere* 1, no. 1 (2011): 32: "Such forms of cultural policy represent a liberal tradition in the arts, which promotes reforms aimed to help the working classes but also to improve them. This follows a Victorian logic that Tony Bennett has analysed in his book *Culture: A Reformer's Science*, in which art is enlisted to 'govern at a distance' by creating frameworks in which individuals

will voluntarily regulate their own behaviour to achieve specific social ends rather than needing to be subjected to forced direction."

37. Gill, "Something Biblical for the Weekend?" 6.

38. Artangel, "About Artangel," http://www.artangel.org.uk/about_us. This text has since changed, and now reads as follows: "Artangel has always gone where others fear to tread. We collaborate with artists who defy boundaries to give form to extraordinary ideas. The art we produce boldly responds to the environment in which we live. It's often unlike anything you have experienced before."

39. See Maeve Connolly's 2013 examination of Artangel's history, "Artangel and the Changing Mediascape of Public Art," *Journal of Curatorial Studies* 2, no. 2 (2013): 196–217, which reviews the 2011 media commentary marking twenty years of Lingwood and Morris's stewardship of the organization.

40. Robert Hewison, "Light in the Darkness," *The Times*, October 18, 1992.

41. Malcolm Miles, "Community Murals in Britain," in *Art for Public Places: Critical Essays*, ed. Malcolm Miles (Winchester, UK: Winchester School of Art Press, 1989), 76.

42. Connolly, "Artangel and the Changing Mediascape of Public Art," 200.

43. For example, the TSWA Four Cities Project (1990) in Derry, Glasgow, Newcastle, and Plymouth. Regarding the project's intervention in Glasgow, the artist Cedric Tai writes ("The 1990 TSWA Four Cities Projects in Glasgow and the Proposals That Never Materialised," April 17, 2013): "This effort took place between the Glasgow Garden Festival and the City of Culture designation at a time where public art was being solicited to bring more attention to the city, but also being critiqued as needing to stake out its own advancement beyond community art or activist art."

44. "A Conversation between Michael Craig-Martin, Lisa Jardine, James Lingwood, and Michael Morris," in *Off Limits: 40 Artangel Projects*, ed. Gerrie van Noord (London: Merrell, 2002), 10.

45. Cultural Industry, "Cultural Industry," http://www.culturalindustry.co.uk/pages/cultural_industry.html.

46. Michael Church, "The Rise of a Quiet Achiever: Arts Interview: Michael Morris: A Softly Spoken Impresario, He Once Proclaimed the Death of 'Literary Theatre.' Michael Church Talks to a Prime Mover in the Jungle of Avant-Garde Culture," *Financial Times*, November 2, 2002, 6.

47. "Artangel," Artangel brochure (London: Artangel, 2006), 1.

48. "Michael Morris: From a Conversation with Brian Eno in January 2007," in *The Producers: Alchemists of the Impossible*, ed. Kate Tyndall (London: Arts Council England and Jerwood Charitable Foundation, 2007), 62.

49. Michael Ratcliffe, "The Magus of Clink Street: Adored Abroad but Hardly Known Here: Robert Wilson Is Plotting His First Major British Show, writes Michael Ratcliffe," *The Observer*, September 3, 1995, 11.

50. Melanie Counsell, "Coronet Cinema," Artangel, https://www.artangel.org.uk/project/coronet-cinema/.

51. Artangel, "Seizure," https://www.artangel.org.uk/project/seizure/.

52. "A Conversation between Michael Craig-Martin, Lisa Jardine, James Lingwood, and Michael Morris," 15. Particularly relevant to this discussion are the artist-curated response to New Labour's delivery of social policy

through the mechanisms of cultural policy; see Mary Warnock and Mark Wallinger, *Art for All? Their Policies and Our Culture* (London: Peer, 2000); and the special edition "Inclusion Under Pressure" of the *Engage Review: Promoting Greater Understanding and Enjoyment of the Visual Arts*, Winter 2001, 1–72. For a reading of the National Gallery's acquisition of Raphael's *Madonna of the Pinks* and its justification of the £22 million expenditure in terms of "public benefit," see Helen Rees Leahy, "New Labour, Old Masters," *Cultural Studies*, 4-5 (2007): 695–717.

53. "A conversation between Michael Craig-Martin, Lisa Jardine, James Lingwood, and Michael Morris," 12.

54. James Lingwood, introduction to *Rachel Whiteread: House*, ed. James Lingwood (London: Phaidon, 1995), 7; James Lingwood, "Our House Is a Very Nice House," *The Times*, November 27, 1993.

55. "Letter: Timetable for Bow Sculpture: From Cllr. Eric Flounders," *The Independent*, November 25, 1993.

56. "Letter: Private Prejudice, Public Interest, and Bow's *House*: From Mr. James Lingwood," *The Independent*, November 30, 1993.

57. Patrick Wright, "In Your Space: They're Big. You've Paid for Them. And They're Meant to Make You Feel Better. But Ever Since the Sixties, Britain's Public Art Developments Have Caused More Aggro Than Uplift," *The Guardian*, August 25, 1995, 2.

58. Wright, "In Your Space," 2.

59. Richard Cork, *Breaking Down the Barriers: Art in the 1990s* (New Haven, CT: Yale University Press, 2003), 50.

60. Wright, "In Your Space," 2.

61. Peter Lennon, "Home Truths from a Street Fighter: Tower Hamlets Council Leader, Who Is Nearly Always in the Line of Fire, Talks to Peter Lennon," *The Guardian*, December 4, 1993.

62. Malcolm Miles, *Art, Space, and the City: Public Art and Urban Futures* (London: Routledge, 1997), 206. A bigger image can be found on p. 149 featuring a placard reading "HOME IS WHERE THE HEART IS | IF WE LOSE OUR HOMES WE LOSE OUR HEARTS."

63. Doreen Massey, "Space-Time and the Politics of Location," in *Architecturally Speaking: Practices of Art, Architecture, and the Everyday*, ed. Alan Read (London: Routledge, 2000), 59.

64. Massey, "Space-Time," 59, 57.

65. Massey, "Space-Time," 60.

66. Massey, "Space-Time," 57.

67. Smith, *Contingencies of Value*, 126.

68. Lingwood, "Our House Is a Very Nice House."

69. Lingwood, introduction to Rachel Whiteread: House, 8.

70. Kwon, *One Place after Another*, 79–80.

71. "Lesley Greene, James Lingwood, Declan McGonagle, Malcolm Miles, chaired by Mel Gooding," in *TSWA Four Cities Project: New Works for Different Places*, ed. James Lingwood (Plymouth, UK: TSWA, 1990), 152.

72. Justin Lewis, *Art, Culture, and Enterprise: The Politics of Art and the Cultural Industries* (London: Routledge, 1990), 112.

73. Miles, "Community Murals in Britain," 70.

74. For Walls with Tongues, "Free Form—Martin Goodrich," https://www.forwallswithtongues.org.uk/artists/free-form-martin-goodrich/.

75. "Lesley Greene, James Lingwood, Declan McGonagle, Malcolm Miles," 152.

76. "Lesley Greene, James Lingwood, Declan McGonagle, Malcolm Miles," 152.

77. "Cable Street Mural—a Continuing Story—30 Years in the Making," *AND Journal*, October 20, 2011, http://www.and.org.uk/2011/10/cable-street-mural-a-continuing-story-30-years-in-the-making/.

78. David Rosenberg, "'An Antidote to the Far Right's Poison'—the Battle for Cable Street's Mural," *The Guardian*, September 21, 2016; Simon Demissie and Vicky Iglikowski-Broad, "'No Pasarán': The Battle of Cable Street," *The National Archives*, October 4, 2016, https://blog.nationalarchives.gov.uk/no-pasaran-battle-cable-street/.

79. London Mural Preservation Society, "The Battle of Cable Street," http://londonmuralpreservationsociety.com/murals/battle-cable-street/, "Cable Street Mural—a Continuing Story—30 Years in the Making."

80. London Mural Preservation Society, "The Battle of Cable Street"; Miles, "Community Murals in Britain," 72; Rosenberg, "An Antidote to the Far Right's Poison."

81. Rosenberg, "An Antidote to the Far Right's Poison."

82. London Mural Preservation Society, "The Battle of Cable Street."

83. "Lesley Greene, James Lingwood, Declan McGonagle, Malcolm Miles," 152; Sara Selwood, *The Benefits of Public Art: The Polemics of Permanent Art in Public Places* (London: Policy Studies Institute, 1995), 37–38.

84. Arts Council of Great Britain, *An Urban Renaissance: The Role of the Arts in Urban Regeneration: The Case for Increased Public and Private Sector Co-operation* (1988). Cited in Keith D. Peacock, *Thatcher's Theatre: British Theatre and Drama in the 1980s* (Westport, CT: Greenwood, 1999), 54.

85. Selwood, *The Benefits of Public Art*, 37.

86. Selwood, *The Benefits of Public Art*, 37.

87. "A Conversation between Michael Craig-Martin, Lisa Jardine, James Lingwood, and Michael Morris," 10, 19. For an account of Glasgow City of Culture and a developing cultural policy of economic enterprise, see Matthew Reason, "Glasgow's Year of Culture and Discourses of Cultural Policy on the Cusp of Globalisation," *Contemporary Theatre Review* 16, no. 1 (2006): 73–85.

88. "Michael Morris: From a Conversation with Brian Eno in January 2007," 58.

89. Michael Hardt and Antonio Negri, *Empire* (Cambridge, MA: Harvard University Press, 2000), 293.

90. Lewis, *Art, Culture, and Enterprise*, 115.

91. Owen Kelly, "In Search of Cultural Democracy," *Arts Express*, October 1985, https://jubileeartsarchive.com/wp-content/uploads/2015/03/In-Search-of-Cultural-Democracy.pdf.

92. "A Conversation between Michael Craig-Martin, Lisa Jardine, James Lingwood, and Michael Morris," 13.

93. In "'Art and Social Context': Its Background, Inception, and Development" (2010), Chris Crickmay, the leader of the Art and Social Context program

at the Dartington College of Arts (1978–91), suggests Joseph Beuys as an important influence in the development of community arts practices in Britain.

94. Hewison, "Light in the Darkness."

95. "A Conversation between Michael Craig-Martin, Lisa Jardine, James Lingwood, and Michael Morris," 11.

96. Claire Bishop, "'As If I Was Lost and Someone Suddenly Came to Give Me News about Myself,'" in *Off Limits: 40 Artangel Projects*, ed. Gerrie van Noord (London: Merrell, 2002), 22.

97. "A Conversation between Michael Craig-Martin, Lisa Jardine, James Lingwood, and Michael Morris," 11.

98. Bishop, "As If I Was Lost," 26, 25. The *London A-Z* is a pocketbook map of London, once invaluable for navigating its complex streets, but now superseded by smartphone apps.

99. Paul Pfeiffer, *The Saints* program, 2007, 2.

100. Pfeiffer, The Saints program.

101. Wiebke Gronemeyer, "October 2007: Paul Pfeiffer, *The Saints*," *Whitehot Magazine*, October 2007, https://whitehotmagazine.com/index.php?action=articles&wh_article_id=959.

102. Bishop, "As If I Was Lost," 27.

103. Neil Smith, "Gentrification and Uneven Development," *Economic Geography* 58, no. 2 (1982): 139–40.

104. "A Conversation between Michael Craig-Martin, Lisa Jardine, James Lingwood, and Michael Morris," 10.

105. Feargus O'Sullivan, "The Pernicious Realities of 'Artwashing,'" CityLab, June 24, 2014, http://www.citylab.com/housing/2014/06/the-pernicious-realities-of-artwashing/373289/; David Harvey, "The 'New' Imperialism: Accumulation by Dispossession," *Socialist Register* (2004): 63–87. In October 2014, *The Guardian* reported on protests outside the Mipim investor conference in west London's Olympia (Oliver Wainwright, "Protests Disrupt Property Fair in London," *The Guardian*, October 15, 2014): "the international property fair has gained a reputation among its critics as a champagne-soaked jamboree where local authority chiefs are wined and dined by investors. Staged in Cannes for the past 25 years, it is being held in the UK for the first time this year, where it is projected to attract 4,000 delegates."

106. Anna Krausova, "Elephant and Castle: Mapping (Super-)Diversity in the 2011 UK Census," Centre on Migration, Policy and Society, working paper no. 142, University of Oxford, 2018, 27, https://www.compas.ox.ac.uk/wp-content/uploads/WP-2018-142-Krausova_Elephant-and-Castle-2.pdf.

107. "Southwark Notes: Whose Regeneration? | Heygate Estate," https://southwarknotes.wordpress.com/heygate-estate/.

108. Peter Walker, "Heygate Pyramid: London Estate's Evicted Residents Damn Art Plan," *The Guardian*, December 12, 2013.

109. Alberto Duman, "Not Here, Right Now / Right Here, Not Now: Unfolding the Context in Alana Jelinek's *This Is Not Art*," *Journal of Visual Art Practice* 13, no. 3 (2014): 214.

110. Duman, "Not Here, Right Now," 214. Artangel commissioned Richard Wentworth's *An Area of Outstanding Unnatural Beauty* (2002), a response to London's gentrifying King's Cross district.

111. Gregory Sholette, "Mysteries of the Creative Class; or, I Have Seen the Enemy and They Is Us," *MUTE*29: The Precarious Issue* (2005): 2–3, http://www.gregorysholette.com/wp-content/uploads/2011/04/03_mysteries1.pdf.

112. Sholette, "Mysteries of the Creative Class."

113. Sholette, "Mysteries of the Creative Class."

114. Duman, "Not Here, Right Now," 214.

115. John K. Walton, *The British Seaside: Holidays and Resorts in the Twentieth Century* (Manchester: Manchester University Press, 2000), 143.

116. Walton, *The British Seaside*, 4.

117. Walton, *The British Seaside*, 5.

118. See Richard Clements's *Margate* (2009), John Clancey's *Kent's Seaside Resorts through Time* (2012), and Anthony Lane's *Isle of Thanet through Time* (2013)—local history texts which consist of archival images, some repeated across the texts, with short historical glosses.

119. Barker et al., *Margate's Seaside Heritage*, 31–34.

120. James Walvin, *Beside the Seaside: A Social History of the Popular Seaside Holiday* (London: Allen Lane, 1978), 164; James Walvin, *Leisure and Society: 1830–1950* (London: Longman, 1978), 70–82.

121. Quoted in Walvin, *Beside the Seaside*, 48.

122. Stephen V. Ward, *Selling Places: The Marketing and Promotion of Towns and Cities, 1850–2000* (Abingdon, UK: Spon, 1998), 31–32, 51.

123. "A Date with the Sun (1965)," https://www.youtube.com/watch?v=SCc0RP6n37w; "All Go Margate (1970)," https://www.youtube.com/watch?v=TSgGHh6zap0.

124. Walton, *The British Seaside*, 3.

125. John Walton, introduction to *Coastal Regeneration in English Resorts—2010*, ed. John Walton and Patrick Browne (Waterside South, UK: Coastal Communities Alliance, 2010), 2, https://www.coastalcommunities.co.uk/wp-content/uploads/2015/07/coastal-regeneration-handbook.pdf.

126. Turner Contemporary, "About | Who We Are," https://turnercontemporary.org/about/.

127. From the beginnings of its gradual closure in the early 2000s, Dreamland represented an important focus of struggle over the future of tourism in Margate. A locally organized campaign to save Dreamland was launched in 2003. In 2009, the campaign successfully negotiated a grant of £3.7 million from the government's Sea Change fund for the site's redevelopment as a heritage visitor attraction, and this was consolidated in 2011 by the upgrading of the Scenic Railway from Grade II to Grade II* status, a category for "particularly important buildings of more than special interest" (Historic England). For documentation of the Save Dreamland campaign, see Joylandbooks.com, "Save Dreamland," https://www.joylandbooks.com/scenicrailway/.

128. *The Margate Exodus*, http://www.themargateexodus.org.uk/about.html.

129. El-Enany, *(B)ordering Britain*, 15.

130. El-Enany, *(B)ordering Britain*, 38, 11.

131. For overviews of the transformations of Britain's immigration and asylum policy in the 1990s and 2000s, see Will Somerville, *Immigration under New Labour* (Bristol, UK: Policy, 2007), 1–26; and David J. Whittaker,

Asylum Seekers and Refugees in the Contemporary World (London: Routledge, 2006), 28–41.

132. El-Enany, *(B)ordering Britain*, 143.

133. Indeed, El-Enany reminds us that the compensation scheme for British slave-owners devised in 1835 was the "largest state-sponsored pay-out in British history until it was superseded by the bank bailouts of 2008" (*(B)ordering Britain*, 143), with payments supported by taxation concluding only in 2015 (Kris Manjapra, "When Will Britain Face Up to Its Crimes against Humanity?" *The Guardian*, March 29, 2018).

134. Dover Express, quoted in Vaughan Robinson, Roger Andersson, and Sako Musterd, *Spreading the Burden? A Review of Policies to Disperse Asylum Seekers and Refugees* (Bristol, UK: Policy, 2003), 16.

135. "Would You Know How to Identify a Refugee? Starting Today: Asylum Seekers in Thanet—The Reality and the Myths," *Isle of Thanet Gazette*, April 21, 2000.

136. Mark Bowness, "Our Heritage Is Crumbling," *The Sun*, August 19, 2003, 8.

137. Rosemary Sales, "The Deserving and the Undeserving? Refugees, Asylum Seekers, and Welfare in Britain," *Critical Social Policy* 22, no. 3 (2002): 456.

138. Aitch, "Culture: Plagues of Frogs and Lice."

139. Creative Partnerships, "About CP," http://www.creative-partnerships.com/aboutcp/.

140. Anna Cutler, "Towards a Promised Land," in *Art of Negotiation*, ed. David Butler and Vivienne Reiss (London: Cornerhouse, 2007), 196.

141. Cutler, "Towards a Promised Land," 197.

142. In *The Art of Record: A Critical Introduction to Documentary* (Manchester: Manchester University Press, 1996), 139–54, see John Corner's discussion of Woolcock's controversial film *When the Dog Bites* (1988), her account of de-industrialization in Consett, County Durham, for an analysis of the political consequences of her application of fictional tropes and frames to "real life" events.

143. Michael Morris, prologue to *Towards a Promised Land*, ed. Louise Neri (Göttingen: Steidl, 2006), 16.

144. Katherine Hyde, "Portraits and Collaborations: A Reflection on the Work of Wendy Ewald," *Visual Studies* 20, no. 2 (2005): 172–90.

145. Thanks to Steve Farrier for drawing attention to this similarity. A. A. Gill ("Something Biblical for the Weekend?" 6) comments: "These pictures have echoes of school portraits, the New Deal photographs of the American Depression and Benetton posters," in an implicit reference to Lange's works.

146. To view the images, see Artangel, "Towards a Promised Land," https://www.artangel.org.uk/project/towards-a-promised-land/.

147. Wendy Ewald and Michael Morris, "Towards a Promised Land," in *Towards a Promised Land*, ed. Louise Neri (Göttingen: Steidl, 2006), 144.

148. Cutler, "Towards a Promised Land," 215.

149. Cutler, "Towards a Promised Land," 215–17.

150. Caroline Blunt, in "Neither Last Resort nor Promised Land," *Street Signs* (Autumn 2006), 28–29, writes: "As much as these acts may trigger a

variety of responses of disgust, sympathy, surprise or lack of it, it does not seem to me that the destruction and defacing of children's pictures are acceptable casualties in a process of changing minds and raising consciousness."

151. Cutler, "Towards a Promised Land," 217. The project also staged an audio walk around the town, featuring spoken recordings of the young people's reflections, and two exhibitions—one at the Outfitters' Gallery in 2005, and the second at the Margate Library in 2006, which featured Woolcock's portraits and the young people's own work.

152. Paul Gilroy, *After Empire: Melancholia or Convivial Culture?* (Abingdon, UK: Routledge, 2004), 97.

153. Gilroy, *After Empire*, 116.

154. Films shot in Margate include *The Last Resort* (2000), Pawel Pawlikowski's documentary-style, partially improvised feature about immigration and asylum; and *Gypo* (2005), a Dogme 95 project starring Paul McGann. In "Good Intentions, High Hopes, and Low Budgets: Contemporary Social Realist Film-Making in Britain," *New Cinemas: Journal of Contemporary Film* 5, no. 3 (2007): 240, Samantha Lay advances the view that "in contemporary social realist film-making the seaside towns of England, long abandoned by the tourists, have become the new symbolic locations of the nation's fragmentation and decay."

155. "The Making of Exodus," DVD, dir. Andrew Palmer, 2007, in *Exodus*, DVD, dir. Penny Woolcock, Soda Pictures, 2007.

156. *Exodus*, DVD, dir. Penny Woolcock, Soda Pictures, 2007.

157. *Exodus*, DVD.

158. Jon Savage, "Two Tribes Go to War," *BBC: Culture*, October 21, 2014, https://www.bbc.com/culture/article/20140515-when-two-tribes-went-to-war.

159. Iain Aitch, "Exodus Fires Up the Imagination of Thousands," *Isle of Thanet Gazette*, October 6, 2006.

160. Lingwood, introduction to Rachel Whiteread: House, 8.

161. "Vogue Loves," *Vogue*, September 2006, 122; Michael White, "Reveling in a Wrathful Exodus, Plagues and All," *New York Times: The Arts*, October 2, 2006.

162. Georgina Cotton, "Previews: The Promised Land beside the Seaside: Film 'The Margate Exodus,'" *The Independent*, September 25, 2006.

163. Aitch, "Culture: Plagues of Frogs and Lice."

164. Chris Denham, "Margate Exodus Is More Than a Great Arts Event," *Thanet Extra*, September 15, 2006.

165. TurneroundMargate.com, "The Lasting Legacy of Exodus," March 22, 2007, http://www.turneroundmargate.com/the-lasting-legacy-of-exodus/. The *TurneroundMargate* website is now defunct; see http://margateneverruns.com/about, accessed April 2022.

166. "Your Chance to Be a Star," *Isle of Thanet Gazette*, June 9, 2006; Kathy Bailes, "Be a Star in Movie of Town," *Isle of Thanet Gazette*, May 12, 2006; "Chance for All to Shine with Film Project," *Isle of Thanet Gazette*, June 16, 2006; "Your Invitation to Create an Art Legend," *Isle of Thanet Gazette*, August 11, 2006.

167. David Chater, "TV Choice," *The Times: The Knowledge*, December 2, 2006.

168. Anthony Gormley, "Waste Man, 2006," https://www.antonygormley.com/projects/item-view/id/260#p0.

169. Michael Balfour, "Refugee Performance: Encounters with Alterity," *Journal of Arts and Communities* 2, no. 3 (2010): 186.

170. Madeleine Bunting, "Culture, Not Politics, Is Now the Heart of Our Public Realm: The Cynics Who Ridiculed Margate's Exodus Day Miss the Point: Art Has Broken Its Elitist Leash to Inspire Collective Purpose," *The Guardian*, October 3, 2006, 30.

171. Lyn Gardner, "The Margate Exodus," *The Guardian: Guide*, September 30, 2006.

172. Eve Light Honthaner, *The Complete Film Production Handbook*, 4th edition (Oxford: Focal Press, 2010 [1993]), 274.

173. "The Making of Exodus," DVD.

174. Maddy Costa, "Reviews: Film Sets and Reality Blur into One as Margate Takes Starring Role," *The Guardian*, October 2, 2006.

175. Costa, "Reviews: Film Sets and Reality Blur."

176. Nield, "Siting the People," 223.

177. Michael Morris, "G2: Yes, but . . . : Michael Morris, Co-director of Artangel," *The Guardian*, October 11, 2006, 21.

178. Artangel, "Exodus Venice," received via e-mail September 1, 2007.

179. "Michael Morris: From a Conversation with Brian Eno in January 2007," 59.

180. Nicholas Garnham, "Afterword: The Cultural Commodity and Cultural Policy," in *The UK Cultural Sector: Profile and Policy Issues*, ed. Sara Selwood (London: Policy Studies Institute, 2001), 450.

181. Artangel, "Jeremy Deller, The English Civil War: Part II (2002)," http://www.artangel.org.uk//projects/2001/the_battle_of_orgreave/background/the_english_civil_war_part_ii.

182. Jeremy Deller, "The Battle of Orgreave," https://www.jeremydeller.org/TheBattleOfOrgreave/TheBattleOfOrgreave_Video.php.

183. Morris, "G2: Yes, but, . . . : Michael Morris, Co-director of Artangel."

184. Lennon, "Home Truths from a Street Fighter."

185. Aitch, "Exodus Fires Up Imagination of Thousands."

186. Morris, "G2: Yes, but, . . . : Michael Morris, Co-director of Artangel," 21.

187. Cameron, "Geographies of Welfare and Exclusion: Social Inclusion and Exception," 397.

188. Cameron, "Geographies of Welfare and Exclusion: Social Inclusion and Exception," 401.

189. "Campaigners Plan to Exploit Margate Movie," *Kent News*, September 29, 2006.

190. Thomas Piketty, *Capital in the Twenty First Century*, trans. Arthur Goldhammer (Cambridge, MA: Belknap Press of Harvard University Press 2014), 20.

191. Tracy C. Davis's essay "Theatricality and Civil Society," in *Theatricality*, ed. Tracy Davis and Thomas Postlethwaite (Cambridge: Cambridge University Press, 2003), examines "theatricality" as a historical problematic connected to the public sphere as a construct. The alternative definition she formulates for

the *Oxford English Dictionary* aptly characterizes the representational effect I describe here: "Theatricality: n. A spectator's dédoublement resulting from a sympathetic breach (active dissociation, alienation, self-reflexivity) effecting a critical stance toward an episode in the public sphere, including but not limited to the theatre" (Davis, "Theatricality and Civil Society," 145).

Chapter 3

1. Jamie Peck and Nik Theodore, "Still Neoliberalism?" *South Atlantic Quarterly* 118, no. 2 (2019): 259.

2. The British and Brazilian political cultures and models of citizenship have markedly different histories. Leslie Bethell's detailed review of Brazil's governmental history from the nineteenth century on, "Politics in Brazil: From Elections without Democracy to Democracy without Citizenship," in *Brazil since 1985: Politics, Economy and Society*, ed. Maria D'Alva Kinzo and James Dunkerley (London: Institute of Latin American Studies, 2003), 21–41, encompasses the abolition of slavery, the provision of access to the franchise, Brazil's twentieth-century dictatorships, and the institutions and practices of citizenship, which, he argues, have been underscored by "the personalism and authoritarianism deeply rooted in the country's political culture" (30). In "An Ugly Democracy? State Violence and the Rule of Law in Postauthoritarian Brazil," in *Democratic Brazil: Actors, Institutions, and Processes*, ed. Peter R. Kingstone and Timothy J. Power (Pittsburgh, PA: University of Pittsburgh Press, 2000), 217–35, Anthony W. Pereira discusses the uses of state violence in Brazil in the post-dictatorship period of the late twentieth century, arguing that "much of it has targeted the poor, the socially marginal and the non-white, from whose ranks the 'criminally suspect' are disproportionately drawn" (218). For a historicization of the appropriation of "citizenship" as a value by criminal drug gangs in Brazil, see James Holston, "Dangerous Spaces of Citizenship: Gang Talk, Rights Talk, and Rule of Law in Brazil," Working Paper 21: Centre for Latin American Studies, University of California, Berkeley, August 2008, 1–23.

3. Cameron and Palan, *The Imagined Economies of Globalization*, 147.

4. Cameron, "Geographies of Welfare and Exclusion: Social Inclusion and Exception," 403.

5. Cameron and Palan, *The Imagined Economies of Globalization*, 158.

6. Patrick Neate and Damian Platt, *Culture Is Our Weapon: Making Music and Changing Lives in Rio de Janeiro* (London: Penguin, 2010).

7. Augusto Boal, *The Rainbow of Desire: The Boal Method of Theatre and Therapy* (London: Routledge, 1995), 43.

8. Warren Linds, "Metaxis: Dancing (in) the In-between," in *A Boal Companion: Dialogues on Theatre and Cultural Politics*, ed. Jan Cohen-Cruz and Mady Schutzman (New York: Routledge, 2006), 114.

9. Interview with Derek Richards, Rich Mix.

10. Elizabeth Burns, *Theatricality: A Study of Convention in the Theatre and in Social Life* (New York: Harper Torchbooks, 1972), 21.

11. Iris Marion Young, *Inclusion and Democracy* (Oxford: Oxford University Press, 2002), 5.

12. Young, *Inclusion and Democracy*, 13.

13. Young, *Inclusion and Democracy*, 13.

14. Young, *Inclusion and Democracy*, 13.

15. For example: "although the notion of *cultural difference* has worldwide currency in making claims to respect, inclusion, participation, and citizenship, it has different *uptake* in different societies" (Yúdice, The Expediency of Culture, 44, emphasis in original); "The politics of representation seeks to transform institutions not only by means of inclusion but also by the images and discourses generated by them" (164); "difference is what drives conceptions and practices of 'cultural citizenship,' such as making claims for inclusion and participation in specific countries, and even transnationally via the 'global civil society' projected in the discourse of NGOs, foundations, and intergovernmental organizations like UNESCO" (217). An exception is Yúdice's quotation of an essay by David Rieff, who "gives words of comfort to conservatives who worry that multiculturalism is a bid for power when it is nothing short of 'a demand for inclusion, for a piece of the capitalist pie' " (160).

16. See the tabulation of terms in Loïc Wacquant and Pierre Bourdieu, "NewLiberalSpeak," *Radical Philosophy*, no. 105 (2001): 2. Cameron and Palan provide a similar model in The Imagined Economies of Globalization (16).

17. Cameron, "Geographies of Welfare and Exclusion: Social Inclusion and Exception," 397.

18. Regina Gagnier, *The Insatiability of Human Wants: Economics and Aesthetics in Market Society* (Chicago: University of Chicago Press, 2000), 105.

19. Adam Arvidsson, *Brands: Meaning and Value in Media Culture* (Abingdon, UK: Routledge, 2006), 82.

20. Angus Cameron, "Geographies of welfare and exclusion: reconstituting the 'public,' " *Progress in Human Geography* 31, no. 4 (2007): 519. Cameron writes that "the rebranding of poverty as exclusion and the invocation of 'inclusion' as intertwined sociopolitical acts are narratives about the fundamental relationship between the state and its citizens." Despite AfroReggae's own citation of it, the discourse of exclusion was taken up unevenly in Brazil in this period. At the 2004 conference *Overcoming Social Exclusion: Brazil in Comparative Perspective* in 2004, Peter Townsend noted (in response to a paper about social credit programs given by Marcelo Cortes Neri) that Brazil "had come relatively late to this [the social exclusion] debate" (9). A World Bank publication by Estanislao Gacitúa Marió and Michael Woolcock, *Social Exclusion and Mobility in Brazil* (Washington, DC: World Bank, 2008), opens by stating that as part of research into the incidence of poverty in Brazil "little attention has been given to social exclusion processes to explain why certain groups lack equal access to resources." See also Bryan R. Roberts, "Citizenship, Social Policy, and Population Change," in *Exclusion and Engagement: Social Policy in Latin America*, ed. Christopher Abel and Colin M. Lewis (London: Institute of Latin American Studies, 2002), 115–18.

21. Joy G. Dryfoos, *Adolescents at Risk: Prevalence and Prevention* (New York: Oxford University Press, 1991), 3. For discussions of the concept of "youth at risk," see Peter Kelly, "Youth at Risk: Processes of Individualisation and Responsibilisation in the Risk Society," *Discourse: Studies in the Cultural Politics of Education* 22, no. 1 (2001): 23–33; Peter Kelly, "The

Entrepreneurial Self and 'Youth at-Risk': Exploring the Horizons of Identity in the Twenty-First Century," *Journal of Youth Studies* 9, no. 1 (2006): 17–32; Simon Bradford, "The Management of Growing Up: Youth Work in Community Settings," in *Youth in Society*, 2nd edition, ed. Jeremy Roche, Stanley Tucker, Rachel Thomson, and Ronny Flynn (London: Sage, 2004), 245–54; and Claire Smith, Wendy Stainton Rogers, and Stan Tucker, "Risk," in *Youth in Context: Frameworks, Settings, and Encounters*, ed. Martin Robb (London: Sage, 2007), 219–50.

22. Dryfoos, *Adolescents at Risk*, 3.

23. Dryfoos, *Adolescents at Risk*, 3.

24. Peter Kelly, "The Dangerousness of Youth-at-Risk: The Possibilities of Surveillance and Intervention in Uncertain Times," *Journal of Adolescence*, no. 23 (2000): 465.

25. World Bank, "Brazil: Youth at Risk in Brazil, Volume I: Policy Briefing," May 10, 2007, 3, https://openknowledge.worldbank.org/handle/10986/7763. For example, World Bank (2007, 1): "These include school repetition and early school leaving, inactivity (neither attending school nor working), substance use, violent behaviour, early sexual initiation, and unsafe sexual practices. For the unfortunate few, these risky kinds of behaviour result in negative outcomes, such as HIV/AIDS, early pregnancy, lifetime poverty, or death, affecting not just the risk-taker but also society in general." No mention is made in this document of the favelas or the problems of drug trafficking and police violence attending them beyond a general reference to "poor neighbourhoods" (26).

26. *OED Online*, December 2022, s.v "at-risk, adj.," https://www-oed-com.ezproxy.lib.bbk.ac.uk/view/Entry/275705?rskey=HdiQok&result=1&isAdvanced=false#eid.

27. In "The Formation of an Underclass or Disparate Processes of Social Exclusion? Evidence from Two Groupings of Vulnerable Youth," in *Youth, the "Underclass," and Social Exclusion*, ed. Robert Macdonald (Abingdon, UK: Routledge, 1997), 83–95, Debbie Baldwin, Bob Coles, and Wendy Mitchell note that the 1989 Children's Act frames children and young people taken into care in terms of being "seen to be 'at risk of significant harm' " (91). Though criminological risk discourses play an important role in this collection and other academic literature addressing young people, the specific term "at risk" does not seem to have gained currency in policy and critique in Britain until the 2000s.

28. HM Government/DfES, *Every Child Matters: Change for Children* (Nottingham, UK: Department for Education and Skills, 2004), 4.

29. Dawn E. Stephen, "Community Safety and Young People: 21st-Century *Homo Sacer* and the Politics of Injustice," in *Community Safety: Critical Perspectives on Policy and Practice*, ed. Peter Squires (Bristol, UK: Policy, 2006), 219–36.

30. Arts Council England, *The Arts and Young People at Risk of Offending* (London: Arts Council England, 2005), 17. For an analysis of the 2001 Youth Crime Prevention Strategy of the Youth Justice Board for England and Wales, see Derrick Armstrong, "A Risky Business? Research, Policy, and Governmentality and Youth Offending," *Youth Justice*, no. 4 (2004): 103–4.

31. Hall, "New Labour's Double Shuffle," 19.

32. Paul Heritage, *Intense Dreams: Reflections on Brazilian Culture and Performance* (London: People's Palace Projects, 2009), 17.

33. Larry Rohter, *Brazil on the Rise: The Story of a Country Transformed* (New York: Palgrave Macmillan, 2011), 59–79; Yúdice, *The Expediency of Culture*, 114–15.

34. Rohter, *Brazil on the Rise*, 107–38.

35. Oswald de Andrade, "Manifesto antropófago," *Revista de Antropofágia* (São Paulo), no. 1 (1928): 3, https://icaa.mfah.org/s/en/item/771303#?c=&m=&s=&cv=&xywh=-1250%2C-101%2C3982%2C2228.

36. "M53: Oswald de Andrade, *Cannibalist Manifesto* (1928)," in *100 Artists' Manifestos: From the Futurists to the Stuckists*, ed. Alex Danchev (London: Penguin, 2011), 262.

37. Styliane Philippou, "Modernism and National Identity in Brazil, or How to Brew a Brazilian Stew," *National Identities* 7, no. 3 (2005): 245–64, esp. 253, 250.

38. Else Ribeiro Pires Vieira, "Liberating Calibans: Readings of *Antropofagio* and Haroldo de Campos' Poetics of Transcreation," in *Post-Colonial Translation: Theory and Practice*, ed. Susan Bassnett and Harish Trivedi (London: Routledge, 1998), 95–113, esp. 95.

39. According to Philippou ("Modernism and National Identity," 253): "In the 1930s, *mestiço* nationalism replaced earlier nationalist ideologies centring on the supremacy of white colonial culture. By the end of the Old Republic and the beginning of the authoritarian Vargas regime (1930–1945), all Brazil recognised the emblems of its national identity. *Samba de morro* or *favela samba* became the symbol par excellence of the emerging 'hopeful fiction that Brazil has transcended race prejudice' (Vianna, 1999: xiv). A series of national icons became firmly established: carnival, 'replete with African and Amerindian orgiastic survivals' (Freyre, 1970: xix), especially that of Rio de Janeiro, acquired the status of national celebration par excellence; the black bean *feijoada* of the black slaves, which Tarsila do Amaral had offered her Parisian guests in the 1920s, was adopted as the national dish; *guaraná*, black coffee and Parati *cachaça* (sugar-cane liquor) became the national drinks, and guava paste and cheese the national dessert; previously illegal *capoeira* was pronounced by Vargas the national sport in 1937; and *candomblé* was decriminalised in 1938. The *mestiço* Nossa Senhora da Conceição Aparecida was chosen as the patron saint of Brazil, and the architect and sculptor Aleijadinho (i.e., 'little cripple,' born Antonio Francisco Lisboa, 1730–1814): the natural son of a Portuguese master builder and a black slave, was consecrated as the paradigmatic Brazilian artist—the national artistic genius, the noble ancestor of all Brazilian artists."

40. Cynthia Canejo, "The Resurgence of Anthropophagy," *Third Text* 18, no. 1 (2004): 62–63.

41. Idelber Avelar and Christopher Dunn, "Introduction: Music as Practice of Citizenship in Brazil," in *Brazilian Popular Music and Citizenship*, ed. Idelber Avelar and Christopher Dunn (Durham, NC: Duke University Press, 2011), 1.

42. Yúdice, *The Expediency of Culture*, 115.

43. Frederick Moehn, "'We Live Daily in Two Countries': Audiotopias of Postdictatorship Brazil," in *Brazilian Popular Music and Citizenship*, ed. Idelber Avelar and Christopher Dunn (Durham, NC: Duke University Press, 2011): 115–18.

44. Will Hodgkinson, "A Totally Tropicália Revolution," *The Times: The Knowledge*, February 4–10, 2006, 24.

45. Hodgkinson, "A Totally Tropicália Revolution," 24.

46. Gilberto Gil, "Ministro Gilberto Gil no Fórum de Amigos da Cultura do Brasil na Europa," address in Rome, Itály, July 21, 2003, Ministry of Culture, Brazil, http://cultura.gov.br/ministro-gilberto-gil-no-forum-de-amigos-da-cultura-do-brasil-na-europa-35658/; Anonymous, "Gil integra comitiva de Lula a Portugal," Agência Brasil, July 8, 2003, http://memoria.ebc.com.br/agenciabrasil/noticia/2003–07–08/gil-integra-comitiva-de-lula-portugal.

47. "A ideologia neo-liberal, ideologia da globalização, quer nos fazer crer que não há mais nada a fazer. Que o destino da humanidade está para sempre selado. E isto é fundamentalmente falso" (Gil 2003).

48. "setor dinâmico da economia" (Gil 2003).

49. "frente de combate à exclusão social" (Gil 2003).

50. "espaço de realização plena da cidadania" (Gil 2003).

51. "filho e produto da primeira grande maré planetária da globalização" (Gil 2003).

52. "transfusões culturais" (Gil 2003).

53. "Em decorrência do tráfico transatlântico de escravos, gentes de países como a Nigéria, o Benin e Gana estão presentes em nossos códigos genético e simbólico. Como se sabe, apesar de toda a violência sistêmica do escravismo colonial, negros dessas regiões e seus descendentes foram sujeitos ativos e vitais nos processos de construção e invenção do Brasil e da cultura brasileira. De Zumbi a Pelé" (Gil 2003).

54. "Cultura não apenas como o reduzido conjunto das formas culturais tradicionais canonizadas pela cultura ocidental-européia. Mas como constelação dinâmica na qual se inscrevem todos os atos criativos de nosso povo. Da arquitetura ao candomblé, da capoeira à literatura, do samba ao teatro, do urbanismo ao artesanato, do patrimônio histórico à poesia a laser, da estética das favelas às técnicas culinárias, dos fragmentos culturais dos meninos de rua à vida no sistema social xinguano, do futebol ao carnaval, da pesquisa científica ao saber dos pajés amazônicos" (Gil 2003).

55. Gilberto Gil, "'Experimentation, Memory, and Invention': Inaugural Address Delivered by Minister Gilberto Gil on Being Sworn into Office, Brasília, January 2, 2003," in *Living Culture: National Culture, Education, and Citizenship Program*, http://colecoes.inpa.gov.br/sb/docs/english.pdf. In this speech, there is continuity with Gil's earlier work. Santuza Cambraia Naves, in "From Bossa Nova to Tropicália: Restraint and Excess in Popular Music," in *Imagining Brazil*, ed. Jessé Souza and Valter Sinder (Lanham, MD: Lexington Books, 2005), 251–65, writes that with the exception of early *bossa nova*, whose modernist precision derived from and coincided with "a time of assertion of industrial modernity" (263), artists of the 1960s such as Gil, Chico Buarque, and Edu Lobo "privileged *inclusion* as their major procedure" (261, emphasis in original). Gil's expansive definition of culture as a member of

the government resonates with that espoused decades earlier by the *tropicália* movement of which Gil was an important figure, in which, in Naves's account, concepts of "resource," "nation," and "culture" bled into one another: "The Tropicalista notion of 'cultural wealth' encompasses everything from rock, that ubiquitous cultural import, to established regional rhythms, and is flexible enough to accommodate kitsch as one more component of the nation's treasure" (261). Frederick Moehn, in "Music, Mixing, and Modernity in Rio de Janeiro." *Ethnomusicology Forum* 17, no. 2 (2008): 198, suggests that Gil's speech and its rhetoric of tolerance and peace "adapted national allegories of mixture to the post 9/11 context."

56. Raymond Williams, *Communications*, rev. ed. (Harmondsworth, UK: Penguin 1966), 18.

57. Adrian Ellis, "Valuing Culture," speech given at the "Valuing Culture" symposium, National Theatre Studio, June 17, 2003, https://www.demos.co.uk/files/File/VACUAEllis.pdf.

58. Ellis, "Valuing Culture."

59. Smith, *Contingencies of Value*, 126.

60. Nicholas Hytner, "Valuing Culture," speech given at the "Valuing Culture" symposium, National Theatre Studio, June 17, 2003, http://www.demos.co.uk/files/File/VACUNHytner.pdf.

61. Hytner, "Valuing Culture."

62. Chris Smith, "Valuing Culture," speech given at the "Valuing Culture" symposium, National Theatre Studio, June 17, 2003, https://www.demos.co.uk/files/File/VACUCSmith.pdf.

63. David Lloyd and Paul Thomas, *Culture and the State* (London: Routledge, 1998), 48; Jean-Christophe Agnew, *Worlds Apart: The Market and the Theatre in Anglo-American Thought, 1550–1750* (Cambridge: Cambridge University Press, 1986), 6–7; Guillory, *Cultural Capital*, 269–340. I discuss Guillory's critique and historicization of the concept of "cultural value" in the introduction.

64. Oval House ("History," 2013): "The roots of Oval House can be traced back to the 1930s and its foundations, as Christ Church (Oxford) Clubs, by the graduates of Christchurch College, Oxford. The young people from disadvantaged areas in South London were able to use the space for sports activities and were taken on away days, along with skills training which they could use for the future. Since that time Oval House has pioneered enabling forms of education and artistic endeavour. . . . Oval House has played a key part in supporting the experimental theatre companies of the '60s and '70s, the emergence of gay and lesbian and women's theatre in the 1970s and '80s, and the development of new Black and Asian writing in the '90s and into the next millennium."

65. Commission for Racial Equality. Established in 1976, the CRE was replaced in 2007 by the Equality and Human Rights Commission.

66. Deborah Bestwick, "Valuing Culture," speech given at Valuing Culture, National Theatre Studio, June 17, 2003, http://www.demos.co.uk/files/File/VACUDBestwick.pdf.

67. Gilroy, *After Empire*, 20.

68. Yúdice, *The Expediency of Culture*, 115; Frederick Moehn, "Music, Citizenship and Violence in Postdictatorship Brazil," *Latin American Music*

Review 28, no. 2 (2007): 187; João H. Costa Vargas, "When a Favela Dared to Become a Gated Condominium: The Politics of Race and Urban Space in Rio de Janeiro," *Latin American Perspectives* 33, no. 4 (2006): 49–81.

69. Patrick Wintour and Vikram Dodd, "Blair Blames Spate of Murders on Black Culture," *The Guardian*, April 12, 2007. A database search (Proquest) for the phrase "knife crime" in the pages of British broadsheets turned up 41 articles for the period January 1, 2000, to January 1, 2005. Between 2005 and 2009, 1,398 articles were published that contained the phrase, the bulk of them (1,001) in 2008 and 2009. The relation between this frenzy of reporting and the emergence of the financial crisis is conspicuous.

70. Louise Owen, "'In Tune with the Beat of Where They Are': The Afro-Reggae UK Partnership in 2007," *PPP Research Bulletin* 4 (2008): 1–14.

71. AfroReggae UK Partnership, "Can Culture Be Our Weapon? Raising the Stakes in the Fight against Gun Crime and Gang Culture," Monday, May 14, 2007, Garden Room, Barbican Centre.

72. Moehn, "Music, Citizenship, and Violence in Postdictatorship Brazil," 185.

73. *Nenhum motiva explica a guerra*, DVD, dir. Cacá Diegues e Rafael Dragaud, Warner Music, 2006.

74. In "Black Movements and the 'Politics of Identity' in Brazil,'" in *Cultures of Politics, Politics of Cultures: Re-visioning Latin American Social Movements*, ed. Sonia E. Alvarez, Evelina Dagnino, and Arturo Escobar (Boulder, CO: Westview, 1998), 238, Olivia Maria Gomes da Cunha writes: "The founders of the journal [AfroReggae Noticias] had diverse educational backgrounds. During the period that this research was conducted (1994–1996), the group's governing board consisted of an unemployed chemical technician who made his living selling cassette tapes, compact discs, and silk-screened shirts; a mid-level public servant; a young man who had previously driven a taxi and delivered newspapers; a graduate student in the social sciences; a graduate student in education; a journalist; and a dentist."

75. Enrique Desmond Arias, *Drugs and Democracy in Rio de Janeiro: Trafficking, Social Networks, and Public Security* (Chapel Hill: University of North Carolina Press, 2006), 141–42.

76. Arias, *Drugs and Democracy in Rio de Janeiro*, 154–56; José Júnior, *Da favela para o mundo: Grupo Cultural AfroReggae* (Rio de Janeiro: Aeroplano Editora, 2004), 60–62. Arias offers the alternative spelling "Mocovide" for the name of the group.

77. For an extensive history and contextualization of AfroReggae, see Neate and Platt's *Culture Is Our Weapon: Making Music and Changing Lives in Rio de Janeiro*; and Zuenir Ventura, *Cidade Partida* (São Paulo: Companhia das Letras, 1994).

78. *Nenhum motiva explica a guerra*.

79. Elizabeth Leeds, "Rio de Janeiro," in *Fractured Cities: Social Exclusion, Urban Violence, and Contested Spaces in Latin America*, ed. Kees Koonings and Dirk Kruijt (London: Zed Books, 2007), 25. Janice Perlman's pioneering anthropological text *The Myth of Marginality: Urban Poverty and Politics in Rio de Janeiro* (Berkeley: University of California Press, 1976) offers deep insight into the history of the favelas, and an activist counter-argument to

the "myth of marginality" prevalent in scholarship of the period. Perlman revisited this work in *Favela: Four Decades of Living on the Edge in Rio de Janeiro* (Oxford: Oxford University Press, 2010) to examine changes to the favelas and the impact of those changes on individual life histories; for the association of the favelas with criminality, see especially pp. 24–40. See also Julio Cesar Pino, *Family and Favela: The Reproduction of Poverty in Rio de Janeiro* (Westport, CT: Greenwood, 1997), 37–58; and "From the Marginality of the 1960s to the New Poverty of Today: An LARR Research Forum," *Latin American Research Review* 39, no. 1 (2004): 183–203.

80. Damian Platt, *Nothing by Accident: Brazil on the Edge* (London: Independent Publishing Network, 2020), 56.

81. Arias, *Drugs and Democracy in Rio de Janeiro*, 31.

82. Leeds, "Rio de Janeiro," 26.

83. Luke Dowdney, *Children of the Drug Trade: A Case Study of Children in Organised Armed Violence in Rio de Janeiro* (Rio de Janeiro: 7 Letras, 2003), 213–14.

84. Da Cunha, "Black Movements and the 'Politics of Identity' in Brazil," 241.

85. Silvia Ramos, "Brazilian Responses to Violence and New Forms of Mediation: The Case of the Grupo Cultural AfroReggae and the Experience of the Project Youth and the Police," *Ciênca & Saúde Coletiva* 11, no. 2 (2006): 423.

86. Da Cunha, "Black Movements and the 'Politics of Identity' in Brazil," 242.

87. "Ouvíamos várias tendências musicais de dentro and de fora do Brasil. Tudo era bom, tudo dava ser aproveitado: drum'n'bass, maracatu, rap." Júnior, *Da favela para o mundo*, 126–27.

88. In *¡Cocinando! Fifty Years of Latin Album Cover Art* (New York: Princeton Architectural Press, 2005), 172, Pablo Yglesias offers this fascinating commentary on the cover of *Gilberto Gil* (1968), which was designed by Rogério Duarte with the American photographer David Drew Zingg: "At first glance he [Gil] appears to be dressed as an African dictator surrounded by radiating liberation colors of red, gold, and green. Gil is in fact making a deeper, more nuanced statement. In the centre photo he is dressed in the official attire of the Brazilian Academy of Letters, a group of forty peer-elected 'immortals' consisting at that time entirely of white males. He is wearing bifocals similar to those used by Machado de Assis, the first president of the academy (1897–1908), who was of partial African descent. On the left Gil is brandishing a cane as if to ridicule the real dictators, and on the right he seems to be steering a vehicle without a body, commenting on the disastrous route the elite was taking as the 1960s drew to a close."

89. Da Cunha, "Black Movements and the 'Politics of Identity' in Brazil," 240.

90. Beatriz Olivon, "O que o Santander pode ensinar sobre o Complexo do Alemão," *Exame*, March 12, 2010.

91. While acknowledging that all those negotiating this context are subject to "performative injunctions" (The Expediency of Culture, 53), Yúdice argues that the valuable outcomes of AfroReggae's ambiguous negotiations are its efficacious "community-building activities," and its efforts to enable young

people living in poverty to "become a recognisable part of the city and partake in some modest way of its assets" (156). In making this argument, he suggests that "community" represents a zone at least partially untouched by "spectacle and performativity" (156).

92. Patrick Neate, *Where You're At: Notes from the Frontline of a Hip Hop Planet* (London: Bloomsbury, 2003), 200; Neate and Platt, *Culture Is Our Weapon*, 150.

93. Juliana Borges, "Eles fazem muito com pouco," *Exame*, December 18, 2009; Ramos, "Brazilian Responses to Violence," 423.

94. "Usamos roupas de marca, porque gostamos e porque assim também despertamos a cobiça, a vaidade e a auto-estima dos meninos. O objetivo maior é que os jovens das favelas não tenham mais só traficantes como seus idolos. Em vez de fuzis, ofereciamos instrumentos musicais. O nosso poder não era o da morte, mas o da vida. Faziamos o tráfico dos sonhos, das possibilidades e da cultura." Júnior, *Da favela para o mundo*, 128.

95. *Nenhum motiva explica a guerra.*

96. *Nenhum motiva explica a guerra.*

97. J. L. Austin, *How to Do Things with Words*, 2nd ed., ed. J. O. Urmson and Maria Sbisa (Cambridge, MA: Harvard University Press, 1975 [1962]), 7.

98. PPP, "About PPP," https://peoplespalaceprojects.org.uk/en/about/#about.

99. The Shoreditch Trust was one of the first New Deal for Communities (NDC) programs set up by the New Labour government in 1998, targeted to address particular areas of deprivation. It is now a registered charity which works to "support communities in Hackney and neighbouring boroughs to improve their health and well-being, develop social networks, and build skills and opportunities for meaningful employment."

100. Jamie Peck, "Geography and Public Policy: Constructions of Neoliberalism," *Progress in Human Geography* 28, no. 3 (2004): 400.

101. Sandeep Dwesar, "Taking Greater Risks to Reach New Heights," *Barbican Annual Review 06/07*, 52.

102. Interview with Malin Forbes, Barbican Centre, December 2007.

103. Graham Sheffield was artistic director of the Barbican from 1995 to 2010.

104. AfroReggae UK Partnership, "Can Culture Be Our Weapon?"

105. Smith, *Contingencies of Value*, 126.

106. Dwesar, "Taking Greater Risks, 51.

107. Mark Espiner, "Shows of Strength," *Barbican at 25*, pamphlet, 107.

108. Espiner, "Shows of Strength," 107.

109. Espiner, "Shows of Strength," 108.

110. Interview with Karen Taylor, Arts Council England, December 2007.

111. Ellis, "Valuing Culture."

112. Interview with Richard Ings, May 2007.

113. Interview with Richard Ings.

114. Cameron, "Geographies of Welfare and Exclusion: Social Inclusion and Exception," 396.

115. Cameron, "Geographies of Welfare and Exclusion: Social Inclusion and Exception," 397.

116. Richard Ings, *From the Favela to Our Manor: Translating AfroReggae: The Impact and Implications of an International Intervention in Arts Work with Young People at Risk* (London: People's Palace Projects, 2007), 13.

117. Ings, *From the Favela to Our Manor*, 14.

118. Ings, *From the Favela to Our Manor*, 29.

119. Ings, *From the Favela to Our Manor*, 35.

120. Ings, *From the Favela to Our Manor*, 33.

121. David McNally, *Global Slump: The Economics and Politics of Crisis and Resistance* (Oakland, CA: PM Press, 2011), 118.

122. Ministry of Justice, "Story of the Prison Population: 1993–2012, England and Wales," January 2013, 1, https://assets.publishing.service.gov.uk/government/uploads/system/uploads/attachment_data/file/218185/story-prison-population.pdf.

123. Ings, *From the Favela to Our Manor*, 54–55.

124. Elizabeth Burney, *Making People Behave: Anti-Social Behaviour, Politics, and Policy* (Cullompton, UK: Willan, 2005), 13.

125. John Muncie, "Youth Justice: Responsibilisation and Rights," in *Youth in Society*, 2nd ed., ed. Jeremy Roche, Stanley Tucker, Rachel Thomson, and Ronny Flynn (London: Sage, 2004), 136.

126. Ings, *From the Favela to Our Manor*, 75.

127. David Harvey, "Flexible Accumulation through Urbanization: Reflections on 'Post-Modernism' in the American City," in *Post-Fordism: A Reader*, ed. Ash Amin (Oxford: Blackwell, 1994 [1987]), 371.

128. Robyn Travis, *Prisoner to the Streets* (London: X Press, 2013).

129. Dowdney, *Children of the Drug Trade*, 134.

130. David Harvey, "Flexible Accumulation through Urbanization," 371.

131. Pierre Bourdieu, *The Logic of Practice*, trans. Richard Nice (Cambridge: Polity, 1990 [1980]), 66–68.

132. AfroReggae UK Partnership, Mini-Projects showcase, artist seminar, Rich Mix, Wednesday, June 27, 2007.

133. Interview with Carla Martins, AfroReggae, October 2007.

134. An interesting example is the ArtsCatalyst loyalty card scheme established by teachers at another school in the London borough of Hackney, to incentivize attendance from "at risk" pupils, with the reward being to participate in AfroReggae workshops—a model which effectively imagined the pupil as a utility-maximizer. As teaching staff described it to me in our interviews, the scheme was a great success, the cards themselves being viewed by pupils as "presents."

135. Immediate Theatre, http://www.immediate-theatre.com/.

136. Interview, Jo Carter, Immediate Theatre, December 2007.

137. Shoreditch Trust, "Shoreditch Trust Delivery Plan 2007–08," 2006, 47.

138. Interview, Damian Atkinson, Shoreditch Trust, January 2008.

139. Taru Arts, https://taru.org.uk/.

140. Tom MacInnes and Peter Kenway, *London's Poverty Profile* (London: City Parochial Foundation and New Policy Institute, 2009), 9.

141. Hackney, "Hackney Local Implementation Plan LIP (2006–2011)," http://www.hackney.gov.uk/local_implementation_plan_-_section_1_-_local_socio-economic_impact.pdf.

142. Hoxton Hall is one of a handful of music halls of the late nineteenth century to have survived, and remains a fully functioning local arts resource. A detailed architectural history of it can be found at the Theatres Trust website, https://database.theatrestrust.org.uk/resources/theatres/show/1983-hoxton-hall.

143. Interview, E. J. Trivett, Immediate Theatre, December 2007.

144. Shoreditch Trust, "Shoreditch Trust Delivery Plan 2007–08," 2.

145. Shoreditch Trust, "Shoreditch Trust Delivery Plan 2007–08," 47.

146. Immediate Theatre meeting, December 12, 2007; Shoreditch Trust, "Shoreditch Trust Delivery Plan 2007–08," 48. In our 2007 interview, Peter Leigh of Sound Connections also discussed at length the reluctance of young people to leave their local areas to participate in projects run by the organization.

147. Interview, Karen Taylor.

148. Meeting: AfroReggae in Shoreditch, Immediate Theatre, December 2007.

149. Tony Jeffs, "Changing Their Ways: Youth Work and 'Underclass' Theory," in *Youth, the "Underclass," and Social Exclusion*, ed. Robert MacDonald (London: Routledge, 1997), 163.

150. Claire Bishop, *Artificial Hells: Participatory Art and the Politics of Spectatorship* (London: Verso, 2012), 190.

151. Jeffs, "Changing Their Ways," 157. On the Youth Service in Britain after 1945, Jeffs writes: "Denied lavish funding, it gained, by way of compensation, the freedom to develop small pockets of radical practice and, above all, the space and privacy in which to address sensitive issues. It employed informal education and group work techniques to enable young people to discuss and learn about those issues and topics excluded from the school curriculum and which few schoolteachers would dare to broach" (157).

152. Yúdice, *The Expediency of Culture*, 156.

153. Yúdice, *The Expediency of Culture*, 155.

154. "queria ver favelados maltrapilhos, criancas de nariz sujo and dentes cariados." Junior, *Da favela para o mundo*, 142.

155. Miranda Joseph, *Against the Romance of Community* (Minneapolis: University of Minnesota Press, 2002), 96.

156. Grupo Cultural AfroReggae, *We Are AfroReggae: No Reason Justifies War*, 13.

157. Neate and Platt, *Culture Is Our Weapon*, 153.

158. Barbican, "Favelization," http://www.barbican.org.uk/theatre/event-detail.asp?ID=7378.

Chapter 4

1. Beatriz García, "Cultural Policy and Urban Regeneration in Western European Cities: Lessons from Experience, Prospects for the Future," *Local Economy* 19, no. 4 (2004): 312–26; Stuart Wilks-Heeg and Peter North, "Editorial: Cultural Policy and Urban Regeneration: A Special Edition of *Local Economy*," *Local Economy* 19, no. 4 (2004): 305–11.

2. For example, Richard Morrison, in "Power to the People, Write On," *The Times*, October 8, 2005, 4: "Hytner's National has been at the forefront of the

post 9/11 renaissance in political theatre and its even newsier sibling, 'verbatim theatre' (where playwrights use real quotes)"; Kate Kellaway, in "Theatre of War: The Iraq War Has Energised Dramatists, with David Hare's New Play the Latest in a Surge of Political Theatre," *The Observer*, August 29, 2004, 5: "it is not satire, it is verbatim theatre that has recently made political theatre high profile"; and Lyn Gardner, in "Guantanamo," *The Guardian*, June 29, 2004, 18: "Verbatim theatre is apparently the new journalism . . . The relentless rise of verbatim theatre over the past couple of years has once again put theatre centre stage."

3. Deirdre Heddon, *Autobiography and Performance* (Basingstoke, UK: Palgrave Macmillan, 2008), 129.

4. Alison Forsyth and Chris Megson, introduction to *Get Real: Documentary Theatre Past and Present*, ed. Alison Forsyth and Chris Megson (Basingstoke, UK: Palgrave Macmillan, 2009), 2.

5. In *Theatre-Making: Interplay between Text and Performance in the 21st Century* (Basingstoke, UK: Routledge, 2013), Duška Radosavljević opens a chapter (119) on verbatim theater by noting that following its early twenty-first-century upsurge, "this popularity has since waned somewhat." Yet in 2014, at least eleven verbatim theater productions were staged in Britain: Tess Berry-Hart, *Sochi 2014*, King's Head Theatre; *Bloody Trams: A Rapid Response*, Traverse Theatre; Rani Moorthy, *States of Verbal Undress: The Voice of Britain Today*, Lowry Centre; James Graham, *Privacy*, Donmar Warehouse; Paper Birds, *Broke*, Pleasance Dome; Vocal Point Theatre Company, *Bloom*, Underbelly; Alecky Blythe, *Little Revolution*, Almeida; Govanhill Theatre Group, *The Battle of Calder Street*, Govanhill Baths, Glasgow; DV8, *John*, National Theatre; Jonny Woo, *The East London Lecture*, Transport Theatre Company/Mill Co Project; and *Mamela*, Live Theatre Newcastle.

6. Stephen Bottoms, "Putting the Document into Documentary: An Unwelcome Corrective?" *TDR: The Drama Review* 50, no. 3 (2006): 67.

7. Jacques Derrida, quoted in Rebecca Schneider, "Patricidal Memory and the Passerby," *The Scholar and Feminist Online* 2, no. 1: "Public Sentiments" (2003), http://sfonline.barnard.edu/ps/schneide.htm.

8. Rebecca Schneider, "Performance Remains," *Performance Research* 6, no. 2 (2001): 101.

9. Schneider, "Performance Remains," 101.

10. Phil Hubbard, "Revenge and Injustice in the Neoliberal City: Uncovering Masculinist Agendas," *Antipode* 36, no. 4 (2004): 678. In "Should Lap Dancing Be Run Out of Town?" a piece for the *Guardian* on March 8, 2009, Rachel Cooke (24) sketches an industrial history of private lap-dancing clubs: the first club opened in Britain in 1995, and during the 2000s, loopholes in the Licensing Act 2003, which granted the same status to lap dancing clubs as to café-bars, saw the number of lap-dancing clubs double, from 150 in 2004 to 300 in 2008. The title of her article demonstrates the proprietarial logic that informs debate about sex work: "Should lap dancing be run out of town? With a new venue opening every week, lap dancing has spread into British culture. Rachel Cooke talks to the men behind the boom, the women lured by the promise of easy money, and the campaigners battling to stop the clubs opening on your doorstep."

11. Angela McRobbie, *The Aftermath of Feminism: Gender, Culture, and Social Change* (Los Angeles: Sage Books, 2009), 1.

12. McRobbie, *The Aftermath of Feminism*, 1.

13. McRobbie, *The Aftermath of Feminism*, 1.

14. McRobbie, *The Aftermath of Feminism*, 122.

15. Julia Laite, "Paying the Price Again: Prostitution Policy in Historical Perspective," *History and Policy*, Policy Paper 46 (2006): 1, https://www.historyandpolicy.org/policy-papers/papers/paying-the-price-again-prostitution-policy-in-historical-perspective.

16. Lisa E. Sanchez, "The Global E-rotic Subject, the Ban, and the Prostitute-Free Zone: Sex Work and the Theory of Differential Exclusion," *Environment and Planning D: Society and Space*, no. 22 (2004): 861.

17. Kate Kellaway, "Review: Theatre: Both Sides Now: The Latest Addition to the Growing Canon of Verbatim Theatre Examines the Question of Terrorism from All Angles to Impressive, Moving Effect," *The Observer*, May 1, 2005, 9.

18. Jane Shenton, "Man-in-Street Script," *Liverpool Daily Post*, May 16, 1967.

19. Shenton, "Man-in-Street Script."

20. Shenton, "Man-in-Street Script."

21. Doreen Tanner, "Play That Just Grew," *Liverpool Daily Post*, May 18, 1967.

22. Tanner, "Play That Just Grew."

23. Gillete A. Elvgren Jr., "Documentary Theatre at Stoke-on-Trent," *Educational Theatre Journal* 26, no. 1 (1974): 97.

24. Elvgren Jr., "Documentary Theatre," 88.

25. Elvgren Jr., "Documentary Theatre," 89.

26. Derek Paget, "'Verbatim Theatre': Oral History and Documentary Techniques," *New Theatre Quarterly*, no. 12 (1987): 317; Paola Botham, "From Deconstruction to Reconstruction: A Habermasian Framework for Contemporary Political Theatre," *Contemporary Theatre Review* 18, no. 3 (2008): 312; Heddon, *Autobiography and Performance*, 127; and Radosavljević, *Theatre-Making*, 128.

27. Paget, "Verbatim Theatre," 317.

28. Paget, "Verbatim Theatre," 317.

29. Paget, "Verbatim Theatre," 317.

30. Paget, "Verbatim Theatre," 318–19. See also Peter Cheeseman, "A Community Theatre-in-the-Round," *Theatre Quarterly*, no. 1 (1971): 71–82; Cheeseman, "Production Casebook No. 1: The Staffordshire Rebels," *Theatre Quarterly*, no. 1 (1971): 86–102; Anna Seymour, "Culture and Political Change: British Radical Theatre in Recent History," *Theatre Research International* 21, no. 1 (1996): 8–16; Alan Filewod and David Watt, *Workers' Playtime: Theatre and the Labour Movement in Australia, Canada, and the United Kingdom 1970–1997* (Sydney: Currency, 2001); and David Watt, "'The Maker and the Tool': Charles Parker, Documentary Performance, and the Search for a Popular Culture," *New Theatre Quarterly* 19, no. 1 (2003): 41–66.

31. Paget, "Verbatim Theatre," 317, 322.

32. Paget, "Verbatim Theatre," 322.
33. Paget, "Verbatim Theatre," 319.
34. Paget, "Verbatim Theatre," 329.
35. Peter Cheeseman, quoted in Paget, "Verbatim Theatre," 322.
36. Cheeseman, "A Community Theatre-in-the-Round," 77.
37. Jen Harvie, *Staging the UK* (Manchester: Manchester University Press, 2005), 20–22.
38. Harvie, *Staging the UK*, 21.
39. Paget, "Verbatim Theatre," 335.
40. Paget, "Verbatim Theatre," 320.
41. Paget, "Verbatim Theatre," 336.
42. Chris Megson, "Verbatim Practices in Contemporary Theatre: Symposium Report," *Contemporary Theatre Review* 16, no. 4 (2006): 530.
43. Megson, "Verbatim Practices," 529–30.
44. David Edgar, "Doc and Dram: Why Has This Decade Seen the Rise of a Vibrant Theatre of Reportage? Playwright David Edgar Points to a Decline in Conventional Journalism and TV Documentary," *The Guardian*, September 27, 2008, 18.
45. Chris Megson, "*Half the Picture*: 'A Certain Frisson' at the Tricycle Theatre," in *Get Real: Documentary Theatre Past and Present*, ed. Alison Forsyth and Chris Megson (Basingstoke, UK: Palgrave Macmillan, 2009), 195–208.
46. In "Verbatim Theatre (Verbatim)," the conversation introducing *The Tricycle: Collected Tribunal Plays 1994–2012* (London: Oberon, 2014), Nicolas Kent comments (5): "Well, I suppose, going back quite a long way, I'd always been interested in verbatim theatre, or certainly big public enquiries or trials."
47. Richard Norton-Taylor, "Arts: Theatre: Blair in the Dock," *The Guardian*, April 16, 2007, 26.
48. For example, Richard Norton-Taylor, "Out of the Shadows," *The Guardian*, June 8, 1994; Richard Norton-Taylor, "On the Trail of the Trial," *The Guardian*, May 1, 1996, 213; and Richard Norton-Taylor, "The Truth Will Out," *The Guardian*, December 23, 1998, 13.
49. "Theatre Check," *The Times*, June 19, 1994.
50. Charles Spencer, "The Arts: Lifting the Curtain on Arms to Iraq: The Scott Inquiry Is Brilliantly Enacted at the Tricycle," *The Daily Telegraph*, June 17, 1994, 19.
51. Mark Lawson, "Theatre: Nothing but the Truth: You Couldn't Make It Up. For Centuries the Book-Reading, Theatre-Going Public Want Nothing but Fiction—Then Suddenly Only True-Life Stories Will Do. What's So Great about Reality, Asks Mark Lawson," *The Guardian*, October 9, 1996, 12.
52. Susannah Clapp, "Arts: The Year Ahead; Theatre in '99; Four Legs Good," *The Observer*, January 3, 1999, 8.
53. Alastair Macaulay, "No Happy Endings in Real Life: The Colour of Justice, Tricycle Theatre, London NW6," *Financial Times*, January 14, 1999, 26; Alastair Macaulay, "Going Public in a Way That Makes a Difference: Alastair Macaulay Meets Nicolas Kent, the Man behind 'The Colour of Justice,'" *Financial Times*, September 20, 1999, 19.

54. Jeremy Kingston, "Trials of a Court Reporter: All the World's Crime is a Stage for Nicolas Kent," *The Times*, October 7, 1996, 1.

55. David Thomas, David Carlton, and Anne Etienne, *Theatre Censorship: From Walpole to Wilson* (Oxford: Oxford University Press, 2007), 230.

56. Nicholas Wroe, "Profile: Nicolas Kent: Courtroom Dramas," *The Guardian*, July 24, 2004, 16.

57. Megson, "Verbatim Practices," 530.

58. In "A Search for New Realities: Documentary Theatre in Germany," *TDR: The Drama Review* 50, no. 3 (2006), Thomas Irmer (24) translates *Wartesaal Deutschland* as *German Waiting Room*, which substantially alters its meaning.

59. The Royal Court's interventions in shaping the contemporary field of verbatim theater practices have been decisive both in Britain and internationally, particularly in Russia. In "New Documentarism on Stage: Documentary Theatre in New Times," *ZAA* 56, no. 2 (2008), Derek Paget (134) notes that in 1990, the theatre re-mounted *Falkland Sound* along "with a new semi-verbatim play, *Gibraltar Spirit*. The bill containing these two short plays compared and contrasted official fictions and eye-witness realities from the Falklands War of 1982 and the 1988 'Death on the Rock' incident (when an IRA team were shot by British special forces)"—a project constructed in a similar way to the subsequent *Rita, Sue and Bob Too/A State Affair* duet. Three years later, with the Royal Court and Nottingham Playhouse as co-producers, DV8 created *MSM* (1993), a dance-documentary exploring the practices and motivations of men who have sex with men, but do not identify as homosexual. The piece was based on interviews with men conducted by the company. MSM, "Press Release," https://www.dv8.co.uk/projects/archive/msm/press-release.

60. "Robin Soans," in *Verbatim Verbatim: Contemporary Documentary Theatre*, ed. Will Hammond and Dan Steward (London: Oberon Books, 2008), 15–44.

61. "Robin Soans," in *Verbatim Verbatim*, 22.

62. "Robin Soans," in *Verbatim Verbatim*, 22.

63. Elaine Aston and Janelle Reinelt, "Building Bridges: Life on Dunbar's Arbor, Past and Present," *Theatre Research International* 26, no. 3 (2001): 286, 292.

64. Lyn Gardner, "Waiting Room Germany," *The Guardian*, November 13, 1995, 9.

65. Lyn Gardner, "Reviews: Theatre: Rita, Sue/A State Affair: Everyman, Liverpool (4/5 stars)," *The Guardian*, October 26, 2000, 25.

66. Phil Daoust, "Reviews: Theatre: Rita, Sue/A State Affair; Soho Theatre, London (5 stars)," *The Guardian*, December 9, 2000, 29.

67. Aston and Reinelt, "Building Bridges," 292.

68. Daoust, "Reviews," 29.

69. "Robin Soans," in *Verbatim Verbatim*, 22.

70. Thomas Irmer, "A Search for New Realities: Documentary Theatre in Germany," *TDR: The Drama Review* 50, no. 3 (2006): 24.

71. Irmer, "A Search for New Realities," 24.

72. Megson, "Verbatim Practices," 532.

73. Edgar, "Doc and Dram," 18.

74. For an insightful discussion of this piece in terms of testimony and trauma, see Amanda Stuart Fisher, "Trauma, Authenticity, and the Limits of Verbatim," *Performance Research* 16, no. 1 (2011): 112–22.

75. Alastair Macaulay, "Theatre," *Financial Times*, February 18, 2006, 38.

76. Similar in this respect is *Charlie Victor Romeo* (1999), presented by its creators, the New York-based theater company Collective: Unconscious, at Udderbelly's Pasture in August 2008, which went on to be adapted for cinema in 2012. This piece utilized transcriptions of recordings from aircraft black box recorders.

77. Ben Brantley, "Theater Review: Someone Else Committed Their Crimes," *New York Times*, October 11, 2002, https://www.nytimes.com/2002/10/11/movies/theater-review-someone-else-committed-their-crimes.html.

78. Edgar, "Doc and Dram," 18. In "*Half the Picture*," Chris Megson (207) shows that *Half the Picture* was an exception in staging monologues and other reflexive strategies to punctuate "the experience of live television coverage . . . the seductive illusion of uninterrupted verisimilitude."

79. Wroe, "Profile: Nicolas Kent," 16.

80. Edgar, "Doc and Dram," 18.

81. Megson, "*Half the Picture*," 197.

82. Bella Merlin, "*The Permanent Way* and the Impermanent Muse," *Contemporary Theatre Review* 17, no. 1 (2007): 41–49.

83. Bella Merlin, "Acting Hare: *The Permanent Way*," in *The Cambridge Companion to David Hare*, ed. Richard Boon (Cambridge: Cambridge University Press, 2007), 127.

84. Merlin, "*The Permanent Way*," 41.

85. Bella Merlin, "Interview with Max Stafford-Clark for the National Theatre Educational Website *on The Permanent Way*," cited in Merlin, "Acting Hare," 124.

86. "David Hare and Max Stafford-Clark," in *Verbatim Verbatim: Contemporary Documentary Theatre*, ed. Will Hammond and Dan Steward (London: Oberon Books, 2008), 51.

87. David Hare, *The Permanent Way, or La Voie Anglaise* (London: Faber and Faber, 2003), 19, 26, 50.

88. Brian Logan, "Why Do We Still Run with the Hare?" *The Times*, November 27, 2006, 14.

89. Bottoms, "Putting the Document into Documentary," 59–60.

90. Stephen Bottoms' analysis of *Counted* (2010), a verbatim theater piece he made in collaboration with Look Left Look Right about participation in the electoral process, examines how the interview form played its part in the devising of the show. The show's uses of the form departed from the understanding that "far from being a transparent medium for the transmission of the subject's true, unguarded feelings and beliefs, the interview is a form of dramatic encounter conducted according to certain established (though not always acknowledged) behavioural conventions" (Bottoms, "Staging the Democratic Deficit; or, Three Uses of the Interview," *Contemporary Theatre Review* 25, no. 2 [2015]: 193). For a fascinating examination of a range of actorly approaches to verbatim theater, see Tom Cantrell, *Acting in Documentary Theatre* (Basingstoke, UK: Palgrave Macmillan, 2013).

91. Merlin, "Acting Hare," 131.

92. Moises Kaufman, *The Laramie Project*, Sound Theatre W1; Tanika Gupta, *Gladiator Games*, Sheffield Crucible; Alecky Blythe/Recorded Delivery, *All the Right People Come Here*, New Wimbledon Studio; Fermin Cabal, *Tejas Verdes (Green Gables)*, Gate Theatre, Notting Hill; Alecky Blythe/Recorded Delivery, *The Day of All Days*, Flight 5065 Festival, London Eye; Alan Rickman and Katharine Viner, *My Name Is Rachel Corrie*, Royal Court; Richard Norton-Taylor, *Bloody Sunday*, Tricycle Theatre; Robin Soans, *Talking to Terrorists*, Royal Court; Davey Anderson, *Tipping Point*, 7:84/Scottish Trades Union Congress Centre, Glasgow.

93. Alfred Hickling, "The Shipman Inquiry Revisited: Beyond Belief," *The Guardian*, October 28, 2004, 28.

94. Lyn Gardner, "Come Out Eli," *The Guardian*, September 9, 2003, 26.

95. "Alecky Blythe," in *Verbatim Verbatim: Contemporary Documentary Theatre*, ed. Will Hammond and Dan Steward (London: Oberon Books, 2008), 80.

96. Alfred Hickling, "Geoff Dead: Disco for Sale," *The Guardian*, October 18, 2008, 40.

97. "Alecky Blythe," in *Verbatim Verbatim*, 81.

98. Gregory Burke, *Black Watch* (London: Faber and Faber, 2010), 7.

99. Stephen Hoggett, quoted in Heddon, *Autobiography and Performance*, 141.

100. Kate Bassett, "So, Exactly What Did Neil Hamilton Do 13 Years Ago?" *The Independent*, September 30, 2007, 54.

101. Lyn Gardner, "Edinburgh: Theatre: A Fresh Look at the London Bombings: Yesterday Was a Weird Day / Sweet on the Grassmarket," *The Guardian*, August 17, 2005, 20.

102. Kirk Williams, "Anti-Theatricality and the Limits of Naturalism," in *Against Theatre: Creative Destructions on the Modernist Stage*, ed. Alan Ackerman and Martin Puchner (Basingstoke, UK: Palgrave Macmillan, 2006), 97.

103. Kenneth Pickering and Jayne Thompson, *Naturalism in Theatre: Its Development and Legacy* (Basingstoke, UK: Palgrave Macmillan, 2013), 211.

104. Williams, "Anti-Theatricality," 97.

105. Paget, "New Documentarism on Stage," 132.

106. Paget, "Verbatim Theatre," 326.

107. Derek Paget, *True Stories? Documentary Drama on Radio, Screen, and Stage* (Manchester: Manchester University Press, 1990), 21.

108. Paget, "New Documentarism on Stage," 138–39.

109. Adrian Turpin, "Reality Check: Plays Using the Words of Real-Life Protagonists Will Abound on the Edinburgh Fringe. Do They Take Us Closer to the Truth?" *Financial Times*, July 22, 2006, 36.

110. Charlotte Higgins, "Cultural News Round-up: National Rediscovers Politics," *The Guardian*, October 7, 2004, 16.

111. Ron Griffiths, "City/Culture Discourses: Evidence from the Competition to Select the European Capital of Culture 2008," *European Planning Studies* 14, no. 4 (2006): 415–30; Paul Jones and Stuart Wilks-Heeg, "Capitalising Culture: Liverpool 2008," *Local Economy* 19, no. 4 (2004): 341–60.

112. Pete Clark, Mark A. Bellis, and Karen Tocque, "Consultation on a Managed Zone for Sex Trade Workers in Liverpool: Views from Residents, Businesses and Sex Trade Workers in the City of Liverpool: Executive Summary, June 2004," Liverpool John Moores University, 2004, 2.

113. Clark, Bellis, and Tocque, "Consultation on a Managed Zone," 1, 2. Philip Howell, David Beckingham, and Franscesca Moore, "Managed Zones for Sex Workers in Liverpool: Contemporary Proposals, Victorian Parallels," *Transactions of the Institute of British Geographers*, no. 33 (2008): 234.

114. Alfred Hickling, "Sex and the City: Can a Play Make a Difference to the Lives of Prostitutes? Alfred Hickling Investigates," *The Guardian*, March 14, 2006, 21.

115. Diane Taylor, "My Daughter: 'Not Just a Prostitute': Dianne Parry Hoped Her Heroin-Addicted Daughter Would Wake Up One Morning, See Sense, and Come Home. But Hanane Never Did—She Was Murdered, Aged 19, while Working as a Prostitute," *The Guardian*, August 5, 2006.

116. Hickling, "Sex and the City," 21; Suzanne Bell, preface to *Unprotected*, by Esther Wilson, John Fay, Tony Green, and Lizzie Nunnery (London: Josef Weinberger Plays, 2006).

117. Lyn Gardner, "Unprotected," *The Guardian: Guide*, July 29, 2006, 38.

118. Gardner, "Unprotected," 38.

119. Bell, preface to Unprotected.

120. Bell, preface to Unprotected.

121. Elizabeth Burns, *Theatricality: A Study of Convention in the Theatre and in Social Life* (New York: Harper Torchbooks, 1972), 21.

122. John Frow, "Cultural Studies and the Neoliberal Imagination," *Yale Journal of Criticism* 12, no. 2 (1999): 428.

123. Sophie Nield, "On the Border as Theatrical Space: Appearance, Dislocation, and the Production of the Refugee," in *Contemporary Theatres in Europe: A Critical Companion*, ed. Joe Kelleher and Nicholas Ridout (Abingdon, UK: Routledge, 2006), 64.

124. Nield, "On the Border as Theatrical Space," 65.

125. Julia O'Connell Davidson, "The Rights and Wrongs of Prostitution," *Hypatia* 17, no. 2 (2002): 86.

126. Davidson, "The Rights and Wrongs of Prostitution," 86.

127. Julia O'Connell Davidson, *Prostitution, Power, and Freedom* (Ann Arbor: University of Michigan Press, 1998), 121.

128. Phil Hubbard, Roger Matthews, and Jane Scoular, "Regulating Sex Work in the EU: Prostitute Women and the New Spaces of Exclusion," *Gender, Place and Culture* 15, no. 2 (2008): 144.

129. Hilary Kinnell, *Violence and Sex Work in Britain* (Cullompton, UK: Willan Publishing, 2008), xxii.

130. Kinnell, *Violence and Sex Work in Britain*, 37.

131. Hubbard, Matthews, and Scoular, "Regulating Sex Work in the EU," 137–52.

132. Sanchez, "The Global E-rotic Subject," 872.

133. Sanchez, "The Global E-rotic Subject," 869–70.

134. Phil Hubbard and Teela Sanders, "Making Space for Sex Work: Female Street Prostitution and the Production of Urban Space," *International Journal*

of Urban and Regional Research 27, no. 1 (2003): 81. See also Hilary Kinnell's detailed analysis (93–109) in *Violence and Sex Work in Britain*, which exposes the complex racial, religious, and local politics surrounding the events in Balsall Heath.

135. Sanchez, "The Global E-rotic Subject," 871–72.

136. Hickling, "Sex and the City," 21.

137. Sanchez, "The Global E-rotic Subject," 863.

138. Giorgio Agamben, *Homo Sacer: Sovereign Power and Bare Life*, trans. Daniel Heller-Roazen (Stanford, CA: Stanford University Press, 1998), 110, 181.

139. Nield, "On the Border as Theatrical Space," 69.

140. Sanchez, "The Global E-rotic Subject," 866.

141. Sanchez, "The Global E-rotic Subject," 868.

142. Sanchez, "The Global E-rotic Subject," 867.

143. Agamben, cited in Sanchez, "The Global E-rotic Subject," 868.

144. Sanchez, "The Global E-rotic Subject," 868.

145. Sanchez, "The Global E-rotic Subject," 868.

146. Schneider, "Performance Remains," 100–101.

147. Schneider, "Performance Remains," 104.

148. Schneider, 'Performance Remains," 104.

149. Jacques Derrida, *Archive Fever: A Freudian Impression*, trans. Eric Prenowitz (Chicago: University of Chicago Press, 1996), 84.

150. Schneider, "Performance Remains," 105.

151. Though here the "domicile" does not connote the domestic dwelling, these are processes implicated too in the feminized domain of socially reproductive labor. Thanks to Broderick Chow for this observation.

152. Sanchez, "The Global E-rotic Subject," 861.

153. Carol Midgley, "Sex, the City, and a Red Light Ghetto," *The Times*, January 29, 2005, 27.

154. Midgley, "Sex, the City, and a Red Light Ghetto."

155. "Prostitution Zones Approved: Home Office Should Approve Plan . . . but There Must Be Safeguards, Insists MP," *Daily Post*, January 27, 2005, 6. See also Howell, Beckingham, and Moore, "Managed Zones for Sex Workers in Liverpool," 247.

156. Midgley, "Sex, the City, and a Red Light Ghetto."

157. Hubbard, "Revenge and Injustice in the Neoliberal City," 681.

158. Hubbard, 'Revenge and Injustice in the Neoliberal City," 682–83.

159. Charles Landry and Phil Wood, *Harnessing and Exploiting the Power of Culture for Competitive Advantage: A Report by Comedia for the Liverpool City Council and the Core Cities Group* (Stroud, UK: Comedia, 2003), 12.

160. Phil Key, "Liverpool Crowd Won Star Status on a Party Night to Remember: Capital of Culture People's Year Celebration," *Daily Post*, January 12, 2008, 6.

161. David Harvey, *The Enigma of Capital and the Crises of Capitalism* (London: Profile Books, 2011), 16; Tony Lane, *Liverpool: Gateway of Empire* (London: Lawrence and Wishart, 1987), 48–49; Stuart Wilks-Heeg, "From World City to Pariah City? Liverpool and the Global Economy, 1850–2000,"

in *Reinventing the City? Liverpool in Comparative Perspective*, ed. Ronaldo Munck (Liverpool: Liverpool University Press, 2003), 36–52. The droll framing of the artists and politicians as freight would likely now be unstageable, in the light of more recent and widely reported instances of the uses of shipping containers in trafficking people, which have resulted in many deaths. See Anoosh Chakelian, "'Horrified, but Not Shocked': How 39 Deaths Exposed a Cruel Underworld in an Essex Town," *New Statesman*, October 30, 2019. For video footage of the launch, see WalkthePlanktv, "Liverpool 08, European Capital of Culture: The People's Opening and Transition," October 12, 2010, https://www.youtube.com/watch?v=h3lx_hNq91M.

162. Alfred Hickling, "G2: Arts: Follow That Spider! It Had 7,000 Events, Involving 10,000 Artists and 60 Premieres. But Was Liverpool's Year of Culture a Success? Alfred Hickling Gives His Verdict," *The Guardian*, January 5, 2009, 24. For images, see the blog *That's How the Light Gets In*, January 19, 2009, https://gerryco23.wordpress.com/2009/01/10/transition/.

163. Hickling, "G2: Arts: Follow That Spider!"

164. Paul Kingsnorth, *Real England: The Battle Against the Bland* (London: Portobello Books, 2008), 172–81.

165. Helen Ochyra, "Liverpool: Capital of Culture 2008: Rookie's Guide: Well-Heeled City: Looking for an Exciting City Break with Flair, Elegance, and Just a Touch of Luxury? Liverpool Has All You Need for a Chic Weekend, as Helen Ochyra Discovers," *The Guardian: Magazine*, April 5, 2008, 4.

166. Hickling, "G2: Arts: Follow That Spider!"

167. Ben Schofield and Barry Turnbull, "City Shopping Figures Go 'Through the Roof,'" *Daily Post*, December 24, 2008, 1.

168. Richard Down, "Rallying Call as Culture Year Ends," *Daily Post*, January 1, 2009, 6.

169. *Liverpool's Third Cathedral: The Liverpool Everyman Theatre in the Words of Those Who Were, and Are, There*, ed. Ros Merkin (Liverpool: Liverpool and Merseyside Theatres Trust Limited in association with Liverpool John Moores University, 2004); Lynne Walker, "Theatre: The Quality of Mersey: Gemma Bodinetz and Deborah Aydon, the New Team at the Liverpool Everyman and Playhouse, Are Determined to Put the Two Theatres Back on the Map. Lynne Walker Hears How They Plan to Do It," *The Independent*, January 15, 2004, 12.

170. Mary Luckhurst, *Dramaturgy: A Revolution in Theatre* (Cambridge: Cambridge University Press, 2006), 239.

171. Walker, "Theatre: The Quality of Mersey."

172. Paul Taylor, "Review of the Year 2004: Arts: Theatre," *The Independent*, December 27, 2004, 40; Alfred Hickling, "G2: Theatre: 'We Don't Have to Whinge Anymore': It's Boom Time for Regional Theatre. Alfred Hickling Profiles the Playhouses That Are Leading the Way," *The Guardian*, June 2, 2004, 8.

173. Hickling, "G2: Theatre: 'We Don't Have to Whinge Anymore,'" 8.

174. "Capital Date for City's Write Stuff," *Liverpool Daily Post*, October 24, 2003.

175. Liverpool Everyman and Playhouse Theatres, "Mission," http://www.everymanplayhouse.com/about-us/mission.asp.

176. "'Uncelebrated Voices': Part of the Two-Day Symposium 'Verbatim Practice in Contemporary Theatre' Held at Central School of Speech and Drama, 13–14 July 2006," http://www.crco.cssd.ac.uk/25/1/CEN_V_unceleb_edit.pdf.

177. Interview, Esther Wilson, Everyman Theatre, April 2008. This phrase is also included on the front cover of the production's press cuttings pack.

178. Interview, Suzanne Bell, Everyman Theatre, April 2008; Interview, Esther Wilson.

179. "Uncelebrated Voices."

180. "Uncelebrated Voices."

181. Bell, preface to Unprotected.

182. *Unprotected* was broadcast on BBC Radio 4 on March 17, 2006.

183. A5 flyer, *Unprotected*, Traverse Theatre, August 2006.

184. Esther Wilson, John Fay, Tony Green, and Lizzie Nunnery, *Unprotected* (London: Josef Weinberger Plays, 2006), 1.

185. Wilson et al., *Unprotected*, 2.

186. As the academic ethnographer Will Van Den Hoonaard writes in "Is Anonymity an Artifact in Ethnographic Research?" *Journal of Academic Ethics* 1 (2003): 141: "the fetish of individualism creates its ironic counterpart: the individual as the source of data may not be revealed." But the person who grants consent for the use of the nonfictional speech, whom the production frames as authentic, is not the "real" "Ali," but her fictional counterpart. This representational peculiarity—like that of Councillor Clucas publicly discussing her participation in the research process, but not appearing as "herself"—implicitly points to the performative powers of theatrical representation.

187. Interview with Esther Wilson.

188. Traverse Theatre, "About Us," http://www.traverse.co.uk/about-us/.

189. Judith R. Walkowitz, *Prostitution and Victorian Society: Women, Class, and the State* (Cambridge: Cambridge University Press, 1980), 5.

190. Bottoms, "Putting the Document into Documentary," 67.

191. Wilson et al., *Unprotected*, 67.

192. Heddon, *Autobiography and Performance*, 133.

193. "'Uncelebrated Voices.'"

194. "'Uncelebrated Voices.'"

195. "'Uncelebrated Voices.'"

196. Taylor, "My Daughter."

197. A5 flyer, *Unprotected*.

198. Hickling, "G2: Theatre: 'We Don't Have to Whinge Anymore,'" 8.

199. Sam Lister, "We're Well on Course," *Liverpool Daily Post*, May 8, 2006, 6.

200. Philip Key, "Liverpool Artists Stage an Invasion of Edinburgh," *Liverpool Daily Post*, August 8, 2006, 17.

201. Everyman and Playhouse Theatres, "New Writing," http://www.everymanplayhouse.com/new-writing/index.asp.

202. McRobbie, *The Aftermath of Feminism*, 122.

203. Bottoms, "Putting the Document into Documentary," 67.

204. Schneider, "Performance Remains," 104.

205. Paget, "New Documentarism on Stage," 138–39.

206. Turpin, "Reality Check," 36.
207. Sanchez, "The Global E-rotic Subject," 861.
208. "Uncelebrated Voices."
209. Interview with Esther Wilson.
210. Gardner, "Unprotected," 38.
211. Radosavljević, *Theatre-Making*, 145–46.
212. Cheeseman, "A Community Theatre-in-the-Round," 77.

Conclusion

1. David Randall, "A Journey: The Ed Miliband Story," *The Independent*, September 26, 2010.

2. Mark Fisher and Jeremy Gilbert, "Capitalist Realism and Neoliberal Hegemony: A Dialogue," *New Formations*, no. 80–81 (2013): 90.

3. Fisher and Gilbert, "Capitalist Realism and Neoliberal Hegemony," 90–91.

4. Fisher and Gilbert, "Capitalist Realism and Neoliberal Hegemony," 91.

5. Jamie Peck and Nik Theodore, "Still Neoliberalism?" *South Atlantic Quarterly* 118, no. 2 (2019): 259.

6. Jeremy Gilbert, "The Second Wave: The Specificity of New Labour Neoliberalism," *jeremygilbertwriting*, November 3, 2004, https://jeremygilbertwriting.wordpress.com/2004/11/03/the-second-wave-the-specificity-of-new-labour-neoliberalism/.

7. Jamie Peck, "Explaining (with) Neoliberalism," *Territory, Politics, Governance* 1, no. 2 (2013): 135–36.

8. Vanessa Thorpe, "Cultural Figures and Teachers Denounce the Abolition of Arts in Schools Project," *The Observer*, January 9, 2011.

9. "The former Sandfield School closed in 1993 and was then taken over by the Nottinghamshire Arts Support Service and later by the Nottinghamshire Education Advisory Service. Following local government reorganization, the Centre was used by the City's Children's Services Department as offices. Also on the site were a theatre and a Community Wardrobe facility used by a range of organisations. The Centre was substantially vacated in 2010 as part of the Workplace Strategy programme. The theatre closed in April 2011 and then finally Nottingham Community Wardrobe vacated in August 2011." Nottingham City Council, "Development of Sandfield Centre, Sandfield Road, Nottingham," http://open.nottinghamcity.gov.uk/comm/download3.asp?dltype=inline&filename=52591/sandfieldreport.pdf; "Planning Committee 20th December 2017: Report of Chief Planner: Site of the Sandfield Centre, Sandfield Road," http://committee.nottinghamcity.gov.uk/documents/s66378/Site%20Of%20The%20Sandfield%20Centre%20Sandfield%20Road.pdf.

10. Tom Marshall, "Rich Mix Saved after Tower Hamlets Council Drops £850k Lawsuit," *Evening Standard*, September 29, 2015.

11. "Dance Development Takes a Hit in NPO Funding Round," *Arts Professional*, June 30, 2017, https://www.artsprofessional.co.uk/news/dance-development-takes-hit-npo-funding-round.

12. Arts Council England and ComRes, "Arts Council England: Sector Dialogue on Funding 2018 and Beyond," July 2016, 17, https://www.artscouncil.org.uk/sites/default/files/download-file/Arts-Council-England_Sector-dialogue-on-funding-2018-and-beyond.pdf.

13. Equity, "Performance for All Arts Policy 2019," 2019, 9, 12, https://www.equity.org.uk/media/3370/equity_arts-policy-2019_final-web.pdf.

14. Patrick Butler, "Councils Say More Arts Cuts Inevitable Amid Rising Social Care Need," *The Guardian*, January 28, 2019.

15. Dany Louise, "Arts Funding: The New Reality?" *AMAculturehive*, 2019, https://www.culturehive.co.uk/resources/arts-funding-the-new-reality/.

16. Barker et al., *Margate's Seaside Heritage*, 38.

17. Ian Aitch, "Bohemian Private School in Area of Child Poverty Divides Residents," *The Guardian*, December 11, 2018.

18. Michael Smith, "How Margate Became the New Hipster's Paradise," *Esquire*, April 4, 2015, https://www.esquire.com/uk/food-drink/travel/news/a8101/how-margate-became-the-new-hipsters-paradise/.

19. Clive Martin, "Thanet Earth: Margate Is like London Before It Turned into Angel," *Vice*, September 9, 2014, https://www.vice.com/en_uk/article/gq8mk3/thanet-earth-margate-is-the-place-to-be-0000412-v21n8. Angel is a now-upscale area in north London with numerous shops, bars, and restaurants.

20. Barker et al., *Margate's Seaside Heritage*, 46.

21. Jon Burnett, "Racial Violence and the Brexit State," *Race & Class* 58, no. 4 (2017): 85–97.

22. Eleonora Belfiore, "'Defensive Instrumentalism' and the Legacy of New Labour's Cultural Policies," *Cultural Trends* 21, no. 2 (2012): 109.

23. Belfiore, "Defensive Instrumentalism," 110.

24. Peck, "Explaining (with) Neoliberalism," 142, 147.

25. Mary O'Hara, *A Journey to the Sharp End of Cuts in the UK* (Bristol, UK: Policy, 2015); Alison Flood, "Britain Has Closed Almost 800 Libraries since 2010, Figures Show," *The Guardian*, December 6, 2019.

26. Stuart Hall, "The Neoliberal Revolution," *Cultural Studies* 25, no. 6 (2011): 705, 715.

27. Hall, "The Neoliberal Revolution," 719–21, 723.

28. Peck, "Explaining (with) Neoliberalism," 154.

29. Peck, "Explaining (with) Neoliberalism," 154.

30. Ann Pettifor, *The Production of Money: How to Break the Power of Bankers* (London: Verso, 2017), x.

31. Jeremy Gilbert, "This Conjuncture: For Stuart Hall," *New Formations* 96–97 (2019): 16.

32. Simon English, 'How Labour wooed the City: Keir Starmer's offensive is working on business', *Evening Standard*, July 25, 2023.

33. Adam Tooze, *Shutdown: How Covid Shook the World's Economy* (London: Allen Lane, 2021), 22.

34. Meadway, "Neoliberalism Is Dying": "Neoliberalism might be dying, but this is no reason for complacency. Some of what is now happening points to a decisively worse world: digitally enabled authoritarianism and overtly discriminatory government policy, for example."

35. Hall, "The Neoliberal Revolution," 705.

36. John Frow, "Cultural Studies and the Neoliberal Imagination," *Yale Journal of Criticism* 12, no. 2 (1999): 428.

37. Frow, "Cultural Studies and the Neoliberal Imagination," 428.

38. Frow, "Cultural Studies and the Neoliberal Imagination," 429.

BIBLIOGRAPHY

Archival Materials

AfroReggae UK Partnership. "Can Culture Be Our Weapon? Raising the Stakes in the Fight against Gun Crime and Gang Culture." Monday, May 14, 2007, Garden Room, Barbican Centre.

AfroReggae UK Partnership Mini-Projects showcase. Artist seminar, Wednesday June 27, 2007.

Artangel. "Exodus Venice," received via e-mail September 1, 2007.

Artangel brochure. London: Artangel 2006.

Artsadmin Events. "La Ribot Comes to Greenwich," received via e-mail September 27, 2005.

Dance4. "Exciting Opportunity to Perform at Nottdance06," publicity flyer, 2006.

Espiner, Mark. "Shows of Strength." *Barbican at 25* (2007), 107–8.

Everyman Theatre. *Unprotected*, A5 flyer, Thursday, August 3, to Sunday, August 20, 2006, Traverse Theatre.

Greenwich Dance Agency, promotional DVD.

La Ribot. *40 espontaneos*, publicity flyer, 2005–6.

"La Ribot." In *Panorama Rioarte de Danca Workshops: La Ribot—Pacitti Company—Gary Stevens*, DVD, directed by Nelson Enohata. London: British Council, 2004.

The Margate Exodus, recruitment flyer.

Pfeiffer, Paul. *The Saints* program, 2007.

Interviews

Interview, Brendan Keaney, Greenwich Dance Agency, April 2006.

Interview, Carla Martins, AfroReggae, October 2007.

Interview, Damian Atkinson, Shoreditch Trust, January 2008.

Interview, E. J. Trivett, Immediate Theatre, December 2007.

Interview, Esther Wilson, Liverpool Everyman Theatre, April 2008.

Interview, Jo Carter, Immediate Theatre, December 2007.

Interview, Karen Taylor, Arts Council England, December 2007.

Interview, Malin Forbes, Barbican Centre, December 2007.

Interview, Nicky Childs, Artsadmin, July 2006.

Interview (e-mail), Nicky Molloy, Dance4, July 2006.

Interview, Peter Leigh, Sound Connections, November 2007.
Interview, Richard Ings, May 2007.
Interview, Suzanne Bell, Liverpool Everyman Theatre, April 2008.
40 espontáneos e-mail questionnaire, May 2006.

Secondary Sources

Ackerman, Alan, and Martin Puchner. "Introduction: Modernism and Anti-Theatricality." In *Against Theatre: Creative Destructions on the Modernist Stage*, ed. Alan Ackerman and Martin Puchner, 1–17. New York: Palgrave, 2006.

"After Neoliberalism, with James Meadway." *Politics, Theory, Other*, July 25, 2021. https://soundcloud.com/poltheoryother/after-neoliberalism-w-james-meadway.

Agamben, Giorgio. *Homo Sacer: Sovereign Power and Bare Life*. Stanford, CA: Stanford University Press, 1998.

Agnew, Jean-Christophe. *Worlds Apart: The Market and the Theatre in Anglo-American Thought, 1550–1750*. Cambridge: Cambridge University Press, 1986.

Aitch, Ian. "Bohemian Private School in Area of Child Poverty Divides Residents." *The Guardian*, December 11, 2018.

———. "Culture: Plagues of Frogs and Lice . . . and Artists, including Antony Gormley and Rufus Wainwright, Have Descended on Margate. Ian Aitch on a Huge Project That's Transforming the Town." *The Guardian*, September 26, 2006.

———. "Exodus Fires Up the Imagination of Thousands." *Isle of Thanet Gazette*, October 6, 2006.

"All Go Margate (1970)." https://www.youtube.com/watch?v=TSgGHh6zap0.

Andrade, Oswald de. "Manifesto antropófago." *Revista de Antropofágia* (São Paulo) 1 (1928): 3–7. https://icaa.mfah.org/s/en/item/771303#?c=&m=&s=&cv=&xywh=-1250%2C-101%2C3982%2C2228.

Anonymous. "Gil integra comitiva de Lula a Portugal." *Agência Brasil*, July 8, 2003. http://memoria.ebc.com.br/agenciabrasil/noticia/2003–07–08/gil-integra-comitiva-de-lula-portugal.

Arias, Enrique Desmond. *Drugs and Democracy in Rio de Janeiro: Trafficking, Social Networks, and Public Security*. Chapel Hill: University of North Carolina Press, 2006.

Armstrong, Derrick. "A Risky Business? Research, Policy, and Governmentality and Youth Offending." *Youth Justice* 4 (2004): 100–116.

Artangel. "About Artangel." http://www.artangel.org.uk/about_us.

———. "Coronet Cinema." Artangel. https://www.artangel.org.uk/project/coronet-cinema/.

———. "The English Civil War: Part II (2002)." Artangel. http://www.artangel.org.uk//projects/2001/the_battle_of_orgreave/background/the_english_civil_war_part_ii.

———. "Seizure." https://www.artangel.org.uk/project/seizure/.

———. "Towards a Promised Land." https://www.artangel.org.uk/project/towards-a-promised-land/.

Arts Council England. *The Arts and Young People at Risk of Offending*. London: Arts Council England, 2005.

Arts Council England and ComRes. "Arts Council England: Sector Dialogue on Funding 2018 and Beyond." July 2016. https://www.artscouncil.org.uk/sites/default/files/download-file/Arts-Council-England_Sector-dialogue-on-funding-2018-and-beyond.pdf.

Arts Council of Great Britain. *Opera and Dance: Report of the Study Group: February 1983*. London: Arts Council of Great Britain, 1983.

Artsadmin Events. "La Ribot Comes to Greenwich," received via e-mail, September 27, 2005.

Arvidsson, Adam. *Brands: Meaning and Value in Media Culture*. Abingdon, UK: Routledge, 2006.

Aston, Elaine, and Janelle Reinelt. "Building Bridges: Life on Dunbar's Arbor, Past and Present." *Theatre Research International* 26, no. 3 (2001): 285–93.

Austin, J. L. *How to Do Things with Words*. 2nd edition, ed. J. O. Urmson and Maria Sbisa. Cambridge, MA: Harvard University Press 1975 (1962).

Avelar, Idelber, and Christopher Dunn. "Introduction: Music as Practice of Citizenship in Brazil." In *Brazilian Popular Music and Citizenship*, ed. Idelber Avelar and Christopher Dunn, 1–27. Durham, NC: Duke University Press, 2011.

Bailes, Kathy. "Be a Star in Movie of Town." *Isle of Thanet Gazette*, May 12, 2006.

Baldwin, Debbie, Bob Coles, and Wendy Mitchell. "The Formation of an Underclass or Disparate Processes of Social Exclusion? Evidence from Two Groupings of Vulnerable Youth." In *Youth, the "Underclass," and Social Exclusion*, ed. Robert Macdonald, 83–95. Abingdon, UK: Routledge, 1997.

Balfour, Michael. "Refugee Performance: Encounters with Alterity." *Journal of Arts and Communities* 2, no. 3 (2010): 177–95.

Barbican. "Favelization." http://www.barbican.org.uk/theatre/event-detail.asp?ID=7378.

Barker, Nigel, Allan Brodie, Nick Dermott, Lucy Jessop, and Gary Winter. *Margate's Seaside Heritage*. Swindon, UK: English Heritage, 2007. https://historicengland.org.uk/images-books/publications/margates-seaside-heritage/margates-seaside-heritage/.

Bartlett, Ken. "A Workforce for the Future?" *Animated* (2009): 32–35.

Bassett, Kate. "So, Exactly What Did Neil Hamilton Do 13 Years Ago?" *The Independent*, September 30, 2007, 54.

Bauer, Una. "The Movement of Embodied Thought: The Representational Games of the Stage Zero of Signification in Jérôme Bel." *Performance Research* 13, no. 1 (2008): 35–41.

Beckett, Andy. *When the Lights Went Out: What Really Happened to Britain in the Seventies*. London: Faber and Faber, 2009.

Belfiore, Eleanora. "Auditing Culture: The Subsidised Cultural Sector in the New Public Management." *International Journal of Cultural Policy* 10, no. 2 (2004): 183–202.

———. "'Defensive Instrumentalism' and the Legacy of New Labour's Cultural Policies." *Cultural Trends* 21, no. 2 (2012): 103–11.

Belgrade Theatre Coventry. "About Us | History." http://www.belgrade.co.uk/about-us/history/.

Bell, Suzanne. Preface to *Unprotected*, by Esther Wilson, John Fay, Tony Green, and Lizzie Nunnery. London: Josef Weinberger Plays, 2006.

Bestwick, Deborah. "Valuing Culture." Speech given at the "Valuing Culture" symposium, National Theatre Studio, June 17, 2003. http://www.demos.co.uk/files/File/VACUDBestwick.pdf.

Bethell, Leslie. "Politics in Brazil: From Elections without Democracy to Democracy without Citizenship." In *Brazil since 1985: Politics, Economy and Society*, ed. Maria D'Alva Kinzo and James Dunkerley, 21–41. London: Institute of Latin American Studies, 2003.

Birringer, Johannes. "Dance and Not Dance." *PAJ: A Journal of Performance and Art* 27, no. 2 (2005): 10–27.

Bishop, Claire. *Artificial Hells: Participatory Art and the Politics of Spectatorship*. London: Verso, 2012.

———. "'As If I Was Lost and Someone Suddenly Came to Give Me News about Myself.'" In *Off Limits: 40 Artangel Projects*, ed. Gerrie van Noord, 22–29. London: Merrell, 2002.

Blakeley, Grace. "Covid-19 Is Not the End of Neoliberalism." *Tribune*, May 28, 2021. https://tribunemag.co.uk/2021/05/covid-19-is-not-the-end-of-neoliberalism.

Blunt, Caroline. "Neither Last Resort nor Promised Land." *Street Signs*, Autumn 2006, 28–29.

Blythe, Alecky. "Alecky Blythe." In *Verbatim Verbatim: Contemporary Documentary Theatre*, ed. Will Hammond and Dan Steward, 77–102. London: Oberon Books, 2008.

Boal, Augusto. *The Rainbow of Desire: The Boal Method of Theatre and Therapy*, trans. Adrian Jackson. London: Routledge, 1995.

Boas, Taylor C., and Jordan Gans-Morse. "Neoliberalism: From New Liberal Philosophy to Anti-Liberal Slogan." *Studies in Comparative International Development* 44, no. 2 (2009): 137–61.

Borges, Juliana. "Eles fazem muito com pouco." *Exame*, December 18, 2009.

Botham, Paola. "From Deconstruction to Reconstruction: A Habermasian Framework for Contemporary Political Theatre." *Contemporary Theatre Review* 18, no. 3 (2008): 307–17.

Bottoms, Stephen. "Putting the Document into Documentary: An Unwelcome Corrective?" *TDR: The Drama Review* 50, no. 3 (2006): 56–68.

———. "Staging the Democratic Deficit; or, Three Uses of the Interview." *Contemporary Theatre Review* 25, no. 2 (2015): 190–204.

Bourdieu, Pierre. *The Logic of Practice*, trans. Richard Nice. Cambridge: Polity, 1990 (1980).

Bowness, Mark. "Our Heritage Is Crumbling." *The Sun*, August 19, 2003.

Bradford, Simon. "The Management of Growing Up: Youth Work in Community Settings." In *Youth in Society*, 2nd edition, ed. Jeremy Roche, Stanley Tucker, Rachel Thomson, and Ronny Flynn, 245–54. London: Sage, 2004.

Brantley, Ben. "Theater Review: Someone Else Committed Their Crimes." *New York Times*, October 11, 2002. https://www.nytimes.com/2002/10/11/movies/theater-review-someone-else-committed-their-crimes.html.

Brinson, Peter. "The Audience of the Future: The Royal Ballet Demonstration Group's Work and Progress." *Dancing Times* 56, no. 669 (June 1966): 455–56.

———. "A Culture of Mind and Body." *Dance Now* 2, no. 3 (1993): 51–59.

———. *Dance as Education: Towards a National Dance Culture*. London: Falmer, 1991.

———. "The Making of Dance Animateurs." *Dance Theatre Journal* 3, no. 3 (1985): 26.

———. "The Nature of Collaboration." *New Dance* 22 (June 1982): 8–11.

———. "Reaching Out from London: Gulbenkian Grant for the Opera House." *Dancing Times* 54, no. 642 (March 1964): 290.

———. "Stimulating Audiences: Peter Brinson Talks to Dance and Dancers about Ballet for All." *Dance and Dancers* 18, no. 11 (November 1967): 22–23.

Brinson, Peter, and Clement Crisp. *Ballet for All: A Guide to One Hundred Ballets*. London: Pan Books, 1970.

Brinson, Peter, and Fiona Dick, *Fit to Dance? The Report of the National Inquiry into Dancers' Health and Injury*. London: Calouste Gulbenkian Foundation, 1996.

Brown, Wendy. *Undoing the Demos: Neoliberalism's Stealth Revolution*. New York: Zone Books, 2005.

Bunting, Madeleine. "Culture, Not Politics, Is Now the Heart of Our Public Realm: The Cynics Who Ridiculed Margate's Exodus Day Miss the Point: Art Has Broken Its Elitist Leash to Inspire Collective Purpose." *The Guardian*, October 3, 2006, 30.

Burke, Gregory. *Black Watch*. London: Faber and Faber, 2010.

Burnett, Jon. "Racial Violence and the Brexit State." *Race & Class* 58, no. 4 (2017): 85–97.

Burney, Elizabeth. *Making People Behave: Anti-Social Behaviour, Politics, and Policy*. Cullompton, UK: Willan, 2005.

———. *Theatricality: A Study of Convention in the Theatre and in Social Life*. New York: Harper Torchbooks, 1972.

Burt, Ramsay. "Preferring to Laugh." *Parallax* 14, no. 1 (2008): 15–23.

Butler, Patrick. "Councils Say More Arts Cuts Inevitable amid Rising Social Care Need." *The Guardian*, January 28, 2019.

"Cable Street Mural—a Continuing Story—30 Years in the Making." *AND Journal*, October 20, 2011. http://www.and.org.uk/2011/10/cable-street-mural-a-continuing-story-30-years-in-the-making/.

Cameron, Angus. "Geographies of Welfare and Exclusion: Social Inclusion and Exception." *Progress in Human Geography* 30, no. 3 (2006): 396–404.

———. "Geographies of Welfare and Exclusion: Reconstituting the 'Public.' " *Progress in Human Geography* 31, no. 4 (2007): 519–26.

Cameron, Angus, and Ronen Palan. *The Imagined Economies of Globalization*. London: Sage, 2004.

"Campaigners Plan to Exploit Margate Movie." *Kent News*, September 29, 2006.

Canejo, Cynthia. "The Resurgence of Anthropophagy." *Third Text* 18, no. 1 (2004): 61–68.

Cantrell, Tom. *Acting in Documentary Theatre*. Basingstoke, UK: Palgrave Macmillan, 2013.

"Capital Date for City's Write Stuff." *Liverpool Daily Post*, October 24, 2003.

Chakelian, Anoosh. "'Horrified, but Not Shocked': How 39 Deaths Exposed a Cruel Underworld in an Essex Town." *New Statesman*, October 30, 2019.

"Chance for All to Shine with Film Project." *Isle of Thanet Gazette*, June 16, 2006.

Chater, David. "TV Choice." *The Times: The Knowledge*, December 2, 2006.

Cheeseman, Peter. "A Community Theatre-in-the-Round." *Theatre Quarterly* 1 (1971): 71–82.

Chisenhale Dance Space. "History." https://www.chisenhaledancespace.co.uk/about/our-history/.

Church, Michael. "The Rise of a Quiet Achiever: Arts Interview: Michael Morris." *Financial Times*, November 2, 2002.

Clancey, John. *Kent's Seaside Resorts through Time*. Stroud, UK: Amberley, 2012.

Clapp, Susannah. "Arts: The Year Ahead; Theatre in '99; Four Legs Good." *The Observer*, January 3, 1999, 8.

Clark, Pete, Mark A. Bellis, and Karen Tocque. "Consultation on a Managed Zone for Sex Trade Workers in Liverpool: Views from Residents, Businesses and Sex Trade Workers in the City of Liverpool: Executive Summary, June 2004." Liverpool John Moores University, 2004.

Clements, Richard. *Margate*. Stroud, UK: History, 2009 (1992).

Connolly, Maeve. "Artangel and the Changing Mediascape of Public Art." *Journal of Curatorial Studies* 2, no. 2 (2013): 196–217.

"A Conversation between Michael Craig-Martin, Lisa Jardine, James Lingwood, and Michael Morris." In *Off Limits: 40 Artangel Projects*, ed. Gerrie van Noord, 10–20. London: Merrell, 2002.

Cooke, Rachel. "Should Lap Dancing Be Run Out of Town? With a New Venue Opening Every Week, Lap Dancing Has Spread into British Culture." *The Observer*, March 8, 2009, 24.

Cork, Richard. *Breaking Down the Barriers: Art in the 1990s*. New Haven, CT: Yale University Press, 2003.

Corner, John. *The Art of Record: A Critical Introduction to Documentary*. Manchester: Manchester University Press, 1996.

Costa, Maddy. "Reviews: Film Sets and Reality Blur into One as Margate Takes Starring Role." *The Guardian*, October 2, 2006.

Cotton, Elizabeth. "Self-Employment Is Precarious Work." *LSE: Surviving Work in the UK*, September 12, 2016. https://blogs.lse.ac.uk/businessreview/2016/09/12/self-employment-is-precarious-work.

Cotton, Georgina. "Previews: The Promised Land beside the Seaside: Film 'The Margate Exodus.'" *The Independent*, September 25, 2006.

Coult, Tony. "Agents of the Future: Theatre-in-Education." In *Dreams and Deconstructions: Alternative Theatre in Britain*, ed. Sandy Craig, 76–85. Ambergate, UK: Amber Lane, 1980.

Creative Partnerships. "About CP." http://www.creative-partnerships.com/aboutcp/.

Crickmay, Chris. "'Art and Social Context': Its Background, Inception, and Development." 2010. *Demanding Conversations*. http://www.demandingconversations.org.uk/wp-content/uploads/2010/08/Art-and-Social-Context-by-Chris-Crickmay.pdf.

Cultural Industry. "Cultural Industry." http://www.culturalindustry.co.uk/pages/cultural_industry.html.

Cutler, Anna. "Towards a Promised Land." In *Art of Negotiation*, ed. David Butler and Vivienne Reiss, 187–223. London: Cornerhouse, 2007.

Cvejić, Bojana. "Collectivity? You Mean Collaboration." *Transversal Texts*, January 2005. https://transversal.at/transversal/1204/cvejic/en.

Da Cunha, Olivia Maria Gomes. "Black Movements and the 'Politics of Identity' in Brazil." In *Cultures of Politics, Politics of Cultures: Re-visioning Latin American Social Movements*, ed. Sonia E. Alvarez, Evelina Dagnino, and Arturo Escobar, 220–51. Boulder, CO: Westview, 1998.

"Dance Development Takes a Hit in NPO Funding Round." *Arts Professional*, June 30, 2017. https://www.artsprofessional.co.uk/news/dance-development-takes-hit-npo-funding-round.

Daoust, Phil. "Reviews: Theatre: Rita, Sue / A State Affair; Soho Theatre, London (5 stars)." *The Guardian*, December 9, 2000, 29.

"A Date with the Sun (1965)." https://www.youtube.com/watch?v=SCc0RP6n37w.

Davidson, Julia O'Connell. *Prostitution, Power, and Freedom*. Ann Arbor: University of Michigan Press, 1998.

———. "The Rights and Wrongs of Prostitution." *Hypatia* 17, no. 2 (2002): 85–98.

Davis, Tracy C. "Theatricality and Civil Society." In *Theatricality*, ed. Tracy Davis and Thomas Postlethwaite, 127–55. Cambridge: Cambridge University Press, 2003.

DCMS/DfES. "Government Response to the Culture, Media, and Sport Select Committee Report on Arts Development: Dance (HC 587), Session 2003–2004," 1–10. London: TSO, 2004.

Deller, Jeremy. "The Battle of Orgreave." www.jeremydeller.org/TheBattleOfOrgreave/TheBattleOfOrgreave_Video.php.

Demissie, Simon, and Vicky Iglikowski-Broad. "'No Pasarán': The Battle of Cable Street." *The National Archives*, October 4, 2016. https://blog.nationalarchives.gov.uk/no-pasaran-battle-cable-street/.

Denham, Chris. "Margate Exodus Is More Than a Great Arts Event." *Thanet Extra*, September 15, 2006.

Dent Coad, Emma. "Artistic Patronage and Enterprise Culture." In *Spanish Cultural Studies: An Introduction: The Struggle for Modernity*, ed. Helen Graham and Jo Labanyi, 373–76. Oxford: Oxford University Press, 1996.

Department for Culture, Media, and Sport. "Building on PAT 10: Progress Report on Social Inclusion." London, 2001.

———. "Culture at the Heart of Regeneration." London, 2003.

———. "Policy Action Team 10: A Report to the Social Exclusion Unit." London, 1999.

Derrida, Jacques. *Archive Fever: A Freudian Impression*, trans. Eric Prenowitz. Chicago: University of Chicago Press, 1996.

Dowdney, Luke. *Children of the Drug Trade: A Case Study of Children in Organised Armed Violence in Rio de Janeiro*. Rio de Janeiro: 7 Letras, 2003.

Down, Richard. "Rallying Call as Culture Year Ends." *Daily Post*, January 1, 2009, 6.

Drummond, John, and Nicholas Thompson. *The Turn of Dance? A Feasibility Study towards the Establishment of a National Dance House*. London: Arts Council of Great Britain, 1984.

Dryfoos, Joy G. *Adolescents at Risk: Prevalence and Prevention*. New York: Oxford University Press, 1991.

Duman, Alberto. "Not Here, Right Now/Right Here, Not Now: Unfolding the Context in Alana Jelinek's *This Is Not Art*." *Journal of Visual Art Practice* 13, no. 3 (2014): 203–26.

Dunn, Bill. "Against Neoliberalism as a Concept." *Capital and Class* 41, no. 3 (2017): 435–54.

Dwesar, Sandeep. "Taking Greater Risks to Reach New Heights." *Barbican Annual Review 06/07*.

Eaton, George. "Is the Neoliberal Era Finally Over?" *New Statesman*, June 16, 2021. https://www.newstatesman.com/politics/economy/2021/06/neoliberal-era-finally-over.

Edgar, David. "Doc and Dram: Why Has This Decade Seen the Rise of a Vibrant Theatre of Reportage? Playwright David Edgar Points to a Decline in Conventional Journalism and TV Documentary." *The Guardian*, September 27, 2008.

El-Enany, Nadine. *(B)ordering Britain: Law, Race, and Empire*. Manchester: Manchester University Press, 2020.

Ellis, Adrian. "Valuing Culture." Speech given at the "Valuing Culture" symposium, National Theatre Studio, June 17, 2003. https://www.demos.co.uk/files/File/VACUAEllis.pdf.

Ellis, Samantha. "Spontaneous Co-operation: Maria Ribot Takes on Untrained Performers for Her Dance Work about Bullfight Spectators, Reports Samantha Ellis." *What's On in London*, October 26, 2005.

Elvgren, Gillete A., Jr. "Documentary Theatre at Stoke-on-Trent." *Educational Theatre Journal* 26, no. 1 (1974): 86–98.

English, Simon. 'How Labour wooed the City: Keir Starmer's offensive is working on business." *Evening Standard*, July 25, 2023.

Equity. "Performance for All Arts Policy 2019." 2019, pp. 9, 12. https://www.equity.org.uk/media/3370/equity_arts-policy-2019_final-web.pdf.

Evans, Graeme, and Phyllida Shaw. "The Contribution of Culture to Regeneration in the UK: A Review of Evidence." London: Department for Culture, Media, and Sports, 2004.

Everyman and Playhouse Theatres. "Mission." http://www.everymanplayhouse.com/about-us/mission.asp.

———. "New Writing." http://www.everymanplayhouse.com/new-writing/index.asp.

Ewald, Wendy, and Michael Morris. "Towards a Promised Land." In *Towards a Promised Land*, ed. Louise Neri, 141–52. Göttingen: Steidl, 2006.

Exodus. DVD, directed by Penny Woolcock. Soda Pictures, 2007.

Féral, Josette, "Foreword." *SubStance* 31, no. 2-3 (2002): 3–13.

Filewod, Alan, and David Watt. *Workers' Playtime: Theatre and the Labour Movement in Australia, Canada, and the United Kingdom 1970–1997*. Sydney: Currency, 2001.

Finlayson, Alan. "Tony Blair and the Jargon of Modernisation." *Soundings* 10 (1998): 11–27.

Fisher, Mark, and Jeremy Gilbert. "Capitalist Realism and Neoliberal Hegemony: A Dialogue." *New Formations* 80/81 (2013): 89–101.

Forsyth, Alison, and Chris Megson. Introduction to *Get Real: Documentary Theatre Past and Present*, ed. Alison Forsyth and Chris Megson, 1–5. Basingstoke, UK: Palgrave Macmillan, 2009.

Foucault, Michel. *The Birth of Biopolitics: Lectures at the Collège de France 1978–79*, ed. Michel Senellart. Basingstoke, UK: Palgrave Macmillan, 2008.

Foundation for Community Dance. "Mapping Community Dance: A Research Report of the Foundation for Community Dance." Leicester, 2001.

"Free Form—Martin Goodrich." *For Walls with Tongues*. https://www.forwallswithtongues.org.uk/artists/free-form-martin-goodrich/.

"From the Marginality of the 1960s to the New Poverty of Today: An LARR Research Forum." *Latin American Research Review* 39, no. 1 (2004): 183–203.

Frow, John. *Cultural Studies and Cultural Value*. Oxford: Clarendon, 1995.

———. "Cultural Studies and the Neoliberal Imagination." *Yale Journal of Criticism* 12, no. 2 (1999): 424–30.

———. *Genre*. New York: Routledge, 2006.

Gacitúa Marió, Estanislao, and Michael Woolcock. *Social Exclusion and Mobility in Brazil*. Washington, DC: World Bank, 2008. https://openknowledge.worldbank.org/handle/10986/6340.

Gagnier, Regina. *The Insatiability of Human Wants: Economics and Aesthetics in Market Society*. Chicago: University of Chicago Press, 2000.

García, Beatriz. "Cultural Policy and Urban Regeneration in Western European Cities: Lessons from Experience, Prospects for the Future." *Local Economy* 19, no. 4 (2004): 312–26.

Gardner, Lyn. "Come Out Eli." *The Guardian*, September 9, 2003.

———. "Edinburgh: Theatre: A Fresh Look at the London Bombings: Yesterday Was a Weird Day / Sweet on the Grassmarket." *The Guardian*, August 17, 2005, 20.

———. "Guantanamo." *The Guardian*, June 29, 2004, 18.

———. "The Margate Exodus." *The Guardian: Guide*, September 30, 2006.

———. "Reviews: Theatre: Rita, Sue / A State Affair: Everyman, Liverpool (4/5 stars)." *The Guardian*, October 26, 2000, 25.

———. "Unprotected." *The Guardian: Guide*, July 29, 2006, 38.

———. "Waiting Room Germany." *The Guardian*, November 13, 1995, 9.

Garland, David. "What Is a 'History of the Present'? On Foucault's Genealogies and Their Critical Preconditions." *Punishment & Society* 16, no. 4 (2014): 365–84.

Garnham, Nicholas. "Afterword: The Cultural Commodity and Cultural Policy." In *The UK Cultural Sector: Profile and Policy Issues*, ed. Sara Selwood, 445–58. London: Policy Studies Institute, 2001.

———. "From Cultural to Creative Industries: An Analysis of the Implications of the 'Creative Industries' Approach to Arts and Media Policy-Making in the United Kingdom." *International Journal of Cultural Policy* 11, no. 1 (2005): 15–29.

Giddens, Anthony. *Beyond Left and Right: The Future of Radical Politics.* Cambridge: Polity, 1994.

Gil, Gilberto. "'Experimentation, Memory, and Invention': Inaugural Address Delivered by Minister Gilberto Gil on Being Sworn into Office, Brasília, January 2, 2003." *Living Culture: National Culture, Education, and Citizenship Program.* http://colecoes.inpa.gov.br/sb/docs/english.pdf.

———. "Ministro Gilberto Gil no Fórum de Amigos da Cultura do Brasil na Europa." Address in Rome, Italy, July 21, 2003. http://cultura.gov.br/ministro-gilberto-gil-no-forum-de-amigos-da-cultura-do-brasil-na-europa-35658/.

Gilbert, Jeremy. "'Neoliberalism' and 'Capitalism'—What's the Difference?" *jeremygilbertwriting*, July 14, 2015. https://jeremygilbertwriting.wordpress.com/2015/07/14/neoliberalism-and-capitalism-whats-the-difference/.

———. "The Second Wave: The Specificity of New Labour Neoliberalism." *jeremygilbertwriting*, November 3, 2004. https://jeremygilbertwriting.wordpress.com/2004/11/03/the-second-wave-the-specificity-of-new-labour-neoliberalism/.

———. "This Conjuncture: For Stuart Hall." *New Formations* 96–97 (2019): 5–37.

———. "What Kind of Thing Is Neoliberalism?" *New Formations* 80/81 (2013): 7–22.

Gill, A. A. "Something Biblical for the Weekend? As Margate Prepares for a Plague of Frogs and Lice, A. A. Gill Asks: Can They Be Serious?" *Sunday Times: Culture*, August 27, 2006.

Gilroy, Paul. *After Empire: Melancholia or Convivial Culture?* Abingdon, UK: Routledge, 2004.

Gormley, Anthony. "Waste Man, 2006." https://www.antonygormley.com/projects/item-view/id/260#p0.

Goumarre, Laurent. "Die Another Day." In *La Ribot*, vol. 2, ed. Claire Rousier, 60–69. Pantin: Centre National de la Danse, 2004.

Griffiths, Ron. "City/Culture Discourses: Evidence from the Competition to Select the European Capital of Culture 2008." *European Planning Studies* 14, no. 4 (2006): 415–30.

Gronemeyer, Wiebke. "October 2007: Paul Pfeiffer, *The Saints.*" *Whitehot Magazine*, October 2007. https://whitehotmagazine.com/index.php?action=articles&wh_article_id=959.

Guilding, Ruth. "Unforgettable Fire." *The Spectator*, October 7, 2006.

Guillory, John. *Cultural Capital: The Problem of Literary Canon Formation.* Chicago: University of Chicago Press, 1993.

Hackney. "Hackney Local Implementation Plan LIP (2006–2011)." http://www.hackney.gov.uk/local_implementation_plan_-_section_1_-_local_socio-economic_impact.pdf.

Hall, Stuart. "The Neoliberal Revolution." *Cultural Studies* 25, no. 6 (2011): 705–28.

———. "New Labour's Double Shuffle." *Soundings* 24 (2003): 10–24.

Hall, Stuart, Doreen Massey, and Michael Rustin. "After Neoliberalism: Analysing the Present." In *After Neoliberalism? The Kilburn Manifesto*, 1–20. Chadwell Heath, UK: Soundings, 2013. https://www.lwbooks.co.uk/sites/default/files/00_manifestoframingstatement.pdf.

Hancox, Dan. "Revealed: Creeping Privatization of London Parks in Summer." *The Guardian*, July 5, 2019.

Hardt, Michael, and Antonio Negri. *Empire*. Cambridge, MA: Harvard University Press, 2000.

Hare, David. *The Permanent Way, or La Voie Anglaise*. London: Faber and Faber, 2003.

Hare, David, and Max Stafford-Clark. "David Hare and Max Stafford-Clark." In *Verbatim Verbatim: Contemporary Documentary Theatre*, ed. Will Hammond and Dan Steward, 45–75. London: Oberon Books, 2008.

Hargreaves, Martin. "Laughing, Crying, Contagion, Collapse." *Dance Theatre Journal* 20, no. 2 (2004): 34–37.

Harvey, David. *A Brief History of Neoliberalism*. Oxford: Oxford University Press, 2005.

———. *The Condition of Postmodernity: An Enquiry into the Origins of Cultural Change*. Malden, MA: Blackwell, 1990.

———. *The Enigma of Capital and the Crises of Capitalism*. London: Profile Books, 2011.

———. "Flexible Accumulation through Urbanization: Reflections on 'Post-Modernism' in the American City." In *Post-Fordism: A Reader*, ed. Ash Amin, 361–86. Oxford: Blackwell, 1994.

———. "The 'New' Imperialism: Accumulation by Dispossession." *Socialist Register* (2004): 63–87.

Harvie, Jen. *Fair Play: Art, Performance and Neoliberalism*. Basingstoke, UK: Palgrave Macmillan, 2013.

———. *Staging the UK*. Manchester: Manchester University Press, 2005.

Haurant, Sandra. "Average House Price Breaks £200,000 Barrier." *The Guardian*, November 8, 2006.

Heathfield, Adrian. "After the Fall: Dance-Theatre and Dance-Performance." In *Contemporary Theatres in Europe: A Critical Companion*, ed. Joe Kelleher and Nicholas Ridout, 188–98. Abingdon, UK: Routledge, 2006.

———. "In Memory of Little Things." In *La Ribot*, vol. 2, ed. Claire Rousier, 21–27. Pantin: Centre National de la Danse, 2004.

Heddon, Deirdre. *Autobiography and Performance*. Basingstoke, UK: Palgrave Macmillan, 2008.

Heritage, Paul. *Intense Dreams: Reflections on Brazilian Culture and Performance*. London: People's Palace Projects, 2009.

Hesmondhalgh, David, Melissa Nisbett, Kate Oakley, and David Lee. "Were New Labour's Cultural Policies Neo-Liberal?" *International Journal of Cultural Policy* 21, no. 1 (2015): 97–114.

Hewison, Robert. *Cultural Capital: The Rise and Fall of Creative Britain*. London: Verso, 2014.

———. "Light in the Darkness." *The Times*, October 18, 1992.

Hewison, Robert, and John Holden, *Experience and Experiment: The UK Branch of the Calouste Gulbenkian Foundation, 1956–2006*. London: Calouste Gulbenkian Foundation, 2006.

Hewitt, Andy. "Privatizing the Public: Three Rhetorics of Art's Public Good in 'Third Way' Cultural Policy." *Art and the Public Sphere* 1, no. 1 (2011): 19–36.

Hickling, Alfred. "Geoff Dead: Disco for Sale." *The Guardian*, October 18, 2008, 40.

———. "G2: Arts: Follow That Spider! It Had 7,000 Events, Involving 10,000 Artists and 60 Premieres. But Was Liverpool's Year of Culture a Success? Alfred Hickling Gives His Verdict." *The Guardian*, January 5, 2009, 24.

———. "G2: Theatre: 'We Don't Have to Whinge Anymore.'" *The Guardian*, June 2, 2004, 8.

———. "Sex and the City: Can a Play Make a Difference to the Lives of Prostitutes? Alfred Hickling Investigates." *The Guardian*, March 14, 2006, 21.

———. "The Shipman Inquiry Revisited: Beyond Belief." *The Guardian*, October 28, 2004, 28.

Higgins, Charlotte. "Cultural News Round-up: National Rediscovers Politics." *The Guardian*, October 7, 2004, 16.

Historic England. "Listed buildings." https://historicengland.org.uk/listing/what-is-designation/listed-buildings/.

———. "Meridian House (Former Greenwich Town Hall)." http://list.historicengland.org.uk/resultsingle.aspx?uid=1213855.

HM Government, Department for Education and Skills. "Every Child Matters: Change for Children." Nottingham, UK: Department for Education and Skills, 2004.

Hodgkinson, Will. "A Totally Tropicália Revolution." *The Times: The Knowledge*, February 4–10, 2006.

Hoffmann, Beth. "Radicalism and the Theatre in Genealogies of Live Art." *Performance Research* 14, no. 1 (2009): 95–105.

Holston, James. "Dangerous Spaces of Citizenship: Gang Talk, Rights Talk, and Rule of Law in Brazil." Working Paper 21. Center for Latin American Studies, University of California, Berkeley, August 2008, 1–23.

Hope, Sophie. "From Community Arts to the Socially Engaged Art Commission." In *Culture, Democracy, and the Right to Make Art: The British Community Arts Movement*, ed. Alison Jeffers and Gerri Moriarty, 203–21. London: Bloomsbury Methuen, 2017.

House of Commons, Communities and Local Government Committee. *Coastal Towns: Second Report of Session 2006–07*. London: Stationery Office, 2007. https://publications.parliament.uk/pa/cm200607/cmselect/cmcomloc/351/351.pdf.

Houston, Sara. "Participation in Community Dance: A Road to Empowerment and Transformation?" *New Theatre Quarterly* 21, no. 2 (2005): 166–77.

Howell, Philip, David Beckingham, and Francesca Moore. "Managed Zones for Sex Workers in Liverpool: Contemporary Proposals, Victorian Parallels." *Transactions of the Institute of British Geographers* 33 (2008): 233–50.

Hubbard, Phil, "Revenge and Injustice in the Neoliberal City: Uncovering Masculinist Agendas." *Antipode* 36, no. 4 (2004): 665–86.

Hubbard, Phil, Roger Matthews, and Jane Scoular. "Regulating Sex Work in the EU: Prostitute Women and the New Spaces of Exclusion." *Gender, Place and Culture* 15, no. 2 (2008): 137–52.

Hubbard, Phil, and Teela Sanders. "Making Space for Sex Work: Female Street Prostitution and the Production of Urban Space." *International Journal of Urban and Regional Research* 27, no. 1 (2003): 75–89.

Hutera, Donald. "Pregnant with Possibilities." *Dance Umbrella News*, Autumn 2005.

Hyde, Katherine. "Portraits and Collaborations: A Reflection on the Work of Wendy Ewald." *Visual Studies* 20, no. 2 (2005): 172–90.

Hytner, Nicholas. "To Hell with Targets." *The Observer*, January 12, 2003.

———. "Valuing Culture." Speech given at the "Valuing Culture" symposium, National Theatre Studio, June 17, 2003. http://www.demos.co.uk/files/File/VACUNHytner.pdf.

Immediate Theatre. http://www.immediate-theatre.com/.

Imrie, Rob, and Mike Raco. "Community and the Changing Nature of Urban Policy." In *Urban Renaissance? New Labour, Community, and Urban Policy*, ed. Rob Imrie and Mike Raco, 3–36. Bristol, UK: Policy, 2003.

"Inclusion under Pressure." *Engage Review: Promoting Greater Understanding and Enjoyment of the Visual Arts*, Winter 2001, 1–72.

"India House: A Short History, Compiled by Ian Priston, Boys & Maughan Solicitors, September 2017." https://www.margatelocalhistory.co.uk/Articles/India%20House%20by%20Ian%20Priston.pdf.

Ings, Richard. *From the Favela to Our Manor: Translating AfroReggae: The Impact and Implications of an International Intervention in Arts Work with Young People at Risk*. London: People's Palace Projects, 2007.

Irmer, Thomas. "A Search for New Realities: Documentary Theatre in Germany." *TDR: The Drama Review* 50, no. 3 (2006): 16–28.

Jackson, Shannon. *Social Works: Performing Art, Supporting Publics*. Abingdon, UK: Routledge, 2011.

Jancovich, Leila. "Great Art for Everyone? Engagement and Participation Policy in the Arts." *Cultural Trends* 20, no. 3-4 (2011): 271–79.

Jasper, Linda. "Tensions in the Definition of Community Dance." In *Border Tensions: Dance and Discourse: Proceedings of the Fifth Study of Dance Conference, University of Surrey, 20–23 April 1995*, ed. Janet Adshead-Lansdale, 181–90. Guildford, UK: University of Surrey, 1995.

Jeffers, Alison. "The Community Arts Movement 1968–1986." In *Culture, Democracy, and the Right to Make Art: The British Community Arts Movement*, ed. Alison Jeffers and Gerri Moriarty, 35–64. London: Bloomsbury Methuen, 2017.

———. Introduction to *Culture, Democracy, and the Right to Make Art: The British Community Arts Movement*, ed. Alison Jeffers and Gerri Moriarty, 1–31. London: Bloomsbury Methuen, 2017.

———. "Then and Now: Reflections on the Influence of the Community Arts Movement on Contemporary Community and Participatory Arts." In *Culture, Democracy, and the Right to Make Art: The British Community Arts Movement*, ed. Alison Jeffers and Gerri Moriarty, 133–59. London: Bloomsbury Methuen, 2017.

Jeffs, Tony. "Changing Their Ways: Youth Work and 'Underclass' Theory." In *Youth, the "Underclass," and Social Exclusion*, ed. Robert MacDonald, 153–66. London: Routledge, 1997.

Jermyn, Helen. *The Art of Inclusion*. Research Report 35. London: Arts Council of England, 2004.

———. *The Arts and Social Exclusion: A Review Prepared for the Arts Council of England*. London: Arts Council of England, 2001.

Johnson, Dominic. "Introduction: The What, When, and Where of Live Art." *Contemporary Theatre Review* 22, no. 1 (2012): 4–16.

Jones, Alice. "Arts: Behind Closed Doors: Installation: Gregor Schneider's Mysterious Terrace-Based Project Is Set to Intrigue." *The Independent*, September 21, 2004.

Jones, Paul, and Stuart Wilks-Heeg. "Capitalising Culture: Liverpool 2008." *Local Economy* 19, no. 4 (2004): 341–60.

Jordan, Stephanie. *Striding Out: Aspects of Contemporary and New Dance in Britain*. London: Dance Books, 1992.

Joseph, Miranda. *Against the Romance of Community*. Minneapolis: University of Minnesota Press, 2002.

Jowell, Tessa. *Government and the Value of Culture*. London: Department for Culture, Media, and Sport, 2004.

Joylandbooks.com. "Save Dreamland." https://www.joylandbooks.com/scenicrailway/.

Júnior, José. *Da favela para o mundo: Grupo Cultural AfroReggae*. Rio de Janeiro: Aeroplano Editora, 2004.

Keidan, Lois. "This Must Be the Place: Thoughts on Place, Placelessness, and Live Art since the 1980s." In *Performance and Place*, ed. Leslie Hill and Helen Paris, 8–16. Basingstoke, UK: Palgrave Macmillan, 2006.

Keidan, Lois, and Daniel Brine. "Live Art in London." *Performing Arts Journal* 81 (2005): 74–82.

Kellaway, Kate. "Review: Theatre: Both Sides Now: The Latest Addition to the Growing Canon of Verbatim Theatre Examines the Question of Terrorism from All Angles to Impressive, Moving Effect." *The Observer*, May 1, 2005, 9.

———. "Theatre of War: The Iraq War Has Energised Dramatists, with David Hare's New Play the Latest in a Surge of Political Theatre. Pinter, Frayn and Others on the Front Line Talk to Kate Kellaway." *The Observer*, August 29, 2004, 5.

Kelly, Owen. "In Search of Cultural Democracy." *Arts Express*, October 1985. https://jubileeartsarchive.com/wp-content/uploads/2015/03/In-Search-of-Cultural-Democracy.pdf.

Kelly, Peter. "The Dangerousness of Youth-at-Risk: The Possibilities of Surveillance and Intervention in Uncertain Times." *Journal of Adolescence* 23 (2000): 463–76.

———. "The Entrepreneurial Self and 'Youth at-Risk': Exploring the Horizons of Identity in the Twenty-First Century." *Journal of Youth Studies* 9, no. 1 (2006): 17–32.

———. "Youth at Risk: Processes of Individualisation and Responsibilisation in the Risk Society." *Discourse: Studies in the Cultural Politics of Education* 22, no. 1 (2001): 23–33.

Kent County Council. "Regeneration of East Kent Coastal Towns: A Review by a Select Committee Appointed by the Strategic Planning Policy Overview Committee." August 2004.

Kershaw, Baz. "Discouraging Democracy: British Theatres and Economics, 1979–1999." *Theatre Journal* 51 (1999): 267–83.

———. *The Politics of Performance: Radical Theatre as Cultural Intervention.* Abingdon, UK: Routledge, 1992.

Key, Philip. "Liverpool Artists Stage an Invasion of Edinburgh." *Liverpool Daily Post*, August 8, 2006, 17.

———. "Liverpool Crowd Won Star Status on a Party Night to Remember: Capital of Culture People's Year Celebration." *Daily Post*, January 12, 2008, 6.

Kingsnorth, Paul. *Real England: The Battle against the Bland.* London: Portobello Books, 2008.

Kingston, Jeremy. "Trials of a Court Reporter: All the World's Crime Is a Stage for Nicolas Kent." *The Times*, October 7, 1996, 1.

Kinnell, Hilary. *Violence and Sex Work in Britain.* Cullompton, UK: Willan, 2008.

Klein, Gabriele. "Dance in a Knowledge Society." In *Knowledge in Motion: Perspectives of Artistic and Scientific Research in Dance*, ed. Sabine Gehm, Pirkko Husemann, and Katharina von Wilcke, 25–36. New Brunswick, NJ: Transaction, 2007.

Koram, Kojo. *Uncommon Wealth: Britain and the Aftermath of Empire.* London: John Murray, 2022.

Krausova, Anna. "Elephant and Castle: Mapping (Super-)Diversity in the 2011 UK Census." Centre on Migration, Policy and Society, working paper no. 142, University of Oxford, 2018, 27. https://www.compas.ox.ac.uk/wp-content/uploads/WP-2018-142-Krausova_Elephant-and-Castle-2.pdf.

Kwon, Miwon. *One Place after Another: Site-Specific Art and Locational Identity.* Cambridge, MA: MIT Press, 2004.

"La Ribot." In *Panorama Rioarte de Danca Workshops: La Ribot—Pacitti Company—Gary Stevens*, DVD, directed by Nelson Enohata. London: British Council, 2004.

La Ribot. http://www.laribot.com.

———. "*40 espontáneos.*" https://www.laribot.com/work/12.

———. "Los cuarentones son más auténticos con sus cuerpos." *El Culturales*, October 19, 2006. https://www.laribot.com/work/12.

———. "Panoramix." In *Live: Art and Performance*, ed. Adrian Heathfield, 28–37. London: Tate Publishing, 2004.

Labour. *Create the Future: A Strategy for Cultural Policy, Arts, and the Creative Economy*. Labour Party, 1997.

———. "Labour Party Rule Book 2013." http://labourlist.org/wp-content/uploads/2013/04/Rule-Book-2013.pdf.

Lacey, Stephen. "British Theatre and Commerce, 1979–2000." In *The Cambridge History of British Theatre*, vol. 3: *Since 1895*, ed. Baz Kershaw, 426–47. Cambridge: Cambridge University Press, 2004.

Laite, Julia. "Paying the Price Again: Prostitution Policy in Historical Perspective." History and Policy, Policy Paper 46 (2006). https://www.historyandpolicy.org/policy-papers/papers/paying-the-price-again-prostitution-policy-in-historical-perspective.

Landry, Charles, and Phil Wood. *Harnessing and Exploiting the Power of Culture for Competitive Advantage: A Report by Comedia for the Liverpool City Council and the Core Cities Group*. Stroud, UK: Comedia, 2003.

Lane, Anthony. *Isle of Thanet through Time*. Stroud, UK: Amberley, 2013.

Lane, Tony. *Liverpool: Gateway of Empire*. London: Lawrence and Wishart, 1987.

Lawson, Mark. "Theatre: Nothing but the Truth: You Couldn't Make It Up. For Centuries the Book-Reading, Theatre-Going Public Want Nothing but Fiction—Then Suddenly Only True-Life Stories Will Do." *The Guardian*, October 9, 1996, 12.

Lay, Samantha. "Good Intentions, High Hopes, and Low Budgets: Contemporary Social Realist Film-Making in Britain." *New Cinemas: Journal of Contemporary Film* 5, no. 3 (2007): 231–44.

Leahy, Helen Rees. "New Labour, Old Masters." *Cultural Studies* 4-5 (2007): 695–717.

Lee, Anthony. *Margate in the Georgian Era: Pleasures and Pursuits in a Seaside Town*. Margate, UK: Droit House, 2012.

Leeds, Elizabeth. "Rio de Janeiro." In *Fractured Cities: Social Exclusion, Urban Violence, and Contested Spaces in Latin America*, ed. Kees Koonings and Dirk Kruijt, 23–34. London: Zed Books, 2007.

Leigh Foster, Susan. "Dancing Bodies." In *Meaning in Motion: New Cultural Studies of Dance*, ed. Jane C. Desmond, 235–57. Durham, NC: Duke University Press, 1997.

Lennon, Peter. "Home Truths from a Street Fighter: Tower Hamlets Council Leader, Who Is Nearly Always in the Line of Fire, Talks to Peter Lennon." *The Guardian*, December 4, 1993.

Lepecki, André. "Concept and Presence: The Contemporary European Dance Scene." In *Rethinking Dance History: A Reader*, ed. Alexandra Carter, 170–81. London: Routledge, 2004.

———. *Exhausting Dance: Performance and the Politics of Movement*. London: Routledge, 2006.

"Lesley Greene, James Lingwood, Declan McGonagle, Malcolm Miles." In *TSWA Four Cities Project: New Works for Different Places*, ed. James Lingwood, 151–55. Plymouth, UK: TSWA, 1990.

"Letter: Private Prejudice, Public Interest, and Bow's *House*: From Mr. James Lingwood." *The Independent*, November 30, 1993.

"Letter: Timetable for Bow Sculpture: From Cllr. Eric Flounders." *The Independent*, November 25, 1993.

Levitas, Ruth. *The Inclusive Society? Social Exclusion and New Labour*. 2nd edition. Basingstoke, UK: Palgrave Macmillan, 2005 (1998).

Lewis, Justin. *Art, Culture, and Enterprise: The Politics of Art and the Cultural Industries*. London: Routledge, 1990.

Lewis, Veronica. "Fundamentally Embodied." *Animated*, Autumn-Winter 2016/17. https://www.communitydance.org.uk/DB/animated-library/fundamentally-embodied?ed=41635.

Light Honthaner, Eve. *The Complete Film Production Handbook*. 4th edition. Oxford: Focal, 2010 (1993).

Linds, Warren. "Metaxis: Dancing (in) the In-Between." In *A Boal Companion: Dialogues on Theatre and Cultural Politics*, ed. Jan Cohen-Cruz and Mady Schutzman, 114–24. New York: Routledge, 2006.

Ling, Tom. "Delivering Joined-up Government in the UK: Dimensions, Issues, and Problems." *Public Administration* 80, no. 4 (2002): 615–42.

Lingwood, James. Introduction to *Rachel Whiteread: House*, ed. James Lingwood, 7–11. London: Phaidon, 1995.

———. "Our House Is a Very Nice House." *The Times*, November 27, 1993.

Lister, Sam. "We're Well on Course." *Liverpool Daily Post*, May 8, 2006, 6.

Lloyd, David, and Paul Thomas. *Culture and the State*. London: Routledge, 1998.

Logan, Brian. "Why Do We Still Run with the Hare?" *The Times*, November 27, 2006, 14.

London Mural Preservation Society. "The Battle of Cable Street." http://londonmuralpreservationsociety.com/murals/battle-cable-street/.

Long, Jonathan, Mel Welch, Peter Bramham, Jim Butterfield, Kevin Hylton, and Eddy Lloyd. *Count Me In: The Dimensions of Social Inclusion through Culture and Sport*. London: Department for Culture, Media, and Sport, 2002.

Louise, Dany. "Arts Funding: The New Reality?" 2019. *AMAculturehive*. https://www.culturehive.co.uk/resources/arts-funding-the-new-reality/.

Luckhurst, Mary. *Dramaturgy: A Revolution in Theatre*. Cambridge: Cambridge University Press, 2006.

"M53: Oswald de Andrade, *Cannibalist Manifesto* (1928)." In *100 Artists' Manifestos: From the Futurists to the Stuckists*, ed. Alex Danchev, 262–66. London: Penguin, 2011.

Macaulay, Alastair. "Going Public in a Way That Makes a Difference: Alastair Macaulay Meets Nicolas Kent, the Man behind 'The Colour of Justice.'" *Financial Times*, September 20, 1999, 19.

———. "No Happy Endings in Real Life: The Colour of Justice, Tricycle Theatre, London NW6." *Financial Times*, January 14, 1999, 26.

———. "Theatre." *Financial Times*, February 18, 2006, 38.

Mackrell, Judith. *Out of Line: The Story of British New Dance*. Binstead, UK: Dance Books, 1992.

———. "Post-Modern Dance in Britain: An Historical Essay." *Dance Research: The Journal of the Society for Dance Research* 9, no. 1 (1991): 40–57.

Mahoney, Grace. "Art Changes Lives." *New Moves*. http:/www.newmoves.co.uk/PageAccess.aspx?id=36.

"The Making of Exodus." DVD, directed by Andrew Palmer, in *Exodus*, DVD, directed by Penny Woolcock, Soda Pictures, 2007.

"Manifesto for a European Performance Policy (2002)." http://www.freietheater.at/?page=kulturpolitik&detail=61304&jahr=2002.

Manjapra, Kris. "When Will Britain Face Up to Its Crimes against Humanity?" *The Guardian*, March 29, 2018.

Marazzi, Christian. *Capital and Language: From the New Economy to the War Economy*, trans. Gregory Conti. Los Angeles: Semiotext(e), 2008.

The Margate Exodus. http://www.themargateexodus.org.uk/about.html.

Margate Never Runs. "About." http://margateneverruns.com/about.

Marshall, Tom. "Rich Mix Saved after Tower Hamlets Council Drops £850k Lawsuit." *Evening Standard*, September 29, 2015.

Martin, Clive. "Thanet Earth: Margate Is like London before It Turned into Angel." *Vice*, September 9, 2014. https://www.vice.com/en_uk/article/gq8mk3/thanet-earth-margate-is-the-place-to-be-0000412-v21n8.

Martin, Randy. *An Empire of Indifference: American War and the Financial Logic of Risk Management*. Durham, NC: Duke University Press, 2007.

———. "A Precarious Dance, a Derivative Sociality." *TDR* 56, no. 4 (2012): 62–77.

Massey, Doreen. "Space-Time and the Politics of Location." In *Architecturally Speaking: Practices of Art, Architecture, and the Everyday*, ed. Alan Read, 49–61. London: Routledge, 2000.

Matarasso, François. *Regular Marvels: A Handbook for Animateurs, Practitioners, and Development Workers in Dance, Mime, Music and Literature*. Leicester, UK: Community Dance & Mime Foundation, 1994.

———. *Use or Ornament? The Social Impact of Participating in the Arts*. Stroud, UK: Comedia, 2003.

McGuigan, Jim. "Neoliberalism, Culture, and Policy." *International Journal of Cultural Policy* 11, no. 3 (2005): 229–41.

McMaster, Sir Brian. *Supporting Excellence in the Arts: From Measurement to Judgement*. London: Department for Culture, Media, and Sports, 2008.

McNally, David. *Global Slump: The Economics and Politics of Crisis and Resistance*. Oakland, CA: PM, 2011.

McRobbie, Angela. *The Aftermath of Feminism: Gender, Culture, and Social Change*. Los Angeles: Sage Books, 2009.

Meadway, James. "Neoliberalism Is Dead—and Something Even Worse Is Taking Its Place." *Novara Media*, June 29, 2021. https://novaramedia.com/2021/06/29/neoliberalism-is-dead-and-something-even-worse-is-taking-its-place/.

———. "Neoliberalism Is Dying—Now We Must Replace It." *Open Democracy*, September 3, 2021. https://www.opendemocracy.net/en/oureconomy/neoliberalism-is-dying-now-we-must-replace-it/.

Meer, Nasar, and Tariq Modood. "The Multicultural State We're In: Muslims, 'Multiculture,' and the 'Civic Re-Balancing' of British Multiculturalism." *Political Studies* 57 (2009): 473–97.

Megson, Chris. "*Half the Picture*: 'A Certain Frisson' at the Tricycle Theatre." In *Get Real: Documentary Theatre Past and Present*, ed. Alison Forsyth and Chris Megson, 195–208. Basingstoke, UK: Palgrave Macmillan, 2009.

———. "Verbatim Practices in Contemporary Theatre: Symposium Report." *Contemporary Theatre Review* 16, no. 4 (2006): 529–32.

Menon, Jisha. "Palimpsestic City: Nostalgia in Neoliberal Bangalore." In *Neoliberalism and Global Theatres*, ed. Lara D. Nielsen and Patricia Ybarra, 237–52. Basingstoke, UK: Palgrave Macmillan, 2012.

Merkin, Ros, ed. *Liverpool's Third Cathedral: The Liverpool Everyman Theatre in the Words of Those Who Were, and Are, There*. Liverpool: Liverpool and Merseyside Theatres Trust Limited and Liverpool John Moores University, 2004.

Merlin, Bella. "Acting Hare: *The Permanent Way*." In *The Cambridge Companion to David Hare*, ed. Richard Boon, 123–37. Cambridge: Cambridge University Press, 2007.

———. "*The Permanent Way* and the Impermanent Muse." *Contemporary Theatre Review* 17, no. 1 (2007): 41–49.

"Michael Morris: From a Conversation with Brian Eno in January 2007." In *The Producers: Alchemists of the Impossible*, ed. Kate Tyndall, 55–62. London: Arts Council England and Jerwood Charitable Foundation, 2007.

Midgley, Carol. "Sex, the City, and a Red Light Ghetto." *The Times*, January 29, 2005, 27.

Miles, Malcolm. *Art, Space, and the City: Public Art and Urban Futures*. London: Routledge, 1997.

———. "Community Murals in Britain." In *Art for Public Places: Critical Essays*, ed. Malcolm Miles, 61–78. Winchester, UK: Winchester School of Art Press, 1989.

Miles, Steven, and Ronan Paddison. "The Rise and Rise of Culture-led Urban Regeneration." *Urban Studies* 42, no. 5-6 (2005): 833–39.

Minihan, Janet. *The Nationalization of Culture: The Development of State Subsidies to the Arts in Great Britain*. London: Hamish Hamilton, 1977.

Ministry of Justice. "Story of the Prison Population: 1993–2012, England and Wales." January 2013. https://assets.publishing.service.gov.uk/government/uploads/system/uploads/attachment_data/file/218185/story-prison-population.pdf.

Moehn, Frederick. "Music, Citizenship, and Violence in Postdictatorship Brazil." *Latin American Music Review* 28, no. 2 (2007): 181–219.

———. "Music, Mixing, and Modernity in Rio de Janeiro." *Ethnomusicology Forum* 17, no. 2 (2008): 165–202.

———. "'We Live Daily in Two Countries': Audiotopias of Postdictatorship Brazil." In *Brazilian Popular Music and Citizenship*, ed. Idelber Avelar and Christopher Dunn, 109–30. Durham, NC: Duke University Press, 2011.

Morris, Estelle. "Estelle Morris: 'There Is Something Inherently Good and Valuable in Art': From a Speech by the Arts Minister at the Cheltenham Festival of Literature." *The Independent*, October 17, 2003.

Morris, Michael. "G2: Yes, but . . . : Michael Morris, Co-Director of Artangel." *The Guardian*, October 11, 2006.

———. Prologue to *Towards a Promised Land*, ed. Louise Neri, 15–17. Göttingen: Steidl, 2006.

Morrison, Richard. "Power to the People, Write On." *The Times*, October 8, 2005, 4.

MSM. "Press Release." https://www.dv8.co.uk/projects/archive/msm/press-release.

Muncie, John. "Youth Justice: Responsibilisation and Rights." In *Youth in Society*, 2nd edition, ed. Jeremy Roche, Stanley Tucker, Rachel Thomson, and Ronny Flynn, 131–44. London: Sage, 2004.

Naves, Santuza Cambraia. "From Bossa Nova to Tropicália: Restraint and Excess in Popular Music." In *Imagining Brazil*, ed. Jessé Souza and Valter Sinder, 251–65. Lanham, MD: Lexington Books, 2005.

Neate, Patrick. *Where You're At: Notes from the Frontline of a Hip Hop Planet*. London: Bloomsbury, 2003.

Neate, Patrick, and Damian Platt. *Culture Is Our Weapon: Making Music and Changing Lives in Rio de Janeiro*. London: Penguin, 2010.

NEF. "Coasting Along: A Study of Business Impacts and Regeneration in South East Coastal Towns: A Report from NEF (the New Economics Foundation) for the South East England Development Agency (SEEDA)." August 2005.

Nenhum motiva explica a guerra. DVD, directed by Cacá Diegues e Rafael Dragaud. Warner Music, 2006.

New Moves. http://www.newmoves.co.uk/PageAccess.aspx?id=345.

Nicholson, Helen. *Theatre and Education*. Basingstoke, UK: Palgrave Macmillan, 2009.

Nield, Sophie. 'On the Border as Theatrical Space: Appearance, Dis-location, and the Production of the Refugee." In *Contemporary Theatres in Europe: A Critical Companion*, ed. Joe Kelleher and Nicholas Ridout, 61–72. Abingdon, UK: Routledge, 2006.

———. "Siting the People: Power, Protest, and Public Space." In *Performing Site-Specific Theatre: Politics, Place, Practice*, ed. Anna Birch and Joanne Tompkins, 219–32. Basingstoke, UK: Palgrave Macmillan, 2012.

Norton-Taylor, Richard. "Arts: Theatre: Blair in the Dock." *The Guardian*, April 16, 2007, 26.

———. "Out of the Shadows." *The Guardian*, June 8, 1994.

———. "On the Trail of the Trial." *The Guardian*, May 1, 1996, 213.

———. "The Truth Will Out." *The Guardian*, December 23, 1998, 13.

"Not Conceptual." Symposium held on February 22, 2007, presented by Jonathan Burrows at Siobhan Davies Studios, part of Parallel Voices 2007: A Public Season of Talks and Events. https://www.youtube.com/watch?v=EkdI-87T2z0.

Nottingham City Council. "Development of Sandfield Centre, Sandfield Road, Nottingham." 2012. http://open.nottinghamcity.gov.uk/comm/download3.asp?dltype=inline&filename=52591/sandfieldreport.pdf.

———. "Planning Committee 20th December 2017: Report of Chief Planner: Site of the Sandfield Centre, Sandfield Road." http://committee.nottinghamcity.gov.uk/documents/s66378/Site%20Of%20The%20Sandfield%20Centre%20Sandfield%20Road.pdf.

Nugent, Ann. "In Memoriam: Peter Brinson (Born Lladudno, Wales, 1923—Died London, 1995)." *Dance Research Journal* 28, no. 1 (1996): 126–29.

Ochyra, Helen. "Liverpool: Capital of Culture 2008: Rookie's Guide." *The Guardian: Magazine*, April 5, 2008, 4.

Office of the Deputy Prime Minister, Social Exclusion Unit. "Breaking the Cycle: Taking Stock of Progress and Priorities for the Future: A Report by the Social Exclusion Unit." London, 2004.

O'Hara, Mary. *Austerity Bites: A Journey to the Sharp End of the Cuts in the UK*. Bristol, UK: Policy, 2015.

Olivon, Beatriz. "O que o Santander pode ensinar sobre o Complexo do Alemão." *Exame*, March 12, 2010.

O'Malley, Pat. *Risk, Uncertainty, and Government*. London: Glasshouse, 2004.

"On the Concept of Laughter in *Laughing Hole*: An Interview with La Ribot, Edited by Abi Weaver." *Contemporary Theatre Review* 23, no. 2 (2013): 256–61.

O'Sullivan, Feargus. "The Pernicious Realities of 'Artwashing.'" *CityLab*, June 24, 2014. http://www.citylab.com/housing/2014/06/the-pernicious-realities-of-artwashing/373289/.

Osborne, R. C. *The Margate Guide; Or, Isle of Thanet Directory* (1835). https://www.google.co.uk/books/edition/The_Margate_Guide_Or_Isle_of_Thanet_Dire/rqhYAAAAcAAJ?hl.

Oval House. "History." 2013. http://www.ovalhouse.com/about/our-history.

"Overcoming Social Exclusion: Brazil in Comparative Perspective." Conference held at St. Antony's College, Oxford, June 22, 2004. http://www.guystanding.com/files/documents/Summary_Oxford_June_2004.pdf.

Owen, Louise. "'In Tune with the Beat of Where They Are': The AfroReggae UK Partnership in 2007." *PPP Research Bulletin*, 4 (May 2008): 1–13.

———. "The Witness and the Replay: London Bubble." In *Performance and Community: Commentary and Case Studies*, ed. Caoimhe McAvinchey, 155–87. London: Bloomsbury Methuen, 2014.

Paget, Derek. "New Documentarism on Stage: Documentary Theatre in New Times." *ZAA* 56, no. 2 (2008): 129–41.

———. *True Stories? Documentary Drama on Radio, Screen, and Stage*. Manchester: Manchester University Press, 1990.

———. "'Verbatim Theatre': Oral History and Documentary Techniques." *New Theatre Quarterly* 12 (1987): 317–36.

Peacock, Keith D. *Thatcher's Theatre: British Theatre and Drama in the 1980s*. Westport, CT: Greenwood, 1999.

Peck, Jamie. *Constructions of Neoliberal Reason*. Oxford: Oxford University Press, 2010.

———. "Explaining (with) Neoliberalism." *Territory, Politics, Governance* 1, no. 2 (2013): 132–57.

———. "Geography and Public Policy: Constructions of Neoliberalism." *Progress in Human Geography* 28, no. 3 (2004): 392–405.

Peck, Jamie, and Nik Theodore. "Still Neoliberalism?' *South Atlantic Quarterly* 118, no. 2 (2019): 245–65.

Peck, Jamie, and Adam Tickell. "Neoliberalizing Space." *Antipode* 34, no. 3 (2002): 380–404.

People Dancing: The Foundation for Community Dance. "Dance Agencies." https://www.communitydance.org.uk/useful-contacts-and-links/dance-agencies.

Peppiatt, Anthony. "Speaking in Tongues." *Dance Theatre Journal* 3, no. 3 (1985): 27–28.

———. "What Is a Framework and Why Does It Matter?" In *Thinking Aloud: In Search of a Framework for Community Dance*, ed. Chris Jones, 2–3. Leicester, UK: Foundation for Community Dance, 1996.

Pereira, Anthony W. "An Ugly Democracy? State Violence and the Rule of Law in Postauthoritarian Brazil." In *Democratic Brazil: Actors, Institutions, and Processes*, ed. Peter R. Kingstone and Timothy J. Power, 217–35. Pittsburgh, PA: University of Pittsburgh Press, 2000.

Perlman, Janice E. *Favela: Four Decades of Living on the Edge in Rio de Janeiro*. Oxford: Oxford University Press, 2010.

———. *The Myth of Marginality: Urban Poverty and Politics in Rio de Janeiro*. Berkeley: University of California Press, 1976.

Pettifor, Ann. *The Production of Money: How to Break the Power of Bankers*. London: Verso, 2017.

Philippou, Styliane. "Modernism and National Identity in Brazil, or How to Brew a Brazilian Stew." *National Identities* 7, no. 3 (2005): 245–64.

Phillips, Caryl. *The Atlantic Sound*. London: Vintage, 2001.

Pickering, Kenneth, and Jayne Thompson. *Naturalism in Theatre: Its Development and Legacy*. Basingstoke, UK: Palgrave Macmillan, 2013.

Piketty, Thomas. *Capital in the Twenty First Century*. Translated by Arthur Goldhammer. Cambridge, MA: Belknap Press of Harvard University Press, 2014.

Pino, Julio Cesar. *Family and Favela: The Reproduction of Poverty in Rio de Janeiro*. Westport, CT: Greenwood, 1997.

Poynor, Helen. "Yes, But Is It Dance?" In *An Introduction to Community Dance Practice*, ed. Diane Amans, 87–98. Basingstoke, UK: Palgrave Macmillan, 2008.

PPP. "About PPP." https://peoplespalaceprojects.org.uk/en/about/#about.

Pristaš, Goran Sergej. "'Whispering with Our Bodies': Interview with La Ribot." *Frakcija magazin za izvedbene un jetnosti: Performing arts magazine*, 24/25 (2002): 18–23.

"Production Casebook No. 1: The Staffordshire Rebels." *Theatre Quarterly* 1 (1971): 86–102.

"Prostitution Zone Approved: Home Office Should Approve Plan . . . but There Must Be Safeguards, Insists MP." *Daily Post*, January 27, 2005, 6.

Quinn, Ruth-Blandina M. *Public Policy and the Arts*. Aldershot, UK: Ashgate, 1998.

Radosavljević, Duška. *Theatre-Making: Interplay between Text and Performance in the 21st Century*. Basingstoke, UK: Routledge, 2013.

Rainer, Yvonne. "Some Retrospective Notes on a Dance for 10 People and 12 Mattresses Called 'Part of Some Sextets.' Performed at the Wadsworth

Atheneum, Hartford, Connecticut, and Judson Memorial Church, New York, in March 1965." *Tulane Drama Review* 10, no. 2 (1965): 168–78.

Ralph, Richard. "Peter Brinson." *Dance Research: The Journal of the Society for Dance Research* 15, no. 1 (1997): 4–12.

Randall, David. "A Journey: The Ed Miliband Story." *The Independent*, September 26, 2010.

Ramos, Silvia, "Brazilian Responses to Violence and New Forms of Mediation: The Case of the Grupo Cultural AfroReggae and the Experience of the Project 'Youth and the Police.' " *Ciênca & Saúde Coletiva* 11, no. 2 (2006): 419–28.

Ratcliffe, Michael. "The Magus of Clink Street: Adored Abroad but Hardly Known Here: Robert Wilson Is Plotting His First Major British Show, Writes Michael Ratcliffe." *The Observer*, September 3, 1995.

Reason, Matthew. "Glasgow's Year of Culture and Discourses of Cultural Policy on the Cusp of Globalisation." *Contemporary Theatre Review* 16, no. 1 (2006): 73–85.

Reich, Robert B. "Entrepreneur or Unemployed?" *New York Times*, June 1, 2010. http://www.nytimes.com/2010/06/02/opinion/02reich.html?_r=0.

Ribeiro Pires Vieira, Else. "Liberating Calibans: Readings of *Antropofagio* and Haroldo de Campos' Poetics of Transcreation." In *Post-Colonial Translation: Theory and Practice*, ed. Susan Bassnett and Harish Trivedi, 95–113. London: Routledge, 1998.

Roberts, Bryan R. "Citizenship, Social Policy, and Population Change." In *Exclusion and Engagement: Social Policy in Latin America*, ed. Christopher Abel and Colin M. Lewis, 111–30. London: Institute of Latin American Studies, 2002.

Robinson, Vaughan, Roger Andersson, and Sako Musterd. *Spreading the Burden? A Review of Policies to Disperse Asylum Seekers and Refugees*. Bristol, UK: Policy, 2003.

Rohter, Larry. *Brazil on the Rise: The Story of a Country Transformed*. New York: Palgrave Macmillan, 2011.

Roms, Heike, and Rebecca Edwards. "Towards a Prehistory of Live Art in the UK." *Contemporary Theatre Review* 22, no. 1 (2012): 17–31.

Rosenberg, David. " 'An Antidote to the Far Right's Poison'—the Battle for Cable Street's Mural." *The Guardian*, September 21, 2016.

Royle, Edward. *Modern Britain: A Social History, 1750–1985*. London: Edward Arnold, 1987.

Saad-Filho, Alfredo, and Deborah Johnston. Introduction to *Neoliberalism: A Critical Reader*, ed. Alfredo Saad-Filho and Deborah Johnston, 1–6. London: Pluto, 2005.

Sales, Rosemary. "The Deserving and the Undeserving? Refugees, Asylum Seekers, and Welfare in Britain." *Critical Social Policy* 22, no. 3 (2002): 456–78.

Samuel, Richard. "Thanet." In *Coastal Regeneration in English Resorts—2010*, ed. John Walton and Patrick Browne, 82–86. Waterside South, UK: Coastal Communities Alliance, 2010. https://www.coastalcommunities.co.uk/wp-content/uploads/2015/07/coastal-regeneration-handbook.pdf.

Sánchez, José A. "Distinction and Humour." In *La Ribot*, vol. 2, ed. Claire Rousier, 39–49. Pantin: Centre National de la Danse 2004.

Sanchez, Lisa E. "The global E-rotic Subject, the Ban, and the Prostitute-Free Zone: Sex Work and the Theory of Differential Exclusion." *Environment and Planning D: Society and Space* 22 (2004): 861–83.

Saunders, Graham. "The Freaks' Roll Call: Live Art and the Arts Council, 1968–73." *Contemporary Theatre Review* 22, no. 1 (2012): 32–45.

Savage, Jon. "Two Tribes Go to War." *BBC: Culture*, October 21, 2014. https://www.bbc.com/culture/article/20140515-when-two-tribes-went-to-war.

Schechner, Richard. *Between Theatre and Anthropology*. Philadelphia: University of Pennsylvania Press, 1985.

Schneider, Rebecca. "Patricidal Memory and the Passerby." *The Scholar and Feminist Online* 2, no. 1, "Public Sentiments" (2003). http://sfonline.barnard.edu/ps/schneide.htm.

———. "Performance Remains." *Performance Research* 6, no. 2 (2001): 100–108.

Schofield, Ben, and Barry Turnbull. "City Shopping Figures Go 'Through the Roof.'" *Daily Post*, December 24, 2008, 1.

Selwood, Sara. *The Benefits of Public Art: The Polemics of Permanent Art in Public Places*. London: Policy Studies Institute, 1995.

Seymour, Anna. "Culture and Political Change: British Radical Theatre in Recent History." *Theatre Research International* 21, no. 1 (1996): 8–16.

Shared Intelligence. "Margate Renewal Study." 2008. https://democracy.kent.gov.uk/documents/s6101/Item%209%20App%202ThanetShared%20Intelligence%20Report.pdf.

Shenton, Jane. "Man-in-Street Script." *Liverpool Daily Post*, May 16, 1967.

Sholette, Gregory. "Mysteries of the Creative Class; or, I Have Seen the Enemy and They Is Us." *MUTE*29: The Precarious Issue* (2005): 2–3. http://www.gregorysholette.com/wp-content/uploads/2011/04/03_mysteries1.pdf.

Shoreditch Trust. "About Us." http://www.shoreditchtrust.org.uk/About-Us/About-Us.

———. "Shoreditch Trust Delivery Plan 2007–08." 2006.

Siegmund, Gerald. "Emblems of Absence: La Ribot's *Piezas distinguidas*." In *La Ribot*, vol. 2, ed. Claire Rousier, 79–87. Pantin: Centre National de la Danse, 2004.

Siobhan Davies Studios. "New Dance and the Visual Arts." *Remembering British New Dance*, June 2012. https://www.siobhandavies.com/relay/events/remembering-british-new-dance/.

Slobodian, Quinn. *Globalists: The End of Empire and the Birth of Neoliberalism*. Cambridge, MA: Harvard University Press 2018.

Slobodian, Quinn. "Hayek's Bastards: The Populist Right's Neoliberal Roots." *Tribune*, June 15, 2021. https://tribunemag.co.uk/2021/06/hayeks-bastards-the-populist-rights-neoliberal-roots.

Smith, Barbara Herrnstein. *Contingencies of Value: Alternative Perspectives for Critical Theory*. Cambridge, MA: Harvard University Press, 1988.

Smith, Chris. *Creative Britain*. London: Faber and Faber, 1998.

———. “Valuing Culture.” Speech given at the “Valuing Culture” symposium, National Theatre Studio, June 17, 2003. https://www.demos.co.uk/files/File/VACUCSmith.pdf.

Smith, Claire, Wendy Stainton Rogers, and Stan Tucker. “Risk.” In *Youth in Context: Frameworks, Settings, and Encounters*, ed. Martin Robb, 219–50. London: Sage, 2007.

Smith, Michael. “How Margate Became the New Hipster’s Paradise.” *Esquire*, April 4, 2015. https://www.esquire.com/uk/food-drink/travel/news/a8101/how-margate-became-the-new-hipsters-paradise/.

Smith, Neil. “Gentrification and Uneven Development.” *Economic Geography* 58, no. 2 (1982): 139–55.

Soans, Robin. “Robin Soans.” In *Verbatim Verbatim: Contemporary Documentary Theatre*, ed. Will Hammond and Dan Steward, 15–44. London: Oberon Books, 2008.

Somerville, Will. *Immigration under New Labour*. Bristol, UK: Policy, 2007.

“Southwark Notes: Whose Regeneration? | Heygate Estate.” https://southwarknotes.wordpress.com/heygate-estate/.

Spencer, Charles. “The Arts: Lifting the Curtain on Arms to Iraq: The Scott Inquiry Is Brilliantly Enacted at the Tricycle.” *The Daily Telegraph*, June 17, 1994, 19.

Stephen, Dawn E. “Community Safety and Young People: 21st-Century *Homo Sacer* and the Politics of Injustice.” In *Community Safety: Critical Perspectives on Policy and Practice*, ed. Peter Squires, 219–36. Bristol, UK: Policy, 2006.

Stevens, Jayne. “The National Association of Dance and Mime Animateurs (1986–9): A Community of Practice.” *Dance Research* 31, no. 2 (2013): 157–73.

Stuart Fisher, Amanda. “Trauma, Authenticity, and the Limits of Verbatim.” *Performance Research* 16, no. 1 (2011): 112–22.

Sulcas, Rosalyn. “Unless You Have Another World, Dance Will Do.” *New York Times*, February 24, 2008. https://www.nytimes.com/2008/02/24/arts/dance/24sulc.html.

Tai, Cedric. “The 1990 TSWA Four Cities Projects in Glasgow and the Proposals That Never Materialised.” *The Glasgow Miracle: Materials for Alternative Histories*, April 17, 2013. http://glasgowmiracle.blogspot.co.uk/2013/04/the-1990-tswa-four-cities-projects-in.html.

Tanner, Doreen. “Play That Just Grew.” *Liverpool Daily Post*, May 18, 1967.

Taru Arts. https://taru.org.uk/.

Taylor, Diane. “My Daughter: ‘Not Just a Prostitute’: Dianne Parry Hoped Her Heroin-Addicted Daughter Would Wake Up One Morning, See Sense, and Come Home. But Hanane Never Did—She Was Murdered, Aged 19, While Working as a Prostitute.” *The Guardian*, August 5, 2006, 3.

Taylor, Paul. “Review of the Year 2004: Arts: Theatre.” *The Independent*, December 27, 2004, 40.

“Theatre Check.” *The Times*, June 19, 1994.

Theatres Trust. “Hoxton Hall.” https://database.theatrestrust.org.uk/resources/theatres/show/1983-hoxton-hall.

Thomas, David, David Carlton, and Anne Etienne. *Theatre Censorship: From Walpole to Wilson*. Oxford: Oxford University Press, 2007.

Thomson, Christopher. "Community Dance: What Community . . . What Dance?" In *Young People Dancing: An International Perspective*, vol. 3: *Dance: A Cultural Phenomenon and Community Dance*, 88–98. Oxford: Dance and the Child International, 1989.

———. Foreword to *An Introduction to Community Dance Practice*, ed. Diane Amans, ix–xi. Basingstoke, UK: Palgrave Macmillan, 2008.

———. "We Are a Dancing Nation." *Animated*, Spring 2006.

Thorpe, Vanessa. "Cultural Figures and Teachers Denounce the Abolition of Arts in Schools Project." *The Observer*, January 9, 2011.

Tolley, Julie. "The Dance Animateur: A British Phenomenon." In *Young People Dancing: An International Perspective*, vol. 3: *Dance: A Cultural Phenomenon and Community Dance*, 103–11. Oxford: Dance and the Child International, 1989.

Tomlin, Liz. *British Theatre Companies, 1995–2014*. London: Methuen, 2015.

Tooze, Adam. *Shutdown: How Covid Shook the World's Economy*. London: Allen Lane, 2021.

Toynbee, Polly. "A Good Home's Where the Art Is." *The Independent*, May 29, 1997, 21.

Tramway. "Tramway—A History." http://www.tramway.org/Pages/Tramway---A-History.aspx.

Traverse Theatre. "About Us." http://www.traverse.co.uk/about-us/.

Travis, Robyn. *Prisoner to the Streets*. X Press Publishing, 2013.

Turner Contemporary. "About | Who We Are." https://turnercontemporary.org/about/.

TurneroundMargate.com. "The Lasting Legacy of Exodus." March 22, 2007. http://www.turneroundmargate.com/the-lasting-legacy-of-exodus/.

Turpin, Adrian. "Reality Check: Plays Using the Words of Real-Life Protagonists Will Abound on the Edinburgh Fringe. Do They Take Us Closer to the Truth?" *Financial Times*, July 22, 2006, 36.

"UK Politics: Tony Blair's Speech in Full." *BBC News*, September 28, 1999. http://news.bbc.co.uk/1/hi/uk_politics/460009.stm.

"'Uncelebrated Voices': Part of the Two-Day Symposium 'Verbatim Practice in Contemporary Theatre' Held at Central School of Speech and Drama, 13–14 July 2006." http://www.crco.cssd.ac.uk/25/1/CEN_V_unceleb_edit.pdf.

Urry, John. *The Tourist Gaze*. 2nd edition. London, Thousand Oaks, and New Delhi: Sage Publications, 2002.

Van Den Hoonaard, Will C. "Is Anonymity an Artifact in Ethnographic Research?" *Journal of Academic Ethics* 1 (2003): 141–51.

Vargas, João H. Costa. "When a Favela Dared to Become a Gated Condominium: The Politics of Race and Urban Space in Rio de Janeiro." *Latin American Perspectives* 33, no. 4 (2006): 49–81.

Vason, Manuel, Lois Keidan, and Ron Athey. *Exposures*. London: Black Dog, 2002.

Ventura, Zuenir. *Cidade partida*. São Paulo: Companhia das Letras, 1994.

"Verbatim Theatre (Verbatim): This Conversation Took Place on 17/06/2014. Present Were: Nicolas Kent, Richard Norton-Taylor, Gillian Slovo and

David Edgar." In *The Tricycle: Collected Tribunal Plays 1994–2012*, 4–40. London: Oberon, 2014.

Virno, Paolo. "General Intellect," entry in Zanini and Fadini, eds., *Lessico Postfordista* (Milan: Feltrinelli, 2001), translation by Arianna Bove, in *Generation Online*. http://www.generation-online.org/p/fpvirno10.htm.

"Vogue Loves." *Vogue*, September 2006.

Wacquant, Loïc, and Pierre Bourdieu. "NewLiberalSpeak." *Radical Philosophy* 105 (2001): 2–5.

Wainwright, Oliver. "Protests Disrupt Property Fair in London." *The Guardian*, October 15, 2014.

Walker, Lynne. "Theatre: The Quality of Mersey: Gemma Bodinetz and Deborah Aydon, the New Team at the Liverpool Everyman and Playhouse, Are Determined to Put the Two Theatres Back on the Map. Lynne Walker Hears How They Plan to Do It." *The Independent*, January 15, 2004, 12.

Walker, Peter. "Heygate Pyramid: London Estate's Evicted Residents Damn Art Plan." *The Guardian*, December 12, 2013.

Walkowitz, Judith R. *Prostitution and Victorian Society: Women, Class, and the State*. Cambridge: Cambridge University Press, 1980.

———. Introduction to *Coastal Regeneration in English Resorts—2010*, ed. John Walton and Patrick Browne, 1–11. Waterside South, UK: Coastal Communities Alliance, 2010. http://www.coastalcommunities.co.uk/.

———. *The English Seaside Resort: A Social History, 1750–1914*. Leicester: Leicester University Press, 1983.

WalkthePlanktv. "Liverpool 08, European Capital of Culture: The People's Opening and Transition." October 12, 2010. https://www.youtube.com/watch?v=h3lx_hNq91M.

Walton, John K. *The British Seaside: Holidays and Resorts in the Twentieth Century*. Manchester: Manchester University Press, 2000.

Walvin, James. *Beside the Seaside: A Social History of the Popular Seaside Holiday*. London: Allen Lane, 1978.

———. *Leisure and Society: 1830–1950*. London: Longman, 1978.

Ward, Stephen V. *Selling Places: The Marketing and Promotion of Towns and Cities, 1850–2000*. Abingdon, UK: Spon, 1998.

Warner, Marina. Foreword to *Off Limits: 40 Artangel Projects*, ed. Gerrie van Noord, 8–9. London: Merrell, 2002.

Warnock, Mary, and Mark Wallinger. *Art for All? Their Policies and Our Culture*. London: Peer, 2000.

Watt, David. "'The Maker and the Tool': Charles Parker, Documentary Performance, and the Search for a Popular Culture." *New Theatre Quarterly* 19, no. 1 (2003): 41–66.

White, Michael. "Blair Defines the New Labour: Leader on the Verge of a Coup over the Clause Four Pledge to Nationalise: Delegates Warm to '90s Socialism." *The Guardian*, October 5, 1994.

———. "Reveling in a Wrathful Exodus, Plagues and All." *New York Times: The Arts*, October 2, 2006.

Whittaker, David J. *Asylum Seekers and Refugees in the Contemporary World*. London: Routledge, 2006.

Wilks-Heeg, Stuart. "From World City to Pariah City? Liverpool and the Global Economy, 1850–2000." In *Reinventing the City? Liverpool in Comparative Perspective*, ed. Ronaldo Munck, 36–52. Liverpool: Liverpool University Press, 2003.

Wilks-Heeg, Stuart, and Peter North. "Editorial: Cultural Policy and Urban Regeneration: A Special Edition of *Local Economy*." *Local Economy* 19, no. 4 (2004): 305–11.

Williams, Kirk. "Anti-Theatricality and the Limits of Naturalism." In *Against Theatre: Creative Destructions on the Modernist Stage*, ed. Alan Ackerman and Martin Puchner, 95–111. Basingstoke, UK: Palgrave Macmillan, 2006.

Williams, Raymond. *Communications*. Revised edition. Harmondsworth, UK: Penguin, 1966.

———. *Keywords: A Vocabulary of Culture and Society*. London: Fontana/Croom Helm, 1976.

Wilson, Esther, John Fay, Tony Green, and Lizzie Nunnery. *Unprotected*. London: Josef Weinberger Plays, 2006.

Wilson, Heidi. "Community Dance in Performance." In *An Introduction to Community Dance Practice*, ed. Diane Amans, 63–75. Basingstoke, UK: Palgrave Macmillan, 2008.

Wintour, Patrick, and Vikram Dodd. "Blair Blames Spate of Murders on Black Culture." *The Guardian*, April 12, 2007.

World Bank. "Brazil: Youth at Risk in Brazil, Volume I: Policy Briefing." May 10, 2007. https://openknowledge.worldbank.org/handle/10986/7763.

Worley, Clare. "'It's Not about Race. It's about the Community': New Labour and 'Community Cohesion.'" *Critical Social Policy* 25, no. 4 (2005): 483–96.

"Would You Know How to Identify a Refugee? Starting Today: Asylum Seekers in Thanet—The Reality and the Myths." *Isle of Thanet Gazette*, April 21, 2000.

Wright, Patrick. "In Your Space: They're Big. You've Paid for Them. And They're Meant to Make You Feel Better. But Ever Since the Sixties, Britain's Public Art Developments Have Caused More Aggro Than Uplift." *The Guardian*, August 25, 1995.

Wroe, Nicholas. "Profile: Nicolas Kent: Courtroom Dramas." *The Guardian*, July 24, 2004, 16.

Yglesias, Pablo. *¡Cocinando! Fifty Years of Latin Album Cover Art*. New York: Princeton Architectural Press, 2005.

Young, Iris Marion. *Inclusion and Democracy*. Oxford: Oxford University Press, 2002.

"Your Chance to Be a Star." *Isle of Thanet Gazette*, June 9, 2006.

"Your Invitation to Create an Art Legend." *Isle of Thanet Gazette*, August 11, 2006.

Yúdice, George. *The Expediency of Culture: Uses of Culture in the Global Era*. Durham, NC: Duke University Press 2003.

INDEX